THE LIGHT OF KAILASH

Volume Two

The LIGHT of KAILASH
A History of Zhang Zhung and Tibet

VOLUME TWO
*The Intermediate Period
Tibet and Zhang Zhung*

CHÖGYAL NAMKHAI NORBU

Translated from the Tibetan and edited by
Donatella Rossi

English editing by
Nancy Simmons

Shang Shung Publications
Merigar
58031 Arcidosso (GR)
Italy
www.shangshunginstitute.org
info@shangshunginstitute.org

Original title: *Zhang bod kyi lo rgyus ti se'i 'od*

Copyright © 2013 Shang Shung Institute
All rights reserved. No portion of this book may be reproduced by any means without prior written permission from the publisher.

ISBN 978-88-7834-132-6

Cover calligraphy: Chögyal Namkhai Norbu
Editor: Nancy Simmons
Cover and interior design: Daniel Zegunis and Fulvio Ferrari
Layout: Tiziana Gottardi
Graphics: Fulvio Ferrari

IPC - 762EN13 - Approved by the International Publications Committee of the Dzogchen Community founded by Chögyal Namkhai Norbu.

339EN

Contents

Translator's Foreword	7
I. ORIGINS OF THE HUMAN GENERATIONS OF ANCIENT TIBET	17
II. ORIGINS OF THE BONPO LINEAGES OF ANCIENT TIBET	41
1. Origin of the word "Bon"	42
2. The Diffusion of Bon at the Time of King Mu-khri bTsan-po	54
III. THE ROYAL LINEAGES OF ANCIENT TIBET	87
1. The Divine Lineage of the First King of Tibet	
2. The Succession of the Tibetan Monarchs from gNya'-Khri bTsan-po to the Dharmarāja Srong-bTsan sGam-po	123
IV. THE WRITTEN LANGUAGE OF ANCIENT TIBET	173
1. The Foremost Diffusion of the Tibetan Written Language	174
2. Did a Tibetan Language Exist Before the Dharmarāja Srong-btsan?	178
V. THE CIVILIZATION OF ANCIENT TIBET	203
1. The Twelve Lores of Bon	203
2. The Three Cardinal Aspects of the Culture of the Intermediate Period	212
3. Royal Castles of Ancient Tibet	228
VI. KINGS, GSHEN-POS, AND BONPOS OF ZHANG ZHUNG	236
1. King sTag-rna gZi-brjid	236
2. Mu-wer bTsad-po	238

3. The Bon gShen-po Dran-pa Nam-mkha' 239
4. The King of Zhang Zhung Lig-mi-rkya lDe-bu 244

Bibliography 260
Indexes
    Tibetan and Zhang Zhung Names and Terms 271
    Textual Sources 299
    Sanskrit Names and Terms 303
    Chinese Names and Terms 305

List of Tables
    Table 1. The Twelve Animals of the Astrological Cycle 31
    Table 2. The Original Clans as mentioned in the *Po ti bse ru*, the *Lho brag chos 'byung*, and the *Rus mdzod* (1) 35
    Table 3. The Original Clans as mentioned in the *Baidūrya dkar po*, and in the *Nyer mkho bum bzang* (2) 35
    Table 4. The Names of the Twelve Lores as recorded in the *Byams ma*, and in the *Dar rgyas gsal sgron* (1) 53
    Table 5. The Names of the Twelve Lores as Recorded in the *rGyal rabs bon 'byung* and in the *Legs bshad mdzod* (2) 54
    Table 6. (1 through 32) The monarchs of the Intermediate Period, from the first king gNya'-khri bTsan-po, up to gNam-ri Srong-btsan, the father of Srong-btsan sGam-po; their royal protectors [*sku gshen*]; and the temples they built, as recorded in eight different textual sources 70
    Table 7. The Divine Lineage of the First King of Tibet as recorded in the *lDe'u rgya bod kyi chos 'byung*, the *lDe'u chos 'byung chen mo*, and the *Srid pa rgyud kyi kha byang* 100
    Table 8. The Succession of the Thirty-Four Tibetan Dynasties of the Intermediate Period according to Twenty Different Sources 133
    Table 9. Stanza 129 from the Eighth Chapter on Meditative Absorption of the *Bodhicaryāvatāra* by the Noble Śāntideva, written in *Lha Babs Yi Ge* (The Language Descended from the Gods) 194
    Table 10. Sample of *Lha Babs Yi Ge* (The Language Descended from the Gods) by Chögyal Namkhai Norbu with Tibetan Equivalent 196
    Table 11. Image of the Yum-bu Bla-sgang Palace 230

Translator's Foreword

CHÖGYAL NAMKHAI NORBU (born 1938), former professor of Tibetan and Mongolian Language and Literature at the University of Naples L'Orientale, has dedicated his academic career to the study of Tibetan culture and has published a number of works, in particular, on its origin.[1] In his findings, the cradle of Tibetan culture is to be looked for in the ancient realm of Zhang Zhung and in the Bon spiritual traditions which flourished within and spread from that kingdom.

According to relevant textual sources, the ancient kingdom of Zhang Zhung, prior to the advent of Buddhism in the seventh century, encom-

---

This is an updated version of the Translator's Foreword found in Volume One.

1 Among these figure *Bod kyi lo rgyus las 'phros pa'i gtam g.yung drung nor bu'i do shal*, Library of Tibetan Works and Archives, Dharamsala, 1981; *La Collana di Zi, Storia e cultura del Tibet*, translated in Italian from the Tibetan and edited by Adriano Clemente, Shang Shung Edizioni, Arcidosso, 1997; *The Necklace of gZi. A Cultural History of Tibet*, LTWA, Dharamsala, 1981 (*Bod rigs gzhon nu rnams la gros su 'debs pa gZi yi phreng ba*, LTWA, Dharamsala, 1982); *The Necklace of Zi, On the History and Culture of Tibet*, translated in English from the Italian by Barrie and Nancy Simmons, Shang Shung Edizioni, Arcidosso, 2004; *Gaṅs ti se'i dkar chag. A Bon-po Story of the Sacred Mountain Ti-se and the Blue Lake Ma-paṅ*, edited by Chögyal Namkhai Norbu, revised, collated, and completed by Ramon Prats, excerpts in English translated by Chögyal Namkhai Norbu and Ramon Prats, Serie Orientale Roma, LXI, IsMEO, 1989; *sGrung lde'u bon gsum gyi gtam e ma ho*, LTWA, Dharamsala, 1989. For a list of the works of Chögyal Namkhai Norbu until 1995, see his *Drung, Deu and Bön. Narrations, symbolic languages and the Bön tradition in ancient Tibet*, translated, edited, and annotated by Adriano Clemente, LTWA, Dharamsala, 1995, pp. 295-297.

passed a vast area including Western and Northern Tibet, with the revered and majestic Mount Kailash as its center and heart. Thus, the author's choice of title for his work is meaningful per se, in that it symbolizes and at the same time emphasizes the rich cultural origin of the Land of Snows.

Tibetan studies have a long and honored history, though only in the second half of the last century did scholars begin to take an interest in the Tibetan Bonpo culture.[2] The reasons for this delay lie primarily in the previous lack of access to textual sources, and in the prevalence of orthodox Buddhist views which not only greatly influenced the attitude of modern Bonpo adherents, but have also been adopted by Western scholars as the unquestioned basis for the study of Tibetan culture as a whole. That attitude resulted in a simplistic view, still maintained by some, according to which Tibet was a savage land before the adoption of Buddhism, even lacking a written language.

Fortunately, a change in the status quo took place in the 1960s, when Professor David Llewellyn Snellgrove invited a group of knowledgeable representatives of the Bon tradition[3] from their refugee settlement in India, and undertook the pioneering task of letting this tradition speak for the first time in its own voice to the Western world.[4]

Soon after, Professor Samten Gyaltsen Karmay published the translation of an outstanding work on the history of Bon, compiled by the famed Bonpo master and scholar, Shar-rdza bKra-shis rGyal-mtshan (1859-1934), which became a seminal text of reference for research

---

2 See for example, Helmut Hoffmann, *Quellen zur Geschichte der tibetischen Bon-Religion*, Akademie der Wissenschaften und der Literatur in Mainz, F.S. Verlag, Wiesbaden, 1950.

3 Lopon Tenzin Namdak, Ven. Sangye Tenzin, and Samten G. Karmay.

4 See *The Nine Ways of Bon. Excerpts from the gZi brjid*, London Oriental Series, vol. 18, Oxford University Press, 1967. A volume dedicated to Prof. Snellgrove, entitled *Bon: the Everlasting Religion of Tibet. Tibetan Studies in Honour of Professor David L. Snellgrove* (papers presented at the International Conference on Bon, 22-27 June 2008, Shenten Dargye Ling, Château de la Modetais, Blou, France, New Horizons of Bon Studies 2, Samten G. Karmay and Donatella Rossi eds.) has been published in EAST AND WEST, IsIAO, as vol. 59, nos. 1-4, 2009.

studies;[5] and in 1974, Professor Emeritus Per Kværne published a study of the Bonpo Canon (*bka' 'gyur*), based on a nineteenth century text.[6]

During the 1980s, two sets of the Bonpo Canon (154 and 192 volumes, respectively) were reprinted in Eastern Tibet (present day Sichuan Province, People's Republic of China), while in the late 1990s, a collection of 300 volumes of ancillary texts (*bka' brten*) of the Bonpo Canon was published in Lhasa by the Venerable Tenpai Nyima.

The availability of this extensive literature has paved the way for a series of analytic cataloguing, research studies, field work, seminars, and so on, that have contributed dramatically to improve understanding about the Bon tradition as a whole.[7] *The Light of Kailash, A History of Zhang Zhung and Tibet* can be considered a highly significant contribution to this body of knowledge.

---

5 *The Treasury of Good Sayings: A Tibetan History of Bon*, London Oriental Series, vol. 26, Oxford University Press, London, 1972.

6 "The Canon of the Tibetan Bonpos," *Indo-Iranian Journal*, vol. 16, Part One, pp. 18-56, Part Two, pp. 96-144.

7 See mainly the following works, produced under the aegis of Prof. Yasuhiko Nagano: *Mandalas of the Bon Religion*, Bon Studies 1, Tenzin Namdak, Yasuhiko Nagano and Musashi Tachikawa eds., Senri Ethnological Reports 12, National Museum of Ethnology, Osaka, 2000; *New Horizons in Bon Studies*, Bon Studies 2, Samten G. Karmay and Yasuhiko Nagano eds., Senri Ethnological Reports 15, National Museum of Ethnology, Osaka, 2000; *New Research on Zhangzhung and Related Himalayan Languages*, Bon Studies 3, Yasuhiko Nagano and Randy J. LaPolla eds., Senri Ethnological Reports 19, National Museum of Ethnology, Osaka, 2001; *A Catalogue of the New Collection of Bonpo Katen Texts*, Bon Studies 4, Samten G. Karmay and Yasuhiko Nagano eds., Senri Ethnological Reports 24, National Museum of Ethnology, Osaka, 2001; *A Catalogue of the New Collection of Bonpo Katen Texts—Indices*, Bon Studies 5, Samten G. Karmay and Yasuhiko Nagano eds., Senri Ethnological Reports 25, National Museum of Ethnology, Osaka, 2001; *The Call of the Blue Cuckoo. An Anthology of Nine Bonpo Texts on Myths and Rituals*, Bon Studies 6, Samten G. Karmay and Yasuhiko Nagano eds., Senri Ethnological Reports 32, National Museum of Ethnology, Osaka, 2002; *A Survey of Bonpo Monasteries and Temples in Tibet and the Himalaya*, Bon Studies 7, Samten G. Karmay and Yasuhiko Nagano eds., Senri Ethnological Reports 38, National Museum of Ethnology, Osaka, 2003; *A Catalogue of the Bon Kanjur*, Bon Studies 8, Dan Martin, Per Kværne and Yasuhiko Nagano eds., Senri Ethnological Reports 40, National Museum of Ethnology, Osaka, 2003; *Feast of the Morning Light. The Eighteenth Century Wood-engravings of Shenrab's Life-stories and the Bon Canon from Gyalrong*, Bon Stud-

The text was originally conceived as a set of university lectures that Chögyal Namkhai Norbu was invited to give at the University of Nationalities in Beijing (Minzu Daxue, former Zhongyang Minzu Xueyuan) in 1988. The contents of the lectures formed a first abridged version of *The Light of Kailash*, which was subsequently enlarged and expanded by the author after further research, until the manuscript, written in his unique calligraphy, became a work of 1,900 pages, divided in three volumes.

The first volume, "The Early Period, the History of Ancient Zhang Zhung," considers the rise of early human generations and the Bon lineages of ancient Zhang Zhung, its dynasties, language, and culture.

The second volume, entitled "The History of the Intermediate Period: Tibet and Zhang Zhung," is focused upon human generations, the Bonpo lineages, the spread of Bon during the lifetimes of the first Tibetan monarchs, the dynasties, written language, and civilization of ancient Tibet, as well as upon the reigns of specific kings, the Bon religion, and Bonpo religious figures (Dran-pa Nam-mkha' in particular) of Zhang Zhung during that period.

The third volume, "The History of the Later Period: Tibet," is concerned with an assessment of the genealogies, Bonpo lineages, royal dynasties (from the first monarch gNya'-khri bTsan-po until the forty-fifth monarch Khri-dar-ma 'U-dum-btsan), language, and civilization of Tibet.[8]

---

ies 9, Samten G. Karmay ed., Senri Ethnological Reports 57, National Museum of Ethnology, Osaka, 2005; *Bonpo Thangkas from Khyungpo*, Bon Studies 10, Tenpa Yundrung, Per Kværne, Musashi Tachikawa and Yasuhiko Nagano eds., Senri Ethnological Reports 60, National Museum of Ethnology, Osaka, 2006; Pasar Tsultrim Tenzin, Changru Tritsuk Namdak Nyima, Gatsa Lodroe Rabsal, *A Lexicon of Zhangzhung and Bonpo Terms*, Bon Studies 11, Yasuhiko Nagano and Samten G. Karmay eds, Senri Ethnological Reports 76, National Museum of Ethnology, Osaka, 2008. For iconographic and artistic perspectives, see Per Kværne, *The Bon Religion of Tibet. The Iconography of a Living Tradition*, Serindia Publications, London, 1995, and *Bon, The Magic Word, The Indigenous Religion of Tibet*, Samten G. Karmay and Jeff Watt eds., Rubin Museum of Art, New York, and Philip Wilson Publishers Ltd, London, 2007.
8 The translation of the third volume will be published in due course.

In the translator's view, this summa of Chögyal Namkhai Norbu's researches is dedicated, first and foremost, to his fellow countrymen and women, and to Tibetan youth in particular. *The Light of Kailash* through meticulous selection and a critical use and analysis of a vast array of literary and often unpublished sources, such as dynastic and religious histories and cycles, myths, articles, and so on, offers an open, daring, holistic, unbiased approach to the study of the cultural and spiritual heritage of Tibet and to the understanding of the origin of this fascinating and endangered civilization. It is my hope that scholars will appreciate the import and interested readers enjoy the content of this amazing trilogy.

In conclusion, I wish to express deep gratitude, above all, to Chögyal Namkhai Norbu, for the invaluable opportunity for study and reflection that this work offered, and also for his great patience in aiding me with the interpretation of difficult or obscure passages. My heartfelt thanks go also to Ponlop Trinley Nyima Rinpoche, the Director of the Dialectic School of New Menri Monastery in Dolanji (Himachal Pradesh, India), for his precious clarifications.

I greatly thank Adriano Clemente, for his excellent advice; Enrico Dell'Angelo, for permitting me to consult his dissertation, in itself a pioneering work;[9] Nancy Simmons, for her skilled and graceful revision of the English text; and Marta Sernesi, for her precision in checking the Indexes. Tiziana Gottardi, Igor Legati, Maurizio Mingotti, and Dan Zegunis have my grateful appreciation for their accurate production work.

In terms of sponsorship, I thank the International Shang Shung Institute, particularly Laurie Marder, Jacqueline Gens, and the late and loved Andrea Sertoli (United States branch), Luigi Ottaviani (Italian branch), and Oliver Leick (Austrian branch); the David Sharpe Bequest; the Italian Ministry of Education, University, and Research; Dick Drury for his unstinting generosity and exceptional commitment to this work; Benedetta Tagliabue who with great bounty underwrit the printing of the first volume; Mark Farrington; and Mark Fulton. At the onset of this project these individuals and institutions made its launching pos-

---

9 *Srid pa'i spyi mdos: Contributo allo Studio dell'Insegnamento di gShen rab Mi bo che* [Contribution to the study of gShen rab Mi bo che's teaching], MA dissertation, Istituto Universitario Orientale di Napoli, Naples, 1982.

sible. Many other people helped in both tangible and intangible ways; I hope they will consider the realization of this work as the token of my recognition for their kindness and support.

Donatella Rossi
September, 2013
Rome, Italy

A Technical Note on the Translation

The translation is based on the original Tibetan manuscript (*Zhang bod kyi lo rgyus ti se'i 'od*). *The Light of Kailash* was published in the People's Republic of China in 1996 in block print form.[10] The text printed in China presents some omissions and imprecisions and for that reason was not used as a main source, though at times it was consulted.

The transliteration used follows the Wylie system. It has been preferred as the most accurate method, despite its notorious difficulty for nonspecialists, since reader-friendly solutions, though more accessible, are notably misleading. A combination of the two seemed cumbersome, in view of the great number of names and terms contained in the text. To facilitate reading by nonspecialists, personal and geographical names have been hyphenated while textual sources and technical terms are written in italics. The name of the ancient kingdom of Zhang Zhung has not been hyphenated in view of the explanation provided by the Author in the text. Similarly the word Bonpo has not been hyphenated, in this case because of its common usage.

Bibliographic references in the text appear as in the original. They are self-explanatory in that they follow a consistent structure: a first syllable for the publishing place, volume letter or number, page or folio

---

10 *Zhang bod kyi lo rgyus ti se'i 'od*, Chinese title: *Gudai xiangxiong yu tufan shi*, The China Tibetology Publishing House, Beijing. Other works by Chögyal Namkhai Norbu have also been published in the People's Republic of China: see *Nam mkha'i nor bu'i gsung rtsom phyogs bsgrigs* (Selected Works of Namkhai Norbu, Tibetan Edition), The China Tibetology Publishing House, Beijing, 1994.

number, and line number. The relevant sources can be found in the bibliographies that follow each of the three volumes.

Translator's notes have been added when deemed necessary and are enclosed in brackets [...]. Similarly, names or terms translated or quoted appear in square brackets in the body of the text.

Responsibility for any defect, error, or imperfection rests solely with the translator.

The LIGHT of KAILASH

VOLUME TWO

Mount Kailash

 I

Origins of the Human Generations of Ancient Tibet

WE CAN ASSESS the way in which the Tibetan genealogies came into being through an investigation of the origins of the people of ancient Tibet. Determining the history of that people is impossible if its connection with the first genealogies of ancient Zhang Zhung described in old Bonpo textual sources is not taken into account. Famous dynastic and religious histories maintain that the first Tibetan king and the Tibetan state [*mnga' sde*] descend from the Indian lord Rūpati who fled to Tibet with his troops, presupposing that both royalty and subjects appeared in the country simultaneously. However, if we examine the real circumstances, this notion cannot be the basis for understanding the development in ancient times of the human generations and of the Tibetan royal dynasties, because it lacks an awareness of the actual history of those origins.

Concerning the origins of the ancient Tibetans, both Bonpo and Buddhist sources as a matter of course refer to specific family lineages. Tibetan genealogies cite four primeval clans: sBra, lDong, 'Bru, and sGa; five, if the rGo are also included; seven, if the dPa-yi-tshan and Zla-yi-tshan clans are included separately; or six, if the last two are grouped as a unit. Zhang Zhung genealogies mention as the first ancestor Sangs-po 'Bum-khri, followed in succession by the Brothers of Primordial Humankind [*srid pa mi rabs mched dgu*] until dBal and Zla from whom arose distinct family lines: the four primeval clans together with the dBal and Zla are known as the Six Family Lines of the Early Human Generations [*mi'u gdung drug*] from which the Zhang/Bod genealogies spread. This fact can not be ignored. Nevertheless, even excluding the sBra and the Khyung clans from which the Zhang Zhung genealogies descended and considering only the evolution of other clans, such as the lDong, 'Bru, sGa, rGo, dBal, and Zla, their locations, and so on, it is obvious that the names of the people descending from those clans, as well as local customs and habits, underwent diverse developments because of the social transitions and changes that occurred during different epochs.

Many historical documents speak of Se, rMu, lDong, and sTong as the four original clans. For example the *lHo brag chos 'byung* [Religious History of lHo-brag] affirms (Pe, sTod, 154, 5):

> The Four Family Lines [*mi'u rigs bzhi*] of Tibet are composed of the Se, rMu, lDong, and sTong clans; when dBra and 'Dru are added, they are known as the Six Family Lines [*mi'u rigs drug*] [of the early human generations].

In this case, dBra and 'Dru are added to the four original clans—Se, rMu, lDong, and sTong—which then become six. According to the unspecified justifications of some, the above quotation infers that the sBra descended from the Se, and the 'Dru or 'Bru from the sTong. The commonly held opinion is that the Se or bSe and the Khyung are the sBra clan; the rMu and the Seng are the sGa; the lDong is the A-spo-ldong, sometimes also known as the sMug-po-gdong; and the sTong is usually identified with the 'Bru. Thus, in actual fact, even if various designations exist for the clans, it seems unlikely that all were not included within the four original family lines.

The custom of referring to the four primeval family lineages as if they were the four cardinal points of a single perspective at the root of human genealogies has turned into a famous postulate, that of "The Four Great Original Clans" [*rus chen bzhi*]. Also, the *lHa bsang rgyag brngan chen mo* [The Great Ritual for Offering *bSang* to the Deities], authored by Teacher Padmasambhava, mentions four distinct clans and the names of their chief protective female deities [Shugs-mgon-mo] (sDe, 10, 4):

[For the] gDong Deity [gDong-lha-mo] of gDong,
delicate smoke offerings [*chung bsang*].
[For the] sBra Deity [sBra-mo] of sBra,
assorted smoke offerings [*khra bsang*].
[For the] 'Bru Deity ['Bru-mo] of 'Bru,
dense smoke offerings [*khrom khrom bsang*].
[For the] sGa Deity [sGa-mo] of sGa,
choice smoke offerings [*le le bsang*].

The *Deb ther dpyid kyi rgyal mo'i glu dbyangs* [The Annals of the Melodious Song of the Queen of Spring[11]] says about the four original clans (Pe, II, 19):

From the four original clans arose four separate family lines:
[that of] Ye-sang dKar-po with the celestial cord;
[that of] Ye-smon Nag-mo, [who is] like a boulder of molten iron;
[that of] sPyang-khrig Ye-shes, [who is like a] lamp of the gods; and
[that of] Mon-rdzu Nag-po with the green drum [made] of dog [skin].

If we examine the words that compose those names, we can be sure that the account we are dealing with originated within the Bon tradition from the names themselves, such as Ye-sang dKar-po and so on, or from the attributes, the celestial cord and so on. The four sentences following the first one, furthermore, describe the extraordinary characteristics of the four tribal ancestors.

The *bShad mdzod chen mo* [The Great Treasury of Exposition] distinguishes four external and four internal family lineages: the external ones refer to populations derived from other, non-Tibetan clans; the internal ones refer to actual Tibetan clans and to the various divisions among them (Thim, 190, 5, 2):

---

11 [That is, the cuckoo bird.]

> The four external family lines [are those from] India and China, sTag-gzig and Ge-sar. The four internal ones are Se and rMu, lDong and sTong.
> [There are also] Li and Bal-po, Hor and Mi-nyag.

The names of the four populations appearing in the last sentence are presented in that order as if to indicate that the people of the Li line descended from the internal Se clan, that the people of the Bal-po line descended from the rMu, the people of the Hor line from the lDong, and the people of the Mi-nyag line from the sTong. Another commonly held view states that the people of the Hor and the Sum-pa lines descended from the sTong, and the people of the Mi-nyag line from the lDong. Whichever view is right, we have a clear indication that the people of the Li, Bal-po, Hor, and Sum-pa lines descended from Tibetan clans.

The Li people spoken of here as descending from the Se refers to an ethnic group that in ancient times were the indigenes of Li-yul [Khotan].[12] That the Li are not considered part of the present day Uigur ethnic group is thus due to precise historical circumstance. The Li-yul-ba of ancient times, notwithstanding their distinctive characteristics, shared the same ancestral origins and had a strong connection with the Tibetan people. However, at some point in time, the kingdom of Khotan [56 BCE-1006 CE] fell under the Turkish dominion. Islamic people of Turkish origin together with Islamic armed forces in great number settled widely in Khotan; the present day Uigurs in that area descend from those Muslim populations. Gradually the Islamic forces conquered the majority of Central Asian territories; that is why believers in the Islamic faith increased in those regions. Thus, even though the Uigurs of later times are not considered descendants of the Se clan, strictly speaking the ancient people of the country of Li that are mentioned in the *Glang ru lung bstan gyi mdo* [The Oxhorn Prophecy

---

12 [Khotan is now part of the Chinese province of Xīnjiāng 新疆, literally, New Territory.]

Sūtra, Sanskrit *Gośṛṅga Vyākaraṇa sūtra*]¹³ and other sources share the same ancestral origins as the Tibetan people.

The major dynastic and religious histories of Tibet contain diverse descriptions and different views about the four or six original clans, the groups that descended from them, and so on. Even their names are written in many different ways. For example, lDong can be written "gDong;" bSe, "Se;" sBra can be written "dBra;" 'Bru, "'Gru" or "'Dru;" rMu, "dMu;" sGa, "rGa" or "dGa';" and dBal, "dPa'."

The *Rus mdzod pad dkar skyed tshal* [The White Lotus Grove, Treasure of Genealogies] describes the way in which the distinction between lords and subjects was made, following the division into good or unsuitable families from among the original clans (rNga, 2, 5):

> Since the people of good families [*rigs bzang po*] were naturally virtuous and presented offerings to the local deities of Tibet with great faith, they were called Zhing-bo. In later times, it seems that they were also known as Zhing-bo lHa-rigs-rgo.
>
> It is said that [the best among the Zhing-bo were] the lHa-rigs-rgo and [that] the best among the bSe [were] the bSe-khyung-sbra. Similarly, the best among the dMu [were said to be] the dMu-tsha-rga. The best among the lDong [were] the A-spo-ldong. The best among the lTong [were] the A-thang-'bru.

Hence, the text mentions five prominent groups: lHa-rigs-rgo, bSe-khyung-sbra, dMu-tsha-rga, A-spo-ldong, and A-thang-'bru.

And also [ibid., 3, 8]:

> These five clans also had the following significant names: lDong Che-gnyan-can, [because] there were four great kings [*rgyal chen mi bzhi*] [among them, who were] extremely powerful [*che gnyan che*]; 'Bru Byas-pa-can, [because they] granted no quarter to enemies; rGa Yig-tshang-can, [because they were] learned; sBra Ming-rna-can, because they possessed abundant riches and cattle; Zhing rGo, [because they were] the ones [who attended] the

---

13 [A prophetic sūtra named after Mount Oxhorn of Khotan that describes the characteristics of the places where the Buddhadharma will be expounded in the future.]

deities. Later on, the unsuitable families [*rigs ngan pa*] that had been separated from the good ones split into two groups; these two groups, the dPa'-yi-tshan and Zla-yi-tshan, [included] the common people [*dmangs*], that is, the nomads and the peasants [*tsha zhing*], [bringing the number of clans] from five [to] seven.

Thus, the text mentions five clans—lDong, 'Bru, rGa, sBra, and rGo—and adds the dPa'-yi-tshan or dBal-yi-tshan and the Zla-yi-tshan, bringing the number of clans to seven.

Whatever divisions may have taken place, according to many renowned histories the people of the three regions of Zhang Zhung—sGo, Phug, and Bar—descended from the sBra or Khyung; the people of 'A-zha descended from the Seng or sGa; the people of Mi-nyag descended from the A-spo-ldong; and the people of Sum-pa descended from the sTong. However, this is only one explanation and does not necessarily imply that the whole of the Tibetan people belonged to those four populations, that is, Zhang Zhung, 'A-zha, Mi-nyag, and Sum-pa; nor that the contrary is true, namely, that the Zhang Zhung, 'A-zha, Mi-nyag, and Sum-pa people are different from the Tibetans. The names of bSe and Khyung are associated with the sBra clan;[14] similarly, rMu and Seng are associated with the sGa; 'Bru and so on are associated with the sTong. Due to numerous and various spatiotemporal circumstances, those clans and family lines—either individually or combined—grew and developed into the broader Tibetan population that expanded in all the principal areas of Central and Eastern Tibet during the course of time. Nonetheless, it can be automatically inferred that many other family lines beside the ones mentioned above must have existed although their circumstances are unknown to us.

The *Baiḍūrya dkar po* [White Beryl] associates the five Tibetan clans with the five elements and also with powerful protectors[15] symbolized by the animals of the twelve year cycle (sDe, 147, 1):

sTong three: Wood, Hare [and] Tiger.

---

14 [On the sBra clan, cf. Vol. One, chap. I, p. 75.]
15 *shugs mgon*: the term refers to deities and protectors that assist an individual in promoting the positive and virtuous aspects of his or her own energy and character.

Se 'A-zha: Fire, Snake [and] Horse.
sBrang [*sic*] Zhang Zhung: Iron, Monkey [and] Bird.
rGyal-drang-rje: Earth, the Four Opposites.¹⁶
lDong Mi-nyag: Water, Pig [and] Mouse.

The first verse of this excerpt, *shing dang stag yos stong gsum zhes* [sTong three: Wood, Hare [and] Tiger] needs clarification. The sentence shows the reading *stong gsum* as the scribes did not understand the real significance of the word and mistakenly opted for its common meaning [literally, three thousand]; actually it should be understood as "*stong sum*", because it refers to the ancient sTong clan and to the Sum-pa population that descended from it.

In the second verse, *me dang rta sbrul se 'a zha* [Se 'A-zha: Fire, Snake [and] Horse], another scribal error is evident: the word *se* is written instead of *seng*. The scribes may have concluded that *se* bore the meaning of bSe-khyung-sbra by considering the next verse, *lcags dang bya sprel sbrang zhang zhung* [sBrang Zhang Zhung: Iron, Monkey [and] Bird]. However, neither *se* nor *bse* is the correct reading here; the Seng and the rMu tribes were part of the sGa clan, and the sGa clan was specifically one of the clans from which the 'A-zha people descended.

The 'A-zha people, descendants from either the sGa or the Seng clan, occupied an area of Eastern Tibet bordered on the south by Sum-pa and on the southwest by Mi-nyag. Today the term 'A-zha is attributed to subject territories that start from the greater inner region of mDo-khams to the east of Central Tibet [dBus-gtsang] and extend southward from Lake Khri-shor rGyal-mo [also known as Koko Nor] to the northwest of sDe-dge, with rGyal-rong to the east and Mongolia [Sog-yul] to the north. The center of the 'A-zha land is called sGa and/or sGa-khog; if this is testimony, as it seems, that the place took its name from the original family line, the same principle could be adopted for researching the old toponymy of the whole area.

In ancient times the majority of the lDong families lived in the vicinity of Lake Khri-shor rGyal-mo; the people that descended from the A-spo-ldong clan, called Mi-nyag, occupied an area to the east of 'A-zha and Sum-pa; later on, due to changes that occurred over time, it

---

16 [*gshed bzhi*: See explanation below, p. 31.]

was said that the Mi-nyag territory roughly corresponded to the present day Province of Qīnghǎi [青海], from the eastern side of Gānsù [甘肃] Province to the northeastern border of Sìchuān [四川] Province. Those people were traditionally known as lDong or lDong-pa; and since they inhabited northern Khams, the Khams-pas would call them lDong Byang [lDong North]. Also the Tibetans living in Central Tibet called them in this way, but since the pronunciation of the Central Tibetan and Khams-pa idioms differ, the words *ldong* and *byang* are also pronounced differently in those dialects; for this reason some Chinese historians[17] attributed to this population the appellation 党项羌 (Dǎng Xiàng Qiāng). A work entitled *Mi nyag gi skor rags tsam gleng ba* [Brief history of the Mi-nyag] describes how the Mi-nyag descended from the lDong and the reason why the name of the Mi-nyag family line descending from the lDong clan came into being (Bod, 5, 9):

> The lDong pas arrived in the area near Lake Khri-shor rGyal-mo. At the beginning they earned their livelihood and supported themselves by hunting. Then, accumulating many animals as livestock, they became nomads and herders. They lived in tents made of yak hair and did not cultivate fields. The male population wore earrings, a felt hat, leather shoes, and a skin coat with long sides tied with a thin rope that served as a belt. The belt held a small knife and flame-igniting objects [flint and steel]. The women wore an elegant woolen garment with long sleeves and the collar folded back called a *bod lwa*. The livestock of these people included yaks, sheep, goats, and cows; their weapons were [bows and] arrows, knives, spears, axes, and slingshots. They nourished themselves by eating meat and drinking milk; they brewed beer (*chang*) from boiled [and fermented] barley. Later, since the families of the lDong-pas grew very large, many tribes went their separate ways. Those who remained in the original location continued to be called rMad and lDong; those who migrated to northern Tibet were called sMad-pa and lDong Byang by the Tibetans.
>
> Furthermore, among the various tribes of Tibet proper, three main groups were distinguished: *bod*, *byang*, and *lho*; Tibetans called

---

17 [Following the Khams-pa dialect.]

Byang-pa the tribes who lived in the north of Tibet and lHo-pa those who lived in the south of the country. However, people belonging to the Byang and lHo tribes did not call themselves Byang-pa or lHo-pa; they used the family names with which they were known to each other. People from dBus-gtsang would pronounce *"byang"* (*zhanga*) as something like *"chang"* (*changa*); for this reason, the Chinese considered the sound *qiang* as primary and used it in their historical records in correspondence with the character 羌 (Qiāng), although accurately it is *byang*. In general, all the people associated with tribes that are designated as Byang are an integral part of the Tibetan race. The one hundred or so Tibetan Byang and lHo tribes that resided in their own specific locations were recognized by the Chinese as belonging to old Tibet; nonetheless, later Chinese generations labeled those tribes as ethnic groups separate from the Tibetans.

The Northern lDong [lDong-byang] were a division of the Tibetan Byang tribes; they inhabited an area northeast of Central Tibet, which today corresponds to southeastern Qīnghǎi Province, southwestern Gānsù, and northwestern Sìchuān. Later, the people of lDong split into eight family lines called the eight original tribes. These tribes were not governed by the same leader. The largest of them had a cavalry of more than five thousand soldiers, while the smaller ones had a cavalry of one thousand soldiers; they were all self-sustained. If enemies appeared, they would assemble from their respective locations to give battle. Every three years they would meet once in council, and during the council they would slaughter yaks and sheep and perform blood offerings [*dmar mchod*] to the deities. The lDong tribes were extremely courageous and greatly enjoyed fierce military action. They were mighty but did not have a written language.

When the Tibetan monarch gNam-ri Srong-btsan ruled, Tibet was unified as a single country. First the nearby regions of Dwags-po, Kong-po, and Myang-po were brought into submission; then came the turn of Zhang Zhung, Sum-pa, 'A-zha, Gru-gu, lDong-byang, and so on. In order to conquer the Northern lDong and the others, King gNam-ri Srong-btsan personally led an army of ten thousand soldiers. When these people were subjugated, they swore allegiance to the king. Salt began to be imported from the region of the Northern lDong. At that time the political might of Tibet was as limitless as the sky, and its status had more solidity than a mountain; this is why the king assumed the name gNam-ri [sky-mountain] Srong-btsan [righteous-solid].

After this king died [ca. 627 CE], although Zhang Zhung and other principalities decided to separate from the greater kingdom of Tibet, the Northern lDong did not, and during the life of King Srong-btsan sGam-po they constituted one of the peripheral principalities of Tibet. They introduced the Tibetan script, afterward modifying their laws and adopting the Buddhist faith. Since the idioms, customs, ways of dressing, and so on, of the lDong-byang and of the Tibetans were similar, the lDong-pas learned written Tibetan, from then on retaining it as their own script. At some point, one of the major Northern lDong tribes betrayed Tibet and as soon as the news reached King Srong-btsan sGam-po, an army was sent to suppress the rebellion. The lDong-pas overwhelmed by the harrowing splendor of the Tibetan army fled and eventually settled as twenty-five large tribes in what presently corresponds to the Chinese areas of Níngxià [宁夏], Shǎnběi [陕北], and Shǎnxī [陕西].

The lDong-pas that did not flee remained peacefully in their own areas and without vindictive feelings continued to loyally obey the laws of greater Tibet. The laudatory title of Mi-nyag [literally, spotless] was bestowed on them. Mi-nyag thus became the name for the lDong Byang people and tribes, and the appellation lDong Byang gradually declined.

The lDong-pas that fled to China had long since established relations with the Hans [Hàn 汉]. The Hans ascribed the name Xī Xià [西夏, literally, Western Xià][18] to all the lDong-pas who inhabited the western regions at that time. After the Xī Xià name was attributed to the lDong-pas, the appellation lDong Byang disappeared completely, like a rainbow vanishing in the sky. As a result, also the lDong-pas who were living in different

---

18 [夏(Xià) is an ancient name for China and also of the homophonous dynasty, which according to the tradition ruled from the twenty-first to the sixteenth century BCE.]

places were called Mi-nyag and Xī Xià. Hence, the names of Mi-nyag and Xī Xià developed from lDong.

The excerpt quoted above is of great value in understanding Tibetan civilization.

As was said, the lDong-pas were absorbed as one of the Tibetan nationalities by the Tibetan King Srong-btsan sGam-po and were awarded the title Mi-nyag. Although the specific reason for giving this appellation is not clear, the Mi-nyags represented one of the lDong-pa's family lines. We can understand this because lCe-tsha mKhar-bu, one of the so-called Eight Great Scholars that appeared in the country of Zhang Zhung before the advent of the eighth Tibetan monarch Gri-gum bTsan-po, bore the family name Mi-nyag. At the time of Srong-btsan, the lDong-pa chieftains that rebelled against Tibet had escaped to China; since the chieftains of the lDong-pa tribes that did not rebel and did not flee belonged to the Mi-nyag family line and were in the majority, it is understandable why that family name was used.

The origin of the ancient Tibetan population and the way in which this is envisioned by Chinese scholars is related in the *rGya'i thang yig rnying ma* [Old Chinese Chronicles] thusly (Dha, I, 6):

> The land called Bod lies eight thousand *lǐ* [里][19] to the west of Cháng'ān [长安, present day] (Xī'ān 西安), the Táng [唐][20] capital. At the time of the Hàn [汉] [dynasty] (before the Common Era),[21] this was the land of people called the Shi'i-'jang whose origin no one is able to define. Some historians say that the Shi'i-'jangs are the descendants of Nan-le or Thu'u-hu-li'i-lo'o-ku of the Shan-sbi'i people. The son of Thu'u-hu-li'i-lo'o-ku was called Hun-nyi. Hun-nyi led his people to the western side of Hre-kri-hru'e (rMa-chu),[22] a vast area to the west of China that extends for thousands of *lǐ*. The capital was

---

19 [A Chinese unit of length corresponding to half a kilometer.]
20 [Táng dynasty (Táng cháo 唐朝), 618-907 CE.]
21 [This is a note contained in the original text. The Western Han (Xī Hàn 西汉) ruled from 206 BCE to 24 CE.]
22 [Situated in present day Qīnghǎi Province, this area is where the Yellow River (Tib. rMa-chu, Chin. Huáng Hé 黄河) rises.]

located in the vicinity of rMa-chen sPom-ra.[23] The kingdom was called Thu'u-hphā; after many years its name changed to Thu'-hphan. Their descendants, growing ever more numerous, conquered the neighboring princedom of 'Jang[24] which made their dominion even greater.

During the reigns of the Zhōu[25] and Súi [26] that preceded the Táng dynasty, no relation whatsoever existed between the 'Jang princedom and the Middle Kingdom. Their king was called bTsan-po; under him, a leadership composed of ministers, divided into major and minor ones, ruled the country.

In another version of the same text (mTsho, 128, 1) we read:

Thu-bhod is a land located eight thousand *lĭ* west of Chang'an. Originally, at the time of the Hàn dynasty, this was the western province of 'Jang. The origins of the tribes and lineages of the latter are not certain. Some say that they are the descendants of Thu'u-hpha-li-lo'u-ku'u of Nan-leng. Li-lo'u-ku'u had a son called 'Phan-myi. When Li-lo'u-ku'u died, since his son 'Phan-myi was still a child, Li-lo'u-ku'u's younger brother called Ru-than was elevated to the throne. 'Phan-myi was entrusted with the leadership of the army [at] An-zhi. During the first year of the reign of Hrin-ros of the Hig-we dynasty, Chē-hpho-kri-'phan of Zhi-qin subjugated Ru-than. Those left of 'Phan-myi's retinue were assembled and entrusted to Che-chid Mang-sung. Mang-sung nominated Chē-hpho-kri-'phan "The-hrig of Lin-sung."

After Mang-sung died, 'Phan-myi, leading his own retinue, moved west, forded the rMa-chu River, passed Mount Ci-hri, and in the land of the 'Jang founded a kingdom that extended for one thousand *lĭ*. Since 'Phan-myi was [a] brilliant and kind [leader], the 'Jang-pas respected [him]. As he treated everyone with kindness, the 'Jang-pas were happy to become his subjects. 'Phan-myi called his lineage sPur-rgyal, and the kingdom was named Thu-hpha; later this name changed into Thu-bhod.

---

23 [A reference to the area adjacent to the famed sacred mountain A-mye rMa-chen (6282 m.).]
24 [Roughly corresponding to present day Yúnnán (云南) Province.]
25 [Northern Zhōu dynasty (Běi Zhōu cháo 北周朝), 557-581 CE.]
26 [Súi dynasty (Súi cháo 隋朝), 581-618 CE.]

The descendants of sPur-rgyal proliferated, conquered with fierce strength, and greatly extended their dominion. From the Krig dynasty until the Sos dynasty they had no contact with the Middle Kingdom, because the 'Jang stood between them. According to their custom, the king was called bTsan-po and the ministers who were divided into greater and lesser ruled.

Except for the information concerning 'Phan-myi contained in the second text, no fundamental differences in the content of the two sources quoted above exist. In essence, these historical sources are the Chinese explanation for the rise of the ancient king of Tibet, a completely anachronistic one because the first year of the Hrin-ros (Shén Ruì 神瑞) era of the Hig We (Hòu Wèi 后魏) dynasty [r. 386-535] corresponds to the male Wood Tiger year of the last *sMe-phreng* [twelve-year cycle] of the thirteenth *sMe-'khor* [sixty-year cycle] (that is, Tibetan year 2331, 414 CE).

The first excerpt above contains an in-text note [see note 11] that mentions "before the Common Era," referring to the earlier part of the Hàn dynasty, and obviously has nothing to do with the supposed time of Nan-le or Thu'u-hu-li'i-lo'o-ku of the Shan-sbi'i people. These two excerpts of Chinese historiography maintain that the origin of the Tibetan people lies within the 'Jang population, that their country was located in the rMa-chu area, and that the capital was near rMa-chen sPom-ra. These beliefs demonstrate that the historians who wrote those texts had no understanding of ancient Tibetan history and that they were unaware even that Tibet had a capital or that the Tibetan king resided in a palace. In a previous passage the 'Jangs are mentioned as not having had any relation with China, an indication of a further misconception, since they abruptly have the Bod appear in the rMa-chu area. At any rate, it is clear that these historical texts see the origin of the 'Jang and the Tibetans as one. Chinese scholars of later times have used the appellation Byang or Chang (Chin. Qiāng 羌) for the lDong-pas, and based on that faulty nomenclature, have mistakenly considered this population as different from the Tibetans. In summation, this discussion should help clarify what the ancient Tibetan documents mean when they say "the Mi-nyags originated from the lDongs."

The "Sum-pa" or "Sum-bha" that originated from the sTong clan, as the *lHo brag chos 'byung* and other sources clearly describe, had their main center in rGya-shod sTag-la-tshal, with gNye-yul Bum-nag to the east, sMri-ti Chu-nag to the south, Yol-zhabs lDing-po-che to the west, and Nag-shod gZi-'phrang to the north. The location corresponded to an area situated northeast of Central Tibet, bordered on the western side by Mi-nyag and on the northwestern side by 'A-zha.

The original clans are the ancestors not only of the Zhang Zhung, 'A-zha, Mi-nyag, and Sum-pa people, but of all Tibetan peoples. An indication that the five original clans are recognized as the ancestors of all Tibetans is found in texts on the astrology of the elements [*'byung rtsi*], which in Tibet are famous and which mention these original clans in a special way. For example the astrological text called *Nyer mkho bum bzang* [The Excellent Vase of Necessary Elements] cites the five great clans of lDong, 'Bru, sBra, sGo, and sGa, as related to a specific element, and associates them with a specific animal that represents their totemic image or their special protector (sDe, 2, 2):

> The gDong [have] Earth [as their] element [and their] soul [*bla*] [is linked] to the Deer.
> The 'Bru [have] Water [as their] element [and their] soul [is linked] to the Yak.
> The sBra [have] Iron [as their] element [and their] soul [is linked] to the rKyang.[27]
> The sGo [have] Fire [as their] element [and their] soul [is linked] to the Goat.
> The sGa [have] Wood [as their] element [and their] soul [is linked] to the Sheep.

Furthermore, the astrological treatise entitled *Baidūrya dkar po* affirms (sDe, 147, 1):

> Mouse, Ox, Tiger, Hare, Dragon, Snake,
> Horse, Sheep, Monkey, Bird, Dog, and Pig
> are the symbolic names.
> sTong three: Wood, Hare[, and] Tiger.
> Se 'A-zha: Fire, Snake[, and] Horse.

---

27 [Onager (*Equus hemionus pallas*).]

CHAPTER 1 ■ ORIGINS OF THE HUMAN GENERATIONS OF ANCIENT TIBET 31

sBrang [*sic*] Zhang Zhung: Iron, Monkey [and] Bird.
rGyal-drang-rje: Earth, the Four Opposites.
lDong Mi-nyag: Water, Pig [and] Mouse.

The word *sbrang* in the verse "sBrang Zhang Zhung: Iron, Monkey[, and] Bird" may appear to have the meaning of honeybee, but in fact it refers to the sBra clan from which the Zhang Zhung people originated; that becomes evident when the order of the words is analyzed.

The penultimate verse "rGyal-drang-rje: Earth, the Four Opposites" refers to the Earth element and to four animals that appear in the twelve year cycle, namely Ox, Dragon, Sheep, and Dog. These four animals are called the Four Opposites because of the pivotal position they occupy in astrological calculations, as is shown in the table below:

Table 1. *The Twelve Animals of the Astrological Cycle*

		South			
	Dragon	Snake	Horse	Sheep	
	Hare			Monkey	
East					West
	Tiger			Bird	
	Ox	Mouse	Pig	Dog	
		North			

rGyal-drang is the name of a region presently known as rGya-rong. The text *Pad dkar skyed tshal* (rNga, 9, I) found in the *gTo 'bum* [Collection of Rituals] says:

As for the man, [he is] rGya-rje Drang-dkar.

rGya-rje-drang has the same meaning as the more common expression rGya-rgyal-rong; *dkar* [white] simply refers to the good deities; furthermore, the name of this place can be written in two ways: rGyal-rong and rGya-rong; the people from this area descended from the family line of the Zhing-po lHa-rigs-rgo and for this reason the special word *rje* [noble] is added to this expression.

The excerpt quoted above where the five Tibetan great clans are associated with the five elements contains the verse "the gDong [have] Earth [as their] element [and their] soul [*bla*] [is linked] to the Deer;" here there is no particular reference to the lHa-rigs-rgo family line, but this family line was in fact a member of the gDong clan. Furthermore, in the *Rus mdzod pad dkar skyed tshal* (rNga, 9, 4) we read:

> If we examine the sentence "The twelve principalities originated from the lineage of King 'Bri of Sam-gha," it would seem that the so-called twelve principalities originated from the land of Sam-gha before the advent of the family lineage of the Tibetan King sPu-rgyal.

Sam-Gha is to be understood as Sum-pa and 'Bri as 'Bru; this can also be inferred from the order of the words. The text means that the principalities that conquered Tibet descended from the Tibetan clans of A-thang-'bru and sTong that were from Sum-pa. It would be incorrect to categorize them as ancient populations of Tibet or as originators of the populations of Zhang/Bod, as it would be incorrect to think that all people in the twelve principalities descended only from the 'Bru family line. In this respect the *Rus mdzod pad dkar skyed tshal* (rNga, 10, 6) says:

> Looking at the [astrological text of the] *gTo-phug*, [we read that] before gNya'-khri bTsan-po, lord of Tibet, there were twelve principalities. They descended from the lDong who [came] from Mi-nyag. Similarly, the 'Bru [came] from Sum-bha, the sBra from Zhang Zhung, the sGa from 'A-zha. This is how the peoples who had the king of Tibet as their leader developed.

The last sentence of this quotation is a bit confusing, because it would seem that the populations that descended from those clans spread and developed all over Zhang Zhung and Tibet and also that the king of Tibet was the most important leader of those clans. It cannot mean that the entire population of Tibet came from the progeny of the king, because this is impossible. The usual course of events is that first a place comes into being; then individuals appear; then gradually more assertive people emerge and prevail with whatever means; then a king or lord becomes the representative of all the people. The *Pad dkar skyed tshal* (rNga, 9, 7) continues:

> When we consider that eighteen family lines developed from the lDong and that nine progenies developed from the Seng, the rGyal, [and] the 'A-zha, it is difficult to categorically maintain that [the Tibetan people] originated from the six Tibetan family lines of the early human generations [*mi'u gdung drug*].

These two important verses explain how populations developed during the course of time in Mi-nyag, rGyal-rong, and 'A-zha from the lDong and the Seng, making it possible to understand how people in Zhang Zhung and Tibet grew and developed out of the mutual interaction of those clans and families. Therefore I do not see why it would be difficult also to identify the original clans.

In this text I have mentioned Sangs-po 'Bum-khri before considering the Four or Six Original Clans. This is not because I am demonstrating faith in the Bon tradition or because I believe that he is the actual progenitor of the people, but to indicate him as a mythological font.

In general, as far as I can see, the narratives of the ancient Bon tradition claim that the universe and sentient beings were generated from a cosmic egg. For me this notion makes much more sense than the idea of human beings descending from apes and chimpanzees, the reason being that in this context the egg has a broader meaning than the appellation itself, inasmuch as it refers to the condition of the collected essence of the five elements. In principle, this notion does not differ from scientific theories about the creation of the world: a definite correspondence can be seen in the way that, for example, human beings are conceived in the mother's womb and need to spend time there until their bodies reach the maturity needed for birth. If our descent is from apes, why do apes of later times not gradually turn into human beings? Also, even if we agree that, due to various spatiotemporal circumstances, apes turned into human beings, why are those circumstances no longer extant? How is it possible to establish such a simplistic idea that human beings descended from apes mainly because of physical similarities?

Research on the history of ancient times accepts as logical evidence documents written by ancient people as well as the objects they crafted, such as *gZi* and *Thog lcags*, rock carvings and images, excavated skeletons, and utensils. Based on comparing artifacts available from previous and later times, by elaborating upon how circumstances may have or have actually evolved, and by speculating upon innermost considerations, such as the belief systems of ancient peoples, we establish history. There is a vast difference between defining history on the basis of what one may believe personally and what ancient people believed. History should not be based on personal convictions, but on understanding concrete circumstances and relevant factors.

It is essential to pay attention to the way of thinking and to the oral traditions of people of very ancient times if we want to shed light on the uncertain issue of their historical origins. In order to do that, I have adopted here the view contained in the *gZi brjid* that represents a vast and profound traditional account. This view considers Sangs-po 'Bum-khri as the source of existence and, in particular, contains the sayings of the forefathers of four thousand years ago—namely, the release of existence from a cosmic egg and the birth from its essence of the Lha of the sky, the gNyen of the atmosphere or the earth, and the Klu of the underworld, leading to the gradual appearance of Srid-pa Sangs-po 'Bum-khri and the creation of humanity.

It is also important to understand that the mention of the four or six clans immediately after the so-called Nine Brothers of Primordial Humankind [*srid pa mi rabs mched dgu*] who were generated by the ancestor Sangs-po 'Bum-khri is an account of the way in which humanity in general came into being and not a method of classification of the various groups.

The following tables are an example of how to compare the six or seven clans mentioned in various literary sources:

Table 2. *The Original Clans, as mentioned in the Po ti bse ru, the Lho brag chos 'byung, and the Rus mdzod (1)*

	Kha byang	Po ti bse ru	lHo brag chos 'byung	Rus mdzod
1	lDong	sPos-chu-ldong	lDong	lDong = A-spo-ldong
2	'Bru sTong	A-lcags-'bru -	'Dru sTong	'Bru sTong = A-thang-'bru
3	sGa rMu	dMu-tsha-dga' -	- rMu	dMu= rGa = dMu-tsha-rga -
4	sBra	-	dBra	-
5	Se	-	Se	-
6	rGo	-	-	Zhing-rgo = Zhing-bo-rgo
7	dPa' Zla	dBal Zla	- -	dPa'-yi-tshan Zla-yi-tshan

Table 3. *The Original Clans, as mentioned in the Baiḍūrya dkar po, and in the Nyer mkho bum bzang (2)*

	Kha byang	Baiḍūrya dkar po (Astrological text)	Nyer bum (Astrological text)
1	lDong	lDong	gDong
2	'Bru	'Bri	'Bru
	sTong	sTong	-
3	sGa	Se = (sGa)	sGa
	rMu	-	-
4	sBra	sBrang = (sBra)	sBra
5	Se	-	-
6	rGo	rJe (lha-rigs)	sGo
7	dPa'	-	-
	Zla	-	-

Many clans descended from the four or six original ones, and from their interaction the population grew and spread to every corner of the vast snowy region of Zhang/Bod. Even so, it is easily understood that a new society did not appear all at once, but was shaped following innumerable changes across time. In an article entitled *"Bod gna' rabs kyi rig gnas dang chos lugs mi rigs bcas kyi 'byung khungs skor gleng ba"* [A discussion concerning the origins of the people, religion, and civilization of ancient Tibet] (*Bod ljong zhib 'jug*, 2-1984, 9, 8) an eminent scholar[28] scrutinizes the conditions of Tibet from the advent of humankind to the rise and development of society:

> Many antecedent Tibetan historical sources maintain that at the time of Buddha Śākyamuni the land of Tibet was covered with water. Some [maintain that] when Pha-dams-pa Sangs-rgyas[29] went to Tibet for the first time at the age of five hundred years or so, Tibet was under water; when he went the second time, nothing but valleys with scattered trees and animals existed; and when he was there for the seventh time, he met Mi-la Ras-pa,[30] and so on.
>
> Since not more than two thousand years have elapsed from the appearance of the Tibetan people until now, statements of this sort are not in accordance with scientific explanations.
>
> The historian 'Gos-lo[-tsa-wa] gZhon-nu-dpal[31] specifies that even if it is said that the country, the people, and so forth of Tibet began, like India, in the *kalpa* of existence [*gnas pa'i bskal pa*],[32] that is not inconsistent from the standpoint of scriptures and logic. Buddhists, on their side, say that from the time in which the world did not exist until the time it was created, three big *dkrigs*, three small *dkrigs*, nine big *gtam* [*ma*], seven small *gtam* [*ma*], seven big *rab bkram*, no [small] *rab bkram*, six big *khrag khrig*, two [small] *khrag khrig*, and four big *ther*

---

28 [The late scholar Dung-dkar Blo-bzang 'Phrin-las (1927-1997).]
29 [An Indian Buddhist master who lived between the end of the eleventh century and the beginning of the twelfth century. He founded the Pacification of Suffering School (*zhi byed*); according to the Tibetan tradition this is one of the Indian Buddhist schools from which the system of *gCod* originated.]
30 [The famous Tibetan yogi and saint who lived from 1040 to 1123.]
31 ['Gos Lo-tsa-wa gZhon-nu-dpal (1392-1481) authored the *Deb gter sngon po*, one of the most famous Tibetan historiographical works. See *The Blue Annals* trans. by George N. Roerich, Asiatic Society, Calcutta, 1953.]
32 [According to Indian cosmology, a period of time after the first cosmic creation.]

'bum³³ elapsed. If we base ourselves on the current scale of one hundred million [*dung phyur*], this [period] would correspond to 397,706,240,000,000,000 human years. The ages [of the world] are divided into four and consist of a first period when the world is created, a second period when the world exists, a third one when the world is destroyed, and a fourth when the world is emptied space. Between the time in which the world is emptied space and the time in which it is created, there is a gap of twenty intermediate *bskal pa* [*bar bskal*], each of them corresponding to 1,728,000,000 human years. After the period in which this world is created starts the period in which the world exists. From when the ancient human race appeared until now, we must consider that a few million years have elapsed. Tibetans, like other people, have moved through prehistory, the Stone Age, the New Stone Age, barbaric epochs, and the Dark Age, into civilization.

Another article in the same review entitled "*Byang gi 'byung khungs la dpyad pa'i thog ma'i bsam tshul*" [Preliminary reflections on the analysis of the origins of Byang] (*Bod ljongs zhib 'jug*, 2-1986, 74, 19) contains historical information about ancient Tibetans and their existence in Upper, Middle, and Lower Tibet since the Stone Age:

> From several Tibetan sites, such as Ya-gyal,³⁴ Nying-khri,³⁵ Me-tog-rdzong, Kha-rub,³⁶ Ding-ri,³⁷ gNya'-nang,³⁸ and so on, old stone implements, tiny stone tools, human bones, petrified bones of vertebrate creatures, fragments of pottery, traces of foundations, and many earthenware containers have been found. Archaeologists have analyzed those relics, and have seen that they bear the same characteristics as relics found in the Central

---

33   [All these represent very large numbers.]
34   [An area located north of Lhasa.]
35   [Also known as Nyang-khri, located east of Lhasa at the lower reaches of the Nyang River.]
36   [Located in Chab-mdo, a vast area in the southeastern part of the Tibetan Autonomous Region.]
37   [Located in the southwestern part of Tibet, toward the Nepalese border.]
38   [Located in the southwestern part of Tibet, toward the Nepalese border.]

> Plains [*dkyil rgyud klung thang*] (Zhōngyuán Dìqū 中愿地区).[39] They acknowledge not only that mutual interconnections certainly existed between Tibet and the Central Plains from ancient times, but also that contacts were established during the third century C.E. by a tribe known as Bon-kyi-rong that, reaching the Central Plains, engaged in disputes and fights with the local tribes. Every time the Rong-pa won, they immediately annexed the conquered encampments, expanding as much as possible; on the contrary, when they lost, they would withdraw to the southwest, establishing residence in areas that correspond to present day Qīnghǎi Province, Sìchuān, and the Tibetan Autonomous Region. This is related in the "History of the Northwest [*Xī Běi Shǐ* 西北史]," contained in the *Dynastic Chronicles of the Later Hans* [*Hòu Hàn Shū* 后汉书].

And also (ibid., 80, 16):

> In the years 1956, 1966, 1976, 1978, and so on, old and more recent stone implements, tiny stone tools, pottery, bones of vertebrate creatures, human bones, fragments of pottery, fossilized bones of small animals, anchor stones used for fishing nets, bones of birds and wild animals, as well as traces of the foundations of dwellings were excavated in Nag-chu,[40] along the banks of the Tho-tho-hu River, a tributary that is one of the sources of the Chángjiāng [长江, 'Bri-chu, also known as the Yangtze River] in Qīnghǎi, as well as in Hu-hu-zhi-li and sGor-mo; in g.Ya'-li of the gNya'-nang district; and in Lug-rar, Shan-rtswa, mTsho-gnyis, Ru-thog, sPu-hreng, sKyid-grong, Kha-rub, Ding-ri, and Nying-khri. These recently found relics definitively show that ancient people appeared in Tibet twenty thousand, if not thirty thousand, years ago. They also prove that eight to five thousand years ago people accumulated groups of horses, cattle, and sheep and would spend their time herding them; and that more than 6,690, if not 6,843, years ago the Tibetans were sedentary and depended on agriculture as their main source of subsistence, with hunting and herding being complementary occupations.

---

39 [Comprising the middle and lower reaches of the Yellow River.]
40 [Located on the northeastern side of Lhasa.]

CHAPTER I ▪ ORIGINS OF THE HUMAN GENERATIONS OF ANCIENT TIBET 39

The following excerpts from the *Deb ther kun gsal me long* (Bod, 4, 16) contain extremely significant information that enables us to gain a general idea about the condition of the ancient Tibetan people:

> During the past few years, many ancient objects have been excavated in Tibet; for example, bones of primeval humans have been found along the banks of the Nyang-chu [River] in Nyi-khri. By analyzing a specific type of those bones that dates back four thousand years ago, experts have determined that it is a bone of the Man of Nyi-khri, and not of the Ape Man. The Man of Nyi-khri belongs to the Stone Age, or, alternatively, to the transition period between the New Stone Age and the Iron Age. Furthermore, relics and human bones excavated in great quantity in gNya'-nang, Ding-ri, Shan-tsha, Me-tog, and especially in Chab-mdo Kha-rub, provide varied and substantial scientific basis for research on the origins and the development of the ancient Tibetan civilization.

And also (ibid., 5, 15):

> Those relics are four or five thousand years old and are objects belonging to the New Stone Age. The objects were recovered from excavation sites measuring about 10,000 cubic meters and are astounding examples of the civilization they represent. Evidence was found not only of two types of dwellings, but also of a circular stone construction used for worship. Many stone implements, pottery including smooth, attractive earthenware vessels adorned with beautiful images, bone utensils, and seeds have also been excavated. The good quality of the ornaments and of the bone implements testifies to the level of culture and craftsmanship reached [by those people], while the seeds are a valid proof that about four thousand years ago agriculture was highly diffused in Tibet.

Several scientists of world reputation have said that originally in ancient times the Asian and American continents were connected and that they gradually separated, a process that took many thousands of years, a process that is confirmed by the jagged configuration of the coastal areas. There is also scientific speculation according to which people and animals migrated to America from the Asian continent. Even if no way exists to know clearly when, why, and how the two continents split apart because the separation occurred so long ago, a great similarity between the American Indians and the Tibetan people certainly exists, particularly in those facets of the American Indian culture which seem to have emerged from the Bon tradition. If we examine those aspects, we can understand that it is possible that the American Indians and Tibetans share those same age-old origins, like many rivers flowing into the same ocean.

Some scholars consider the possibility that the ancient Tibetan people arrived in America by crossing the northern glaciers; at the same time, there is no certainty that the Tibetan population rather than another people may have arrived at that place. Even the fact that several animals on the American continent resemble Tibetan fauna is not an ultimate verification. On the other hand, the striking affinities between the American Indians and the Tibetan people represent a phenomenon that cannot find any justification other than the fact that the two continents were one before their division. In any case, circumstances indicate that the Tibetans are an old population that existed long before the American and the Asian continents separated.

II
Origins of the Bonpo Lineages of Ancient Tibet

To discuss the ancient Bon of Tibet, first of all we have to clearly define what kind of Bon we intend; otherwise it is not possible to understand the meaning of ancient Bon.

All human beings have tried and will always try to find a way to mitigate the innumerable difficulties, fears, and suffering related to their body, energy, and mind. The cardinal problems that human beings struggle to conquer or resolve in whatever way possible are those encountered concretely in the physical body. In the case of the body, one can seek opportunities or create strategies in order to succeed, but dilemmas also arise at the mental and energy levels, and these can not be dispelled with material means, but only after careful consideration of the possible causes. The source of an individual's intentions is the force that resides in the physical body. The foundation of this physical force is air [*rlung*] and its source is rooted in the power of sound [*sgra*]. That is why in the Bon tradition the natural harmonization of a person's body and vital energy is thought necessary to lead a happy life. Generating that force is the element of the *bla*, and since the fundamental force of an individual is ultimately related to sound, the principle of *sgra bla* was developed.

The combined manifestation of air and sound is called speech [*ngag*]; this aggregate can operate as an equalizer of conflicting aspects in a person's environment, and is an indispensable component in the cure or redressing of disruptions. Beings who created mantras with specific functions did so by incorporating sounds endowed with power over the elemental sphere. Any motivated person in need could systematically recite them after having received the proper empowerment in order to produce their functions and, consequently, have the opportunity to deflect or transform the difficulties experienced. Because of that possibility, the recitation of mantras came to be considered the principal way to control the environment.

1. Origin of the Word "Bon"

In Old Tibetan the word *bon* meant to recite [*bzla ba*] and, specifically, to recite mantras. Whoever was accomplished in the recitation of mantras and thus had the power and capacity of dispelling difficulties was designated a *bon po*. The term *bon* was attributed not only to the recitation of magic formulas, but also to the different kinds of rituals that developed in connection with those formulas during the course of time. Therefore, as can be inferred, *bon* was not the name of the tradition proper.

Also the word *gyer*, an archaic Tibetan term [*brda rnying*], has become well-known. Utilized with the same meaning as the Tibetan verb "to chant" [*'don pa*], it is found in expressions such as "reciting the fumigation ritual in this way" [*bsang gi cho ga 'di ltar du gyer*] or "reciting these words for the ransom ritual" [*glud kyi cho ga 'di skad du gyer*]. In the modern idiom, however, the two archaic verbs *bon pa* and *gyer ba* have the specific meanings of *bzla ba* and *'don pa* respectively; the nuances of the two verbs can be inferred from their usages discussed above. In Tibetan eyes, *gyer* is an archaic expression; nevertheless, as the root text and the commentary of the *Srid pa'i mdzod phug* [The Ultimate Treasury of Existence] and other sources make clear, in the Zhang Zhung language *bon* is the equivalent of *gyer*, explaining why *gyer* is a term shared in the Zhang/Bod lexicon.

In fact it can be inferred that this meaning of *bon* is of much earlier origin than the term *bod*, because ancient Bon must have necessarily arisen prior to the Earlier Period and the era of Tibetan political dominion. Nonetheless, the *rGyal po bka'i thang yig* [Chronicles of the Kings] affirms (Pe, 113, 1):

> Then it was ruled by the Klu and the bTsan, and it was called Bod-khams Gling-dgu [Tibet of the nine regions].

If, as it is clearly stated in the text, the term *bod* existed when human beings were not yet ruling Tibet, we can understand that the word *bon* is also very old.

The *Deb ther dkar po* [The White Annals] affirms (Si, 38, 14):

> According to the followers of the Everlasting Bon [*g.Yung drung Bon*], in the beginning the name of the country was Bon, that then became corrupted into Bod. That *bod* and *bon* could be understood as having the same meaning may seem ridiculous, but that is not the case. Before King Nam-ri Srong-btsan, the religious system of the Everlasting Bon had spread everywhere in the country and thus it is not surprising that the name was well-known. In earlier times, the Chinese called Tibet the Country of Phon [*phon gyi yul*], a term phonetically related to *bon*. Furthermore, many examples exist in the old language of the interchangeability of the two consonants *da* and *na* as suffixes, for example in *btsan po* and *btsad po* [king] and in *chun po* and *chud po* [bouquet]; it is possible that this was also the case for *bon* and *bod*. In Mongolia, some call the followers of the Bon religion *bod* or *bo*. Nevertheless, the Islamic religion that spread extensively in Kashmir is called the religion of Kashmir [*kha che'i chos*]; similarly, since the religion of gShen-rab spread in Tibet, it is possible that the name of the country was attached to that of the religion, or that the name of the religion was attached to that of the country. But other than a 2000-year-old forefather, who could answer this question?

As was said, this designation appeared from very early times. That the term Bon and even a Bon system existed prior to the arrival of gShen-rab Mi-bo-che in Tibet is clearly attested to in Bonpo documents. For example the *Legs bshad rin po che'i mdzod* [The Treasury of Good Sayings] says (Pe, 46, 7):

> The demon Phrug-shor-ba rKya-bdun was sent to the gShen country to steal [the gShen's] horses. He stole seven [of them, such as] 'Brug [Dragon], and so forth. [He] drove the herd to Kong, hid them in the subterranean rooms of the castle, and [made] fall seven fathoms [*'dom*] of snow to cover their tracks. gShen-rab knew that; so He followed the horses escorted by his four skillful sons, not because he was attached to the horses, but because he intended to conquer the Srin-po and fight the demons of Tibet.

And also (ibid., 47, 4):

> Then the Teacher arrived where the sources of the Four Rivers of Tibet are concentrated. [He] subjugated the lHa [and the] 'Dre of Tibet, and bestowed [the sūtra called] *bKa' la nyan pa'i chad mdo* [The Promise of Listening to the Word]. At that time, even all the mountain peaks in Tibet bowed in reverence.

This and similar narrations contained in gShen-rab hagiographies explain clearly how the Bon of the so-called Bonpos of Tibet already existed before gShen-rab arrived in Tibet, and when gShen-rab arrived in Tibet about 3,900 years ago. Further, the same text affirms (ibid., 48, 13):

> When [He] arrived pursuing [his] horses, the demonic armies of dBus, Dwags po, [and] Ge-sar Kong-po surrounded [him] on both left and right. All sorts of weapons fell like rain but they could not even approach, let alone reach, the body of the Teacher. This exhausted the demonic armies, and when they were calm, the Teacher said, "If I make you my enemies, it is certain that you will be instantly killed. If you don't believe it, set me a target!" [So] the demons fixed nine iron shields in the ground, one after the other. The Teacher, placing an iron arrow in his bow and standing with his right foot on a big rock, did not [even] shoot the arrow with his right hand [but] with the left one. The arrow utterly pierced the nine iron shields and ended

transfixed in the rock of the facing mountain. The daughter of Kong-rje, Kong-bza' Khri-lcam, removed it with a white silk scarf and gave it back to the Teacher. Where the arrow had struck, a spring appeared that was called "The Spring of the Arrow Shot in the Rock of the Perilous Pass [*dor brag 'phrang la mda' drangs chu mig*];" and on the big rock where the Teacher had put his foot, an amazing brilliant sign appeared.

And also (ibid., 49, 8):

At that point, all declared [their] submission; faith was also born in Kong-rje, who offered Kong-bza' Khri-lcam in marriage [to the Teacher].

Thus the text clearly describes how Kong-rje also became a disciple of gShen-rab Mi-bo-che and not only what kind of primordial Bon and Bonpos existed at that time, but also what teachings of the Everlasting Bon [*g.Yung-drung Bon*] gShen-rab Mi-bo-che imparted, and what religious customs came to be established following the diffusion of his teachings in Tibet.

The *Legs bshad rin po che'i mdzod* informs us briefly about the kind of teachings that gShen-rab Mi-bo-che imparted when he set foot in Tibet (Pe, 47, 7):

To the Bonpos of Tibet, He bestowed the precepts for praying to the gods [*lha gsol ba*], banishing the demons [*'dre bkar ba*], and driving away curses [*yugs phud pa*].

The above-mentioned precepts are definitely part of the so-called Twelve Lores [*shes pa can bcu gnyis*] of Bon; in particular, praying to the gods [*lha gsol ba*] is related to the Bon of the deities, the Lore of Protection [*mgon shes lha bon*]; banishing the demons [*'dre bkar ba*], to the Bon of the *Glud*, the Lore of Beings [*'gro shes glud bon*] and to the gTo Rituals, the Lore of Proclamation [*smrang shes gto dgu*]; and driving away curses [*yugs phud pa*], to the gShen of Existence, the Lore of Funerary Rituals [*'dur shes srid gshen*].

Most Bonpo historical and religious sources maintain that before the advent of the first Tibetan king gNya'-khri bTsan-po, the so-called

Bon of the Fruit [*'bras bu'i bon*] was not diffused in Tibet; but who can say whether this kind of teaching really was not propagated in Tibet during the many years that elapsed between the death of gShen-rab Mi-bo-che and the time that preceded the advent of the first king of Tibet gNya'-khri bTsan-po?

If old Bonpo documents such as the six Vinaya texts of the *'Dul ba rgyud drug* cycle are carefully examined, it would seem that those teachings were available in Tibet at or soon after the time of Mu-khri bTsan-po who came after gNya'-khri bTsan-po. It is not impossible that the texts that are part of the *gSas mkhar spyi spungs* [General Collection of the gSas Palace] cycle were diffused in Tibet in a time precedent to the advent of gNya'-khri. The *rGyal rabs bon gyi 'byung gnas* [Bon Sources for the History of the Royal Lineages] affirms (Thob, 98, 49, 4):

> In Tibet, there were no descendants of the patriarch Seng-ge-'gram [grandfather of the Buddha] who were greatly honored in the world.[41] No royal law existed, but the Bon law was greatly diffused. The country was at ease and happy. That was the time when the gShen Nam-mkha'i mDog-can was residing in Tibet.

Here it is explained that even if no monarchic rule was to be found in Tibet during the period that preceded the arrival of gNya'-khri bTsan-po, the first king of Tibet, during this time the gShen Nam-mkha'i sNang-ba'i mDog-can was residing in Tibet and the country was happy by virtue of the Bon law. Furthermore, in the same text, we read (Thob, 99, 50, 3):

---

41 The progeny of the Gautamas were respected by many. In this regard, the *lDe'u rgya bod kyi chos 'byung* [lDe'u Paṇḍita's Religious History of India and Tibet] says (Bod, 218, 16): The sons of Gautama [were known as] the Sugarcane Ones [Bu-ram Shing-pa, Skt. Ikṣvāku, thus called because they were found in a sugarcane grove]. [The last king of the Ikṣvāku was] 'Phags[pa] sKyes-po [Skt. Virūḍhaka]. He had four sons: sKar-zla-gdong [*sic*, Skt. Ulkāmukha], sNa-lag-can [*sic*, Skt. Karakarṇaka], Glang-chen-'dul [*sic*, Skt. Hasti-niyaṃsa], and dKa'-thub-can [*sic*, Skt. Nūpura]. Also (ibid., 218, 21): dKa'-thub-can's son was gNas-'jog [*sic*, Skt. Vasiṣṭha]. His son was Ba-glang-gnas [Skt. Goṣṭha]. The latter had two sons, Seng-ge-'gram [Skt. Siṃhahanu], and Seng-ge-sgra [Skt. Siṃhanāda].

In Tibet, sGam lHa-sras, Dog-lha Bon-po, and so on, were the Bonpos of the Twelve Lores. They chose the name, performed purification rituals [*khrus gsol*], and there was a king, gNya'-khri bTsad-po. Before that, the gShen Nam-mkha'i mDog-can resided in Tibet. There was no monarchic law, but since [the country] was embraced by the Bon rule, [it means that] the Bonpos were here in Tibet even before the king.

According to what is said here, gShen Nam-mkha'i mDog-can would have resided in Tibet before that time; if that is the case, and since it is implicit that he possessed the Bon teachings of the *sPyi spungs* cycle, what certainty can there be that he did not teach them to the Bonpos of Tibet?

If the *sPyi spungs* teachings were transmitted before the time of the Tibetan King gNya'-khri bTsan-po, this means that also the teachings of the *rDzogs-pa Chen-po*, which are older than all the teachings of the Bon of the Fruit, existed then. This can be understood by reading the content of texts related to that cycle that clearly refer to the characteristic principles of *rDzogs-pa Chen-po*. For example, the tantra *gSas mkhar rin po che spyi spungs gsang ba bsen thub* says (Thob, 197, 99, 2):

> The great Awareness, pure from the beginning,
> is not trapped in obscurations, nor [enticed by] thoughts of deliverance.
> If one realizes the state of Mind devoid of bondage and liberation,
> everything is perfected in the Condition of the Mind [of] *Kun-bzang*.
> The state of *rDzogs-pa Chen-po* is not something which can be investigated.

The *Gab pa srog 'dzin sngags kyi don* affirms (132, 13, 2):

> If one realizes the meaning of [that] Identity,
> how can there be something to protect and someone who protects?
> It is pure, great protection from the very beginning.
> It is protection from the very beginning because it does not exist as [something] to be protected.

> Being held in the Heart-Mind of the Enlightened Beings of the three times,
> it is the very Owner of commitments [*dam tshig*].
> If one goes beyond that Commitment,
> the commitment itself [becomes] the basis of violation.
> Hence, how can acceptance and rejection exist?
> Everything is the Nature [of] *Kun-bzang*.
> Apart from the Enlightened Essence [*sangs rgyas ngo bo*], it is nowhere else.
> One's own Mind, [which is] entirely Pure [and] Perfect [*byang chub*],
> does not conceive of the boundaries of falling into partiality and limitations.

The tantra *gSang ba bsen thub* says (248, 124, 4):

> Perfection as such is devoid of appearance and emptiness.
> Viewed from the inside, it is filled with Bodies and Primordial Wisdom.
> The whirlwind of the mind where afflictions need to be tamed like demons
> shines forth as illusory Bodies and Primordial Wisdoms.
> The five poisons are perfected in the Primordial Wisdoms of the five Bodies.
> Perfection as such is devoid of clarity and obscuration.
> It is the secret Condition, natural bliss.
> The dimension where the objects of knowledge need to be tamed like demons
> shines forth as illusory Method and Discriminating Knowledge.
> It is spontaneously perfected as the Great Self.

Implicit in what can be learned is that when the great gShen Nam-mkha'i mDog-can resided in Tibet and all the people in the Tibetan land were relying on the Bon law, the government of the country was scattered among princes and leaders, more or less powerful, who collaborated among themselves; in order to guarantee the smooth flow of those interactions, people confided in the gShen-pos and Bonpos because they were considered worthy and reliable. The gShen-pos and Bonpos of that time, holding a conference, decided to look for a king who would rule the whole of Tibet. The *lDe'u chos 'byung* describes that event as follows (Bod, 100, 21):

> When the Twelve Princes ruled, none of them was important enough and thus fit to be the Lord of Tibet. The Three Uncles, the Four Ministers,[42] and so on, together with the Twelve Sages of the Lores, having discussed [the matter, decided to] look for a king. They asked Srib-kyi lHa-dkar Mang-po-sde,[43] "Where can we find someone fit to be our king?" He said, "Up above, on the fifth celestial level, there is lDe gNya'-khri bTsan-po, the divine son, nephew of rMu. I will invite him."
>
> Then Kar-ma Yo-lde[44] said, "Lord gNya'-khri bTsan-po, thirty-six places below is a country with no ruler, [but] all those who can talk are able to act as leaders. In heaven there are no yaks, but [there], all animals with horns are considered yaks. The horses are without defects, [but the place is] crisscrossed by ravines. [Nevertheless] please go to Earth to the residence of the fathers." Having made this request, lDe [gNya'-khri bTsan-po] said, "On the Earth below, there is stealing, hate, enmity, yaks, offense, and impediments."[45] [Kar-ma Yo-lde replied]: "For stealing there is punishment; for hate, there is love; for enmity, friendship; for poison, medicines; for yaks, weapons; for offense and impediments, places to escape." After having been told that, the Lord [gNya'-khri bTsan-po] was set to go.

---

42 *zhang gsum blon bzhi*: The *lDe'u chos 'byung chen mo* relates (Bod, 112, 4): "The Three Uncles are sNa-nam, mChims, and 'Bro. The Four Ministers are Khu, 'Gar, sBa, and 'Gos." Although the text says that these individuals lived at the time of King Srong-btsan sGam-po, the Three Uncles and Four Ministers mentioned here may have lived in the era of the first king of Tibet and were entitled to speak in view of their status within the Principalities. In any case, it is certain that both the *lDe'u chos 'byung chen mo* and the *lDe'u rgya bod kyi chos 'byung* are treatises written by mKhas-pa lDe'u.
43 Srib-kyi lHa-dkar Mang-po-sde is the name of a deity, as confirmed by the *lDe'u rgya bod kyi chos 'byung* [223, 19]: "rTsibs-kyi lHa-skar-ma Yol-lde, son of the deity that protects the earth."
44 Kar-ma Yo-lde, Srib-kyi lHa-dkar Mang-po-sde, and rTsibs-kyi lHa-skar-ma Yol-sde are different versions of the same name.
45 *byad dang ltems*: *byad* refers to harm caused by the power of harsh speech; *ltems* represents all sorts of evil spirits that hinder the performance of virtuous actions.

This account relating the way that the Bon gShen-pos empowered the first Tibetan king, after having chosen his name and performed purification rituals, is one of the renowned Bon and Buddhist histories of that event. Furthermore, the *lDe'u chos 'byung* affirms (Bod, 101, 20):

> lDe-glang Ru-kar [produced] the horned headdress.[46]
> rMu-rgyal-tsha of the mTshe-mi gShen placed [it] on [his] head.
> gTso'u-phyag-mkhar put the scepter in [his] hand.
> rMu-'bring Zang-yag took [his] hand.
> Placing [his] feet on the nine steps of the rMu ladder [*rmu skas*], [he] arrived at the peak of lHa-ri Gyang-tho.

A similar account is found in the *g.Yung drung bon gyi rgyud 'bum* [The Hundred Thousand Tantras of the Everlasting Bon] (KA, 18, 10, 2):

> The son of Lord Yab-bla bDal-drug was Khri-bar-la bDun-tshigs.[47]
>
> His middle son was without offspring, so [he] departed to be the ruler of the black-headed people.[48] The Teacher blessed [him] and sent [him] to perform the benefit of beings.
>
> When the Lord was leaving, Bonpos who were bodyguards [*sku srung gi bon po*] appeared from the sky: from the lineage of dMu-bon The-yan, 'Tshe-mi-rgyal appeared; from the lineage of Phywa-bon The-lag, gCo-gshen Phyag-dkar appeared. [The Lord, with the] two Bonpos supporting his right and left hands, went to Yar-lung Sog-ka. This is the first justification [*gtan tshigs*] of the Bonpo called La-li-gu.
>
> Many people raised [the King] and installed [him] on the throne; for that reason, his name was gNya'-khri bTsan-po. 'Tshe-mi placed the crown on [his] head. gCo-bu put the scepter

---

46 *ru'i sbal bdar*. The great royal gShen-pos of ancient Zhang Zhung wore a helmet with horns made of precious materials; perhaps this refers to a similar headdress.

47 Khri-bar-la bDun-tshigs: Yab-bla bDal-drug and rMu-btsun had three elder children and three younger children; Khri-bar-la bDun-tshigs was born as the seventh, hence the name bDun-tshigs [seventh].

48 [*mgo nag mi* is a term indicating lay Tibetans as contrasted with the ordained who had shaved heads.]

in [his] hand. Since the divine son had arrived relying on Bon and had faith in it, Bon was entrusted to the King's care.

The *Srid-pa rgyud kyi kha byang* [Guide to the Lineages of Existence] says (Thob, 78, 40, 4):

> [The King] resided at the Phyi-ba sTag-rtse castle in Yar-lung Sog-ka.
> Of all the places, the one where the Lord arrived was the happiest.
> At that time, the gShen-pos who performed the role of protectors of the royal person [*sku srung gshen po*] were Phya-bon Thang-yag, and Pha-ba mTshe-gco.

The *rGyal gshen ya ngal gyi gdung rabs* [The Lineal Succession of the Ya-ngal Royal gShen-pos] affirms (Thob, 50, 25, 2):

> [All his] actions and manners [were] pure [and] carried out according to the conduct of the gShen[-pos].
> Having requested the *sPyi spungs* Bon cycle from the gShen Nam-mkha' sNang-ba mDog-can, [he] then practiced [it].
> Three were the gShen-pos who protected the royal person: Dag-gtsang Ya-ngal, Tshe, and Co.
> The first location [that was] chosen [was] Yar-lung Sog-kha.
> The first castle [that was] erected [was] Byi-ba sTag-rtse.
> The first king was gNya'-khri bTsan-po.
> The first gShen-pos were Ya-ngal, Tshe, [and] Co.
> The first Bon [teaching was] the secret *sPyi spungs* cycle.

What is written in those texts, namely, that the above-mentioned Bon-pos existed before the arrival of the one who would be the first Tibetan king, that they were there to enthrone him, and also that gNya'-Khri bTsan-po requested the Bon *sPyi spungs* cycle from the great gShen sNang-ba'i mDog-can and practiced it, indicates that at that time not only Bon gShen-pos but also the *sPyi spungs*, profound essence of the Bon teachings, existed.

In the Bonpo culture, the relation of the teachings of the famous Bon of the Cause [*rgyu'i bon*] that were possibly diffused at that time to those of the Bon of the Fruit [*'bras bu'i bon*] and of the Pure Mind [*yang dag pa'i sems bon*], considered the quintessence of Bon, are explained in the *Byams ma skyon gi 'jigs skyobs* [The Merciful Lady who Protects against the Fear of Misfortunes] as follows (mDo, TSHI, 70, 5):

> At the time of gNya'-khri bTsan-po, the teachings of the Bon of the Cause were diffused. They were known and spred as the Twelve Lores:
> [1] the Bon of the Deities—the Lore of Protection [*mgon shes lha bon*];
> [2] the Bon of the Phya—the Lore of Prosperity [*g.yang shes phya bon*];
> [3] the Ransom Rituals- the Lore of Destination [*'dre (sic) shes glud gtong*];
> [4] the gShen of Existence—the Lore of Funerary Rituals [*'dur shes srid gshen*];
> [5] the Exorcism Rituals, - the Lore of Purification [*gtsang shes sel 'debs*];
> [6] the Lore Releasing from Curses [*sgrol shes lda (sic) byad*];
> [7] the Therapeutic Methods—the Lore of Healing [*phan shes sman dpyad*];
> [8] Astrology—the Lore Controlling the Order [of Existence] [*skos shes rtsis mkhan*];
> [9] the *gTo* Rituals—the Lore of Proclamation [of the Origins] [*smra (sic) shes gto rku (sic)*];
> [10] the Deer Rituals—the Lore of Flying [*lding shes sha ba*];
> [11] *Ju thig*—the Lore of Divination [*'phur shes cu (sic) tig (sic)*];
> [12] the Bon of Magic Power—the Lore of Ritual Destruction [*'gro (sic) shes 'phrul bon*].

Thus, the text shows that those Twelve Lores of Bon certainly flourished at the time of the first king of Tibet gNya'-khri bTsan-po.

In that regard, the *lHo brag chos 'byung* provides a list of the Bonpos connected to the Twelve Lores through which we can identify the names of twelve clans (Pe, sTod, 159, 16):

> At that time, some worthy Tibetan people [such as the following ones could] see [and] have insights through the Twelve Lores: the Powerful [*btsan pa*] lHo and gNyags; the Virtuous [*btsun pa*] Khyung and sNubs; the Fierce [*gnyan pa*] Se and sBo. [These

were] the six patrilinear [*yab 'bangs*] lineages. [Then there were] lHa-bo lHa-sras, Se-bon, rMa-bon, Cog-la-bon, Zhang Zhung Bon, Tshe-mi-bon, and so on.

The Twelve Lores are the main Bonpo teachings that developed in Tibet during the Intermediate Period. Therefore, if we want to understand the distinctive nature of the Bon of that period, it is necessary to meticulously research their specific theories and practices.

The reader is invited to consult my book *sGrung lde'u bon gsum gyi gtam e ma ho*[49] where the conclusions of my extensive research on the Twelve Lores of Bon are presented.

The names of the Twelve Lores are recorded with different readings in the *Byams ma*, the *bsTan pa'i rnam bshad dar rgyas gsal ba'i sgron me* [The Bright Lamp that Spreads and Makes Flourish the Explanation of the Teachings], the *rGyal rabs bon kyi 'byung gnas*, and in the *Legs bshad rin po che'i mdzod*. These varied readings are listed in the two tables below.

Table 4. *The Names of the Twelve Lores as recorded in the Byams ma and in the Dar rgyas gsal sgron (1)*

	Byams ma	*Dar rgyas gsal sgron*
1	mGon shes lha bon	mGon shes lha bon
2	g.Yang shes phya bon	g.Yang shes phya bon
3	'Dre shes glud gtong	'Gro shes glud gtong
4	'Dur shes srid gshen	'Dur shes srid gshen
5	gTsang shes sel 'debs	gTsang shes sel 'debs
6	sGrol shes lda byad	sGrol shes gtad byad
7	Phan shes sman dpyad	Phan shes sman dpyad
8	sKos shes rtsis mkhan	sKos shes rtsis mkhan
9	sMra shes gto rku	sMra shes gto
10	lDing shes sha ba	lDing shes sha ba
11	'Phur shes cu tig	'Phur shes ju thig
12	'Gro shes 'phrul bon	'Grol shes 'phrul bon

---

49 *Drung, Deu and Bön. Narrations, Symbolic languages and the Bön tradition in ancient Tibet*, LTWA, Dharamsala, 1995.

Table 5. *The Names of the Twelve Lores as Recorded in the rGyal rabs bon 'byung and in the Legs bshad mdzod (2)*

	rGyal rabs bon 'byung	Legs bshad mdzod
1	mGon shes lha bon	mGon shes lha bon
2	g.Yang shes phya 'dod	g.Yang shes phywa bon
3.	'Gro shes glud gtong	'Gro shes glud gtong
4.	'Dur shes srid gshen	'Dur shes srid gshen
5.	gTsang shes sel 'debs	gTsang shes sel 'debs
6.	sGrol shes lha byad	sGrol shes lta bon
7.	Phan shes sman	Phan shes sman dpyad
8.	lTo shes rtsis mkhan	sKos shes rtsis mkhan
9.	sMra shes gto dgu	sMra shes gto dgu
10.	lDing shes sha ba	lDing shes sha ba
11.	'Phur shes ju thig	'Phur shes ju thig
12.	'Gro shes 'phrul bon	'Gro shes 'phrul bon

2. The Diffusion of Bon at the Time of King Mu-khri bTsan-po

The way in which Bon spread at the time of Mu-khri bTsan-po, son of gNya'-khri bTsan-po, is described in the *Byams ma* as follows (mDo, TSHI, 70, 2):

> His son, Mu-khri bTsad-po, understood the meaning of the instructions, accomplished the purpose of the practice, and realized the meaning of meditation. Experts from countries such as sTag-gzig, and so on, translated [the teachings]. One hundred eight great scholars were invited from Zhang Zhung. Forty-five Bon meeting places [*'du gnas*] were established in Tibet.

The text states that many scholars and translators were invited to Tibet and many Bon teachings were translated, as understood implicitly, into Tibetan. The following excerpts from the *gSas mkhar spyi spungs kyi bshad byang* describe in a succinct manner the way the teachings of Bon and in particular the cycle of the *gSas mkhar spyi spungs* originating from Zhang Zhung together with the teachings called "Four Singles and Eight Pairs" [*ya bzhi zung brgyad*] became widespread and how Bon spiritual communities multiplied in the Intermediate Period during the lifetimes of the second king of Tibet, Mu-Khri bTsan-po, and of the great gShen sNang ba'i mDog-can (rGyud, TA, 99, 6, 2 et seq.; 101, 8, 2 et seq.):

> At the time of King Mu-khri bTsad-po, Nam-mkha' sNang-ba mDog-chen was practicing the precious Bon teachings of the *sPyi spungs g.yung drung thig le dbyings chen* in Khyung-lung dNgul-mkhar, Zhang Zhung. He conquered and bound with an oath all the deities of sky and earth, including their retinues. He would amuse himself with dragons, *khyung*, and lions, and played with blazing fireballs [*dzwa dbal*] as if they were *sGong*.⁵⁰ He subdued arrogant gods and demons and had them swear loyalty to the doctrine. Then he went to King Mu-khri bTsad-po and transmitted in full secret instructions to him. [He] practiced in lHa-ri Gyang-Tho. As ordinary signs of spiritual accomplishment, he would fly in the sky as a bird or walk on water as if he were strolling on earth; he would transform himself into a dragon or a *khyung* and soar in the sky; or, he would become a lion, capable of leaping to the summits of the blinding snow. He controlled the four seasons and showed many other signs of real spiritual accomplishment.
>
> It was then that the group of seven pure and worthy disciples who composed the principal retinue—King Mu-khri bTsad-po, Dhe-ba Za-rong Me-'bar, Bon-mo sTag-wer Li-wer, Zhang Zhung sTong-rgyung mThu-chen, Se-lde Me-gsum, and so on—requested that great and excellent gShen for all the tantric precepts and practices related to the Eight Great Sacred Words [*yi dam bka' chen brgyad*] of the *g.Yung drung thig le dbyings chen gsas mkhar gsang ba sgo dgu*.
>
> At that time, the great and excellent gShen Nam-mkha' sNang-ba mDog-can and the Bon King Mu-khri bTsad-po, together with all the Bon gShen and Wisdom-Holders [*rig 'dzin*],

---

50   *dzwa dbal sgong ltar bsgyur*. The *sgong* was an ancient musical instrument that was played by moving both arms quickly, producing a powerful sound.

practiced the precious instructions of the ultimate Eight Great Sacred Words of the *gSas mkhar rin po che thig le dbyings chen g.yung drung gsang ba* in many places, spreading the teachings, and developing the community of practitioners.

In Zhang Zhung [they practiced] in the three areas of mNga'-ris, namely, Ri-thog, which is surrounded by mountains, Gu-ge, which is surrounded by slate mountains, and sPu-rong, which is surrounded by snowy peaks.

In Upper Tibet [they practiced] in the areas comprised within the Four Divisions of dBus-gtsang: namely, gTsang-chung of the Right Division, Yar-lung and so on of the Middle Division; lHa-rtse and so on of the Border Division; and Nyan-kong and so on of the Left Division.

In Lower Tibet [they practiced] on the six hills of Khams and Amdo [*mdo khams sgang drug*], namely, Bu-'bor-sgang, Rab-sgang, dNgul-zla-sgang, lHo-rdza-sgang, sMar-khams-sgang, and Tsha-ba-sgang. In particular, they created retreat places where the teachings were transmitted and spread, such as the Seven Sister Mountains of Immutable Bon, the Four Nails of the Lazy Ones, the Six Places of Wonderful Talking, and so on.

Furthermore, in the north, they practiced on Mount Ti-tse.

In the border areas of Greater Tibet, they practiced on the snowy mountains of sPu-rgyal; in southern Tibet, they practiced at Yar-lha Sham-po; and also in the heart of Greater Tibet at rDo-thi Gangs-dkar.

At the borders of Tibet and China, they practiced on Kha-ba Glang-ri.

At the borders of Mongolia and Tibet, they practiced at gZer-thung rMa-rgyal sPom-ra.

They also practiced at Ru-dam Zil-khrom, one of the sacred places of Greater Tibet.

At the borders of Ta-zig-rong, they practiced at dBal-gyi Brag-phug dGu-rong.

At the borders with the lands of Klo [and] Mon, they practiced at Kong-po Bon-ri; [and then] at lHa-ri Gyang-tho; at Ri-gsum 'Dus-pa; at Lake Mu-le-khyud, [located] in upper sPu-rong; at Sa-khyon brGya-po Gang-byu in India; at Gyim-shod Shel-brag in Zhang Zhung sGo-mo; in Kha-yug Khyung-lung dNgul-mkhar; at rGyal-sa rGya-mkhar Ba-chod; at gSang-zhol of gNyan-chen Thang-lha; and other retreat places, such as Bam-brag brTsegs-pa, the Seven Sister Mountains, the Nine Sacred Places of Accomplishment, the Sacred Places of Attainment, and so on.

They created meditation places at Dang-ra g.Yu-bun in the north; sPos-ri Ngad-ldan in sTod; 'Phen-yul Brag-dkar in dBus; gNam-mtsho Phyug-mo in Byang; Mang-mkhar lCags-'phrang in La-stod; Gong-bu-me in China; Seng-ge'i sPa-gro sTag-tshang; Drung-gi mTshal-phug in La-stod; and Kha-rag gSang-phug in 'Dzing and so on; and blessed those key places [with their presence].

The fame of the royal gShen naturally spread [everywhere]: from Kha-yug Khyung-lung dNgul-dkar down to dMa'-she-le in India [and] Sum-pa Glang-gi Gyim-shod; and to the south, including Dom-sgro Nag-mo sMyug-ma Bu-'khur.

In the Four Divisions of Tibet from Li-yul-sgang in Byang to 'Jag-ma Glu-len in sTod, [disciples] listened, contemplated, and meditated upon the Bon teachings of the royal gShen and of the Wisdom-Holders and emulated [them]. Thirty-seven main community places were established in order to spread the aural and oral transmissions [*bka' nyan bshad kyi bstan pa*], to create unlimited time [for practice], sever the connections with unfavorable situations, and create a peaceful and pleasant existence.

The thirteen [*sic*] Bon communities in dBus were: Ngan-lam-ral; 'Dam-shod sNar-mo; 'Phen-yul Brag-dkar; Ma-tro Sa-rab; Shun-gyi Brag-dmar; Has-po Khri-Thang; lHa-sa Yer-pa; bSam-yas Khri-thang; gNam-gyi Ru-gdab; gNam-mtsho Do-ring; sTod-ral-lung; sKyi-shod Lung-nag; Re-rkyang Sha-'thab, and mChog-dkon rGyal-mo-khang.

The seven Bon communities in the Left Division [*g.yon ru*] were: 'Ol-kha Shug-gcig; Nyang-phu She-nag; Kong-yul Bre-sna; g.Ya'-lung Gang-bar; Yar-lung Sog-ka; Klung-shod Thong-dmar, and Ma-dros mTsho-shod.

The eight Bon communities in the Right Division [*g.yas ru*] were: 'O-yug Nag-thang; Shangs-kyi Zhing-tshal; Brud-kyi mKhar-gdong; rTa-nag rKyang-bu; rTa-phu Gron-lhas; gTsang-gyi Bye-phug; 'Jad-kyi sKyang-khor, and Zang-zang lHa-brag.

The nine Bon communities of Ru-lag were: Nyang-stod sTag-tshal; Chu-sgro rDo-ring; mKhar-chen Brag-dkar; mTsho-rNgas

Dril-chung; Gram-pa-kha'u; Ra-sa Thang-bdun; Mang-mkhar Bon-phug; Mang-yul Gung-thang, and Brag-dmar Ri-'dus.

All these sites were considered places of spontaneous accomplishment of the Four Actions. They had unsurpassable characteristics, such as sky in the shape of an eight-spoked wheel and earth like an eight-petaled lotus. Each of them had sacred constructions [*gsas mkhar*], a stūpa, [and] excellent theory and practice preceptors; the main temples [*gtsug lag*] were structures modeled on those in the Noble Land of rTag-gzigs [and looked] as if they had been transferred from a joyous heaven.

At that time, [in the] east, folk religion [*gtsug lag*] [was prominent] in China; [in the] north, medicine and diagnosis [*sman dpyad*] [were developed] in Ge-sar; [in the] west, the Doctrinal Collections [*sde snod*, Skt. *piṭaka*] [were diffused] in Ta-zig; [and in the] south, the sacred *Dharma* [was spreading] in India.

In Tibet and Zhang Zhung, the precious Bon teachings of the oral transmission [*bka' brgyud*] [called] the Four Singles and Eight Pairs [were practiced].

The Four Singles [are]: [1] the external teachings of the Vehicle of Discipline [*'dul ba*] and Metaphysics [*mdzod*]; [2] the internal teachings of the Vehicle of Sūtra, *Prajñāpāramitā*, and supporting liturgies; [3] the secret teachings of the rapid Vehicle of Bliss and Mantras; and [4] the very secret teachings of the Unsurpassable Mind Series Vehicle.

Four [of the Eight] Pairs consisted in the teachings of *Phywa*, *Pra*, [and] *Ju-tig*; the four hundred thousand teachings of medicine and diagnosis [*sman dpyad 'bum bzhi*]; those of the astrological sciences [*gab rtse gtsug lag*]; and rituals and methods to purify obstacles and clear disturbances [*gto thabs g.yen sel*].

As we have seen in the *Byams ma* previously quoted, Mu-khri bTsad-po invited one hundred eight scholars from Zhang Zhung and established forty-five major meeting places in Tibet. This data is corroborated by the excerpts just cited, which give us a clear understanding as to how and where communities and meditation places were established from the beginning of the Intermediate Era. This kind of information is important and indispensable in the search for and discovery of cultural vestiges of this period in the history of Tibet.

In the excerpts above we read: "originating from the Noble Land of rTag-gzigs [*'phags yul rtag gzigs kyi yul nas drangs pa*]." Here rTag-gzigs corresponds to the inner region of Zhang Zhung known as Phug-pa; and also: "[in the] west, the Doctrinal Collections [*sde snod*, Skt. *piṭaka*] [were diffused] in Ta-zig [*nub ta zig na sde snod*]." The latter is a distinct place vis-à-vis present day Persia or Iran, evident from its different ways of writing. This is an important element to consider in order to discover whether rTag-gzigs or sTag-gzig is the place from where the teachings of Bon spread and flourished and also to ascertain the actual place of origin of Mu-tsa Dra-he, the translator from sTag-gzig.

The *Byams ma* also describes the way in which the teachings of Bon spread during the time of Mu-khri bTsad-po's son and successors (mDo, TSHI, 70, 4):

> The Six Unsurpassables Teachings[51] spread during the reign of his son Ting-khri bTsad-po, [and of] So-khri bTsad-po, Dar-khri bTsad-po, Ye-khri bTsad-po, and Seng-khri bTsad-po. These were the Unsurpassable Teachings of the Father Tantra [*pha rgyud*], Mother Tantra [*ma rgyud*], Vehicle, Conduct, Fruit, and Ultimate Reality.

The *g.Yung drung bon gyi rgyud 'bum* outlines the way in which the teachings were developed and preserved (Thob, KA, 19, 10, 3):

> At that time, the power of the Lord was great. All the subjects were happy under [his rule], and also the teachings of the Everlasting Bon spread greatly. Twenty-four supreme teachers [*bon chen*] and forty-eight *siddhas* [*sgrub pa po*] appeared. Then came the Four Scholars [*mkhas pa mi bzhi*] who were sTong-rgyung mThu-chen of Zhang Zhung; lCe-tsha mKhar-bu of Me-nyag; lDe Gyim-tsha rMa-chung; and Se Sha-ri U-chen. During the time of those four gShen-pos, thirty-two Bon communities were established from Khyung-lung dNgul-mkhar to Sum-pa Glang-gi Gyim-shod. The influence of Bon increased in large measure.

---

51 *bla ma che drug gi bon*. This expression denotes the Six Unsurpassable Teachings mentioned in the quotation, not teachings imparted by six masters.

The *rGyal gshen ya ngal gyi gdung rabs* informs us briefly about the identity of the royal gShen-pos [*sku gshen*] who were active during the reigns of the so-called Seven Enthroned Ones from Heaven [gNam-gi Khri-bdun], also listing the sacred constructions [*gsas mkhar*] that those monarchs erected, and how those kings protected the Bon doctrine (Thob, 50, 25, 5):

> The first king was gNya'-khri bTsan-po.
> The first gShen-pos were Ya-ngal, Tshe, and Co.

And also (Thob, 51, 26, 2):

> The Lord [gNya'-khri bTsan-po] erected the first[52] temple [called] g.Yung-drung lHa-rtse. After gNya'-khri and [the Queen] departed for the lHa-sman dKar-mo heaven, their son Mu-khri bTsan-po was born. Like [his] father, he descended by way of the dMu staircase [*mu thag*] and the dMu cord, and alighted on the peak of lHa-ri Gyang-mtho. After his father showed him the scriptures of the secret *sPyi spungs* teachings, he requested the initiation from the master [*dpon gsas*] sNang-ba mDog-can. The royal gShen was bCo-bu Phyag-dkar. On the peak of lHa-ri Gyang-mtho, [Mu-khri bTsan-po] erected the temple [called] Khong-ma Ne-chung.

And also (Thob, 54, 27, 5):

> The son of Mu-khri bTsan-po and Khro-ma Ye-sangs was Ding-khri bTsan-po. The royal gShen was Co'u sMin-dkar. At 'Jug-ma'i-rtse, [the king] erected the temple [called] Khong-ma Yang-rTse.
>
> The son of Ding-khri and Khri-ma sTong-cho was So-khri bTsan-po. The royal gShen was Co-bu 'Od-dkar. At Gram-pa-tshal, [the king] erected the temple [called] dBu-khyud.
>
> The son of So-khri and gNam-sman Phyug-mo was Dag-khri bTsan-po. The royal gShen was Co-bu Shel-dkar. At Yar-lungs [*sic*], [the king] erected the temple [called] Zo-bo dBu-dgu.

And also (Thob, 56, 28, 1):

---

52   *rtse mo byung rgyal.* This expression means "the first great one to be created" [*thog ma'i mdzad pa rlabs che ba*].

The son of Dag-khri and Se-snan Phyug-mo was Byang-khri bTsan-po. gShen bCo-na Mi-chen protected the royal person. At Yer-pa-brag [the king] erected the temple [called] g.Yung-drung Khri-brtsegs.

The son of Byang-khri and Ye-byed Gung-rgyal was Khri-lde Yag-pa. The royal gShen was Co-bu Zhal-dkar. At Nya-ro Zla-ba'i-tshal [the king] erected the temple [called] Khong-ma Ru-ring.

The *Ya ngal gdung rabs* contains similar information regarding the eighth Tibetan monarch Gri-rum bTsan-po or Gri-gum bTsan-po (Thob, 57, 29, 2):

The son of Khri-lde Yag-pa and sGrang-za lHa-rgyan was Gri-gum bTsan-po. gShen Co-bu 'Tshams-dkar protected the royal person. At sPa-tshab sGong-phug [the king] erected the temple [called] Sa-le Byed-tshang.

This text, apart from the details quoted above, also provides us with information regarding several issues: the great influence that the Bon gShen-pos had at the time of the enthronement of King Gri-gum bTsan-po at age thirteen; the origin of the Bon teachings practiced by the gShen-pos; and the deep connection existing between the gShen-pos and the kings of Zhang Zhung that in itself was one of the reasons why Bon became so very powerful in the still small kingdom of Tibet. The *Ya ngal gdung rabs* tells us who those powerful figures were (Thob, 58, 29, 1):

At that time, the royal gShen-pos were the four great ministers [*blon chen*] Ya-ngal gSas-skyabs, Thang-nag Bon-po, Tshe-mi g.Yung-drung, and bCo Gyim-bu Lan-tsha. gShen Ya-ngal was displeased because [he considered the court] an unpropitious place to be; thus he left for rKong together with Lord sPu-lde. [He] founded a hermitage at Bon-ri and resided there. Called Bon-ri-dgon, the hermitage is still extant.

Thus it can be understood that the gShen-pos were not happy with the king. The *g.Yung drung bon gyi rgyud 'bum* describes how the conflict between the Bon gShen-pos and the king unfolded (Thob, KA, 23, 13, 6):

> The minister called bTsan-gzher Me-lha said, "Listen, oh Lord! If the hat is bigger than the head, the body looks small. If too much good food is eaten, one feels nauseous. Lice that walk on the legs [soon] aspire to the head. These haughty Bonpos will deprive the Lord of [his] power!"

And also (KA, 24, 13, 2):

> The minister Blo-ngan Bya-mgo said, "Those two speak the truth. Now the Bonpos' word is more important than that of the King, more powerful than that of the ministers. They contradict the King's word. If this is not stopped, no power will be left to the Lord!"

As the excerpt shows, the ministers did not appreciate the influence of the Bon gShen-pos, especially disliking their political power that derived from the relation with the Zhang Zhung king. For these reasons, the teachings of Bon were suppressed for the first time. This is how it happened, according to the *g.Yung drung bon gyi rgyud 'bum* (Thob, KA 24, 13, 7):

> Gru-zha gNam-sras said, "If the divine teachings of the Four Portals [*lha bon sgo bzhi*] are not left as protection, the demise of the king [Gri-gum] will come soon. If [the King] still wants to proceed in this way without one single royal gShen to teach [the Four Portals], [the King] will be as powerful as a virgin."[53]

Except for the divine teachings of the Four Portals that were left in Tibet at the time of King Gri-gum bTsan-po, all the others were suppressed and only two teachers remained to expound them. The *Legs bshad rin po che'i mdzod* describes this momentous event as follows (Pe, 183, 16):

---

53   *lha rgod lcam*. This expression is sometimes utilized with the meaning of *mkha' 'gro* [Skt. Ḍākinī]; however, the word itself is compounded and originates from an old Bonpo term denoting a woman who never had a consort.

The Bon of the Cause was not suppressed. In the *dBang chen* it is written: "The King said, 'In this country there is no room for both my royal governance and your religious authority. Hence, I wish to keep the divine teachings of the Four Portals and request Ge-khod This-'phen and gCo Gyim-bu Lan-tsha to remain as my bodyguards. All others are banned from the Four Divisions of Tibet.' Gyim-bu Lan-tsha said: 'If the divine teachings of the Four Portals are diffused, the life force of the gods [*gsas mkhar*] will be preserved; so it is good that I remain. I am happy that the divine teachings will not be suppressed.'" Of all the teachings he was unwilling to separate from and that he was allowed to keep, one and a half consisted in the teachings of the Bon of the Cause.

The *'Dul ba gling grags* tells how the teachings of the *'Dul ba rgyud drug* [The Six Classes of Discipline] were suppressed and what happened to them (Thob, 125, 6, 1):

> During their time, Ga-chu, Ya-gong, 'Pham-shi, [and] lDe-btsun [were] four [preceptors who through their] teachings [and] communities [of monastic discipline, had become] influential. [However,] since they were greatly envious [of each other], the venerable ones disagreed [about the distribution of] gShen-rab's relics. [Eventually they] split into two communities: Ga-chu and 'Pham-shi assumed the leadership of the first, Ya-gong and lDe-btsun that of the second.
>
> The spiritual son[54] of lDe-btsun [was] bCo Ye-shes. At that time, he requested [the relics and] received [them]. [He then] arranged the relics into five groups and brought [them] to five community places.
>
> At that time, in the temple of 'Dam g.Yung-drung Khri-'dus, the reliquary [*mchod rten*] g.Yung-drung Khri-brtsegs was constructed. [The reliquary] was placed in a crystal chest [*ga'u*] [and] kept as [a symbol of the Teacher's] seat.
>
> In the temple of brGya-ltangs bDud-'dul, the reliquary bDud-'dul dGra-'joms was constructed. It was placed in a silver chest and kept as [a symbolic] support [of the Teachings].

---

54 *mkhan bu*. The child or disciple in the transmission lineage of a preceptor [*mkhan po*] from whom vows have been received.

> rGyal-lde bTsun-rab-gsal took [the relics] to Rag-za g.Yung-drung Rol-po. [There he] built the reliquary Lo-ban-shel with three lids. It was placed in a chest that became the support for funerary ceremonies.
>
> [Furthermore, according to what] rGyal-bco Ye-shes had established, [one hundred relics] were divided into four groups: twenty-five were [taken to and] hidden in the caves of the snow mountains on the borders as [the symbol of the] Ultimate Meaning.
>
> The spiritual son of bCo-btsun, Mu-zi gSal-bzang, hid twenty-five [relics] in places such as Gangs-gnyan sTag-sgo, the crystal stūpa of Ti-se, Srid-pa'i lHa-dgu, [and] Tho-la Da-ma Ga-'go.
>
> Because of the [spiritual] power of the relics, it was impossible for practitioners who resided in those places not to obtain some kind of realization.
>
> Fifty were taken by bCo Ye-shes [who] used [them in his] contemplation [*thugs dam*].
>
> At that time, disputes [arose] within the communities and violations of the monastic rules took place; they also became causes for the dissolution of the Noble *Saṃgha* [*g.yung drung*].⁵⁵

And also (Thob, 126, 7, 5):

> In that time, disputes [arose] within the communities. Those of g.Yung-drung Rol-pa, and so on, split into four major communities and twelve minor ones. The bodily remains [of the teachers] dissolved into light and vanished in the sky. The blessing of the Teacher faded. All monastic rules were violated. Mu-zi gSal-bzang escaped to mDo-smad [Khams] and entered the suspended state.⁵⁶ That was the first time the teachings of Bon were suppressed.

Because King Gri-gum bTsan-po committed grave actions in suppressing the Bon teachings and so forth, he was killed by his minister Lo-

---

55 *g.yung drung*. In this case the expression means noble *saṃgha* [*'phags pa'i dge 'dun*].
56 *'gog pa*. A meditative state in which the flow of conceptuality is suspended, enabling the practitioner to remain in a state of contemplation that can last hundreds of years.

ngam. Having killed Gri-gum, Lo-ngam took political power and ruled Tibet for a number of years. That Lo-ngam acted in that way for the sake of Bon is not clearly stated in either Bon or Buddhist sources in which the circumstances that brought Lo-ngam to kill Gri-gum are presented as only incidental to his suppression of Bon. In fact, it can be understood that he did so precisely because he had faith in and devotion to the Bon teachings and wished to render service to the Bon tradition.

The *rGyal rabs gsal ba'i me long* contains a brief description of the destiny of Gri-gum bTsan-po's sons and of his consort dBal-bza' Khri-btsun-ma during Lo-ngam's rule (Pe, 56, 13):

> The three sons of the King fled to Kong-po, Nyang-po, and sPo-bo [because] in those places the political power of Minister Long-ngam [sic] was not strong.
>
> The King's consort was sent to tend horses. Once after the Queen Mother finished her task, she fell asleep and had a dream. She dreamed that she had intercourse with a white man, an emanation of Yar-lha Sham-po. When she awoke from her dream, she saw a white yak moving away from her pillow and leaving.
>
> Eight months later, the Queen Mother miscarried a trembling bloody mass which had only head and arms. She developed affection for that creature because it came from her own blood. She tried to nurse it, but it had no openings; so she placed it in the warm horn of a wild yak ['*brong*] which she wrapped in the strips[57] of a short garment and left behind. After some days when she went back to see what had happened, she found a baby there. She named him 'Jang-gi-bu Ru-la-skyes [the child of 'Jang born in a horn].
>
> The child at the age of ten asked [his mother], "Where are my father and my elder brothers?" The mother explained the whole story to him in detail.
>
> [Later on,] through various means, Ru-la-skyes retrieved the corpse of his father from the sKya-mo [River, a tributary of the] Nyang-chu, built a tomb for him at Phying-yul Dar-thang,

---

57 *ngar pa*. This is an archaic Tibetan term used specifically to indicate the lower part of a garment that touches the front [*ngar*] of the legs.

killed Minister Long-ngam, and invited his three elder brothers to return.

Sha-khri and Nya-khri did not accept the invitation and continued to rule in Kong-po and Nyang-po [where their] progeny is still found at present. The son Bya-khri came back from sPo-bo and stayed in Yar-lungs where he built the fortress [called] Bying-nga sTag-rtse.

While the mother was holding her son Bya-khri, she addressed a conjuration to the gods. [In that moment,] a voice resounding from the sky said, "Of all [your sons], this is the one who will become king [*bu de kun las rgyal bar 'gyur ro*]!" [The words] *bu de kun las rgyal* [literally, this son, of all, king] was turned into sPu-de Gang-rgyal [*sic*] [and became the name of the king]. This king seized the capital. Ru-la-skyes was his minister.

This clearly shows how the dynasty recouped its power. Furthermore, the *rGyal rabs gsal ba'i me long* relates how once again the Bon teachings were restored in Tibet at the time of sPu-lde Gung-rgyal (Pe, 57, 11):

At the time of this king and of this minister the Everlasting Bon appeared; the teacher named gShen-rab Mi-bo was born in sTag-gzig 'Ol-mo'i Lung-rings.

All the Bon teachings [*bon chos*], such as the *Khams chen po brgyad* [*Prajñāpāramitā*], and so on, [introduced] from the country of Zhang Zhung [and] translated [from the Zhang Zhung language], were propagated and made to flourish.

The teachings were divided into nine groups, four [called] Bon of the Cause and five [called] Bon of the Fruit.

The five Bon of the Fruit are considered the unsurpassable Everlasting Vehicles and are intended to enable one to attain the body of the higher celestial realms.

The four Bon of the Cause are as follows:

the gShen of Existence with the woolen turban [*snang gshen bal thod can*];

the gShen of Magic with the colored threads [*'phrul gshen bal tshon can*];

the gShen of Prediction with the *ju-thig* [strings] [*phywa gshen ju thig can*];

the gShen of Funerals with ritual weapons [*dur gshen mtshon cha can*].

The first one is to summon fortune and prosperity, petition gods and spirits, and produce good fortune and abundance in order to increase wealth.

The second one—which implies crossed-thread healing rituals [*mdos*]—creates stability for existence and its supports, and is for removing all present and future unfavorable conditions.

The third one is to show the way between good and evil, resolve doubts about right and wrong, and dissolve contaminated higher perceptions.

The fourth one is to remove disturbances sent to living people from the deceased, reckon [appropriate times for] burial, conquer the demons who disturb children, observe the heavenly constellations, and subjugate earthly demons.

The text makes evident that at that time numerous and diverse Bon cycles were once again widespread. The sentence "[a]t the time of this king and of this minister the Everlasting Bon appeared; the teacher named gShen-rab Mi-bo was born in sTag-gzig 'Ol-mo'i Lung-rings" does not imply that Bon or Bonpos did not exist in Tibet before then, nor that gShen-rab was born in sTag-gzig 'Ol-mo Lung-rings during the time of that king and that minister. Rather, it can be clearly understood from the following sentence—"[a]ll the Bon teachings [*bon chos*], such as the *Khams chen po brgyad* [*Prajñāpāramitā*], and so on, [introduced] from the country of Zhang Zhung [and] translated [from the Zhang Zhung language], were propagated and made to flourish"—that Bon was thriving in Zhang Zhung and that the teachings pertaining to the Bon of the Cause and to the Bon of the Fruit were developing again during the period in question.

The *Legs bshad rin po che'i mdzod* describes in broad terms how sPu-lde Gung-rgyal and the succeeding Tibetan kings acted toward the fostering of Bon (Pe, 131, 20):

> Since the son of that (Gri-gum) and dBal-za Khri-btsun had body and head covered with bird plumage, as well as a coat of horse and wolf hair, he was given the name sPu-lde'u Gong-rgyal.[58] His royal gShen was gCo'u gNya'-bzhed. [They] built the temple [*gsas khang*] [called] Khri-skor.

---

58 [Literally, the king [*rgyal*] with a mélange [*lde'u*] of hair [*spu*] on top [*gong*].]

And also (ibid., 132, 2):

> The son of sPu-lde and Bum-thang sMad-mtsho was A-sho Legs-rgyal. The royal gShen was sTobs-ra Shib-shang. They built the temple Sa-le lJon-phyug.
>
> The son of A-sho Legs-rgyal and dMu-lcam Dra-ma-na was De-sho Legs-rgyal. The royal gShen was Mi-mo-chung. They built the temple Kho-ma Yang-rtse.
>
> The son of De-sho Legs-rgyal and bTsun-mo Gur-sman was Thi-sho Legs-rgyal. The royal gShen was 'Dzin-bon Khog-der. They built the temple Sa-le Bang-bang.
>
> The son of Thi-sho Legs-rgyal and mTsho-sman 'Brang-ma was Gu-rum Legs-rgyal. The royal gShen was mTshes-pa gNam-'dul. They built the temple Rin-chen Zur-mang.
>
> The son of Gu-rum Legs-rgyal and sMan-bu-mo was 'Brang-zhi Legs-rgyal. The royal protector [*sku srung*] was lHa-bon Ye-gshen bDud-'dul.
>
> The son of 'Brang-zhi Legs-rgyal and Klu-lcam Mi-mo was I-sho Legs-rgyal.

The text continues by listing the successors of I-sho Legs-rgyal, indicating that each built a temple and had a royal gShen until Tho-ri Lung-btsan, giving no specific indication in that last regard, apart from saying, "The mTsho-bon dGu-brgyud acted [as] royal gShen[-pos]."

We also read (ibid., 133, 1):

> The royal protectors of lHa-tho-tho Ri-snyan-shal were gCo'u g.Yang-skyes and mTshe-mi 'Du-'phro.

And also (ibid., 133, 6):

> (Klu-gnyan gZung-btsan) was also known as Khri-gnyan gZung-btsan. The royal gShen was Zhang Zhung Tsha-la-rgyung.
>
> The son of Khri-gnyan gZung-btsan was 'Brang-snyan-lde'u. The royal gShen was Phon-po Ma-rgyung.
>
> The son of 'Brang-snyan-lde'u was born blind, but after the gShen-po performed a ritual practice for his organ of vision, he fully regained his eyesight [to the degree that he could] see

[*gzigs*] a wild *snyan*[59] on a distant mountain. For that reason he was named sTag-gong sNyan-gzigs. The gShen [of sTag-gong sNyan-gzigs] was Ra-sangs Khri-ne-khod.

And also (ibid., 133, 20):

The son of sTag-gong sNyan-gzigs was gNam-ri Srong-btsan. The royal gShen was Za-lha dBang-phyug.

The following tables present in a comparative manner:

1. the monarchs of the Intermediate Period - from the first king gNya'-khri bTsan-po until the father of Srong-btsan sGam-po, gNam-ri Srong-btsan,
2. their royal protectors [*sku gshen*], and
3. the temples they built.

The lists are based upon data retrieved from the following textual sources:

a. *Dar rgyas gsal sgron,*
b. *Srid rgyud,*
c. *lDe'u rgya bod kyi chos 'byung,*
d. *Nyang gi chos 'byung me tog snying po,*
e. *sGrags pa rin chen gling grags,*
f. *Bon 'byung,*
g. *Gleng gzhi bstan pa'i 'byung khungs,* and
h. *Legs bshad rin po che'i mdzod.*

---

59 [The *snyan* or *gnyan* is a variety of wild sheep. According to a personal communication from the Author, this animal has very long horns and when aged, can drown as it drinks because of the weight of its head.]

Table 6. *(1 through 32) The monarchs of the Intermediate Period, from the first king gNya'-khri bTsan-po, up to gNam-ri Srong-btsan, the father of Srong-btsan sGam-po; their royal protectors [sku gshen]; and the temples they built, as recorded in eight different textual sources*

Text	King	Royal gShen	Temple [1]
Dar rgyas	1. gNya'-khri bTsan-po	'Tshe-mi dMu-rgyal, Co'u Phyag-dkar	---
Srid rgyud	1. gNya'-khri bTsad-po	Phya-bon Thang-yag, Pha-ba mTshe-gco	---
lDe'u	1. lDe gNya'-khri bTsan-po	---	---
Nyang 'byung	1. gNya'-khri bTsan-po [6. gNya' Khri-po ?]	Co-na Phyag-gar-tsha, 'Tshe-mi gShen-bu rGyal-tsha	---
Gling grags	1. gNya'-khri bTsan-po	mTshe-mi-rgyal, gCo Phyag-dkar	---
Bon 'byung	1. gNya'-khri bTsad-po	Sa-lha Bon-po	---
Gleng 'byung	1. gNya'-khri bTsad-po	gCo-ldan mTshe-'gro	g.Yung-drung lHa-rtse
Legs bshad	1. gNya'-khri bTsad-po	mTshe-mi dMu-rgyal, gCo'u Phyag-dkar	g.Yung-drung lHa-rtse

Chapter II ▪ Origins of the Bonpo Lineages of Ancient Tibet

Text	King	Royal gShen	Temple [2]
Dar rgyas	2. Mu-khri bTsan-po	bCo'u Lan-tsha	---
Srid rgyud	2. Mu-khri bTsad-po	gCo-dbu-dkar	---
lDe'u	2. Mug-khri bTsan-po	---	---
Nyang 'byung	2. Mu-khri bTsan-po	gShen-po Tshe-rgyal	---
Gling grags	2. Mu-khri bTsan-po	dPon-gas Gru-bon Kha-'bar, sKu-gshen gCo Gyim-bu Phyag-dkar	Khong-ma Ne-chung
Bon 'byung	2. Mu-khri bTsan-po	---	---
Gleng 'byung	2. Mu-khri bTsad-po	gCo'u Phyag-dkar	Kho-ma Ne-chung
Legs bshad	2. Mu-khri bTsan-po	gCo'u Lan-tsha	Kho-ma Ne'u-chung

Text	King	Royal gShen	Temple [3]
Dar rgyas	3. Ding-khri bTsan-po	bCo'u sMin-dkar	---
Srid rgyud	3. Ting-khri bTsad-po	gCo-phyag-dkar	---
lDe'u	3. Ding-khri bTsan-po	---	---
Nyang 'byung	3. Ding-khri bTsan-po	Zhang Zhung Kun-'dus Theg-chen	---
Gling grags	3. Ding-khri bTsan-po	dPon-gsas 'Ol-bon sPyan-gcig, sKu-gshen gCo'u sMin-dkar	Khong-ma Yang-rtse
Bon 'byung	3. Ding-khri bTsan-po	gCo'u sMin-dkar	---
Gleng 'byung	3. Ding-khri bTsad-po	Co'u sMin-dkar	Kho-ma Yang-rtse
Legs bshad	3. Ding-khri bTsan-po	gCo'u sMin-dkar	Kho-ma Yang-rtse

Text	King	Royal gShen	Temple [4]
Dar rgyas	4. So-khri bTsan-po	gCo'u 'Od-dkar	---
Srid rgyud	4. So-khri bTsad-po	gCo-smin-dkar	---
lDe'u	4. So-khri bTsan-po	---	---
Nyang 'byung	4. Sribs-khri bTsan-po	Zhang Zhung Kun-rigs rGyal-po	---
Gling grags	---	---	---
Bon 'byung	4. So-khri bTsan-po	gCo'u 'Od-dkar	---
Gleng 'byung	4. Mu-khri bTsan-po	gCo'u 'Od-dkar	dGu-ra dGu-khyud
Legs bshad	4. So-khri bTsan-po	gCo'u 'Od-dkar	rMur-dgu-khyung

Text	King	Royal gShen	Temple [5]
Dar rgyas	5. Dar-khri bTsan-po	mTsho-mi Zung-smon	---
Srid rgyud	5. Byang-khri bTsad-po	gCo-zhal-dkar	---
lDe'u	---	---	---
Nyang 'byung	6. Khri-pan bTsan-po	Mu-la Kha-'bras	---
Gling grags	5. 'Dar-khri bTsan-po	---	---
Bon 'byung	5. Dar-khri bTsan-po	gCo'u Shang-dkar	---
Gleng 'byung	5. Dar-khri bTsad-po	gCo'u Shang-dkar	Zo'u-khyung-lag
Legs bshad	5. Dar-khri bTsan-po	mTshe-mi Zung-sman	Zo-bo Khyung-lag

Text	King	Royal gShen	Temple [6]
Dar rgyas	6. Dags-khri bTsan-po	Dag-pa Mi-chen	---
Srid rgyud	6. lDe-khri bTsad-po	gCo-shang-dkar	---
lDe'u	6. gDags-khri bTsan-po	---	---
Nyang 'byung	5. Ye-shes Khri-po	g.Yung-drung rGyal-po	---
Gling grags	---	---	---
Bon 'byung	6. Ye-khri bTsan-po	gTso-na Mi-chen	---
Gleng 'byung	6. Ye-khri bTsad-po	bCo-na Mi-chen	g.Yung-drung lHa-rtse
Legs bshad	6. Dwags-khri bTsan-po	Dag-pa Mi-chen	Yung-drung lHa-rtse

Text	King	Royal gShen	Temple [7]
Dar rgyas	7. Sribs-khri bTsan-po	gCo'u Zhal-dkar	---
Srid rgyud	? Khri-lde Legs-pa	gCo-bon dGu-brgyud	---
lDe'u	7. Sribs-khri bTsan-po	---	---
Nyang 'byung	7. Sribs-khri bTsan-po	Zhang Zhung lHa-'od	---
Gling grags	---	---	---
Bon 'byung	7. Seng-khri bTsan-po	gCo'u Zhal-dkar	---
Gleng 'byung	7. Seng-khri bTsan-po	Zhal-dkar	Khong-ma Ru-rings
Legs bshad	7. Srib-khri bTsan-po	gCo'u Zhal-dkar	Kho-ma Ru-ring

Text	King	Royal gShen	Temple [8]
Dar rgyas	1. Gri-rum bTsan-po	Pha-ba 'Tshe-gco	---
Srid rgyud	Dri-gum bTsad-po	gCo-tshem-dkar	---
lDe'u	7. Gri-gum bTsan-po	---	---
Nyang 'byung	---	---	---
Gling grags	1. Dri-rum bTsan-po	dPon-sas Li-bon sPungs-rgyud, sKu-gshen gCo'u Zhal-dkar	Khong-ma Ru-rings
Bon 'byung	---	----	---
Gleng 'byung	1. Gri-rum bTsan-po = Ge-mun bTsan-po	Co'u Tshe-dkar	Sa-le Bye'u-tshang
Legs bshad	1. Gri-rum bTsan-po	gCo'u-tshoms-dkar	Sa-le Bye'u-tshang

Text	King	Royal gShen	Temple [9]
Dar rgyas	2. sPu-lde Gung-rgyal	Zhang Zhung Tshe'i rGyal-po	---
Srid rgyud	1. sPu-lde Gong-rgyal	gCo-bon gNyan-dkar Legs-pa	---
lDe'u	2. 'U-de Gung-rgyal	----	---
Nyang 'byung	2. sPu-rje Gung-rgyal	Dar-ha-to	---
Gling grags	2. sPu-lde Gung-rgyal	Dran-pa Nam-mkha', Khyung-po sTag-sgra Dun-tsug, lHa-bon bTso-mo Gung-rgyal	Khri-rtse dGu-rtsegs
Bon byung	---	---	---
Gleng 'byung	sPu-rgya lDe-gung-rgyal	gCo'u gNyan-bzher	Khri-skor lDem-nyag
Legs bshad	sPu-lde'u Gong-rgyal	gCo'u gNya'-bzhed	Khri-skor

Text	King	Royal gShen	Temple [10]
Dar rgyas	1. A-sho-legs	Zhang Zhung mKhas-pa Nyi-shu	---
Srid rgyud	3. bTsad-po A'i-sho-yag	sTong-re Shib-shang	---
lDe'u	1. Sho-legs	---	Phying-sa sTag-rtse
Nyang 'byung	1. A-sho-legs	Tshe-mi Kun-snang	---
Gling grags	1. I-sho-legs	dPon-gsas Mun-sangs, lHa-bon gCo-stag Klu-gsas	---
Bon 'byung	1. A-sho Legs-rgyal bDud-'dul	---	---
Gleng 'byung	1. A-sho Legs-rgyal	sTobs-ra Shib-shang	Sa-le lJon-phyug
Legs bshad	1. A-sho Legs-rgyal	sTobs-ra Shib-shang	Sa-le lJon-byug

Text	King	Royal gShen	Temple [11]
Dar rgyas	2. De-sho-legs	---	---
Srid rgyud	5. bTsad-po 'O-ru-yag	'Dzi-bon Khod-ge	---
lDe'u	2. De-sho-legs	---	---
Nyang 'byung	2. E-sho-legs	A-la Dun-tshe	---
Gling grags	1. De-sho-legs	Li-shu sTag-ring, lHa-bon bTso-nyag gZher-thod-dkar	---
Bon 'byung	---	---	---
Gleng 'byung	2. De-sho Legs-rgyal	Mi-mo-chung	Kho-ma Yang-rtse
Legs bshad	2. De-sho Legs-rgyal	Mi-mo-chung	Khom-yang-rtse

Text	King	Royal gShen	Temple [12]
Dar rgyas	3. The-sho-legs	---	---
Srid rgyud	2. bTsad-po Tho-yag	gCo bDud-kyi mDud-bkrol	---
lDe'u	5. The-sho-legs	---	g.Yu-rtse
Nyang 'byung	6. The-sho-legs	A-la Dun-tsug	---
Gling grags	5. Thi-sho-legs	dPon-gsas Khu-lung Gru-'dzin, lHa-bon Seg-gshen bDud-'dul	---
Bon 'byung	---	---	---
Gleng 'byung	5. Thi-sho Legs-rgyal	lHa-bon Ye-gshen bDud-'dul	---
Legs bshad	3. Thi-sho Legs-rgyal	'Dzin-bon Khog-der	Sa-le Bang-bang

Text	King	Royal gShen	Temple [13]
Dar rgyas	4. 'Gu-ru-legs	---	---
Srid rgyud	---	---	---
lDe'u	3. Gor-bu-legs	---	dBu-rtse
Nyang 'byung	3. Go-ru-legs	A-so gTsug-spud	---
Gling grags	---	---	---
Bon 'byung	---	---	---
Gleng 'byung	3. Go-ru Legs-rgyal	'Dzin-bon Khog-dor	Si-le Bang-ba
Legs bshad	4. Gu-rum Legs-rgyal	mTshes-pa gNam-'dul	Rin-chen Zur-mang

Text	King	Royal gShen	Temple [14]
Dar rgyas	5. 'Brong-bzher-legs	---	---
Srid rgyud	4. bTsad-po 'Brong-'dzin-yag	mChes-pa rNam-rgyal	---
lDe'u	4. 'Bro-bzhi-legs	---	Khri-rtsig 'Bum-stug
Nyang 'byung	5. 'Brang-rje-legs	Zhang Zhung Khri-lde	---
Gling grags	4. 'Brong-bzhi-legs	dPon-gsas Gu-rum Tsan-de Mi-ser, lHa-bon gCo-snyan-rings	---
Bon 'byung	---	---	---
Gleng 'byung	4. 'Brong-rje Legs-rgyal	'Tshos-pa rNam-'dul	Rin-chen Zur-mangs
Legs bshad	5. 'Brang-zhi Legs-rgyal	Ye-gshen bDud-'dul	---

Text	King	Royal gShen	Temple [15]
Dar rgyas	6. Sho-legs	---	---
Srid rgyud	6. Yag-drug bTsan-po	'Dzi-bon Kha-tor	---
lDe'u	6. I-sho-legs	---	mThong-rtse
Nyang 'byung	4. dGe-sho-legs	Don-rtogs rGyal-po	---
Gling grags	1. gNya'-khri bTsan-po	'Tshe-mi-rgyal, gCo-phyag-dkar	---
Bon 'byung	---	---	---
Gleng 'byung	6. I-sho Legs-rgyal	---	---
Legs bshad	6. I-sho Legs-rgyal	---	---

Text	King	Royal gShen	Temple [16]
Dar rgyas	1. Za-nam Zin-lde	Zhang Zhung g.Yung-drung rGyal-po	lHun-grub dByings-kyi gSas-khang
Srid rgyud	1. rGyal-zi Nam-'dzin	mTshe-bon 'Od-dkar	---
lDe'u	1. rGyal Zan-nam Zin-lde	---	---
Nyang 'byung	1. rGyal Sa-nam Zin-te	Khu-mang bZher-gnyan	---
Gling grags	1. Za-nam-zin	dPon-gsas Gyim-thang rMa'o, lHa-bon sTong-dra Zhing-sha	---
Bon 'byung	---	---	---
Gleng 'byung	1. 'Bi-sho 'Ching-rgyal	---	---
Legs bshad	1. Zin-nam Zin-lde	---	---

Chapter II ▪ Origins of the Bonpo Lineages of Ancient Tibet

Text	King	Royal gShen	Temple [17]
Dar rgyas	2. lDe Nam-'phrul gZhung-btsan	Zhang Zhung 'Tshe-mi Kun-snang	---
Srid rgyud	2. lDe-bo gNam-gzhungs bTsad-po	mTshe-bon 'Ug-ru	---
lDe'u	2. lDe-'phrul-po Nam-gzhung-btsan	---	---
Nyang 'byung	2. gNam-spu'o gZhung-btsan-lde	Khu-mang bZher-gnyan	---
Gling grags	2. gNam-khri gZhung-btsan	dPon-gsas Sum-la Mu-phya, lHa-bon gShen-thang Mi-chung	---
Bon 'byung	---	---	---
Gleng 'byung	3. lDe-'phrul Bon-rgyal	---	---
Legs bshad	2. lDe'u-'phrul gZhung-btsan	---	---

Text	King	Royal gShen	Temple [18]
Dar rgyas	3. Se-snol gNam-lde	Zhang Zhung Don-rtogs rGyal-po	---
Srid rgyud	3. lDe-'od-nam bTsad-po	mTshe-bon Ba-nam	---
lDe'u	6. bSe-lde gNol-nam	---	---
Nyang 'byung	3. lDe-sprul gNam-gzhung-btsan	Dar-ha-ni	---
Gling grags	3. bSe-bon-la gNam-rings	dPon-gsas drag-po Kun-'dul, lHa-bon Ches-pa gnam-'dul	---
Bon 'byung	---	---	---
Gleng 'byung	2. lDe-rnol rNol-nam	---	---
Legs bshad	3. Se-snol gNam-lde	---	---

Text	King	Royal gShen	Temple [19]
Dar rgyas	4. Se sNol-lde	Zhang Zhung A-so gTsug-phud	---
Srid rgyud	4. lDe 'O-rnal bTsad-po	mTshe-bon Yag-rgyal	---
lDe'u	5. bSe-lde gNol-po	---	---
Nyang 'byung	6. lDe So-pha-nam	'Tshe-mi Bon-po 'Du-'phrod	---
Gling grags	---	---	---
Bon 'byung	---	---	---
Gleng 'byung	5. lDe gSer-gnon-rgyal	---	---
Legs bshad	4. Se sNol-po-lde	---	---

Text	King	Royal gShen	Temple [20]
Dar rgyas	5. lDe sNol-nam	Zhang Zhung A-la Dan-ci	---
Srid rgyud	---	---	---
lDe'u	4. lDe gNol-nam	---	---
Nyang 'byung	4. lDe sNol-nam	Ka-ra bDun-tshe	---
Gling grags	---	---	---
Bon 'byung	---	---	---
Gleng 'byung	4. lDe 'Od-rnol-nam	---	---
Legs bshad	5. lDe'u Nam-'od	---	---

Text	King	Royal gShen	Temple [21]
Dar rgyas	6. lDe rNol-po	Zhang Zhung Da-ra Ma-ha-ti	---
Srid rgyud	---	---	---
lDe'u	3. lDe gNol-po	---	---
Nyang 'byung	7. lDe rGyal-nam	'Tshe-mi Bon-po 'Du-'phrod	---
Gling grags	---	---	---
Bon 'byung	---	---	---
Gleng 'byung	6. lDe gSer-nam rGyal-po	---	---
Legs bshad	6. lDe'u sNol-po	---	---

Text	King	Royal gShen	Temple [22]
Dar rgyas	7. lDe rGyal-po	Zhang Zhung Nga-sa Ha-ti	---
Srid rgyud	5. rGyal-srid bTsad-po	mTshe-bon gSas-chen	---
lDe'u	7. lDe rGyal-po	---	---
Nyang 'byung	5. lDe rGyal-po	Kun-'dus Rigs-pa	---
Gling grags	---	---	---
Bon 'byung	---	---	---
Gleng 'byung	---	---	---
Legs bshad	7. lDe'u rGyal-po	---	---

Text	King	Royal gShen	Temple [23]
Dar rgyas	8. lDe Srin-btsan	Zhang Zhung Mu-la Ma-ho	---
Srid rgyud	---	---	---
lDe'u	1. rGyal-po sPrin-btsan	---	---
Nyang 'byung	8. lDe Srid-btsan	Bha'i Bon-po Shog-'brag	---
Gling grags	rGyal-po Srin-btsan	dPon-gsas sTag-sgra dGe-bshes, lHa-bon Yi-za Khod-grags	---
Bon 'byung	---	---	---
Gleng 'byung	1. Dar-rgyal Srin-btsan	'Tsho-bon dGu-rgyud	---
Legs bshad	8. lDe'u sPrin-btsan	---	---

Text	King	Royal gShen	Temple [24]
Dar rgyas	1. rGyal To-ro Lo-btsan	Zhang Zhung Ta-ra La-ha-te	---
Srid rgyud	1. Tho-lde Lo-rog bTsad-po	mTshe-bon 'Phrul-gsas	---
lDe'u	2. rGyal sTo-re Lo-btsan	---	---
Nyang 'byung	1. rGyal Thod-re Long-btsan	'Bum-khri Dar-ba	---
Gling grags	1. rGya-wer Li-lod-btsan	dPon-gsas sTong-sgra Kun-'dul, lHa-bon gCo'u 'Od-dkar	---
Bon 'byung	---	---	---
Gleng 'byung	2. rGyal-btsan	---	---
Legs bshad	1. To-ro Lo-btsan	mTsho-bon dGu-brgyud	---

Text	King	Royal gShen	Temple [25]
Dar rgyas	2. Khri-btsan-nam	Zhang Zhung Mu-la Ha-rgyal	---
Srid rgyud	2. Khri-btsan-nam	mTshe-bon g.Yag-zhu	
lDe'u	3. Khri-btsan-nam	---	---
Nyang 'byung	2. Khri-btsan-nam	dKar-dun-rtse	---
Gling grags	---	---	---
Bon 'byung	---	---	---
Gleng 'byung	3. Khri-btsan	---	---
Legs bshad	2. Khri-btsan-nam	mTsho-bon dGu-brgyud	---

Text	King	Royal gShen	Temple [26]
Dar rgyas	3. Khri sGra-dpung-btsan	Zhang Zhung Mu-la Ha-rgyal	---
Srid rgyud	3. Khri Ka-g.yu-btsan	mTshe-bon Bya-slag-can	---
lDe'u	4. Khri sGra-sgrungs-btsan	---	---
Nyang 'byung	3. Khri sGra-dpung-btsan	dKar-dun-rtse	---
Gling grags	---	---	---
Bon 'byung	---	---	---
Gleng 'byung	4. dMu-btsan	---	---
Legs bshad	3. Khri sGra-dpung-btsan	mTsho-bon dGu-brgyud	---

Text	King	Royal gShen	Temple [27]
Dar rgyas	5. gNam-ri Srong-btsan	gCo'i Bon-po Khri-phyung Grags-pa	---
Srid rgyud	---	---	---
lDe'u	gNam-ri Srong-btsan	---	---
Nyang 'byung	5. gNam-ri Srong-btsan	Shes-rab lDems-pa	---
Gling grags	---	---	---
Bon 'byung	5. gNam-ru Gong-btsan	Za-lha dBang-phyug	---
Gleng 'byung	5. gNam-ra sTong-btsan	Za-lha dBang-phyug	---
Legs bshad	4. gNam-ri Srong-btsan	Za-lha dBang-phyug	---

Text	King	Royal gShen	Temple [28]
Dar rgyas	4. sTag-re sNyan-gzigs	Ra-sangs Khri-ne-khod	---
Srid rgyud	4. sNya-gzi bTsad-po	sTong-bzangs lHa-phug, 'Or-bon 'Phan-grag	---
lDe'u	2. sTag-gu gNyan-gzigs	---	---
Nyang 'byung	3. sTag-ri gNyan-gzigs	Ra-sangs Khre-ne-khred	---
Gling grags	---	---	---
Bon 'byung	3. sTag-gu gNyan-gzigs	Sangs Khre-ne-khod	---
Gleng 'byung	3. sTag-gung gNyan-gzigs	Ra-sangs Khri-na-khod	---
Legs bshad	3. sTag-gong sNyan-gzigs	Ra-sang Khri-ne-khod	---

Text	King	Royal gShen	Temple [29]
Dar rgyas	3. 'Grong-snyan lDe-ru	Khu'i Bon-po Mang-rje Lod-po	---
Srid rgyud	3. 'Brong-gnyen lDem-ru	Sho-tse dMar-yag	---
lDe'u	1. 'Bro-snyan lDe-ru	---	---
Nyang 'byung	4. 'Brong-gnyan-lde'u	Khu'i Bon-po Mang-rje lHa-'od	---
Gling grags	---	---	---
Bon 'byung	4. 'Brong-gnyan-lde'u	Bon-mong Mang-rung	---
Gleng 'byung	4. 'Brong-gnyan lDe-ru	Bon-mo Mang-rgyud	---
Legs bshad	---	---	---

Text	King	Royal gShen	Temple [30]
Dar rgyas	2. Khri-gnyan gZung-btsan	Khu'i Bon-po Mang-sgra Legs-pa	---
Srid rgyud	2. Khri sNya-zungs bTsan-po	---	---
lDe'u	7. Khri gNya'-gzung-btsan	Zhang Zhung Bon-po Mi-tshe Lang-rung	---
Nyang 'byung	---	---	---
Gling grags	---	---	---
Bon 'byung	2. Klu-gnyan Gung-btsan	Zhang Zhung Tsha	---
Gleng 'byung	2. Klu-gnyan gZung-btsan	Zhang Zhung Tsha-la-rung	---
Legs bshad	2. Klu-gnyan gZung-btsan	Zhang Zhung Tsha-la-rgyung	---

Text	King	Royal gShen	Temple [31]
Dar rgyas	1. Tho-tho Ri'i-snyan-btsan	gCo-bon g.Yang-skyes, mTshe-bon 'Dul-srong, 'Bri-bon Shod-tri	---
Srid rgyud	1. lHa Tho-to sNyan-gshal	rMu'i Bon-po sKye-ngo-mtshar	---
lDe'u	6. lHa Tho-tho Ri-snyan-shal	---	---
Nyang 'byung	1. lHa Tho-tho Ri-snyan-shal	Co-bon gSang-skyes	---
Gling grags	---	---	---
Bon 'byung	1. Tho-tho Ri-gnyan-btsan	gCo-bon, 'Du-'phrod	---
Gleng 'byung	1. Tho-re Long-btsan	gCo-bon g.Yang-skyes	---
Legs bshad	1. Tho-ri Lung btsan	gCo'u g.Yang-skyes, mTshe-mi 'Du-'phro	---

Text	King	Royal gShen	Temple [32]
Dar rgyas	4. Khri Thob-rje Thog-btsan	Zhang Zhung Mu-la Ha-rgyal	---
Srid rgyud	4. Khri Thog-rje Thog-btsan	mTshe-gshen lDe-grags	---
lDe'u	5. Khri Thog-rje Thog-btsan	---	---
Nyang 'byung	4. Khri Thog-rje Thog-btsan	dKar-dun-rtse	---
Gling grags	Khri Thog-rje Thog-btsan	dPon-gsas lJang-tsha 'Phan-snang, lHa-bon Tha-tsha Khog-'phar	---
Bon 'byung	---	---	---
Gleng 'byung	5. rJe-btsan	---	---
Legs bshad	4. Khri Thog-rje-btsan	mTsho-bon dGu-brgyud	---

 III

The Royal Lineages of Ancient Tibet

AN UNDERSTANDING of the historical origins of the Tibetan monarchy in the Intermediate Period can be based only upon what was known to the Bonpos of ancient Tibet since in the early Intermediate Period the teaching of the Buddha was not yet established in Tibet and consequently no Buddhist historians existed to record their opinions. It is for these reasons that it is difficult to retrieve accurate historical data about the events of that epoch without the support of the Bonpo tradition.

Concerning what was known in classical times about the origin of the first king of Tibet, the *Blon po bka'i thang yig* [Chronicles of the Ministers] presents two main views [Pe, 435, 8]:

> [According to] the proclaimed Bonpo version, [the king] descended from the gods.
> [According to] the secret version [available to] ministers and subjects, [the king] descended [from] the The'u-brang.

The *lDe'u chos 'byung chen mo* [The Greater Religious History by lDe'u] speaks of three views [Bod, 99, 10]:

> According to the secret Buddhist version, [the king] descended from King [Rūpati].

According to the proclaimed Bonpo version, [the king] descended from the gods.

According to the most secret version, [the king] descended from the The-brang.

Concerning the proclaimed version according to which the king descended from the gods, the *lDe'u rgya bod kyi chos 'byung* [The Indo-Tibetan Religious History by lDe'u] affirms [Bod, 227, 15]:

> Initially, [during] the intermediate kalpa,[60] when Srid-pa was not active yet,[61] a [being] called Phywa Ye-mkhyen Chen-po appeared in order to arrange existence through the Phywa. After him was Legs-pa'i Hor-drug, [son] of Kho-ma 'Bro-rje. His face[62] had a pleasant scent, [he had] a wrathful gaze, [his] hair [was] sparse and ragged. [At that point] the sky and the earth were not separate; [he] exhaled and [his breath] blew them apart, so that the sky above had thirteen strata[63] like layers of canopies and the earth below had thirteen strata[64] like a stack of cushions. Inside the juncture of sky and earth [*gnam sa ga'u kha sbyor*], two lights, one white and one black, appeared. The white one held an opening toward Existence [*yod*], the black one held an opening toward Nonexistence [*med*]. Out of the expansion and contraction of Existence and Nonexistence a golden yellow flower and a turquoise blue lotus appeared. The golden yellow flower created the paternal cause, the turquoise blue lotus created the maternal cause. Out of the emanation

---

60 *bskal pa bas bskal*. According to the Abhidharma system, every two small *bskal pa* alternate with one *bskal pa* called the intermediate one [*bar gyi bskal pa*] that lasts 16,798,000 human years.

61 *srid pas ma srid tsam*. This may refer to a time in which Srid-pa Phywa'i rGyal-po was not yet in charge of the manifestation of Existence.

62 *spyan gyi sgros ma* has the same meaning of *spyan gyi gzigs stang* [look].

63 *gnam rim pa bcu gsum*. These thirteen strata are inhabited by the so-called Thirteen gNyan-po of the Upper Sphere [*yar g.yen gnyan po bcu gsum*]. According to the *gZer mig*, these are dBal, Yogs, and Khrin, gNyer, 'O, and mTshams, dMu, bDud, and bTsan, Srid, sKos, Phywa, and gNyan-po-lha. This is a famous ancient Bonpo worldview.

64 *sa rim pa bcu gsum*: I have not seen a description of an arrangement of the thirteen earth levels, but since the sky has thirteen levels, the thirteen earthly ones could be understood or thought of as support for each of the heavenly ones.

and absorption of the father and mother, the divine lord of Existence Kha-dang sKyol-med was born. He had a son with dByings-kyi sKyol-med, Mes-rnam-la Kar-gsum. Mes-rnam-la Kar-gsum and Phywa-za Ye-thang-ma had a son, sKar-ma Yol-lde. He and g.Yu-ri Phyug-mo had the Four Divine Brothers [*lha rabs mched bzhi*] dKar-nam rGyal-ba, lTing-rgyu dKar-po, lHa-khri Shel-dkar, and Tha-chung rTser-rtser.

And also (ibid., 228, 13):

> From Khri-shel dKar-po came the three brother deities [*mgul lha mched gsum*], Phyi-lha Thog-dkar, Bar-lha 'Od-'bar, and Nang-lha Gul-rgyal. When they spat into the sky, their saliva formed a white cloud like a little tent. In its center a man the size of a fist made of white conch shell with turquoise horns appeared. He was given the name gNam-then-che. His son was rGung-then-che; the son of that [man] was sPrin-then-che; the son of that [man] was Zil-then-che; the son of that [man] was Char-then-che; the son of that [man] was Mong-then-che; the son of that [man] was gNam-la Rong-rong; that son and dByal-cha Ma-ting had a son who was called Yab sTag-cha Yal-yol.

And also (ibid., 229, 9):

> The sons of that one and of the mother Tshe-za Khyad-khyud were the Four Ancestral Brothers of Divine Descent [*srid pa'i lha rabs mched bzhi*], Yab-lha brDal-drug, Phywa-lha Bram-chen, rGya-la 'Brong-nam, and 'O-de Gung-rgyal.

Thus, the text specifies that sTag-cha Yal-yol had four sons and also says that Yab-lha brDal-drug had seven sons and one daughter (ibid., 230, 18):

> The eldest, Yab-lha brDal-drug, was the lord of all the gods of the thirteen strata of the sky. At the highest [level,] he was the ruler of the Yogs; [at the] lowest [level,] he was the ruler of all the ornaments [and of] the first portion [of] victuals [*za ma phud*]. He and the mother rMu-btsun Gri-sman had eight children. These were the Three Elder Ones of Above—Rong-rong rTsol-po, Khri-rga sTag-gzigs, and Than-tsho Zo-'brang—and

the Three Younger Ones of Below—lHe-rje Gung-rtsan, lHe-rje Thog-rtsan, and lHe-rje Zin-gdags; the seventh was Khri-bar-gyi bDun-tshigs; and the eighth one was [their] sister Tha-nga lHa-mo.

And also (ibid., 232, 6):

Bar-gyi bDun-tshigs was sent away to the country of rMu. [His] son was gNya'-khri Gar-gyi bDun-tshigs. Since on the one hand the son was harming [his] father and elder brother, and on the other, his behavior was disagreeable to [his] mother and younger sibling, he was ordered to go to the country of Zhang Zhung. He did not want to go, so he was given a large retinue that included the seven Blo'u Rin-chen brothers[65] [as] bodyguards and lHa-ga-ya, Mu-ya, lHe-glang Ru-kar, and Dung-'phar-po 'Phar-chung [as] deities that protect the body [*sku lha*]. Thus he left for Ngam-'brang lCang-brang, the land of the maternal uncle [*zhang po*] rMu-rje bTsan-po, where he resided at the top of the thirteen levels of the sky.

The son of Khri-gar-gyi bDun-tshigs and Phu-mo Dre-rmu Dre-btsan-mo, [who was] one of the three daughters of Thang-thang in the maternal uncle's country of rMu, spoke from inside the mother's womb saying, "Oh mother, listen! If I were to emerge from above, the mother would die. If I were to emerge from below, the son would be contaminated. Let me exit from the back!" Then he moved to [her] right shoulder and came out from the mother's neck [*gnya' ba*]. That is why he was given the name gNya'-khri bTsan-po.

The text says that the son of Khri-gar-gyi bDun-tshigs, son of Yab-lha brDal-drug, was called gNya'-khri because he was born from the neck of the mother; that clarifies the name "the deity who came from the neck" [*gnya' ba nas byon pa'i lha*] by which he is also known. Furthermore, we read (ibid., 233, 10):

65　*blo'u rin chen mched bdun*. This may be the name of a group of seven siblings who were protectors of the dMu.

> At that time the nine paternal family lines[66] of Central and Eastern Tibet did not countenance the power of the Twelve Minor Kingdoms. They gathered in council and thus debated, "If we need to look for a true leader, mighty and gifted with magical powers, where can we find him?" [Suddenly] from the sky the sound of a divine voice proclaimed, "If you wish to appoint a leader for the black-headed Tibetan subjects, on the seventh stratum of the sky in the land of rMu in a place called Ngam-'brang lCang-brang in a golden castle with turquoise frost there is Lord gNya'-khri bTsan-po of the divine lineage of rMu. Invite him to be the leader of the black-headed ones!"

And also (ibid., 235, 8):

> Then, the fathers Thag-ring rTse-dgu La-dgu, 'Tshe-mis 'Tshe-btsugs, [and] Dung-'phar-po 'Phar-chung exhorted [gNya-khri in this way], "Seize the rMu scepter,[67] with [your] feet take nine steps on the rMu staircase, and magically walk into the sky. This will be the first descent."
>
> Thus [he] opened the expanse of the sky, parted the clouds, and gazed at the earth. Looking at the mountain ranges, he saw no high and secure spot [to descend] except for lHa-ri Gyang-do. Looking at the flatlands, he saw nothing wide and well arranged but only square and empty plains. Looking at the land, he saw no good and fertile [fields] but only square patches. Looking at the highlands, he saw nothing good except pastures. Looking at the waters, he saw nothing pure except for the blue waters [of the] gTsang[-po] and [other] shallow rivers.
>
> So [he] went to g.Yu-yul g.Yam-khang.
> Then he went to g.Yu-yul Drang-pa.
> Then he went to g.Yu-yul Bar-do.
> Then he went eastward to La-do.

And also (ibid., 236, 3):

---

66 *bod khams pha dgu*. This expression indicates that at that time nine paternal family lines existed in the dominions of Central and Eastern Tibet [Bod Khams], but it is not clear which they were.

67 *rmu 'brang zangs yag*. *'Brang* refers to objects of great importance; here it may have the meaning of a staff, most probably a copper staff called a *zangs yag*, a significant dMu or rMu object.

> Then he went to Gyang-thog Thog-yangs.
> Then he went to Bla-'brum Gyang-mdo.
> Then he went to Nags-ma Bya-tshang-can.
> Then he went nearby Shing-mu Le-grum-shing.

And also (ibid., 236, 17):

> The son of Lha-'od-grags called Gung-gzigs performed the Bon of the deities [*lha bon*] for gNya'-khri bTsan-po. Ma-mo Dro-zhal sKyid-lding raised the lamp and held the light in front of [his] eyes. The father Gro-za sKyid-rgyal offered a banner with long fringes.[68] [He] cast off the resplendent divine garments [*lha gos bsil le ma*] and donned human clothes of fine silk; he put aside the divine inner garments [*lha gsang gar bu*] and wore human inner garments [*mi gsang snar mo*].[69] He forwent pure divine nectars and downed brackish human drinks, *ding*[70] and old rice-beer and then went to Mi-yul Gyi-'thing.[71]
>
> > Then he arrived at the shores of [Lake] mTsho-dang-sko.
> > Then he went to Brag-gi dBrag-mar-po.
> > Then he went to Bla-ma Dangs-ma 'Bring-bcu.
> > Then he went to Dogs-mo Dog-mo Dog-nyen.
> > Then he went to Nyag-nyi rGyab-dmar.
> > Then he went to Dwags-yen-mkhar.
> > Then he went to Nga-la g.Ya'-ma-gong.
> > Then he went to Dwags-yul Shing-nag.
> > Then he went to Bra-la sGo-drug.

And also (ibid., 237, 16):

> From Bra-la sGo-drug he went to Shar-la 'Bring-lung.
> > Then he went to Dre-nga Bram-sna.
> > Then he went to lHa-lung sTag-pa.
> > Then he went to Klu-mo sByang-pa.

---

68 *ru tshod sngar ran*. This means *ru mtshon rnga ring* [banner with long tails], that is to say, a banner ornamented with long fringes.

69 *mi gsang snar mo*. A definition of inner garments called *gsang gos*, perhaps referring to underwear made of woven yarn [*snal ma*].

70 *ding*. A synonym of *chang* [beer], a term still used in some villages of dBus and gTsang.

71 *mi yul gyi 'thing*. This may refer to Mi-yul sKyin-thang.

> Then he went to Yar-khyim Sog-ka.
> Then he went to Khyim-bu Gor-gor.
> Then he went to rTsang-thud-gsum.
> Then he went to (Tsan)-dang sGo-bzhi.
> Then he went to 'Phar-po Zo-brang.
> Then the royal palace Yum-bu Bla-sgang was built in a miraculous manner and the king of Sum-pa-shang was conquered.
>
> Then gradually[72] [he] established family ties with the Twelve Minor Princedoms, becoming the ruler of the standing black-headed [Tibetans] and the lord and custodian of animals with a mane.
>
> Thus [he] manifested himself in twenty-seven successive arrivals.
>
> This is the first part of the divine genealogy that completes the history of the *Yo ga lha gyes can* [version].

This explains how the first king of divine descent appeared, became the lord of the Tibetans, arrived near Mu-le Grum-shing, donned human clothes, consumed human food and drink, and eventually traveled to Yar-lung Sog-ka.

Another similar account about the arrival of the first king of Tibet is found in the *lDe'u chos 'byung* (Bod, 99, 19):

> According to the proclaimed version of the divine descent, at the time when this world was not yet in existence, Phya-mi mKhyen-dgu-mkhyen appeared, arranged existence through the *Phywa*, and in succession created heaven and earth. After the universe and the world were gradually ordered, the ancestral god gNam-then Chen-po appeared. From him, the Nine Then [Then dgu], the Four Brothers [mChed bzhi], [and] bDun-tshigs came into being.
>
> The sons of gNam-then-rje were Gung-then-rje, sPrin-then-rje, Char-then-rje, Bal-then-rje, mDa'-then-rje, Mong-then-rje, [and so on], nine in all. His [other] four sons were the Four Brothers of Divine Provenance [*lha rabs mched bzhi*]; they were Yab-lha brDa'-drug, Phywa-lha Bram-chen, 'Od-de Gung-rgyal, [and] rGya-'brom-nam.

---

72 *khad kyis*. This old Tibetan term is similar in meaning to *rim gyis* [gradually].

> The sons of lord Yab-lha brDa'-drug were the Seven Brothers of Divine Provenance [*lha rabs mched bdun*]. The three elder ones were lHa Rong-rong rTsol-po, Khri-ba gNyis-gzig, [and] Than-tsho Zo-'brang; the three younger ones were lHe'u-rje Gung-btsan, lHe-rje Yang-btsan, [and] lHe'u-rje Zin-btsan.
>
> bDun-tshig became the seventh of the seven Khri kings [*khri rgyal po bdun*]; although he was banished to rMu, the country of the maternal uncle, [situated] on the fifth of the thirteen strata of the sky, he did not want to go, so his mother sent him great riches,[73] and [eventually] he left.
>
> The son of Khri-rgyal-ba and 'Dre rMu-khri bTsan-mo was known as Lord gNya'-khri bTsan-po either because he was born from the nape of the neck on a full moon night or because he arrived on a throne carried at neck [height]. Before then, the designation "the king [descended] from the gods [*lha las rgyal po*]" was not included [in his name].

And also (ibid., 102, 3):

> Through his thirty-seven [*sic*] arrivals, [he] generated discipline in the kingdom. [He] descended from the gods of the sky. [He] came as the Lord in the country of human beings. [He] provided all-encompassing positive protection.[74]
>
> Then [he] went to Yum-bu Bla-sgang. From the beginning this construction was much higher [than others]. [To demonstrate its greater importance, its] administrators [were] lHo and sNyags.
>
> Then [he] arrived at Phying-ba sTag-rtse [where] a white silk tent of nine layers was erected and the superior being [*bla'i sku*]

---

73 *skor khang du bskur*. This sentence can mean either "sent many treasures from the storeroom which decided him to go" [*dkor khang gi dngos po du ma bskur nas phebs su bcug pa*] or "the place to perform the ritual for expelling negativities" [*'grul skor byed pa'i las khungs zhig na bskyel bcug*]. Since whether the latter site existed is uncertain, the phrase probably means "sent great riches" [*dkor nor du ma bskur*].

74 *gdags su ni gdugs bdal*. The words *gdags* and *sribs* refer to the positive or negative side, respectively; the parasol [*gdugs*] indicates refuge and protection. Therefore the expression has the meaning of all-encompassing, positive protection.

was surrounded by noblemen. As for a systematic law,[75] only the divine tradition of *sGrung* and *lDe'u* was promulgated.

Since miraculous contemplative knowledge arose,[76] external and internal [issues] were clearly defined[77] in the three types of private consultations.[78]

With the two types of punishment for men[79] and the five legal approaches,[80] Tibetan justice was born.

---

75 *gtsug lag gi thang khrims* means a law that is promulgated in accordance with tradition.
76 *dgongs pa 'phrul gyi ras chags* means the arising of the miraculous eye of secret knowledge, as well as the wisdom of the enlightened mind.
77 *phyi nang gi dmigs phye* are clear duties and procedures for understanding in a detailed way how to rule subjects at home and suppress external enemies.
78 *gsang gros rnam gsum* are private deliberations involving either the king, the nobility, and ministers, or servants and subjects.
79 *mi la chad rnam gnyis*. The text does not specify the nature of these two punishments. However, I think the taking of life is the punishment for great crimes and adequately calibrated chastisements for medium and small ones. The *lHo brag chos 'byung* says (Pe, I, 91, 14), "All [types of] legal sentences are in place. In case of goodness, even if it is the son of an enemy, the good is good and there will be a reward. In case of evil, even if it is one's own son, evil is evil and there will be punishment. [So] it is decided."
80 *bzhed rnam lnga*. The *lDe'u chos 'byung* affirms (Bod, 113, 8): "The five types of law are: the king's law, however bestowed, as the general ruling law; the four ancillary rules of conduct [with respect to] the appointed king, as exemplary laws for the kingdom; the *'Bum gser thang sha ba can* law that relies upon what is written down in the great chronicles of Tibet; the forceful law against criminals who afflict poor and hardworking people; the fifth law is established on the basis of advice derived from religious texts that relate amazing and innovative deeds of wise beings." The ancient foundation of the five laws, said to have appeared at the time of the *Dharmarāja* Srong-btsan sGam-po, is visible in rudimentary form here.

The nine insignia[81] and the eight tokens awarded heroism[82] were gradually bestowed; the four kings of the four borders of the world[83] paid [their] tribute.

This is a clear explanation and the way in which the *bShad mdzod chen mo* and the *lDe'u rgya bod kyi chos 'byung* describe the proclaimed Bon version [*grags pa bon lugs*] shows that probably only some words have been modified.

Famous Buddhist historical documents, such as the *Blon po bka'i thang yig* and the *lHo brag chos 'byung*, quote to a certain extent the history of the proclaimed divine descent and the most secret version of the descent from the The'u-rang, while the two *lDe'u chos 'byung*, the *bShad mdzod chen mo*, and the *Yum bu bla sgang gi dkar chag* simply mention the most secret version, without relating its history.

The origin of the proclaimed version that cites a divine descent is found in various Bonpo sources, such as the *Srid pa'i rgyud kyi kha byang* (*Srid rgyud*), where we read (Thob, 38, 6):

---

81   *yig tshang sde dgu* is either a system for ranking ministers similar to the six insignia [*yig tshang drug*]–gold, turquoise, two alloys, copper, and iron–used at the time of the *dharmarāja* Srong-btsan; or a system similar to that of the nine ministers, originally found at the time of gNya'-khri bTsan-po and described in the *lDe'u rgya bod kyi chos 'byung* (Bod, 263, 2): "As for the nine big ones, they are the nine ministers who take care of all affairs. [They are] the big, medium, and small ministers of the exterior [*dgung*]; the big, medium, and small ministers of the interior; and the big, medium, and small [ministers] who correct violations of the law. Since they are more important than other subjects, they are [called] the Nine Big Ones [Che-dgu]."

82   *dpa' mtshan rnam brgyad* are similar to the recognition accorded heroism that the *lDe'u rgya bod kyi chos 'byung* (Bod, 270, 18) mentions as "the six signs of heroism symbolized by an upper tiger[-skin] [garment and] a lower tiger[-skin] [ornament]; big and small tassels [zar]; tiger- and leopard-skin clothes," namely tiger-skin cloaks and tiger-skin lower fringes, big and small scarves made of gold-threaded silk; and garments made of tiger and leopard skin.

83   *mtha' bzhi'i rgyal po bzhi* are identified by the *lDe'u rgya bod kyi chos 'byung* (Bod, 226, 4) as, "The four untamed kings of the four directions: the king of India who is always coiled like a snake; the king of China who is like a wolf lying in wait for sheep; the king of sTag-gzig who is like a hawk preying on a flock of birds; the king of Gesar who is like an ax gouging wood."

The [first and] only father of all generations was Srid-pa Sangs-po 'Bum-khri.
Chu-lcam rGyal-mo as well was [the first and only] mother.
From their magical union, nine males and nine females came into being.
The eldest of all was Srid-rje 'Brang-dkar.
He took Yod-kyi lHa-mo Gang-grag.
Their son was lHa-rabs gNyan-rum-rje.
The son of lHa-rabs gNyan-rum-rje and Srid-lcam Le-dur was Myes gNam-lha dKar-gsum.
The son of Myes gNam-lha dKar-gsum and Srid-za lHa-mo-thang was lHa-bu gNam-then.
The son of lHa-bu gNam-then and g.Yung-drung Ya-rab rGyal-mo was lHa-bu rGyung-then.
The son of lHa-bu rGyung-then and lHa-mo gSal-skyed-ma was lHa-bu sPrin-then.
The son of lHa-bu sPrin-then and lHa-mo dPal-bskyed-ma was lHa-bu Chags-then.
The son of lHa-bu Chags-then and lHa-mo Gos-dkar-ma was lHa-bu mDa'-then.
The son of lHa-bu mDa'-then and lHa-mo Tshe-'dzin-ma was lHa-bu Drum-then.
The son of lHa-bu Drum-then and lHa-mo rTsad-dkar bDag-mo was lHa-bu Mang-then.
The son of lHa-bu Mang-then and lHa-mo Phya-g.yang bDag-mo was lHa-bu Bal-then.
The son of lHa-bu Bal-then and lHa-mo Zhim-dgu'i Dag-mo was lHa-bu gTsug-then.
The son of lHa-bu gTsug-then and dMu-za Dung-lcam Ral-mo-che was Yab sTag-cha 'Al-'ol. The royal protector [*sku srung*] was dMu-rje Thum-thum rNal-mad.
Before that nine gShen from the country of Ba-rabs acted as royal protectors.
Then, the son of sTag-cha ['Al-'ol] and 'Tsham-za was Lord Yab-bla bDal-drug. His protector was Mu-cho lDem-drug. Also dMu-bon-thugs protected [him].
Phya-rje Yab-bla bDal-drug and dMu-btsun rGyal-mo's children were the Seven lDe'u-rje Brothers [lDe'u-rje mChed-bdun].

> The seventh of those divine sons was also called Khri-sad 'Bar-ba. He was banished to dMu, the country [of his] maternal uncle. He married dMu-za gNyi-mthing-ma. Their son was lDe Nyag-ri bTsad-po who emerged from a single tuft of curled hair in a crease of [his mother's] neck because had he come out from above the mother would have died and had he come out from below the son would have been soiled.

This excerpt describes how the divine genealogy unfolded from Sangs-po 'Bum-khri until gNya'-khri bTsan-po. In this respect, the *rTsa rgyud nyi sgron* affirms (Dhi, 147, 4):

> At that time the consort of Phywa Yab-bla bDal-drug, dMu-lcam mChong-ron-ma, generated the Seven Le'u-rje Brothers [Le'u-rje mChed-bdun]. The seventh was Khri-bar-la bDun-tshig. The father appointed [him] ruler of the Tibetan people. He married dMu-lcam Khab-'bring-ma. The child [begotten] spoke amiably[84] from inside the mother, saying: "If I move upward to be born, the space is too tight; if I move downward, the space is soiled and impure. Is there a direct way out?" The mother said, "Child, do not say that! Do not kill your mother! Come out the natural way!" Even so, he would not listen; then a swelling [appeared] on the mother's neck. With a sharp knife, Phya-bon De-skyong [cut it open and] pulled the child out; dMu-yi Bon-po Gong-chung wrapped [him] in a white silk cloth. The name [given to him] was gNya'-khri bTsan-po. Phya-bon-sngags applied medicinal oil to the opening from where the child had emerged, healing it completely. gNya'-khri bTsad-po arrived on the earth from the sky to be the lord of Tibet. The Teacher conferred a blessing on [him].

Furthermore, the *Dar rgyas gsal sgron* reads (Thob, 636, 71, 7):

> It is said that the progeny of Yab-lha bDal-drug [from] the lineage of Ye-rje sMon-pa, emanation of Srid-pa Sangs-po, is a descendancy respected by many. Here is its history:

---

84 *bu gcig khos srel*. Although *mkhos*, just like *mkhos phab*, literally means "reasonable" or "logically consistent" and *srel* or *bsrel* [past tense] means "holding [*srel ba*] a sharp weapon in the hand," its significance here is an archaic expression meaning "a lovely child."

The head of the ancestral progeny descended to the glorious heart of the world, precious quintessence of the earth, from the gods [in] the pure sphere of existence. When he did so, the divine king had great magic powers and possessed skillful means. He became the lord of all the black-headed [people], protecting all sentient beings in happiness, peace, and welfare, and many honored him. Before that lord became the king of human beings, his name was Tha-tshan Hi-sang-skyes.

Also the *rGyal gshen ya ngal gyi gdung rabs* (Thob, 28, 14, 1) contains similar information. These exegeses clearly consider the first ancestral king Sangs-po 'Bum-khri as the progenitor of Yab-bla bDal-drug's divine lineage, and Phya Yab-bla bDal-drug as the ancestor of the royal progeny of ancient Tibet. Many other Bonpo documents apart from the ones quoted above describe in an expanded or abridged fashion the way in which the first Tibetan king descended from the lineage of Phya Yab-bla bDal-drug.

I could not find details concerning the twenty-seven arrivals, described sketchily in the *lDe'u rgya bod kyi chos 'byung*, or about the thirty-seven arrivals, mentioned in the *lDe'u chos 'byung chen mo*, in either past or contemporary Bonpo documents, but I am certain that the stories quoted above have been drawn from old sources.

The real meaning of the sentence "descended from the gods [which is the] proclaimed [version]" is that the history was not expounded in an ordinary way so as to emphasize the power of the royal progeny and to proclaim the divine origin of the primeval lineage. It also has to be understood that the existence of a subsequent very secret version of the descent from the The'u-rang is solidly based upon that motivation.

1. THE DIVINE LINEAGE OF THE FIRST KING OF TIBET

As it is evident from the discussion of the royal lineages of ancient Zhang Zhung elaborated in the volume dedicated to the Earlier Period, the version of the divine descent of the Tibetan royal lineage as well as the origin of the ancient royal lineage of dMu are corroborated to a certain degree by the history of the Nine 'Then ['Then dgu] and so on.

The following table compares the names of the members of the divine lineage attributed to the first king of Tibet as found in the *lDe'u rgya bod kyi chos 'byung*, the *lDe'u chos 'byung chen mo*, and the *Srid pa rgyud kyi kha byang*.

Table 7. *The Divine Lineage of the First King of Tibet as recorded in the lDe'u rgya bod kyi chos 'byung, the lDe'u chos 'byung chen mo, and the Srid pa rgyud kyi kha byang*

Table 7 – The Divine Lineage of the First King of Tibet [I]					
lDe'u rgya bod kyi chos 'byung		*lDe'u chos 'byung*		*Srid rgyud*	
Father	Mother	Father	Mother	Father	Mother
1. Phya Ye mkhyen Chen-po	Kho-ma 'Bro-rje	Phya-mi mKhyen-dgu-mkhyen	---	Sangs-po 'Bum-khri	Chu-lcags rGyal-mo
2. Legs-pa'i Hor-drug	---	---	---	Srid-rje 'Brang-dkar	Yod-kyi lHa-mo Gang-grag
3. Srid-pa'i lHa-rje Kha-dang sKyol-med	dByings-kyi sKyol-med	---	---	lHa-rabs gNyan-rum-rje	Srid-lcam Le-dur
4. Mes-rnam-la Kar-gsum	Phya-za Ye-than-ma	---	---	Myes gNam-lha dKar-gsum	Srid-za lHa-mo-thang
5. sKar-ma Yol-lde	g.Yu-ri Phyug-mo	---	---	---	---
6. Four Brothers of divine descent [lha rabs mched bzhi]:					
1. dKar-nam rGyal-ba	---	---	---	---	---
2. lTing-rgyu dKar-po	---	---	---	---	---
3. lHa-khri gShel-dkar	---	---	---	---	---
4. Tha-chung rTser-rtser	---	---	---	---	---

Table 7 – The Divine Lineage of the First King of Tibet [2]

lDe'u rgya bod kyi chos 'byung		lDe'u chos 'byung		Srid rgyud	
Father	Mother	Father	Mother	Father	Mother
7. Three Divine Brothers [mgul lha mched gsum]:					
1. Phyi-lha Thog-dkar	---	---	---	---	---
2. Bar-lha 'Od-'bar	---	---	---	---	---
3. Nang-lha Gul-rgyal	---	---	---	---	---
8. gNam-then-che		gNam-then Chen-po	---	gNam-then	g.Yung-drung Ya-rab rGyal-mo
9. rGung-then-che	---	Gung-then-rje	---	rDzung-then	gSal-skyed-ma
10. sPrin-then-che	---	sPrin-then-rje	---	sPrin-then	dPal-bskyed-ma
11. Char-then-che	---	Char-then-rje	---	Chags-then	Gos-dkar-ma
12. ---	---	mDa'-then-rje	---	mDa'-then	Tshe-'dzin-ma
13. Zil-then-che	---	---	---	Drum-then	rTsad-dkar bDag-mo

Table 7 – The Divine Lineage of the First King of Tibet [3]

lDe'u rgya bod kyi chos 'byung		lDe'u chos 'byung		Srid rgyud	
Father	Mother	Father	Mother	Father	Mother
14. Mong-then-che	---	Mong-then-rje	---	Mang-then	Phya-g.yang bDag-mo
15. ---	---	Bal-then-rje	---	Bal-then	Zhim-dgu'i bDag-mo
16. gNam-la Rong-rong	dByal-cha Ma-ting	---	---	gTsug-then	dMu-za Dung-lcam Ral-mo-che
17. Yab sTag-cha Yal-yol	Tshe-za Khyad-khyud	---	---	Yab sTag-cha 'Al-ol	'Tsham-za
18. Four Brothers of the divine ancestral lineage [srid pa'i lha rabs mched bzhi]:		Four Brothers of divine lineage: [lha rabs mched bzhi]:			
1. Yab-lha brDal-drug	rMu-btsun Gri-sman	1. Yab-lha brDa'-drug	sNa-za	rJe Yab-bla bDal-drug	dMu-gtsug rGyal-mo
2. Phya-lha Bram-chen		2. Phywa-lha Bram-chen			
3. rGya-la 'Brong-nam		4. rGya-'brom-nam			
4. 'O-de Gung-rgyal		3. 'Od-de Gung-rgyal			

Table 7 – The Divine Lineage of the First King of Tibet [4]

lDe'u rgya bod kyi chos 'byung		lDe'u chos 'byung		Srid rgyud	
Father	Mother	Father	Mother	Father	Mother
19. Eight Brothers and Sister: [lCam sring brgyad]		Seven Divine Brothers: [lHa rabs mched bdun]		Seven lDe'u-rje Brothers: [lDe'u-rje mched bdun]	
1. Rong-rong rTsol-po		1. lHa Rong-rong rTsol-po		---	
2. Khri-rga sTag-gzigs		2. Khri-ba gNyis-gzig			
3. Than-tsho Zo-'brang		3. Than-tsho Zo-'brang			
4. lHe-rje Gung-rtsan		4. lHe'u-rje Gung-btsan			
5. lHe-rje Thog-rtsan		5. lHe-rje Yang-btsan			
6. lHe-rje Zin-gdags		6. lHe'u-rje Zin-btsan			
7. Khri-bar-gyi bDun-tshigs	Dre-rmu Dre-btsan	7. Khri-rgyal-po = Khri-rgyal-ba	'Dre rMu-khri bTsan-mo	Khri-sad 'Bar-ba (bDun-tshigs)	dMu-za gNyi-mthing-ma
8. Sring-mo Tha-nga lHa-mo					
20. gNya'-khri bTsan-po	gNam-mug-mug	rJe gNya'-khri bTsan-po	gNam-mug-mug	lDe Nyag-ri bTsad-po	gNam-sman Ting-ting

Concerning the very secret version about the descent from the The'u-rang, the *Blon po bka'i thang yig* says (Pe, 435, 9):

> The Nine The'u-rang siblings [The'u-rang sPun-dgu] were born to Mo-btsun Gung-rgyal of the sPu country. Of them, the youngest one was U-pe-ra; [the line of descent] began with him. The son of Khri-rgyal-ba and Dri-dmu Tri-btsan was gNya'-khri bTsan-po, born on full moon. He was also called Nya-khri bTsan-po.

Examining this excerpt we see that the name of the youngest of the nine The'u-brang siblings [The'u-brang sPun-dgu] is U-pe-ra and that gNya'-khri bTsan-po is the son born to Khri-rgyal-ba and Dri-dmu Tri-btsan in his lineage. In this regard, the *Yo ga lha gyes can gyi lo rgyus* calls Khri-bar-gyi bDun-tshigs by the name Khri-rgyal-po, while he is called Khri-rgyal-ba in the *lDe'u chos 'byung* and Khri-sad 'Bar-ba in the *Srid rgyud*. The *lDe'u chos 'byung* calls his mother Dre-rmu Dre-btsan or 'Dre rMu-khri bTsan-mo, whereas the *Srid rgyud* refers to her as dMu-za gNyi-mthing-ma. From this, it can be realized that the person cited above in the excerpt is identical with the one mentioned in the *lDe'u chos 'byung* and in the *Srid rgyud*.

Of all the ancient Tibetan historical documents, the best description of the secret version of the descent from the The'u-rang is found in the *lDe'u rgya bod kyi chos 'byung* (Bod, 226, 14):

> The nine The-brang siblings were born from the womb of sPu'i Mi-mo Mo-btsun of the country of sPu-bo. The youngest one called Ma-snya U-be-ra could cover his face with his tongue and had webbed fingers. He grew up to be very powerful and extremely ruthless. For that reason, the Buddhists and Bonpos of sPu-bo who were in charge said, "Because he has great power and is implacable, it is necessary to banish him!" Thus they enforced the The-brang relocation custom[85] and exiled him to Tibet.
>
> There he met people searching for a ruler for Tibet who asked him, "What kind of person are you?" "I am a man from the country of sPu-bo," he said. Then they asked, "You have a wondrous tongue and fingers. What powers do you have?" He responded, "My magical powers are overwhelming and that is why I was banished." "Well then, we name you our lord!" they replied. So they placed him on a throne [that they carried at] neck [height] and declared, "This is Lord gNya'-khri bTsan-po!"

---

85   *the brang skyas 'debs*. The The-brang or The'u-rang belong to the Ma-sangs class, semidivine beings that bear a close resemblance to humans. Their capacity to damage people in a numerous variety of ways caused a ransom-style custom to be established that allowed the banishment of the The'u-rang to another place. Many different objects and premiums would be collected and entrusted to an individual with a strong connection to the The'u-rang; then the person would be sent away. This ancient tradition remained until later times: it is clearly stated in many histories that prior to 1950 just before Losar, the Tibetan new year, the government would appoint a ransomer who would be recompensed in large measure and sent away from the central region to the borderlands from where he was not allowed to return.

This is the story of the choosing of the sovereign, and that was his hidden flaw or fault.

This excerpt clarifies the real origin of the lineage of the first Tibetan king and the relevant circumstances.

The text calls the youngest of the The'u-rang siblings Ma-snya U-be-ra. The *lDe'u chos 'byung chen mo* says (Bod, 99, 16):

> The very secret [version] is the history of [the lineage] that descends from the The-brang Mang-snya U-be-ra, a [son] generated from the womb of sPu'i Mi-mo-btsan from the country of sPu [sPu-yul], and [of how he] was made lord after having been named gNya'-khri bTsan-po.

If the *lDe'u rgya bod kyi chos 'byung* calls the youngest of the nine The'u-rang siblings Ma-snya U-be-ra, the "Mang-snya U-be-ra" of the *lDe'u chos 'byung chen mo* is most probably the same person. In the extended and abridged versions of the *lDe'u chos 'byung*, Mang-snya U-be-ra is said to be gNya'-khri bTsan-po, the first of the Tibetan rulers. However, since the *Blon po bka'i thang yig* clearly states that the progenitor of U-be-ra or U-pe-ra is Khri-rgyal-ba and that his son is gNya'-khri bTsan-po, could it be possible that the history of the order of succession found in the *lDe'u chos 'byung chen mo* and in the *lDe'u rgya bod kyi chos 'byung* is a little discontinuous?

The *Yum bu bla sgang gi dkar chag 'bring po* [Medium Version of the *Yum bu bla sgang* Register] (Bod ljongs zhib 'jug, 1984, No. 4, 14) describes the history of the very secret descent from the The'u-rang in a way that resembles those quoted above:

> Before, in the country of sPu-bo, nine The'u-brang siblings were born from the womb of Bya-mo-btsun. The youngest one was called U-be-ra: the maṇḍala of his face was excellent, his fingers were webbed. Since he was very powerful, all the people of his country banished him.
>
> When he arrived in Tibet, he met with Tibetans who were looking for a ruler in g.Ya'-le-gong on the northern route. "Who are you? Where do you come from?" they asked. "I come from the country of sPu-bo. Now I am going to Tibet." "Well, what kind of powers do you have"? they asked. He said, "The people

of my country banished me because I have great powers." "Well then, would you be capable of ruling Tibet?" "No doubt about it given my miraculous powers! Raise me on a throne to neck [height]." So, in keeping with what he asked, they lifted him to the level of [their] necks, carried him as a lord, and also gave him the name gNya'-khri bTsan-po.

Even if this text also states that U-be-ra is gNya'-khri bTsan-po, in reality no matter how the order of the words is analyzed, the source of the two *lDe'u chos 'byung* and of the *Yum bu bla sgang gi dkar chag 'bring po* can be clearly seen to be the same. In this regard, in the book that is the source of those texts, the presence of Khri-sad 'Bar-ba or Khri-rgyal-ba is not given as evidence of continuity between U-be-ra and gNya'-khri bTsan-po.

A version of this very secret history is also found in the *bShad mdzod chen mo* (Thim, KA, 169, 85, 4):

> Nine The-brang siblings were born from the womb of sPo'i Mi-mo Bya-btsun in the country of sPo-bo. The youngest one was called The-brang Ma-nya U-be-ra. He could cover his face with his tongue, and had webbed fingers. Since he grew to be ruthless and powerful, all the people in the country said, "This is not possible! Wouldn't it be best to banish him?" His father and mother said, "You are not going to banish the youngest of our nine children! If you banish our child, your children should be banished too!" They said this and would not hear of it. Thus the people of the country agreed to send him away in secret. After having gathered the powerful Bonpos and Buddhists of the country of sPo-bo, they enforced the The-brang relocation and exiled him to Tibet. In order to make it impossible for him to live [again] in sPo, [they had him] arrive in Tibet from the opposite side.
>
> At that time, there was no ruler in Tibet and people had set forth to look for one. They met [Ma-nya U-be-ra] at g.Ya'-le-gong on the northern route and asked him, "Who are you? Where do you come from? Where are you going?" He said, "I am from sPo-bo. Now I am going to Tibet." They asked, "What kind of powers do you have?" He said, "The people

of my country exiled me [precisely] because my capacities and magical powers are great." "Well," they said, "we are looking for a ruler for Tibet. Would you be capable [of that]?" He said, "I certainly would, given my great abilities, strength, and magical powers! Carry me on a throne above your shoulders!" So they appointed him [their] lord, and carried him above their shoulders on a throne. They also named him gNya'-khri bTsan-po. This is the very secret history of the descent according to the version of the extremists [*mu stegs lugs*].

Also this story is probably adapted from the *lDe'u chos 'byung*.

> The expression "Bonpos and Buddhists" [*ban bon*] found in both the *lDe'u rgya bod kyi chos 'byung* and the *bShad mdzod chen mo* obviously represents a concept which must have been inserted by the renowned Buddhist scholars who were the authors of those religious histories, because it makes little sense to speak of Buddhists at that time.
>
> Examining the different places that King gNya'-khri bTsan-po of the Mang-snya U-be-ra lineage gradually traversed before arriving in Lha-ri-gyang-tho from the country of sPu-bo, namely, the twenty-seven or thirty-seven places of arrival of the first king of Tibet mentioned in the version of the divine descent or in the *Yo ga lha gyes can*, one can see a strong historical connection or a correspondence with real places that still exist, as indicated by the mention of his coming to Nyag-nyi rGyab-dmar, Dwags-yul Shing-nag, and so on.

Furthermore, the *Bod kyi deb ther dpyid kyi rgyal mo'i glud byangs* (Pe, 12, 5) affirms:

> A special being was born who had hands that looked like wheel spokes, teeth like rows of tiny conch shells, turquoise eyebrows, and poor eyesight. The father, thinking him to be an emanation of gods or demons, banished [him]. Transforming himself into the light of supreme wisdom and holding a white lotus, [this being] arrived on the crest of Lha-ri Gyang-tho.

The excerpt above is given as an example from a Buddhist source. An exemplary excerpt from a Bonpo source is the following quotation from the *Legs bshad rin po che'i mdzod* (Pe, 129, 9), which says:

> [A being] was born [with] swastikas as ears, bird-like eyes, teeth like rows of tiny conch shells, and fingers connected by a web. The queen did not show him to the king because she was ashamed. She put him in a copper casket and abandoned him on the River Gaṅgā. Through the power of karma, he reached the town of Yangs-pa.[86] Everyone marveled at him and he was adopted. Many signs of his great qualities appeared. When he grew up, he went to Tibet, descending to Yar-lung Sog-ka from the top of Lha-ri Gyang-to.

The Bonpo sources quoted here do not indicate that the The'u-brang Mang-snya U-be-ra is the progenitor of the first kings of Tibet, and even though all the versions that attribute the epithet of The'u-brang to gNya'-khri bTsan-po have become the object of controversy, they represent in themselves an element of true historical significance.

Notwithstanding the fact that historical documents agree for the most part that the ancient king of Tibet arrived first at Lha-ri Gyang-tho in Central Tibet and that the ancient Tibetan dynasty originated from there, several present the name Lha-ri Gyang-tho written in different ways. For example the *Tun hong bod kyi lo rgyus yig rnying* [Old Tibetan Chronicles of Dunhuang] (PT 1286, 30) states:

> The divine one who came from the sky above, in the dimension of the sky:
> the sons of Yab-lha bDag-drug were seven in all, three elder brothers and three younger brothers, including the Seventh Khri [Khri'i-bdun-tshigs]. The son of the Seventh Khri was Khri gNya'-khri bTsan-po. He arrived on earth to be the Primordial Lord. He came to be the Primordial Lord of the earth. When he arrived at Lha-ri Gyang-do, Mount Meru [Ri-rab Lhun-po] bowed, trees lowered [their crests], river waters became pure blue, and even big rocks inclined easily.

---

86 [*yangs pa*: Skt. Vaiśālī, capital city of the ancient republic of Licchavi, present day Bihar State.]

This text reads Lha-ri Gyang-do as does the text carved on the rock of De-mo in Kong-po (lines 3, 4), reproduced in the *Bod kyi gna' rabs yig cha gces bsdus* [A Selection of Ancient Tibetan Texts] (Pe, 63, 12) where it says:

> Before, among the sons of Phywa Yab-bla bDag-drug, Nya-khri bTsan-po came to Lha-ri Gyang-do to be the lord of the human world. From that time ...

Moreover, the *rGyal po'i bka' thems shog dril ma* [The Paper Scroll of the Royal Will] says, "He arrived at Lha-ri Gyang-tho." The *rGyal-po'i bka' thems bka' bkol ma* and the *bKa' chems bka' khol ma* [The Written Order of the Royal Will] both say, "He arrived at the top of Lha-ri rGyang-mtho." The *Ma ni bka' 'bum* [a collection of teachings and practices focused on Avalokiteśvara] says, "He walked down the divine staircase from the top of Lha-ri Rol-po in Yar-lung to bTsan-thang sGo-bzhi [the Royal Garden with Four Gates]."

Whether The'u-brang Mang-snya U-be-ra was the real progenitor of the first Tibetan king gNya'-khri bTsan-po or not, that he is said to have come from the country of sPu, also attested to by the name 'O-lde sPu-rgyal written on the stone pillar, has a special significance.

The majority of Bonpo and Buddhist histories speak of the descent of the first Tibetan king from the Indian royal dynasty and affirm that the king arrived at the crest of Lha-ri Gyang-tho. Meeting some Bonpos of the Lores and minor Tibetan rulers, he was asked from where he came, and since he did not know the language, he pointed toward the sky; that gesture led those Bonpos and minor rulers to assume that he was of divine descent. Questioned about who he was, he apparently replied, "I am of royal descent."

These alternative responses are irreconcilable: even an untutored and unsophisticated person would note the contradiction between not knowing the language and pointing toward the sky, and then suddenly comprehending the language and replying, "I am of royal descent." The kings and lords who rule the countries of the world generally originate from the human beings that occupy those very places. The population, praising and respecting individuals who are distinguished for their physical or mental prowess or both, capable of ruling others, and endowed with special skills and wisdom, would attribute to them the title of kings or lords.

Solitary individuals, no matter how powerful, who come from the outside, conquer the local population, and become kings are as rare as a star visible in the daytime sky. Similarly, what need would there be for naming a foreigner and not a member of the Tibetan people as the first king of Tibet? In later times during the seventh century after Buddhism was introduced in Tibet from India and China, a new happiness arose in Tibetan hearts because of the highly respected royal lineage, the Śākya lineage, and so on.

But the Tibetan people of ancient times did not at all have that inclination. Therefore, also the secret Buddhist version according to which the king came from a royal lineage [of the Indian king Rūpati] is far from the facts and lacking in verisimilitude, based on contradictions and unsubstantiated claims.

Needless to say, if the real country of origin of the first Tibetan king was sPu, also the words used in the *Yo ga lha gyes can* version, according to which he descended from the gods, serve no purpose, just as what is claimed in the secret Buddhist version. The *bShad mdzod chen mo* (Thim, I, 156, 22) affirms:

> The lord of human beings was a god; he [came] to the world from another place. Since he was of superior descent, it is not to be [seen as a] dishonor." This statement contained in the very secret version of the nonhuman [descent] is just a different view, it is not a contradiction. For others, [descending from] noble families is not an insult.

The text maintains that if the origin of the Tibetan king is connected to the The'u-brang Mang-snya U-be-ra, it is inappropriate to insult the lineage of the king. However, in a previous passage, the text contradicts itself when it says (Thim, KA, 153, 77, 1):

> The Tibetan king gNya'-khri bTsan-po [is mentioned in the] secret Buddhist version, [and in the] proclaimed Bonpo version. The very secret [version according to which he is a] manifesta-

tion [of a] The-brang is a superficial falsehood. No matter how one proceeds, one [always] arrives at gNya'-khri. [Hence] the very secret history of the The-brang is not to be taken as the truth, while the secret history should be.

We also read (ibid., KA, 171, 86, 4):

> The shortcomings [and] flaws [*ngan 'tshang*] of the king are secret and cannot be discussed.

The text maintains that it is inappropriate to talk about the view according to which the The'u-rang are the origin of the first Tibetan king. Through those words one can reason that it was necessary to speak of a divine descent so as not to reveal a descent from the The'u-rang. An even clearer example is contained in the *lDe'u rgya bod kyi chos 'byung* (Bod, 227, 3):

> That is the shortcoming or flaw [*rngan nam mtshang*] of the king,

which implies that the descent from a The'u-rang is a defect of the king. The text shows that the meaning of *rngan* is *mtshang*. Furthermore we read (Bod, 238, 11):

> It is said that one does not enumerate the shortcomings of the lord. Since the very secret version of the descent from a The-brang is the shortcoming or flaw [*rngan nam mtshang*] of the lord, we people of common understanding are not allowed to talk about it.

rNgan is an old Tibetan term: the meaning is flaw [*mtshang*] or shortcoming [*skyon*]. The sentences "one does not enumerate the shortcomings of the lord [*rje la rngan ma sgrang*], or "one does not expose the flaws of the lord [*rje'i mtshang ma 'bru*], or "one does not unmask the defects of the lord" [*rje'i skyon ma sngogs*] are syntactic variations that indicate changes occurred in connection with the dynastic history of ancient Tibet and that inevitable implications accompanied those changes.

As regards the assumptions that the gods [*lha*] are good and the demons ['*dre*] are bad, the general belief was that besides Tibetans, other beings also existed. As related in old Bonpo sources, existence is comprised of three main classes of entities, namely the lHa [gods] of the sky, the Klu of the underworld, and the gNyan of the atmosphere. The lHa of the sky are special beings living on thirteen celestial strata; the Klu, inferior to the lHa, control the subterranean world and the oceans; and the gNyan, also inferior to the lHa, control either the surface of the earth or the atmosphere.

Among the gNyan, gNyan-chen Thang-lha, rMa-rgyal sPom-ra, and so on are some of the most famous and important gNyan recognized as fierce earthly forces since olden times. From the standpoint of the lHa of the sky, however, their status has always been considered inferior, no matter how powerful they were. Many types of gNyan were also known as Ma-sangs; the latter, as explained in the section on the origin of human generations of ancient Zhang Zhung, closely resembled humans. A number of ancient genealogies state that many human beings descended from the Ma-sangs or describe the generations that originated from the mutual kinship that existed between them.

In particular, concerning one of the names of the Ma-sangs, variously written The'u-brang or The-brang or The'u-rang, the tendency in the Tibetan parlance to add *'dre* as a prefix [*'dre the'u rang*] indicates that those beings are considered as part of the demon class. Therefore, it goes without saying that to consider the Tibetan king as descended from a lofty and distinguished divine lineage or from the class of the 'Dre or the The'u-rang implies not only two different views, but also a fundamental dichotomy between them.

The *rTsa rgyud nyi sgron* affirms (Thob, 150, 4):

> King Gri-gum bTsad-po became an enemy of Bon. Before, he was committed [to Bon], [and would] pursue nonbelievers. Now he is an enemy of the doctrine, and suppresses Bon. Until he was twenty-seven years old he practiced Bon. He built the temple of the Ninety Thousand Offerings to the tutelary deities. Then, due to [past] negative karma, the heart of the king was possessed by a demon [*gdon*]. The minister's thoughts were mistaken. The Indian beggar had a sharp intellect. The queen was foolish and ruthless. The child was young. Abruptly [the king] suppressed Bon without warning. Bon and gShen [priests] were banished to the borderlands. A retribution for banishing

Bon fell upon the king. The king was the incarnation of the The'u-rang Mang-snya Mu-wer. The subject Lo-ngam rTa-rdzi, who was an emanation of sTag-la Me-'bar, broke [the king's] neck and killed him.

The *g.Yung drung bon gyi rgyud 'bum* affirms (Thob, KA, 23, 12, 2):

> At that time in the country Myang-ro sTag-tshal at the palace Nyang-ro Sham-po, King Khri-rje Yag-pa and Queen sBrang-bza' lHa-rgyan had an inauspicious dream. [Then,] a child of the The-rang Mang-snya dBu-wer was conceived; after nine months and ten days, he was born. The child that came out of the mother's womb [*rum*] had various dagger [*gri*] scars[87] [on his body], red hair, round eyes, a ruddy complexion, and a black mole on the palm of the right hand. He liked evil, coveted weapons, and spoke malignly. The two royal gShen [*sku gshen*], Pha-ba and 'Tshe-gco, gave him the name Gri-rum bTsan-po.

In a similar fashion the *Dar rgyas gsal ba'i sgron ma* says (Thob, 651, 78, 4):

> In that respect, the meaning of Gri-rum is as follows. The *sGra 'grel* says, "At that time, in the country of Nyang-ro sTag-tshal at the palace Nyang-ro Sham-po, an emanation of the The'u-rang Ma-snya U-wer was conceived by King Khri-lde Yags-pa and Queen sGrang-za lHa-rgyan. After nine months and ten days, a son was born. In a month, he grew as much as [would normally take] a year. He had red hair, round eyes, and a black mole on the palm of the right hand. He spoke murderous words, longed for evil, and coveted weapons. Since he was marked with dagger scars [*gri*] [when he emerged] from the mother's womb [*rum*], the royal gShen [*sku gshen*], Pha-ba 'Tshe-gco, gave him the name Gri-rum bTsan-po."

From these excerpts we can ascertain that Gri-gum bTsan-po was degradingly referred to as an emanation of the The'u-rang Ma-snya U-wer because he was a bad king and had harmed the Bon teachings.

If the The'u-rang origin of the first Tibetan king were to be discussed, it would display irreverence toward the Tibetan king, and unmasking the defects or exposing the flaws of the king would be con-

---

87 [The texts suggest these gashes indicate a violent nature.]

sidered an erroneous act in the common worldview. Therefore, in the sentence "one does not enumerate the shortcomings of the lord" [*rje la rngan ma sgrang*], if no one had any doubt that gNya'-khri bTsan-po was the first Tibetan king, the fact that he descended from a The'u-rang would be perceived as his flaw or defect. If the story of the king's origin contained in the very secret version where it is said that "we people with common understanding are not allowed to talk about it" ['*o skol rmangs phal pa rnams kyis gleng la mi 'thad pa lags skad do*] is taken as genuine, whatever could be kept secret was kept secret, so that later historians were completely unclear as to that history, and had no idea of it.

In reality, if we think clearly, a firm conviction or real confirmation as to the true origin can be derived from the assumption that the The'u-rang descent is considered a defect of the king, as exemplified in the sentence quoted above, "it is the shortcoming or flaw of the lord" [*rje'i rngan nam mtshang lags so*]. Moreover, one can clearly understand from the sentence "one does not enumerate the shortcomings of the lord" [*rje la rngan ma sgrang*] that also the *Yo ga lha gyes can* history that is based upon the special argument that [the king] came to be the ruler of the black-headed people from a divine lineage is just a fabrication.

Even so, how could the history contained in the *Yo ga lha gyes can* have been fabricated randomly without reason and basis? That history is an extensive and articulated history primarily dealing with the coming into being of the different classes of the gods of the sky, namely, how the Lord of Phywa, Phywa-rje Yab-bla brDal-drug, came into existence, and how the primordial divine generations descending from his lineage appeared.

For example, concerning the coming into being of the primordial divine generations of Zhang Zhung that descended from Rong-rong rTsol-po, the son of Yab-bla brDal-drug, the *lDe'u rgya bod kyi chos 'byung* relates thusly (Bod, 231, 5):

> The Nine Brothers, sons begotten by Rong-rong rTsol-po and Khab-rmu-bza' mThing-khug-sman, came into the world as the gods of Zhang Zhung: Ge-god, Me-dur, Tshangs-lha, Pha-'brum, rMa-tshes, Pho-'brang, rMa-ge-god, Yo-phyal ...

The designation of sPu-rgyal appears in relation to the name of the first Tibetan king gNya'-khri bTsan-po. If this special designation was truly meant to reveal the origin of the first king, it has nonetheless been recorded under different forms in old historical texts, as indicated by the following two examples. The *Deb ther sngon po* [The Blue Annals] says (Si, Vol. One, 60, 17):

> In old writings from afore, the original name of this place was Pu-rgyal.

In this case, the syllable *Pu* is written without the superscribed consonant *sa*.

Within the corpus of the *bKa' thang sde lnga*, the *rGyal po bka'i thang yig* has (Pe, 113, 8):

> Brought completely under control by the sPur-rgyal king.

In this case, the syllable *sPu* is written with the final consonant *ra*. In the ancient Tibetan language, a word with a superscribed letter *sa* would have a notably different pronunciation tone, demonstrated by the way present day Amdo and Ladaki people pronounce words, a way in which the resulting difference in meaning is even more emphasized. In Tibetan grammar, the consonants *ka, ca, ta, pa,* and *tsa* are considered root letters of male gender; therefore, whether a consonant *sa* is superscribed or not on the radical *pa*, the basic hard tone remains unchanged.

In later phonetics, superscribed letters were used to enhance the tone of root letters, but since the actual sound of the superscribed consonant was not pronounced, "Pu" could be written either *sPu* or *Pu*. In Tibetan, words such as *rDo rJe*, where the first syllable does not have a suffix *ra*, but a *ra* superscribed on the second syllable [*rJe*], are sometimes pronounced as if the superscribed letter *ra* was affixed to the first syllable *Dor-je*. Therefore, the letter *ra* affixed to *sPu* in the word *sPur rgyal* is easily recognizable as a copying error perpetuated by generations of scribes unfamiliar with the meaning of sPu rgyal.

Another name of sPu-rgyal is 'O-lde sPu-rgyal or 'O-de sPu-rgyal as engraved on the eastern side of the stele [*rdo ring*] (5-9) situated in front of the Lhasa Temple and recorded in the *Bod kyi gna' rabs yig cha gces bsdus* (Pe, 10, 6):

> The magic, divine lord 'O-lde sPu-rgyal,
> [Who] appeared on earth, until [he reached this] country,
> [Was] from that time [established as] the leader of the people,
> The great king of Tibet.
> [At the] center of the high snow mountain,
> [At the] source of the great river,
> In a pure land, [in a] lofty place,
> He has come as the king of the people from the heavenly gods.
> The Great Pillar is erected in eternal memory [of this].

Furthermore, the clear writing appearing on the stele (1, 2) situated in front of the tomb of Khri-lde Srong-btsan at 'Phyongs-rgyas and reproduced in the *Bod kyi rdo ring gi yi ge dang dril bu'i kha byang* [Catalog of Tibetan Bells and Steles Inscriptions], reads (Pe, 101, 9):

> The King,
> Divine son,
> 'O-lde sPu-rgyal,
> Has come from the heavenly gods [to act] as the lord of the people.

The *Tun hong bod kyi lo rgyus yig rnying* [Old Tibetan Chronicles of Dunhuang] say (PT 1287, 28):

> In the end, the political rule of 'O-lde sPu-rgyal was without peer.

The *rGyal po bka'i thang yig* has (Pe, 113, 9):

> 'O-de sPur-rgyal, the king of Tibet,
> Has come from the heavenly gods [to act] as the lord of the people.

These citations confirm the point.

The evidence that sPu-rgyal was a central component in the name of the first king gNya'-khri bTsan-po, and that it was used as a term to indicate a distinct lineage or that other kings descended from his lineage can be found in several literary examples. In the *Tun hong bod kyi lo rgyus yig rnying* [Old Tibetan Chronicles of Dunhuang] we read (PT 1287, 153):

> Myang [and] dBa' dissociated themselves from Zing-po-rje. They became close to King sPu-rgyal, and swore a profound and exacting oath.

And also (PT 1287, 158):

> Being addressed as sPu-rgyal sTag-bu'i-snyan ...

And also (PT 1287, 174):

> Zing-po-rje was left behind, people abandoned [him]. sPu-rgyal was cherished, people accepted [him]. [Zing-po-rje] will never oppose King sPu-rgyal.

And also (PT 1287, 288):

> [He] challenged the father, King sPu-rgyal, the son, Khri-srong-btsan, and [the rest of] the family.

As we can see, the title was attached to the names of the Tibetan kings as an epithet of high praise. Moreover, in the "Song of King 'Dus-srong" contained in the *Tun hong bod kyi lo rgyus yig rnying* [Old Tibetan Chronicles of Dunhuang], we read (PT 1287, 465):

> The sPu-rgyal [lineage] of Tibet
> [Has pursued good] intentions [from] generation [to] generation.
> [I] will not disavow the sPu-rgyal lineage.

In the *rGya bod yig tshang chen mo* [Historical Anthology of Tibet and China] we read (Si, 133, 17):

> The middle one, Bya-khri,[88] [was] at sPo-bo Brag-thog. He was given the name sPo-de Gung-rgyal. Since he was the acting lord of sPo-bo, he was invited and then raised to the throne. Since that time, the country was also known as sPur-rgyal-bod.

---

88 [One of the three sons of Gri-gum bTsan-po].

That the sPur-rgyal epithet originated from the time of sPu-de Gung-rgyal is thus affirmed, showing that the author did not know that this was the name of 'O-lde sPu-rgyal or 'O-de sPu-rgyal, the first Tibetan king, and that he was unaware of the history of the provenance of the first Tibetan king contained in the very secret version of the descent from the The'u-brang.

The well-known name of the ancient king of Tibet gNya'-khri bTsan-po can be written in five different ways: gNya'-khri, sNya-khri, Nyag-ri, Nyag-khri, and Nya-khri. The origin of the reading "gNya'-khri" is thus explained in the *Legs bshad rin po che'i mdzod* (Pe, 129, 17):

> At first some herdsmen saw [him]. "Where are you from?" they asked. He raised a finger toward the sky, and when he laughed, the clear design of a swastika could be seen on his tongue. "Who are you?" they asked. He replied, "I am a nobleman." At that point some of them made a wooden throne, and carried him at neck level. When they presented him to the people, everyone was timorous and frightened. When they presented him to the gShen gCo-ldan [and to the gShen] mTsho-mgron, the latter [two] said, "It is befitting that he be the ruler of Tibet!" The lustral ceremony [*tshan khrus*] was performed, and having given him the name gNya'-khri bTsad-po, Lord of the People, they proceeded toward the Tibetan capital.

The *rGyal rabs gsal ba'i me long* says (Pe, 55, 4):

> The *Bod kyi yig tshang* relates: "First he alighted on the summit of lHa-ri Rol-po. Then he looked with his prophetic sight and saw the heights of the mountain Yar-lha Sham-po and the beauty of the Yar-lung Valley. When he reached the mountain bTsan-thang Gong-ma, he was observed by young herdsmen who were tending the cattle. Curious about his origin, they inquired, 'Where are you from?' He pointed a finger toward the sky. When he did so, they said, 'He is a divine son who comes from Heaven! Let us make him our lord!' So they made a throne, lifted it to neck height, and called him Lord gNya'-khri bTsan-po. He was the first king of Tibet."

As the last two excerpts indicate, the principal reason why the name of the first king of Tibet was gNya'-khri [Neck-throne] is because the Tibetan people built a wooden throne and carried him at the level of the neck out of respect. This way of explaining the gNya'-khri in the king's name has the general assent of the New Bonpos, Buddhists, and historians of Buddhism of the present time.

Another related explanation is contained in the *lDe'u rgya bod kyi chos 'byung* (Bod, 232, 17):

> Since he emerged from his mother's neck, he was given the name gNya'-khri bTsan-po.

Whichever the case, both explanations make sense and are reasonable from the standpoint of the Tibetan language proper, but thinking about it, we can see that they are fundamentally insubstantial. Why? The reasons are manifold: because in Tibet before the advent of King gNya'-khri bTsan-po, the great gShen Nam-mkha'i sNang-ba'i mDog-can played a leading role; because the Bonpos of the Twelve Lores were present; because well-known historical accounts relate the way in which the first king of Tibet received the name gNya'-khri bTsan-po after the Bon gShen-pos gCo, 'Tshe-'gron, and others performed the Bonpo lustral ceremony; and because at the time when gNya'-khri bTsan-po ruled the Tibetan kingdom, except for the Bon from Zhang Zhung, where the great Tibetan forefathers and the art of ruling originated, there was nothing else. The foundation of the Bon culture as well as other cultural characteristics related to the Zhang Zhung language demonstrate this amply.

Hence, from the time of the ancient Tibetan king gNya'-khri bTsan-po until the later dissolution of the Central Tibetan dynasty, every Tibetan king had a royal gShen protector, as explained in the previous chapter. When royal children were born, the child would receive a name, following a Bon lustral ceremony. Also, as a memento indicating that the dynasty was protected by Bon and that its origin was without flaw, the use of names deriving from the Zhang Zhung language was the constant rule. That is why not only the first king gNya'-khri bTsan-po but also the monarchs of Tibet starting from

the kings called the Seven Khri of the Sky [gNam-gyi Khri-bdun]—
Mu-khri bTsan-po, Ding-khri bTsan-po, Dar-khri bTsan-po, Ye-khri
bTsan-po, Seng-khri bTsan-po, and so on—until the kings known as
the Six Legs [Legs-drug]—A-sho-legs, De-sho-legs, Thi-sho-legs, Gu-
rum-legs, 'Brang-zhi-legs, I-sho-legs—down to later kings, such as Khri-
srong lDe'u-btsan and Mu-ne bTsan-po, all had names drawn from
the Zhang Zhung language. The names of those kings appear to lack
sense in the Tibetan language, but as the names of ruling kings, each
of them had a vast and profound meaning.

In Tibetan, the Zhang Zhung word *khri* means deity or the mind
of the deity [*lha, lha'i thugs*]; similarly, *mu* means all-encompassing [*kun
khyab*]; *ding* means space [*klong*]; *dar* means good [*legs pa*]; *ye* means first or
primeval [*thog ma, gdod ma*]; *seng* means lion [*seng ge*]; *a sho* means speech
[*ngag*]; *de sho* means happiness [*bde ba*]; *thi sho* means bright [*gsal ba*]; *gu
rum* or *gu ra* means good qualities [*yon tan*]; *'brang zhi*, or *bri zhal* means
rainbow [*'ja' tshon*]; *i sho*, or *un zhi* means renown [*snyan grags*]; *srong* means
unhindered [*thogs med*]; *lde*, or *lde'u* means knowledge or wisdom [*rig pa,
mkhyen pa*]; *mu ne* means like the sky [*nam mkha' lta bu*]. The meaning of
each of the kings' names can be inferred from these examples.

The word *khri*, which means deity or the mind of the deity, appears in many names, such as those of the ancient Zhang Zhung kings
Khri-wer gSer-gyi Bya-ru-can, Khri-lde lCags-kyi Bya-ru-can, the great
Zhang Zhung Bon gShen Khri-'od-gsas, Ra-sangs Khri-na-khod, Khri-
btsan-po 'Od-ldan, and so on. In the extended version of the life of
gShen-rab Mi-bo-che, the *Dri med gzi brjid*, we find another example
(Thob, KA, 342, 172, 2):

> Six sons were born to rJe-rigs bTsun-po and gTsug-lcam Ngang-
> ma: Khri-wer, Khri-ma, Khri-btsun, Khri-brten, Khri-rje, and
> Khri'u-ra-tsa. They were of high noble birth, possessed the
> marks of excellence, were knowledgeable about creation,[89] and
> came from an uninterrupted lineage of royal ministers.

---

89 *chags shes la mkhas pa*. That is to say, they had the knowledge of the formation
process through which existence arose in the beginning.

As the excerpt shows, epithets in the Zhang Zhung language were in use from former times; hence, the same tradition was kept in naming the Tibetan kings. Given that the epithet *khri* occurred in gNya'-khri's name, it became a matter of prestige for the Tibetan kings that followed to have Zhang Zhung words in their names. It is essential to understand this point.

The reading sNya-khri is thus explained in the *rGyal gshen ya ngal gyi gdung rabs* (Thob, 46, 23, 4):

> We are the children of lHa-rab gNyan-rum. As for myself, I am sNya-khri bTsan-po. If [one asks] why [my name is] sNya-khri bTsan-po, [it is] sNya-khri, because after nine months and ten days [I was born] from [my] mother's neck. It is bTsan-po, because I command the whole of existence.

sNya-ba or *gNya'-ba* means nape of the neck [*rke'i mjing pa*]. This expression is an appropriate one in literary Tibetan and is basically consistent with the meaning of gNya'-khri. In ancient times the word *sNya* would appear in names such as sNya Li-shu. However, if that usage had any relation with the name sNya-khri remains to be investigated, since I have not found other clarifying examples.

The reading *Nyag-ri* is explained in the *Srid pa'i rgyud kyi kha byang* as follows (Thob, 77, 39, 4):

> Phya-rje Yab-bla bDal-drug and dMu-btsun rGyal-mo's children were the Seven lDe'u-rje Brothers [lDe'u-rje mChed-bdun]. The seventh of those divine sons was also called Khri-sad 'Bar-ba. He was banished to the country of dMu [of his] maternal uncle. He married dMu-za gNyi-mthing-ma. Their son, who emerged from a single tuft of curled hair at a crease in [his mother's] neck, because had he emerged from above, the mother would have died, and had he emerged from below, he would have been soiled, was lDe Nyag-ri bTsad-po.

The *Yo ga lha gyes can* version, similar to the above, narrates that Khri-bar-gyi bDun-tshigs, the son of Yab-bla brDal-drug and rMu-btsun Gri-sman, was exiled to rMu-yul. He married Phu-mo Dre-rmu Dre-btsan-mo, the daughter of the maternal uncle Thang-thang. When the child they conceived was in the womb, he addressed his mother in the following terms (232, 15):

> If I were to emerge from above, the mother would die. If I were to emerge from below, the son would be contaminated. Let me leave from the back!" So he moved to [her] right shoulder and then emerged from the mother's neck.

The difference in this version is created by the name of the king, Nyag-ri brTsan-po. It is easily inferred that the reading *Nyag-ri* is a derivative of *Nyag-khri*, in line with the meaning of the Tibetan words that refer to the son as born from a single tuft of curled hair [*skra nyag gcig la 'khril ba*] on the nape of the mother's neck. The reading Nyag-khri also appears in the *Tun hong bod kyi lo rgyus yig rnying* [Old Tibetan Chronicles of Dunhuang] (PT 1287, 31):

> The son of Khri'i bDun-thigs was Khri Nyag-khri bTsan-po.

And also (PT 1287, 43):

> The son of Khri'i bDun-tshigs was lDe Nyag-khri bTsan-po.

In reality *nyag* is an old Tibetan term that is to be understood as *nyag gcig*, meaning unique [*gcig pu*] or that very one [*de kho na*]. In the language of Zhang Zhung, *khri* means deity or the nature of the mind of the deity. If the first meaning of *nyag* is attributed to the expression *Nyag-khri*, the latter would correspond to the Tibetan *lHa gcig*, unique deity, in the sense of a powerful deity [*lha mthu bo che*], such as the fierce Shing-rje and the like. If the second meaning of *nyag* is attributed to the expression *Nyag-khri*, the latter would correspond to "*lHa'i thugs nyid*" [the nature of the mind of the deity] or to *lHa'i dgongs pa* [the state of contemplation of the deity]. Therefore the fundamental meaning of the name Nyag-khri bTsan-po should be interpreted along these lines.

We find an example of the reading Nya-khri on the third and fourth lines of a rock inscription at Kong-po De-mo that reads:

> Since [he] arrived at lHa-ri-Gyang-do, Nya-khri bTsan-po, [born] to the son of Phywa Yab-bla bDag drug, [has acted] as the lord of the human world.

Furthermore, in the *Blon po bka'i thang yig* (Pe 35, 12) we read:

> gNya'-khri bTsan-po was born on full moon [*zla ba nya*]. [This is why] he is also known as Nya-khri bTsan-po.

This quotation shows that the reading *Nya* is also an acceptable one in Tibetan and that the king was called Nya-khri as well because he was born on full moon.

2. The Succession of Tibetan Monarchs from gNya'-khri bTsan-po to the Dharmarāja Srong-btsan sGam-po

When historians disagree about the names and the order of succession of Tibetan kings—particularly in the early Intermediate Period that starts with gNya'-khri bTsan-po and ends with the *dharmarāja* Srong-btsan sGam-po—and the main sources for the history of that period consist of old Bonpo documents, it is necessary to rely upon those sources and to compare them with all relevant historical texts. Only then the true historical sense can be found or determined. This is absolutely indispensable when undertaking research on the history of Tibet.

In this respect, one of the most coherent and essential texts among the several old historical documents pertaining to the Bon tradition is the *bsTan pa'i rnam bshad dar rgyas gsal ba'i sgron ma*. If the explanations contained in this text are taken into account, the order of succession of the Tibetan monarchs appears properly arranged.

The text affirms (Thob 640, 73, 5):

> The son of gNya'-khri and gNam-mu-yug was Mu-khri bTsan-po. The royal gShen was bCo'u Lan-tsha.
> The son of Mu-khri and Sa-sman Ting-ting-ma was Ding-khri bTsan-po. The royal gShen was bCo'u sMin-dkar.
> The son of Ding-khri and Se-za-sman was So-khri bTsan-po. The royal gShen was gCo'u 'Od-dkar.
> The son of So-khri and Dar-za Zhang-zhung-ma was Ding-khri bTsan-po. The royal gShen was mTsho-mi Zung-smon.

> The son of Ding-khri and Dwags-kyi lHa-mo dKar-mo was Dwags-khri bTsan-po. The royal gShen was Dag-pa Mi-chen. The son of Dwags-khri and Sribs-kyi lHa-mo dKar-mo [was Sribs-khri bTsan-po].
> The royal gShen of Sribs-khri bTsan-po was gCo'u Zhal-dkar. These [kings, including gNya'-khri] are called the Seven *Khri* Kings of the Sky.

And also (ibid., 651, 78, 4):

> An emanation of the The'u-rang Ma-snya U-wer was conceived by King Khri-lde Yags-pa (Sribs-khri bTsan-po) and Queen sGrang-za lHa-rgyan. After nine months and ten days, a son was born. In a month, he grew as much as [would normally take] a year. He had red hair, round eyes, and a black mole on the palm of the right hand. He spoke murderous words, longed for evil, and coveted weapons. Since he was covered with dagger [*gri*] scars [when he emerged] from the mother's womb [*rum*], the royal gShen Pha-ba 'Tshe-gco gave him the name Gri-rum bTsan-po.

And also (ibid., 660, 83, 6):

> Tri-rgyal Lo-ngam rTa-rdzi aimed a sharp poisoned arrow with a black notch at the forehead [of King Gri-rum bTsan-po] and killed him.

And also (ibid., 661, 83, 4):

> Lo-ngam took the corpse, put it in a copper coffer, and threw it off the 'Da'-le bridge into the river Nyang. He exiled [Gri-gum's] sons, sPu-lde and Nya-khri to Dwags[-po] [and] rKong[-po], respectively; he killed the minister Drag-pa and banned the others; he relegated the queen to the level of shepherdess; and he married the daughter lHa-lcam and reigned for thirteen years.

The following excerpts from the same text specify the order in the succession of the monarchy (ibid., 651, 78, 7):

> [Gri-gum] and dBal[*sic*]-za Khri-btsun had a son born at midday (*gung*) who had bird [feathers], and horse and wolf hair [*spu*]

covering his head and body. [Because of this,] he was also given the name sPu-lde Gung-rgyal. Tshe'i rGyal-po of Zhang Zhung was his royal protector. These are the two *lDeng* of the middle [Bar-gyi lDeng-gnyis].

And also (ibid., 655, 85, 1):

> The son of sPu-lde and Bum-thang sMan-mtsho was A-sho-legs.
> The son of A-sho-legs and dMu-lcam La-na was De-sho-legs.
> The son of De-sho-legs and Klu-sman Mer-mo was The-sho-legs.
> The son of The-sho-legs and bTsan-mo Gur-sman was 'Gu-ru-legs.
> The son of 'Gu-ru-legs and mTshon-sman 'Brong-mo was 'Brong-bzher-legs.
> The son of 'Brong-bzher-legs and Sa-sman Bu-mo was Sho-legs. During the reign of the Six *Legs* of the Earth [Sa-la Legs-drug], the twenty sages from Zhang Zhung acted as royal protectors.

And also (ibid., 665, 85, 5):

> The son of Sho-legs and dMu-lcam rMang-legs was Za-nam Zin-lde. The royal protector was Zhang Zhung g.Yung drung rGyal-po.
> The son of Zin[*sic*]-nam Zin-lde and mTshon-sman Khri-dkar was lDe-nam 'Phrul-zhung[*sic*]-btsan. The royal protector was Zhang Zhung mTshe-mi Kun-snang.
> The son of lDe-nam 'Phrul-gzhung[*sic*]-btsan and gNyan-mang-mo was Se-snol gNam-lde. The royal protector was Zhang Zhung Don-rtogs rGyal-po.
> The son of Se-snol gNam-lde and Klu-thang Mer-mo was Se-snol-lde. The royal protector was Zhang Zhung A-so gtsug-phud.
> The son of Se-snol-lde and 'O-za Ti-mo-mtsho was lDe-snol-nam. The royal protector was Zhang Zhung A-la Dan-ci.
> The son of lDe-snol-nam and Khri-sman rJe-ma was lDe-rnol-po. The royal protector was Zhang-zhung Dar-ma Ha-ti.
> The son of lDe-rnol-po and Sa-btsun sNyan-rje was lDe-rgyal-po. The royal protector was Zhang-zhung Nga-sa Ha-ti.

The son of lDe-rgyal-po and sMan-btsun Lung-gong was lDe-srin-btsan. The royal protector was Zhang-zhung Mu-la Ma-ho. These are the so-called Eight *lDe* of the Water [Chu-la lDe-brgyad]. [During their time] texts concerning the *'Bum* series spread. Temples such as the lHun-grub dByings-kyi gSas-khang, and so on, were built.

The son of lDe-srin btsan and gNyan-btsun Mang-mo-rje was rGyal To-ro Lo-btsan.

The son of rGyal To-ro Lo-btsan and sMan-za Klu-stengs was Khri Thob-rje-btsan. The royal protector of these three kings [including lDe-srin btsan] was Zhang-zhung Mu-la Ha-rgyal. During the last four years of To-ro Lo-btsan's reign, temples such as the lHun-grub dByings-kyi lHa-khang, and so on, were built at Bye-ma g.Yung-drung-tshal in Zhang Zhung.

The son of Khri Thog-rje-btsan and Ru-yang Za-steng rGyal-nam-mtsho was Tho-tho-ri'i sNyan-btsan.

And also (ibid., 667, 86, 2):

The five kings that came after To-ro Lo-btsan were called the Five *bTsan* of the Middle [Bar-gyi bTsan-lnga]. That king married Gur-sman, but they did not have children. He had a son with the second wife, sNo-za Ma-so-rje, Khri-gnyan gZung-btsan. The royal protector was Khu'i-bon-po Mang-sgra Legs-pa.

The son of Khri-snyan Zung-btsan and 'Brong-za Dar-ma g.Yang-bzher was 'Grong-snyan lDe-ru. The royal protector was Khu'i-bon-po Mang-rje Lod-po. The son of 'Grong-snyan and 'Chin-za Klu-rgyal Ngan-na-mtsho was blind. Khu-bon Mang-rje Lod-po restored his eyesight, and since he was able to see the wild animals on the facing mountain, he was given the name sTag-ri sNyan-gzigs.

And also (ibid., 668, 87, 1):

The son of sTag-ri and 'Om-rgod Za-stong bTsun-'gro-skar was gNam-ri Srong-btsan. The royal protector was gCo'i-bon-po Khri-phyung Grags-pa.

And also (ibid., 668, 87, 3):

Thus, each of the thirty-three monarchs—from Lord gNya'-khri bTsan-po until gNam Khri-srong lDe-brtsan—had a royal protector [*sku gshen*] as guide, a principal translator, and had special temples constructed. This is what the *rNam 'byed 'phrul gyi lde mig* states.

We can see from these excerpts that Tri-rgyal Lo-ngam rTa-rdzi is also included in the succession of the thirty-three Tibetan monarchs.

The dynastic history contained in the *Dar rgyas* which reckons Tri-rgyal Lo-ngam among the Tibetan monarchs is quite unique. I have seen no other dynastic history, either Buddhist or Bonpo, that includes Tri-rgyal Lo-ngam. Nonetheless, any powerful individual capable of completely dominating a country and of being totally in charge, is a *de facto* monarch, and that is why such a person is called a king [*rgyal po* or *btsan po*]. Tri-rgyal Lo-ngam ruled Tibet for thirteen years, and yet he is not given a place in the succession of monarchs. This is an unambiguous sign of the narrow-mindedness and limited view of past Tibetan historians. At best, his inclusion has been considered an entertaining idea on the part of more open-minded scholars. Personally, I am inclined to follow the *Dar rgyas* version and think that historians should give it due consideration.

If we analyze from a historical perspective, only one corpus of texts among the many historical documents pertaining to the renowned Buddhist tradition preserves an ancient flavor, undeniably demonstrating its antiquity, unlike the others. That is the corpus known as the *bKa' thang sde lnga* [Five Biographies], which describes in extensive fashion the unfolding of the Tibetan monarchy. These are the specifics of what is to be read in the *rGyal po bka'i thang yig* (Pe, 113, 20):

> The son of gNya'-khri was Mu-khri bTsan-po.
> His son was Ding-khri bTsan-po.
> His son was So-khri bTsan-po.
> His son was Mer-khri btsan-po.
> His son was gDags-khri bTsan-po.
> His son was sPyi-khri bTsan-po.
> These [including gNya'-khri] are called the Seven *Khri* of the Sky [gNam-la Khri-bdun].
> As for the royal lineage of the [so-called] Six *Legs* of the Earth [Sa-la Legs-drug], we [first] have the three sons of King Gri-

gum: Bya-khri, Sha-khri, and Nya-khri. King Bya-khri moved to Kong-po; King Nya-khri moved to Nyang-po; and King Sha-khri moved to sPo-bo.
Since the father died, the princes were called back; sPu-de Gung-rgyal arrived from sPo-bo.
The son of sPu-de Gung-rgyal was I-sho-legs.
His son was Li-sho-legs.
His son was 'Brong-bzhi-legs.
His son was Thi-sho-legs.
His son was Gu-rum-legs.
His son was Za-nam-legs.
These are the so-called Six *Legs* of the Earth.
The son of King Za-nam-legs was known as King lDe-ru gNam-gzhung-btsan.
His son was sDe-snod-sbas.
His son was sDe-snod-ya.
His son was Sor-rno-nam.
His son was King So-ste.
His son was sPrin-rgyal-btsan.
His son was sTong-ri sTong-btsan.
These are the [so-called] Seven Princedoms [*rgyal rabs sil ma bdun*].
The son of sTong-ri sTong-btsan was Khri-nam-btsan.
His son was Khri-sgra dPungs-btsan.
His son was Khri-thog rJe-btsan.
His son was Tho-tho gNyan-btsan.
His son was Khri-gnyan gZungs-btsan.
These were called the Five *bTsan* of the Middle [Tshigs-la bTsan-lnga].
His son was 'Brong-gnyan lDe-ru.
His son was sTag-ri gNyan-gzigs.
His son was gNam-ri Srong-btsan.

Thirty dynasties elapsed over the time of the Seven *Khri* of the Sky, Gri-gum and sPu-de Gung-rgyal, the Six *Legs* of the Earth, the Seven Princedoms, the Five *bTsan* of the Middle, 'Brong-gNyan lDe-ru, sTag-ri gNyan-gzigs, and gNam-ri Srong-btsan. In this respect the *Tun hong bod kyi lo rgyus yig rnying* [Old Tibetan Chronicles of Dunhuang] states (PT 1287, 44):

lDe Nyag-khri bTsan-po and gNam-mug-mug had the son Mu-khri bTsan-po.

The son of Mug[*sic*]-khri bTsan-po and Sa-ding-ding was Ding-khri bTsan-po.

The son of Ding-khri bTsan-po and So-tham-tham was So-khri bTsan-po.

The son of So-khri bTsan-po was De-khri bTsan-po.

The son of De-khri bTsan-po was Khri-spe bTsan-po.

And also (ibid., 47):

The son of Khri-spe bTsan-po was Dri-gum bTsan-po.

The son of Dri-gum bTsan-po was sPu-de Gung-rgyal.

And also (ibid., 49):

When sPu-de Gung-rgyal died, [he was succeeded by] Grang-mo gNam-gser-bstsig.

The son of gSer-bstsig was Tho-leg bTsan-po.

The son of Tho-leg bTsan-po was Sho-legs bTsan-po.

The son of Sho-legs bTsan-po was Go-ru-legs bTsan-po.

The son of Go-ru-legs bTsan-po was 'Brong-zhi-legs bTsan-po.

The son of 'Brong-zhi-legs bTsan-po was Thi-sho-legs bTsan-po.

The son of Thi-shog-leg [*sic*] was I-sho-legs bTsan-po.

The son of I-sho-leg was Zwa-gnam Zin-te.

The son of Zwa-gnam Zin-te was lDe-phru-bo gNam-gzhung-bstsan.

The son of gNam-gzhung-brtsan was lDe-gol.

The son of lDe-gol was gNam-lde rNol-nam.

The son of gNam-lde rNol-nam was bSe'-rnol-po.

The son of bSe[*sic*]-rnol-po was lDe-rgyal-po.

The son of lDe-rgyal-po was rGyal-srin-bstsan.

The son of rGyal-srin-bstsan was rGyal To-re Longs-bstsan.

The son of rGyal To-re Longs-brtsan [*sic*] was Khri-btsan-nam.

The son of Khri-bstsan[*sic*]-nam was Khri-sgra sPung-bstsan.

The son of Khri-sgra sPung-bstsan was Khri-thog-bstsan.

The son of Khri-thog-bstsan and Ru-yong Za-stong rGyal-mtsho-ma was lHa-tho-do sNya-bstsan.

The son of lHa-tho-do sNya-brtsan[*sic*] and gNo'-za Mang-mo-rje Ji-dgos was Khri-snya Zung-bstsan.

The son of Khri-snya Zung-bstsan and 'Bro'-za Dung-pyang-bzher was 'Bro-mnyen lDe-ru.

The son of 'Bro'[*sic*]-mnyen lDe-ru and mChims-za Klu-rgyal Ngan-mo-mtsho was sTag-bu sNya-gzigs.

The son of sTag-bu sNya-gzigs and 'Ol-god Za-stong Tsun'bro-ga was Slon-btsan Rlung-nam.

These excerpts document the succession of the thirty-one dynasties.

The three texts quoted above provide an account indicative of all known historical documents pertaining to the Bonpo and Buddhist traditions with respect to the identification of the succession of Tibetan monarchs during the Intermediate Period. Discrepancies in the succession shown above where thirty-three dynasties occur in the Bonpo version, whereas the *bKa' thang* counts them as thirty, and the Dunhuang documents as thirty-one, are also reflected in various dynastic documents that take different stances in regard to the identification of the succession of Tibetan monarchs during the Intermediate Period.

The main documents used here as the sources for the history of the Intermediate Period are as follows:

- *Dar rgyas gsal ba'i sgron ma* (abbreviation *Dar rgyas*)
- *bKa' thang sde lnga* (abbreviation *bKa' thang*)
- *Tun hong bod kyi lo rgyus yig rnying* (abbreviation *Dunhuang*)
- *bKa' chems bka' khol ma* (abbreviation *Ka khol*)
- *lDe'u chos 'byung* (abbreviation *lDe'u*)
- *Nyang gi chos 'byung* (abbreviation *Nyang 'byung*)
- *Grags rgyal bod kyi rgyal rabs* (abbreviation *Grags rgyal*)
- *Ne'u paṇḍi ta'i sngon gyi gtam* (abbreviation *Ne'u*)
- *Yar lung jo bo'i chos 'byung* (abbreviation *chos 'byung*)
- *Srid pa rgyud kyi kha byang* (abbreviation *srid rgyud*)
- *Deb ther dmar po* (abbreviation *deb dmar*)
- *rGyal rabs gsal ba'i me long* (abbreviation *gSal me*)
- *Deb ther sngon po* (abbreviation *Deb sngon*)
- *rGyal rabs bon gyi 'byung gnas* (abbreviation *Bon 'byung*)
- *lHo brag chos 'byung* (abbreviation *lHo 'byung*)
- *rGya bod yig tshang chen mo* (abbreviation *Yig tshang*)

- *rGyal rabs 'phrul gyi lde mig* (abbreviation *'Phrul lde*)
- *Deb ther dpyid kyi rgyal mo'i glu dbyangs* (abbreviation *dPyid rgyal*)
- *rGyal rabs gser gyi phreng ba* (abbreviation *gSer phreng*)
- *Legs bshad rin po che'i mdzod* (abbreviation *Legs bshad*)

The *Dar rgyas gsal sgron* was composed by sPa-ston bsTan-rgyal bZang-po in the female Wood Bird year of the first *sMe phreng* of the nineteenth *sMe 'khor* (that is, Tibetan year 3262, Western year 1345); therefore it can not be considered as an ancient text. However, since it draws on old Bonpo documents such as the *Byams ma*, and so on, it becomes clear after a careful analysis that it represents an excellent source for the history of the Intermediate Period.

I have used these sources in order to determine the way in which the Tibetan monarchy of the Intermediate Period came into existence. Obviously many more Bonpo and Buddhist fonts of information exist beyond the ones listed.

In the *Tun hong bod kyi lo rgyus yig rnying* [Old Tibetan Chronicles of Dunhuang] (PT 556, 49) we read:

> When sPu-de Gung-rgyal died, [he was succeeded by] Grang-mo gNam-gser-bstsig.
> The son of gSer-bstsig was Tho-leg bTsan-po.

The text affirms that a so-called Grang-mo gNam-gser-bstsig seized the throne after the death of sPu-de Gung-rgyal, and that that king had a son, Tho-legs bTsan-po. However, absolutely no way exists that a king called Grang-mo gNam-gser-brtsig could appear after sPu-de Gung-rgyal and before the Six *Legs* of the Earth. He does not belong either to the first two *lDeng* or to the group of the Six *Legs* of the Earth. The name of this king does not appear in any other dynastic or religious history of Tibet, nor in any other historical collection. Most probably, he did not exist. It is usually much easier to create something in ancient history that does not exist, rather than to make disappear what is already there. It goes without saying that concerning old historical cycles, innumerable historical documents exist about which we are unsure and whose provenance remains unclear.

The following tables illustrate the succession of the thirty-four Tibetan dynasties of the Intermediate Period—from the first Tibetan king gNya'-khri bTsan-po until the ninth monarch Tri-rgyal Lo-ngam and from the eleventh monarch Grang-mo gNam-gser-brtsig until gNam-ri Srong-btsan—as they are acknowledged in the religious and dynastic sources listed above.

The tables show the various ways in which the succession of monarchs is treated, based upon the lists found in each of the twenty documents cited. The number written together with the name indicates the order of succession as it appears in the list of each document. The numbers at the head of the list indicate the Seven *Khri* of the Sky, the Two *sTeng* of Above, the Six *Legs* of the Earth, the Eight *lDe* of the Water, the Four or Five *bTsan* of the Middle, and so on, as they appear in each textual version.

Table 8. *The Succession of the Thirty-Four Tibetan Dynasties of the Intermediate Period according to Twenty Different Sources*

	The Seven Khri of the Sky [gNam gyi Khri bdun] (I)			
Text	1	1	2	2
	King	Queen	King	Queen
Dar rgyas	1. gNya'-khri bTsan-po	gNam-mu-yug	2. Mu-khri bTsan-po	Sa-sman Ting-ting
bKa' thang	1. gNya'-khri		2. Mu-khri	
Dunhuang	1. lDe Nyag-khri bTsan-po	gNam-mug-mug	2. Mu-khri bTsan-po	Sa-ding-ding
Ka khol	1. gNya'-khri bTsan-po		2. sMu-khri bTsan-po	
lDe'u	1. lDe gNya'-khri bTsan-po	gNam-mug-mug	2. Mug-khri bTsan-po	Sa-ding-deng
Nyang 'byung	1. gNya'-khri bTsan-po		3. Mu-khri bTsan-po	
Grags rgyal	1. rJe lDe gNya'-khri bTsan-po		2. Ding-khri bTsan-po	
Ne'u	1. gNya'-khri bTsan-po		2. Ding-khri bTsan-po	
Yar lung	1. gNya'-khri bTsan-po		2. Mu-khri bTsan-po	
Srid rgyud	1. lDe gNya'-khri bTsad-po	gNam-sman Ting-ting	2. Mu-khri bTsad-po	So-tham-tham
Deb dmar	1. gNya'-khri bTsan-po		2. Mu-khri bTsan-po	
gSal me	1. rJe gNya'-khri bTsan-po		2. Mu-khri bTsan-po	
Deb sngon	1. Khri-btsan-po 'Od-lde		2. Mu-khri bTsan-po	
Bon 'byung	1. gNya'-khri bTsad-po	2. Mu-khri bTsad-po		
lHo 'byung	1. gNya'-khri bTsan-po	gNam-mug-mug	2. Mu-khri bTsan-po	Sa-ding-ding
Yig tshang	1. gNya'-khri bTsan-po		2. Mu-khri bTsan-po	
'Phrul lde	1. mNya'-khri bTsan-po		2. Mu-khri bTsan-po	

dPyid rgyal	1. gNya'-khri bTsan-po	gNam-mug-mug	2. Mu-khri bTsan-po	Sa-ding-ding
gSer phreng	1. gNya'-khri bTsad-po		2. Mu-khri bTsan-po	
Legs bshad	1. gNya'-khri bTsan-po	gNam-za Mug-mug	2. Mu-khri bTsan-po	Sa-slan Ting-ting-ma

The Seven Khri of the Sky [gNam gyi Khri bdun] (2)				
Text	3	3	4	4
	King	Queen	King	Queen
Dar rgyas	3. Ding-khri bTsan-po	Se-za-sman	4. So-khri bTsan-po	Dar-za Zhang-zhung-ma
bKa' thang	3. Ding-khri bTsan-po		4. So-khri bTsan-po	
Dunhuang	3. Ding-khri bTsan-po	So-tham-tham	4. So-khri bTsan-po	
Ka khol	3. lHa-khri bTsan-po		4. Deng-khri bTsan-po	
lDe'u	3. Deng-khri bTsan-po	So-tham-tham	4. So-khri bTsan-po	Dog-mer-mer
Nyang 'byung	3. Mu-khri bTsan-po		4. Sribs-khri bTsan-po	
Grags rgyal	3. Mu-khri bTsan-po		4. Sri-khri bTsan-po	
Ne'u	3. Mu-khri bTsan-po		4. Sribs-khri bTsan-po	
Yar lung	3. Ding-khri bTsan-po	So-tham-tham	4. So-khri bTsan-po	Thog-mer-mer
Srid rgyud	3. Ting-khri bTsad-po	Sa-mug-mug	4. So-khri bTsad-po	gDags-kyi rTsis-byang Bu-mo
Deb dmar	3. Ding-khri bTsan-po		4. So-khri bTsan-po	
gSal me	3. Ding-khri bTsan-po		4. So-khri bTsan-po	
Deb sngon	3. Ding-khri-bTsan-po		4. So-khri bTsan-po	
Bon 'byung	3. Ding-khri bTsad-po		4. So-khri bTsan-po	

lHo 'byung	3. Ding-khri	So-tham-tham	4. So-khri		Dog-mer-mer
Yig tshang	3. Deng-khri bTsan-po		4. So-khri bTsan-po		
'Phrul lde	3. Ding-khri bTsan-po		4. So-khri bTsan-po		
dPyid rgyal	3. Ding-khri bTsan-po	So-tham-tham	4. So-khri bTsan-po		Dog-mer-mer
gSer phreng	3. Ding-khri bTsad-po				
Legs bshad	3. Ding-khri bTsan-po	Se-za-sman	4. So-khri bTsan-po		Dar-za Zhang-zhung-ma

The Seven Khri of the Sky [gNam gyi Khri bdun] (3)				
Text	5	5	6	6
	King	Queen	King	Queen
Dar rgyas	5. Dar-khri bTsan-po	Dwags-kyi lHa-mo dKar-po	6. Dwags-khri bTsan-po	Sribs-kyi lHa-mo dKar-mo
bKa' thang	5. Mer-khri bTsan-po		6. gDags-khri bTsan-po	
Dunhuang	5. De-khri bTsan-po		6. Khri-spe bTsan-po	
Ka khol	5. Dos-khri bTsan-po		6. Khri-pe bTsan-po	
lDe'u	5. Dog-khri bTsan-po	gDags-kyi lHa-mo	6. gDags-khri bTsan-po	Sribs-kyi lHa-mo
Nyang 'byung	5. Ye-shes Khri-po		6. gNya'-khri-po	
Grags rgyal	5. gDags-khri bTsan-po		6. Khris-ye bTsan-po	
Ne'u	5. gDags-khri bTsan-po		6. Khri-so bTsan-po	
Yar lung	5. Mer-khri bTsan-po	gDags-kyi lHa-mo dKar-mo	6. gDags-khri bTsan-po	Sribs-kyi lHa-mo
Srid rgyud	5. Byang-khri bTsad-po	lDer-za bTsun-mo	6. lDe-khri bTsad-po	'Brom-za lHa-rgyan
Deb dmar	5. Mer-khri bTsan-po		6. gDags-khri bTsan-po	

gSal me	5. Me-khri bTsan-po		6. gDags-khri bTsan-po	
Deb sngon	5. Mer-khri bTsan-po		6. gDags-khri bTsan-po	
Bon 'byung	5. Dar-khri bTsan-po		6. Ye-khri bTsan-po	
lHo 'byung	5. Mer-khri	gDags-lha dKar-mo	6. gDags-khri	Sribs-lha sNgon-mo
Yig tshang	5. Da-khri		6. Dhag-khri	
'Phrul lde	5. Mo-khri bTsan-po		6. gDags-khri bTsan-po	
dPyid rgyal	5. Mer-khri	gDags-kyi lHa-mo dKar-mo	6. gDags-khri	Srib-kyi lHa-mo
gSer phreng	5. Me-khri bTsan-po		6. gDags-khri bTsan-po	
Legs bshad	5. Dar-khri bTsan-po	Dwags-kyi lHa-mo	6. Dwags-khri bTsan-po = Ye-khri	Srib-kyi lHa-mo dKar-mo

The Seven Khri of the Sky (4)			The lDeng of the Middle [Bar gyi lDeng] (1)	
Text	7	7	1	8
	King	Queen	King	Queen
Dar rgyas	7. Sribs-khri bTsan-po		1. Gri-rum bTsan-po	dBal-za Khri-btsun
bKa' thang	7. sPyi-khri bTsan-po		1. Gri-gum bTsan-po	
Dunhuang	1. Dri-gum bTsan-po			
Ka khol	7. Gung-khri bTsan-po		1. Gri-gung bTsan-po	
lDe'u	7. Sribs-khri bTsan-po		1. Gri-gum bTsan-po	
Nyang 'byung	7. Khri-pan bTsan-po		1. Gri-gum bTsan-po	
Grags rgyal	7. Khri-gum bTsan-po			
Ne'u	7. Gri-gum bTsan-po			

Yar lung	7. Sribs-khri bTsan-po	Sa-btsun Rlung-rje	I. Gri-gum bTsan-po	Klu-btsan Mer-lcam
Srid rgyud	7. Dri-gum bTsad-po	sPug-za bZang-mo		
Deb dmar	7. Sribs-khri bTsan-po		I. Gri-gum bTsan-po	
gSal me	7. Srib-khri bTsan-po		I. Gri-gum bTsan-po	
Deb sngon	7. Sribs-khri bTsan-po		I. Gri-gum bTsan-po	
Bon 'byung	7. Seng-khri bTsan-po		I. Gri-rum bTsan-po	Bal-bza' Khri-btsun
lHo 'byung	7. Sribs-khri bTsan-po	Sa-btsun Klu-rje	I. Gri-gum bTsan-po	Glu-sring Mer-lcam
Yig tshang	7. Sribs-khri bTsan-po		I. Gri-gum bTsan-po	
'Phrul lde	7. Srib-khri bTsan-po		I. Gri-gum bTsan-po	
dPyid rgyal	7. Srib-khri bTsan-po	Sa-btsun Rlung-rje	I. Gri-gum bTsan-po	Klu-btsan Mer-lcam
gSer phreng	7. Sribs-khri bTsan-po		I. Gri-gum bTsan-po	
Legs bshad	7. Srib-khri bTsan-po = Seng-khri		I. Gri-gum bTsan-po	dPa'-za Khri-btsun

The lDeng of the Middle [Bar gyi lDeng] (2)				
Text	2	9	3	10
	King	Queen	King	Queen
Dar rgyas	2. Tri-rgyal Lo-ngam	Sras-mo lHa-lcam	3. sPu-lde Gung-rgyal	Bum-thang sMan-mtsho
bKa' thang			2. sPu-de Gung-rgyal	
Dunhuang			2. sPu-de Gung-rgyal	
Ka khol			2. sPu-de Gung-rgyal	

lDe'u			2. sPu-de Gung-rgyal	
Nyang 'byung			2. sPu-rje Gung-rgyal	
Grags rgyal			1. sPu-lde Gung-rgyal	
Ne'u			1. 'O-ste sPu-rgyal	
Yar lung			2. sPu-de Gung-rgyal	Bem-thang rMang-mtsho
Srid rgyud			(The Six Yag of the Earth [Sa yi Yag drug])	
Deb dmar			2. sPu-de Gung-rgyal	
gSal me			2. sPu-de Gang-rgyal	
Deb sngon			2. sPu-de Gung-rgyal	
Bon 'byung			2. sPu-de Gung-rgyal	
lHo 'byung			2. Pu-de Gung-rgyal	'Om-thang sMan-mtsho
Yig tshang			2. sPu-de Gung-rgyal	
'Phrul lde			2. Pu-te Gung-rgyal	
dPyid rgyal			2. sPu-de Gung-rgyal	Bom-thang rMang-mnya'
gSer phreng			2. sPu-de Gung-rgyal	
Legs bshad			2. sPu-lde'u Gong-rgyal	Bum-thang sMad-mtsho

CHAPTER III ▪ THE ROYAL LINEAGES OF ANCIENT TIBET

	The Six Legs of the Earth [Sa la Legs drug] (I)			
Text	I	II	I	I2
	King	Queen	King	Queen
Dar rgyas			I. A-sho-legs	dMu-lcam La-na
bKa' thang			I. I-sho-legs	
Dunhuang	I. Grang-mo gNam-gser-brtsig		I. Tho-legs bTsan-po	
Ka khol			I. lHa-sho-legs	
lDe'u			I. Sho-legs	
Nyang 'byung			I. A-sho-legs	
Grags rgyal			I. Ngo-legs	
Ne'u			I. Tho-legs	
Yar lung			I. I-sho-legs	dMu-lcam Bra-ma-na
Srid rgyud			I. sPu-lde Gong-rgyal	sBrang-za Yag-mo
Deb dmar			I. I-sho-legs	
gSal me			I. A-sho-legs	
Deb sngon			I. E-sho-legs	
Bon 'byung			I. A-sho Legs-rgyal	
lHo 'byung			I. I-sho-legs	rMu-lcam Bra-ma
Yig tshang			I. I-sho-legs	
'Phrul lde			I. A-sho-legs	
dPyid rgyal			I. I-sho-legs	rMu-lcam Bra-ma na
gSer phreng			I. A-sho-legs	
Legs bshad			I. A-sho Legs-rgyal	dMu-lcam Dra-ma na

The Six Legs of the Earth [Sa la Legs drug] (2)				
Text	2	13	3	14
	King	Queen	King	Queen
Dar rgyas	2. De-sho-legs	Klu-sman Mer-mo	3. The-sho-legs	bTsan-mo Gur-sman
bKa' thang	2. Li-sho-legs		3. 'Brong-bzhi-legs	
Dunhuang	2. Sho-legs bTsan-po		3. Go-ru-legs bTsan-po	
Ka khol	2. Go-ru-legs		3. 'Brong-zhi-legs	
lDe'u	2. De-sho-legs		3. Gor-bu-legs	
Nyang 'byung	2. I-sho-legs		3. Go-ru-legs	
Grags rgyal	2. 'Og-rgyu-legs		3. Sho-legs	
Ne'u	2. mGo-ru-legs		3. Sho-legs	
Yar lung	2. De-sho-legs	Klu-sman Mer-ma	3. The-sho-legs	Gur-sman
Srid rgyud	2. bTsad-po Tho-yag		3. bTsad-po A'i-sho-yag	dMu-lcam lHa-btsun
Deb dmar	2. De-sho-legs		3. Thi-sho-legs	
gSal me	2. De-sho-legs		3. Thi-sho-legs	
Deb sngon	2. De-sho-legs		3. Thi-sho-legs	
Bon 'byung	2. De-sho Legs-rgyal		3. Go-ru Legs-rgyal	
lHo 'byung	2. De-sho-legs	Klu-lcam Mer-ma	3. Thi-sho-legs	mTshan-mo Gung-sman
Yig tshang	2. De-sho-legs		3. Thi-sho-legs	
'Phrul lde	2. I-sho-legs		3. Do-sho-legs	
dPyid rgyal	2. De-sho-legs	Klu-sman Mer-mo	3. Thi-sho-legs	bTsan-mo Gur-sman
gSer phreng	2. I-sho-legs		2. De-sho-legs	
Legs bshad	2. De-sho Legs-rgyal	Gur-sman	3. Thi-sho Legs-rgyal	mTsho-sman 'Brang-ma

CHAPTER III ▪ THE ROYAL LINEAGES OF ANCIENT TIBET 141

Text	The Six Legs of the Earth [Sa la Legs drug] (3)			
	4	15	5	16
	King	Queen	King	Queen
Dar rgyas	4. 'Gu-ru-legs	mTshon-sman 'Brong-mo	5. 'Brong-bzher-legs	Sa-sman Bu-mo
bKa' thang	4. Thi-sho-legs		5. Gu-rum-legs	
Dunhuang	4. 'Brong-zhi-legs bTsan-po		5. Thi-sho-leg	
Ka khol	4. The-sho-legs		5. Tho-sho-legs	
lDe'u	4. 'Brong-bzhi-legs		5. Tho-sho-legs	
Nyang 'byung	4. dGe-sho-legs		5. 'Brang-rje-legs	
Grags rgyal	4. 'Bro-zhing-legs		5. I-sho-legs	
Ne'u	4. 'Bri-sho-legs		5. I-sho-legs	
Yar lung	4. Go-ru-legs	mTsho-sman 'Brong-ma	5. 'Breng-zher-legs	sMan-bu-mo
Srid rgyud	4. bTsad-po 'Brong-'dzin-yag	'Tshod-za Khri-mo	5. 'O-ru-yag	Phrom-za mTsho-rgyan
Deb dmar	4. Gu-ru-legs		5. 'Brom-zher-legs	
gSal me	4. Gu-ru-legs		5. 'Brong-zher-legs	
Deb sngon	4. Gu-ru-legs		5. 'Brong-zhi-legs	
Bon 'byung	4. 'Brong-rje Legs-rgyal		5. Thi-sho Legs-rgyal	
lHo 'byung	4. Gong-ru-legs	mTsho-sman 'Brong-ma	5. 'Brong-gzher-legs	gNam-sman Bu-mo
Yig tshang	4. Go-ru-legs		5. 'Brom-zher-legs	
'Phrul lde	4. Gu-rub-legs		5. 'Brom-rje-legs	
dPyid rgyal	4. Gu-ru-legs	mTsho-sman 'Brang-ma	5. 'Brong-zhi-legs	sMan-bu-mo
gSer phreng	4. Ghu-ru-legs		5. 'Brong-rje-legs	
Legs bshad	4. Gu-rum Legs-rgyal	sMan-bu-mo	5. 'Brang-zhi Legs-rgyal	Glu-lcam Mi-mo

	The Six Legs of the Earth [Sa la Legs drug] (4) The Eight lDe of the Water [Chu la lDe brgyad] (I)			
Text	6	17	1	18
	King	Queen	King	Queen
Dar rgyas	6. Sho-legs	dMu-lcam rMang-legs	1. Za-nam Zin-lde	mTsho-sman Khri-dkar
bKa' thang	6. Sa-nam-legs		(Seven principalities/king lines)	
Dunhuang	6. I-sho-legs bTsan-po		(From here on the list is unclear)	
Ka khol	6. I-sho-legs		1. Za-nam Zin-te	
lDe'u	6. I-sho-legs		1. rGyal-nam Zin-lde	
Nyang 'byung	6. The-sho-legs		1. rGyal-sa Nam-zin	
Grags rgyal	6. gNam-zi-legs		1. lDe-mnam	
Ne'u	6. Zwa-gnam Zin-legs		1. lDe-gnam 'Phrul-po gZhung-btsan	
Yar lung	6. Sho-legs	dMu-lcam sMang-legs	1. Za-nam Zi-nam-lde	mTsho-sman Khri-dkar
Srid rgyud	6. Yag-drug bTsad-po	gNam-sman dKar-mo	1. rGyal-zi Nam-'dzin	gNam-sman Gong-nga
Deb dmar	6. Sho-legs		1. Za-nam Zin-lde	
gSal me	6. I-sho-legs		1. Za-nam Zin-te	
Deb sngon	6. I-sho-legs		1. Za-nam Zi-lde	
Bon 'byung	6. I-sho Legs-rgyal		1. 'Bi-sho 'Ching-rgyal	
lHo 'byung	6. Sho-legs	rMu-lcam rMang-legs	1. Za-nam Zin-lde	mTsho-sman Khri-dkar
Yig tshang	6. A-sho-legs		1. Za-nam Zi-lde	
'Phrul lde	6. Tho-sho-legs		1. rGyal-sa Zin-te	

dPyid rgyal	6. I-sho-legs	rMu-lcam sMad-legs	I. Za-nam Zin-lde	mTsho-sman Khri-dkar
gSer phreng	6. Thong-sho-legs		I. Zin-lde	
Legs bshad	6. I-sho Legs-rgyal	dGu-lcam sMad-legs	I. Zin-nam Zin-lde	

The Eight lDe of the Water [Chu la lDe brgyad] (2)				
Text	2	19	3	20
	King	Queen	King	Queen
Dar rgyas	2. lDe Nam-'phrul-bZhung-btsan	gNyan-mang-mo	3. Se-snol Nam-lde	Klu-thang Mer-mo
bKa' thang	1. lDe-ru gNam-gzhung-btsan		2. sDe-snod-sbas	
Dunhuang	Zwa-gnam Zin-te		lDe Phru-bo gNam-gzhung-bstsan	
Ka khol	2. lDe 'Phrul-po		3. gNam-zhung-btsan	
lDe'u	2. lDe 'Phrul-po		3. gNam-gzhung-btsan	
Nyang 'byung	2. gNam Yu-bo gZhung-btsan-lde		3. lDe sPrul-gnam gZhung-btsan	
Grags rgyal	2. 'Phrul-po gZhung-btsan		3. lTo-rman-bum	
Ne'u	2. lDe-rmul-bu		3. lDe-rnol-nam	
Yar lung	2. lDe 'Phrul-nam gZhung-btsan	bSe-gnyan Mang-mo	3. Se-snol Nam-lde	Klu-mo Mer-ma
Srid rgyud	lDe-bo gNam-gzhung bTsad-po		lDe 'Od-nam bTsad-po	gNam-sman Rung-mo
Deb dmar	2. lDe 'Phrul-nam gZhung-btsan		3. Se-snol lHam-lde	

gSal me	2. lDe 'Phrul-nam gZhung-btsan		3. Se-bsnol Nam-lde	
Deb sngon	2. lDe 'Phrul-nam gZhung-btsan		3. Se-nol Nam-lde	
Bon 'byung	2. lDe-snol rNam-rgyal		3. lDe-'phrul Bon-rgyal	
lHo 'byung	2. 'Phrul-nam gZhung-btsan-lde	Se-gnyan Mer-mo	3. Se-snol Nam-lde	Klu-mo Mer-mo
Yig tshang	2. lDe 'Phrul-nam gZhung-can		3. sNol-nam-lde	
'Phrul lde	2. lDe 'Phrul-nam gZhung-btsan		3. Se-rnol rNam-lde	
dPyid rgyal	2. lDe 'Phrul-nam gZhung-btsan	Se-snyan Mang-ma	3. Se-snol gNam-lde	Klu-mo Mer-ma
gSer phreng	2. lDe 'Phrul-nam gZhung-btsan		3. lDe rGyal-po-btsan	
Legs bshad	2. lDe'u-'phrul gZhung-btsan		3. Se-snol gNam-lde	

CHAPTER III — THE ROYAL LINEAGES OF ANCIENT TIBET

	The Eight lDe of the Water [Chu la lDe brgyad] (3)			
Text	4	21	5	22
	King	Queen	King	Queen
Dar rgyas	4. Se-snol-lde	'O-za Ting-mo-mtsho	5. lDe-snol-nam	Khri-sman rJe-ma
bKa' thang	3. sDe-snod-ya		4. Sor-rno-nam	
Dunhuang	lDe-gol		gNam-lde rNol-nam	
Ka khol	4. sDe-rnol-po		5. sDe-rnol-nam	
lDe'u	4. lDe-rnol-nam		5. bSe-rnol gNam-lde	
Nyang 'byung	4. lDe-snol-nam		5. lDe-rgyal-po	
Grags rgyal	4. lHo-snol-nam		5. lDe-snol-po	
Ne'u	4. lDe-rnol-lo		5. lDe-bis sNol-gnam	
Yar lung	4. Se sNol-po-lde	'O-za Te-mo-mtsho	5. lDe-snol-nam	Khri-sman rJe-ma
Srid rgyud	lDe 'O-rnal bTsad-po		rGyal-srid bTsad-po	gNam-sman Ju-ge
Deb dmar	4. Se sNol-po-lde		5. lDe-snol-nam	
gSal me	4. lDe-bsnol-nam		5. lDe-bsnol-bo	
Deb sngon	4. Se rNol-po-lde		5. lDe-rnol-nam	
Bon 'byung	4. lDe-'od rNam-rgyal		5. lDe-gser gNon-rgyal	
lHo 'byung	4. Se sNor-po-lde	'O-za Te-mo-mtsho	5. lDe-nor-nam	Khri-sman rJe-mo
Yig tshang	4. sNol-bo-lde		5. lDe-snol-nam	
'Phrul lde	4. Se rNol-po-lde		5. lDe-rnol-rnam	
dPyid rgyal	4. Se rNol-po-lde	'O-ma Te-mo-mtsho	5. lDe-snol-nam	Khri-sman rJe-ma
gSer phreng	4. Se sNol-nam-lde		5. Se-snol-po-lde	
Legs bshad	4. Se sNol-po-lde		5. lDe'u-nam-'od	

The Eight lDe of the Water [Chu la lDe brgyad] (4)				
Text	6	23	7	24
	King	Queen	King	Queen
Dar rgyas	6. lDe-rnol-po	Sa-btsun sNyan-rje	7. lDe-rgyal-po	sMan-btsun Lung-gong
bKa' thang	5. rGyal-po So-ste		6. sPrin-rgyal-btsan	
Dunhuang	bSe'-rNol-po		lDe-rgyal-po	
Ka khol	6. bSe-rnol-nam		7. bSe-rnol-po	
lDe'u	6. bSe rNol-po-lde		7. lDe-rgyal-po	
Nyang 'byung	6. lDe So-pha-nam		7. lDe-rgyal-nam	
Grags rgyal	6. lDe Se-snol-nam		7. lDe Se-rnol-po	
Ne'u	6. lDe rMu-la-gnam		7. lDe Se-rnol-po	
Yar lung	6. lDe-snol-po	Sa-btsun gNyan-rje	7. lDe-rgyal-po	sMan-btsun Lug-skong
Srid rgyud	(The list of the Six Yag that follows at this point is not clear)			
Deb dmar	6. lDe-snol-po		7. lDe-rgyal-po	
gSal me	6. lDe-rgyal-po		7. lDe-sprin-btsan	
Deb sngon	6. lDe-rnol-po		7. lDe-rgyal-po	
Bon 'byung	6. lDe gSer-nam rGyal-po	(After the Six Legs of the Water, the Six bTsan of the Middle):		
lHo 'byung	6. lDe-snol-po	Khri Se-btsun gNyan-mo	7. lDe-rgyal-po	sMan-btsun Lug-skong
Yig tshang	6. lDe-snol-po		7. lDe-rgyal-po	
'Phrul lde	6. lDe-rnol-po		7. lDe-rgyal-po	
dPyid rgyal	6. lDe-rnol-po	Se-btsan gNyan-rje	7. lDe-rgyal-po	sMan-btsun Lug-sgong
gSer phreng	6. lDe-lam		7. lDe-snol-po	
Legs bshad	6. lDe'u-snol-po		7. lDe'u-rgyal-po	

	The Eight lDe of the Water [Chu la lDe brgyad] (5) The Five bTsan of the Middle [Bar gyi bTsan lnga] (I)			
Text	8	25	I	26
	King	Queen	King	Queen
Dar rgyas	8. lDe-srin-btsan	gNyan-btsun Mang-mo-rje	I. rGyal To-ro Lo-btsan	'O-ma lDe-sa Khri-btsun-ma
bKa' thang	7. sTong-ri sTong-btsan		I. Khri-nam-btsan	
Dunhuang	rGyal-srin-bstsan		rGyal To-re Longs-bstsan	
Ka khol	8. sDe-rgyal-po		I. rGyal-po sPrin-btsan	
lDe'u	8. rGyal-po sPrin-btsan-sde		I. rGyal To-to-re Long-btsan	rMa-za Klu-rgyal
Nyang 'byung	8. lDe-srid-btsan		I. rGyal Thod-re Long-btsan	
Grags rgyal	8. lDe-rgyal-po	(Four bTsan):	I. rGyal Tho-los-btsan	Khri-rgyal Na-bu
Ne'u	8. lDe-rgyal-po		I. rGyal Tho-long-btsan	rGyal-za 'O-ma-lde
Yar lung	8. lDe-sprin-btsan	Nyi-btsun Mang-ma-rje	I. rGyal Te-ro Long-btsan	'O-ma lDe-za Khri-btsun Byang-ma
Srid rgyud	8.		I. Tho-lde Lo-rog bTsad-po	gNam-sman Ju-ten
Deb dmar	8. lDe-sprin-btsan		I. rGyal lDe-re Long-btsan	
gSal me	8. lDe-sprin-btsan	(The Three bTsan of Below ['Og gi bTsan gsum]):		
Deb sngon	8. lDe-sprin-btsan		I. rGyal To-ri Long-btsan	
Bon 'byung	I. Dar-rgyal Srin-btsan		2. rGyal-btsan	
lHo 'byung	8. lDe-sprin-btsan	Nye-btsun Mang-ma-rje	I. To-re Long-btsan	'O-ma lDe-za Khri-btsun Byang-ma

Yig tshang	8. lDe-sprin-btsan		1. rGyal To-re Long-btsan	
'Phrul lde	8. lDe-sprin-btsan	(The three bTsan of Below ['Og gi bTsan gsum]):		
dPyid rgyal	8. lDe-sprin-btsan	Nyi-btsun Mang-ma-rje	1. rGyal To-ri Long-btsan	'O-ma lDe-bza' Bri-btsun Byang-ma
gSer phreng	8. sPrin-btsan-lde		(The list below is not clear):	
Legs bshad	8. lDe'u-sprin-btsan		1. To-ro Lo-btsan	

The Five bTsan of the Middle [Bar gyi bTsan lnga] (2)				
Text	2	27	3	28
	King	Queen	King	Queen
Dar rgyas	2. Khri-btsan-nam	Sa-khri-dkar	3. Khri-dgra dPung-btsan	sMan-za Klu-stengs
bKa' thang	2. Khri-sgra dPung-btsan		3. Khri Thog-rje-btsan	
Dunhuang	Khri-bstsan-nam		Khri-sgra sPung-bstsan	
Ka khol	2. Tho-re Long-btsan		3. Khri-btsan-nam	
lDe'u	2. Khri-btsan-nam	Khri-sgra Ngan-chung	3. Khri-sgra bsGrungs-btsan	rMa-za Klu-rlungs-btsan
Nyang 'byung	2. Khri-btsan-nam		3. Khri-sgra dPung-btsan	
Grags rgyal	2. Khri-btsan-nam	sMan-bza' Klu-rgyal-dbang	3. Khri-sgra sPungs-btsan	sMan-bza'
Ne'u	2. Khri-btsan	sMan-gza' Klu-rgyal	3. Khri-sgra sPungs-btsan	dBang-gza' sMan-klu-rgyal
Yar lung	2. Khri-btsan-nam	sMan-za Khri-dkar	3. Khri-sgra sPungs-btsan	sMan-bza' Klu-stengs
Srid rgyud	2. Khri-btsan-nam	gNam-sman Phu-ge	3. Khri Ka-g.yu-btsan	gNam-sman Khrung-dkar

CHAPTER III ▪ THE ROYAL LINEAGES OF ANCIENT TIBET

Deb dmar	2. Khri-btsan-nam		3. Khri-sgra sPungs-btsan	
gSal me	1. Khri-btsan-nam		2. Khri-dgra dPung-btsan	
Deb sngon	2. Khri-btsan-nam		3. Khri-sbra dPungs-btsan	
Bon 'byung	3. Khri-btsan		4. dMu-btsan	
lHo 'byung	2. Khri-btsan-nam	sMan-za Khri-dkar	3. Khri-sgra sPungs-btsan	sMan-gsum Klu-steng
Yig tshang	2. rJe Khri-btsan-nam		3. rJe Khri-sgra sPungs-btsan	
'Phrul lde	1. Khri-btsan-nam		2. Khri-dgra dPung-btsan	
dPyid rgyal	2. Khri-btsan-nam	sMan-bza' Khri-dkar	3. Khri-sgra dPung-btsan	sMan-bza' Klu-steng
gSer phreng	Tho-tho Re-long-btsan	sMa-tsha Klu-rgyal	Khri-btsan	
Legs bshad	2 Khri-btsan-nam		3. Khri-sgra dPung-btsan	

The Five bTsan of the Middle [Bar gyi bTsan lnga] (3)				
Text	4	29	5	30
	King	Queen	King	Queen
Dar rgyas	4. Khri-thog rJe-btsan	Ru-yang Za-steng rGyal-nam-mtsho	5. Tho-tho Ri'i-snyan-btsan	Gur-sman and rNo-za Ma-mo-rje
bKa' thang	4. Tho-tho gNyan-btsan		5. Khri-gnyan gZungs-btsan	
Dunhuang	Khri-thog-bstsan	Ru-yong Za-stong rGyal-mtsho-ma	lHa-tho-do sNya-bstsan	gNo'-za Mang-mo-rje
Ka khol	4. Khri-sgra sPung-btsan		5. Thog-rje Thog-btsan	gNyan-mo Gung-sman
lDe'u	4. Khri Thog-rje Thog-btsan	Ru-spong gZa'-stong rGyal-mtsho	5. lHa-tho-tho Re-snyan-btsan	rNo-za Mang-mo-rje

Nyang 'byung	4. Khri Thog-rje Thog-btsan		5. lHa Tho-tho-ri	
Grags rgyal	4. Khri Thog-rje Thog-tsan	Ru-gyong bZa'-steng rGya-mtsho-ma	Tho-tho Ri-snyan-btsan	lHa-lung-bza' Ma-mo-rje
Ne'u	4. Khri Thog-rje Thog-btsan	sTeng-rgyal mTsho-mo	5. lHa mTho-tho Ri-snyan-btsan	Lung-gza' Ma-mo-rje
Yar lung	4. Khri-Thog-rje Thog-btsan	Ru-yongs-za sTong-rgyal Na-mo-mtsho	5. lHa Tho-tho Ri-gnyan-btsan	1) Grangs-yul Gur-sman 2) rNo-za Mang-po-rje (child)
Srid rgyud	4. Khri Thog-rje Thog-btsan	Ru-yong-za sTong-rgyal mTsho-mo	5. lHa-tho-to sNyan-gshal	rNo-za Mang-mo-rje
Deb dmar	4. Khri Thog-rje Thog-btsan		5. lHa-tho-tho Re-gnyan-btsan	
gSal me	3. Khri-de Thog-btsan		1. lHa-tho-tho Ri-snyan-shal	
Deb sngon	4. Khri Thog-rje Thog-btsan		5. lHa-tho-tho Ri-gnyan-btsan	
Bon 'byung	5. rJe-btsan		6. Tho-re-lo bTsan = lHa Tho-tho-ri	
lHo 'byung	4. Khri Thog-rje Thog-btsan	Ru-yong Za-stong rGyal-mo-mtsho	5. Tho-tho-ri gNyan-btsan	rNo-za Mang-dgar
Yig tshang	4. Khri Thog-rje Thog-btsan	Ru-yongs gZa'-stong rGya-mtsho	5. lHa-mTho-do Re'i-gnyen-rtsa	
'Phrul lde	3. Khri Thog-rje Thog-btsan		lHa-tho-tho Ri-gnyan-btsan	
dPyid rgyal	4. Khri-thog rJe-btsan	Ru-yong-bza' sTong-rgyal Na-mo-tsho	5. lHa-tho-tho Ri-gnyan-btsan	rNo-za Mang-mo-rje

CHAPTER III ▪ THE ROYAL LINEAGES OF ANCIENT TIBET   151

gSer phreng	3. Khri Thog rJe Thog-btsan		lHa-tho-tho Re-snyan-bshal	
Legs bshad	4 Khri Thog-rje-btsan		5. Tho-re Lung-btsan	

The Four Bonpo Kings of Prosperity [Phug sum tshogs pa'i Bon rgyal bzhi] (I)				
Text	1	31	2	32
	King	Queen	King	Queen
Dar rgyas	1. Khri-gnyan gZung-btsan	'Brong-za Dar-ma g.Yang-bzher	2. 'Brong-snyan lDe-ru	'Chin-za Klu-rgyal Ngan-ma-mtsho
bKa' thang	'Brong-gnyan lDe-ru		sTag-ri gNyan-gzigs	
Dunhuang	Khri-snya Zung-bstsan	'Bro'-za Dung-pyang-bzher	'Bro-mnyen lDe-ru	mChims-za Klu-rgyal Ngan-mo-mtsho
Ka khol	Khri-gnyan bZung-btsan		sTag-gu gNyan-gzigs	
lDe'u	Khri-snya Zungs-btsan	'Bro-sa Rlugs-yang-bzhed	'Bro-gnyen lDe'u	Dwags-po'i Chims-za Klu-rgyal-mtsho
Nyang 'byung	Khri-gnyan gZung-btsan		sTag-ri gNyan-gzigs	
Grags rgyal	Khri-gnyen bZung-btsan	'Brom-bza' Byang-gnyen Ti-pa	'Bro-gnyen lDe-ru	mChims-bza' Klu-rgyal Ngan-bu-'tsho
Ne'u	Khri-gnyan gZung-btsan	'Bro-gza' Byang-gnyen-phreng	Brong-gnyen lDe-ru	
Yar lung	Khri-gnyan Zung-btsan	'Bro-za-mo Dur-yang-gzher	'Bro-gnyen lDe-ru	
Srid rgyud	Khri-snya Zungs-btsad-po	'Brong-za 'Phan-mo-skar	'Brong-gnyen lDem-ru	mChim-za lHa-rgyal Mang-mo-btsun
Deb dmar	2. Khri-gnyan bZung-btsan		sTar-ri gNyan-gzigs	

gSal me	Khri-snyan gZugs-btsan		'Brang-snyan lDe-ru Klu-rgyal	Dwags-po'i mChims-bza'
Deb sngon	Khri-gnyan gZungs-btsan		'Bro-gnyan lDe'u	
Bon 'byung	(Tho-re Lo-btsan is counted as two above and below)		Klu-gnyan gZung-btsan	
lHo 'byung	Khri-gNyan gZungs-btsan	'Bro-za Ngur-yang-bzhin	'Brong-gnyan lDe-ru	
Yig tshang	Khri-gnyan gZung-btsan		'Bro-gnyan lDe-ru	
'Phrul lde	Khri-gnyan bZung-btsan		'Brong-gnyan lDe-ru	Klu-mo
dPyid rgyal	Khri-gnyan gZung-btsan	'Brong-bza' Mo-dur Yangs-bzher	'Gro-gnyan lDe'u	mChims-bza' Klu-rgyal Ngan-bu-mtsho
gSer phreng	Khri-snyan bZung-btsan		'Brong-snyan lDe-ru	
Legs bshad	Klu-gnyan gZung-btsan		'Brang-snyan lDe'u	

CHAPTER III • THE ROYAL LINEAGES OF ANCIENT TIBET   153

Text	The Four Bonpo Kings of Prosperity [Phug sum tshogs pa'i Bon rgyal bzhi] (2)			
	3	33	4	34
	King	Queen	King	Queen
Dar rgyas	3. sTag-ri sNyan-gzigs	'Om-rgod-za sTong-btsun 'Gro-skar	4. gNam-ri Srong-btsan	Tshe-spungs-za 'Bri-ma Thod-dkar
bKa' thang	3. gNam-ri Srong-btsan			
Dunhuang	sTag-gu sNya-gzigs	'Ol-kod-za sTong-tsun 'Bro-ga	Slon-btsan Rlung-nam	Tshes-pong-za 'Bring-ma-thog
Ka khol	gNam-ri Srong-btsan	Tshe-srong-bza' 'Bri-mo Thod-dkar		
lDe'u	sTa-gu sNyan-gzigs	'Ol-go-gza' bTsun-sgron	'gNam-ri Srong-btsan	Tshe-spong-gza' 'Bri-ma Thod-dkar
Nyang 'byung	'Bro-gnyan lDe'u		gNam-ri Srong-btsan	Tshe-spongs-bza' 'Bring-mo Thod-dkar
Grags rgyal	sTag-ri gNyen-gzigs	Bol-gol-bza' sTong-btsun-gyi 'Bro-sman	gNam-ri Srong-btsan	Tshe-spong-bza' 'Bri-ma Tog-this-skong
Ne'u	rGyal sTag-ri gNya'-gzigs	'Ol-sko sTong-btsun	gNam-ri Srong-btsan	Tshes-spong-bza' 'Bri-ma Tho-ga
Yar lung	sTag-ri gNyan-gzigs	'Ol-god-bza' sTong-btsun 'Bro-dkar	gNam-ri Srong-btsan	Tshe-spong-za 'Bri-ma Thod-dkar
Srid rgyud	sNya-gzi bTsad-po	Pho-yong-za 'Bri-thog-khon		
Deb dmar	gNam-ri Srong-btsan	Tshe-spong-za 'Bri-ma Thod dkar		
gSal me	sTag-gong sNyan-gzigs		gNam-ri Srong-btsan	'Bri-bza' Thod-dkar

Deb sngon	sTag-ri gNyan-gzigs		gNam-ri Srong-btsan	
Bon 'byung	sTag-gu gNyan-gzigs		gNam-ra sTong-btsan	
lHo 'byung	sTag-ri gNyan-gzigs	sTong-btsun 'Bro-dkar	gNam-ri Srong-btsan	'Bri-bza' Thod-dkar
Yig tshang	sTag-ri gNyan-gzigs		gNam-ri Srong-btsan	Tshe-spong-bza' Bri-ma Thod-dkar
'Phrul lde	sTag-ri gNyan-gzigs		gNam-ri Srong-btsan	
dPyid rgyal	sTag-ri gNyan-gzigs	'Ol-gong-bza' sTong-btsun 'Gro-dkar	gNam-ri Srong-btsan	Tshe-spong-bza' 'Bri-ma Thod-dkar
gSer phreng	sTag-ri sNyan-gzigs		gNam-ri Srong-btsan	
Legs bshad	sTag-gong sNyan-gzigs		gNam-ri Srong-btsan	

The importance and superior accuracy of the dynastic list found in the *Dar rgyas gsal sgron* becomes evident confronting it with the lists cited in other texts, the majority of which contain a number of unclear as well as inconsistent entries, even where the known facts are unequivocal.

> For example the *rGyal po bka'i thang yig* (Pe, 113, 18) has Seven *Khri* of the Sky, Six *Legs* of the Earth, Seven Princedoms, and Five *bTsan* of the Middle.
>
> The *Tun hong bod kyi lo rgyus yig rnying* [Old Tibetan Chronicles of Dunhuang], except for mentioning the Seven *Dri* [sic] of the Sky and the Six *Legs* of the Earth, do not contain additional entries.
>
> The *bKa' chems ka khol ma* (Kan, 84, 4) mentions Seven *Khri* of the Sky, Two *sTengs* of the Middle, Eight *sDe* of the Water, Six *Legs* of the Earth, and Five *bTsan* of the Middle.
>
> The *lDe'u chos 'byung chen mo* lists Seven *Khri* of the Sky, Two *sTeng* of the Middle, Six *Legs* of the Earth, Eight *sDe*, Five *bTsan* of the Middle, and Two *sTeng* of Below.
>
> The *Nyang gi chos 'byung* refers only to the Seven *Khri* of the Sky, Six *Legs*, Eight *lDe* of the Water, and Four *Tshigs* of the Middle.
>
> The *Grags rgyal bod kyi rgyal rabs* (sDe, TA, 196, 4, 6) says, "The Tibetan kings are Seven *Khri*, one *lDeng*, Six *Legs*, Eight *lDe*, and Four *bTsan*. These are the twenty-six earlier kings."
>
> The *Ne'u sngon 'byung gi gtam* lists Seven *Khri*, One *sTengs*, Six *Legs*, Eight *lDe*, and Five *bTsan*.
>
> The *Yar lung jo bo'i chos 'byung* mentions Seven *Khri* of the Sky, Two *sTengs* of Above, Six *Legs* of the Earth, Eight *lDe*, Five *bTsan*, and Two *sTengs* of the Middle.
>
> The *Srid pa rgyud kyi kha byang* reckons also Gri-gum bTsan-po among the Seven *Khri* of the Sky, defines sPu-de Gung-rgyal as a *lDeng*, and except for the Six *Yag* of the Earth does not contain other entries.
>
> The *Deb ther dmar po* mentions Seven *Khri* of the Sky, Two *sTengs* of Above, Six *Legs* of the Middle, Eight *sDe* of the Earth, Five *bTsan*, and Two *lTengs* of the Middle.

The *rGyal rabs gsal ba'i me long* refers only to Seven *Khri* of the Sky, Two *sTeng* of Above, Six *Legs* of the Middle, Eight *lDe* of the Earth, and Three *bTsan* of Below.

The *Deb ther sngon po* has only Seven *Khri* of the Sky, Two *lTengs* of the Middle, Six *Legs* of the Earth, and Eight *lDe*.

The *Bon 'byung* (IsMEO, 17, 7) or *Gleng gzhi bstan pa'i byung khungs* has a complete list since it mentions Seven *Khri* of the Sky, Two *lTengs* of the Middle, Six *Legs* of the Earth, Six *lDe* of the Water, Six *bTsan* of the Middle, and the Four Bonpo Kings of Prosperity, but reckons King lHa-tho-tho Ri-snyan-btsan as the last of the Six *bTsan* of the Middle and the first of the Four Bonpo Kings of Prosperity.

The *lHo brag chos 'byung mkhas pa'i dga' ston* mentions Seven *Khri* of the Sky, Two *sTengs* of Above, Six *Legs* of the Earth, Eight *lDe* kings, Five *bTsan*, and Two *sTengs* of the Middle.

The *rGya bod yig tshang chen mo* lists Seven *Khri* of the Sky, the *sNyengs* of Above, Six *Legs* of the Earth, Eight *lDe* of the Middle, Five *bTsan*, and Two *sTengs* of the Middle.

The *rGyal rabs 'phrul gyi lde mig* lists Seven *Khri* of the Sky, Two *sTengs* of Above, Six *Legs* of the Middle, Eight *lDe* of the Earth, and Three *bTsan* of Below.

The *Deb ther dpyid kyi rgyal mo'i glu dbyangs* mentions only Seven *Khri* of the Sky, Six *Legs* of the Earth, and Eight *lDe*.

The *rGyal rabs gser phreng* mentions Seven *Khri* of the Sky, Six *Legs* of the Earth, and Eight *lDe* of the Earth, but no others.

The *Legs bshad rin po che'i mdzod* lists Seven *Khri* of the Sky, Two *lDing* of the Middle, Six *Legs* of the Earth, Eight *lDe* of the Water, Five *bTsan* of the Middle, and the Four Bonpo Kings of Prosperity.

The reason why these last four kings have been called the Four Bonpo Kings of Prosperity [Phun-sum-tshogs-pa'i Bon-rgyal-bzhi] is explained in the *Byams ma* (Tantra Series, TSHI, 71, 5):

During the time of (Tho-do sNyan-shal's) four sons, Khri-gnyan Zung-btsan, sTag-gu Nyan-gzigs, 'Brong-gnyan lDe-ru, and gNam-ri Gong-btsan, firm laws existed and the teaching [activities] were intense. Amazing masters spread the Bon of the Four Transmitted Precepts: innumerable great gShen were knowledgeable about the five expanded *'Bum* series,[90] the six *'Dul ba* Tantras,[91] the four series of *Abhidharma*,[92] and the five series of Philosophy [*mtshan nyid*].[93]

---

90   *rgyas pa 'bum lnga*. The science of arts and crafts; grammar and logic; medicine; knowledge of future times; and the Pure Klu. Each of these series is in turn subdivided into three, so that the total sum comes to fifteen. In this respect the *sKal bzang mgrin rgyan* (Bod, 144, 21) affirms, "First, from the primordial ancestor Sangs-po 'Bum-khri came the three series related to the science of arts and crafts: the series of the wheel of time for the universe and sentient beings; the series of the ancestors of the human generations; and the series of creation, dwelling, destruction, and nothingness." We also read (ibid., 145, 3), "Second, from King Ye-mkhyen sGra-bla came the three series of grammar and logic: the Black series of gods and demons fighting each other; the Variegated series of debate; and the White series of the sacred deities." And also (ibid., 145, 10), "Third, from King Ye-rje sMan-bla came the three series of medicine: the Black series concerning illnesses to be cured; the Variegated series of diagnosis to allow recovery; and the White series of successful remedies." And also (ibid., 145, 13), "Fourth, from King Ye-dbang-sa came the three series related to knowledge of future times: the Black series of gTo [rituals] for existence; the precious Variegated series; and the White *gTsug lag dbal series*." And also (ibid., 145, 16), "Fifth, from King Ye-dbal mThu-stobs came the three series of the Klu: White, Black, and Variegated."
91   *'dul ba rgyud drug*: these are the six tantras called: 1. *Ba' ga yangs ma kun 'byung dbyings dag rgyud*; 2. *'Dul ba kun 'byung dbyings dag rgyud*; 3. *'Dul ba dus chen dus btsan sdom byed rgyud*; 4. *'Dul ba yongs rdzogs rnam dag sdom byed kyi rgyud*; 5. *'Dul ba so sor thar pa'i bye brag rgyud*; and 6. *'Dul ba nyams gso lam sdom rgyud*.
92   *mngon pa sde bzhi*. The *sKal bzang mgrin rgyan* (Bod, 146, 6) says, "Concerning the Bon series of *Abhidharma*, as recorded in the tantra *Srid pa'i mdzod phug g.yung drung las dag rgyud*, four cycles relate to the universe and sentient beings, the first one dealing with the eras of creation, dwelling, destruction, and nothingness; the second one relates to the Base-of-All, transmigration [and] liberation, and deliverance [and] illusion; the third one deals with the secrets of aggregates/constituents/sense bases and defects and good qualities; the fourth one relates to the very secret ultimate reality of the Absolute and phenomena. The four Bon series of the *Abhidharma* are infinite: they sustain [philosophical] justifications; annihilate opposition about the final goal of training and attainment; clarify the four [philosophical] limitations [existence, nonexistence, both, and neither] and the importance of abandoning [them]; and discuss the perfection of pure liberation."
93   *mtshan nyid sde lnga*. These are the two series of the sNang-ldan and Rang-ldan of the Lower Vehicles; the two Mind-Only [Skt. *Cittamātra*, Tib. *Sems tsam*

Some of the lists, such as those contained in the dynastic histories, specify which kings appeared during the Intermediate Period although the majority of the accounts is not clear about the last monarchs. This explains why we can not rely upon those lists for assessing the number of kings that reigned at that time.

Although numerous and extensive narratives about the ancient Tibetan monarchs who appeared during the Intermediate Period and about their political accomplishments exist, the subject matter is difficult to grasp without taking into account historical documents. For example, concerning the reasons why Lo-ngam rTa-rdzi assassinated the eighth Tibetan monarch Gri-gum bTsan-po, a crucial event mentioned in historical sources, the *Tun hong bod kyi lo rgyus yig rnying* [Old Tibetan Chronicles of Dunhuang] (Pl 557, 6) affirm:

> The *lDe* son was like men.[94] He actually went to heaven,[95] and so on. Since he was endowed with great magic powers and glory [*'phrul dang byin tsheng po*], [his] arrogance and pride were hard to match [*drod dang dregs ma thub*]. Defying commands [*btsan 'dran bda'*], he fought, as truculent as a wild yak,[96] the nine male subjects on the father's side and the three female subjects on the mother's side. When [he issued] an order, everyone yielded to his belligerence.

Even if the text affirms that such a situation had occurred due to the great arrogance and pride of Gri-gum bTsan-po, the actual situation is revealed by the *Dar rgyas gsal sgron* that quotes the king as saying (Thob 655, 81, 1):

---

pa] schools which respectively claim senses to be true or false (*rnam bden pa* and *rnam rdzun pa*); and the series called *g.Yung drung sems dpa' spros med pa* [g.Yung-drung Sems-dpa' Beyond Concepts] of the Higher Vehicles. These correspond respectively, as clearly stated in the *sKal bzang mgrin rgyan* (182-193), to the Śrāvaka and Pratyekabuddha or Vaibhāṣika and Sautrāntika of the Hīnayāna Vehicle and to the two branches of the Yogācāra and Madhyamaka of the Mahāyāna Vehicle.

94 *lde sras myi'i myi tshul* means the successor of King lDe had a human demeanor.
95 *mngon bar dgung du gshegs pa* means dying without leaving bodily remains.
96 *g.yag du rdung*. He fought with the same vehemence of two wild yaks attacking each other with their horns.

> There is no room [in this kingdom] for both my might and the power of you Bonpos!

Bon was suppressed because of the great power of the Bon gShen of that time who also had the strong support of Zhang Zhung. The *Yar lung jo bo'i chos 'byung* states (Si, 47, 7):

> At that time, it is said that the king of Zhang Zhung incited the subjects.
> King Gri-gum bTsan-po said to one Lo-ngam Byi-khrom, "You are my adversary!"

Needless to say, the situation had arisen due to the hostile interventions of the king of Zhang Zhung. The *Tun hong bod kyi lo rgyus yig rnying* [Old Tibetan Chronicles of Dunhuang] (Pl 557, 21) report:

> Also the two sons, Sha-khyi and Nya-khyi, were expelled: they were banished and sent to the land of rKong.

And also (ibid., 558, 50):

> The elder, Sha-khyi, departed as the holder of the paternal lineage.[97] Nya-khyi became [the lord of rKong,] rKong-dkar-po.

According to this source, the king had only two sons, although the *lDe'u chos 'byung chen mo* affirms (Bod 103, 9):

> King Gri-gum bTsan-po and the minor king Lo-ngam rTa-rdzi fought each other, and as a consequence Gri-gum bTsan-po was killed. [Lo-ngam] put [Gri-gum bTsan-po's] corpse into a copper [coffer], and threw [it] in the gTsang-po [river]. [He] banished the three sons Sha-khri, Bya-khri, and Nya-khri to gSum-ka, Myang, and Kong. [Lo-ngam] took [Gri-gum's] daughter as his wife. [He] constrained the mother of the four offspring to herd cattle.[98] A child was born during her detention. The minister Khu safe-guarded him[99] so that he could continue his father's lineage. When it was time for the child to take the father's place, the divine

---

97 *sku mtshal gnyer*. This should be understood to mean *gdung rgyud 'dzin pa*.
98 *phyugs zan 'tsho ba*. This should be understood as *gnag phyugs kyi rigs rnams gzas khar 'tsho rdzi byed pa*.
99 *sras kyi gong bcad*. Taking care of the child.

son was brought to the capital. [The middle one,] Bya-khri was invited [to return] from the land of sPu-bo, and for that reason became known as sPu-de Gung-rgyal. The eldest, Sha-khri, was established as the king of rKong-po; the number of his military commanders [zhal ngo] greatly increased to about one hundred.[100] The youngest, Nya-khri, having become the king of Nyang-po, had about fifty military commanders [at his orders].

Since not only this religious history, but also the *Nyang gi chos 'byung* and other texts state that Gri-gum bTsan-po had four children, I think this could be true.

The *bKa' chems ka khol ma* says (Kan, 85, 13):

> King Gri-gum bTsan-po together with the minister dMag-mi Ma-sangs and the subject Li-ngam led the army to the country of Kha-che. He confronted the army of the king of Kha-che. The army of the Tibetan king won.

This excerpt shows that at that time the Tibetan army was present in the kingdom of Kha-che.

Many different and famous texts describe the history of the assassination of Gri-gum bTsan-po by Tri-rgyal Lo-ngam who can aptly be counted as the ninth Tibetan monarch; here the explanation contained in the *lDe'u chos 'byung chen mo* treatise quoted above suffices. As for the length of time during which Lo-ngam remained in power, the *Dar rgyas gsal sgron* says (Thob, 661, 83b, 4):

> [He] exiled the sons sPu-lde and Nya-khri to Dwags and rKong respectively; killed the minister Drag-pa and banned the others; relegated the queen to the role of shepherdess; married the daughter lHa-lcam; and reigned for thirteen years.

This text states that Tri-rgyal Lo-ngam ruled the kingdom for thirteen years. Also the *lDe'u rgya bod kyi chos 'byung* mentions the number of years that Tri-rgyal Lo-ngam remained in power (Bod, 248, 7):

---

100 [In the ancient Tibetan army one commander headed each group of twenty-five soldiers.]

Chapter III ▪ The Royal Lineages of Ancient Tibet

Twelve years [*lo skor gcig*] had elapsed since Gri-gum bTsan-po had been killed before his son 'U-de Gung-rgyal took charge of the kingdom.

That Tri-rgyal Lo-ngam was a minor king of the lHo-brag area is specified in the *Dar rgyas gsal sgron* (Thob, 658, 83, 2):

> A missive was dispatched to Lo-ngam rTa-rdzi of lHo-brag.

Furthermore, as we have seen, the *lDe'u chos 'byung chen mo* says (Bod, 103, 9):

> King Gri-gum bTsan-po and the minor king Lo-ngam rTa-rdzi fought each other.

The *lDe'u rgya bod kyi chos 'byung* says (Bod, 245, 1):

> "Even if I am going to be killed by a dagger's thrust, I am going to fight King Lo-ngam rTa-rdzi!" Having said that, [he] fixed the time of the combat.

These citations show that Lo-ngam was a minor Tibetan king, that he was actually called king, and also that he represented an important and worthy rival for the ruling king at that time.

The origin of the name Tri-rgyal Lo-ngam is clarified by a quotation taken from the *Bon gyi gzhung gri bshad kyi lung* contained in the *Dar rgyas gsal sgron* which reads (Thob, 660, 83b, 6):

> Tri-rgyal Lo-ngam rTa-rdzi aimed a sharp poisoned arrow with a black notch at the forehead [of King Gri-rum bTsan-po] and killed [him].

Concerning the way in which sPu-lde Gung-rgyal obtained power, the *lDe'u rgya bod kyi chos 'byung* affirms (Bod, 246, 8):

> The [queen] shepherdess fell asleep and had a dream in which she had intercourse with one who resembled the offspring of a Klu. It is said that when she awoke from her dream, she saw a yak near her pillow. Then eight months later as she went to fetch water, a bloody mass with only a head and arms came out of her womb. [She did not] kill it, since [after all] it was [her] infant,

nor could she raise it, since it had no limbs. So she placed it in a yak horn and that in turn in the leg of a boot, covered it with a heavy cloth, and kept it hidden. Protected by the heat, a child [eventually] developed inside the horn. She named him "Grown in a horn-kept in the leg [of a boot]-wrapped in a cloth [*rwa las skyes ngar las 'greng yu la brten*]." When the child grew up, he asked his mother, "Who is my father?" The mother replied, "Your father was killed by Long-ngam [*sic*]. He searched for the corpse of the bTsan-po and found that the Klu-srin Bye-ma Lag-ring had it.

And also (ibid., 247, 12):

> Then he went to look for the sons for one to replace the father. When he met the three orphans, he asked who of them wished to be the successor of their father, assume residence at the castle, and become the lord of the black-headed [people] and of the maned beasts. The eldest, Sha-khri, and the youngest, Bya-khri, declined. The middle one, Nya-khri, consented, so Ngar-las-skyes invited him from sPu-bo. After he suppressed hostile demons [*dgra sri*] on the way, his name was changed to 'U-de Gung-rgyal.

This is more or less the common agreement of history. The way in which Ngar-las-skyes, better known as Ru-la-skyes, entrusted the reign to Bya-khri is related in the *lDe'u rgya bod kyi chos 'byung* which says (Bod 247, 19):

> Then Ngar-las-skyes smeared with poison the white coat of a bitch and sent the hound to Long-ngam rTa-rdzi as a present. Long-ngam stroked [the dog], and his hand became poisoned during an assembly of his retinue. Ngar-las-skyes surreptitiously introduced himself into a vulture's nest situated on the mountain where the castle Nyang-ro-sham-po was located. Simulating a vulture, he flung himself onto the roof of the castle and from there descended inside. He killed Lo-ngam's male retinue by crushing their chests with a kettle, and suffocated his female retinue with a copper vessel. Since [Lo-ngam's demise] was the hope [*smon*] of grand and simple [people alike], [Ngar-las-skyes] was given the name sMon-gzung. Since 'U-de Gung-rgyal said, "This is my paternal uncle [*a khu*]," he also became known as Khu-smon-gzung.

The *Yar lung jo bo'i chos 'byung* says (Si, 44, 1):

> The middle one, Bya-khri, was invited and installed in the capital. He was given the name sPu-lde Gung-rgyal.

The ministers elected by the royal mandate of sPu-lde Gung-rgyal, the *Yar lung jo bo'i chos 'byung* informs us, were (Si, 44, 19):

> Ru-la-skyes and his son lHa-bu mGo-dkar.

And also (ibid., 45, 7):

> During the time of these two noble ministers, wild yaks were tamed, canals were dug, land was made arable, silver, copper, and iron were mined, metals were smelted with charcoal, and bridges were built over rivers.

This quotation informs us of pursuits undertaken during the time of the two ministers. Although those activities were previously diffused in Zhang Zhung, the words here would seem to indicate that they became known in Tibet only at that time.

While absent in Tibetan dynastic and religious histories, the eleventh Tibetan monarch Grang-mo gNam-gser-brtsig is nonetheless mentioned in the *Tun hong bod kyi lo rgyus yig rnying* [Old Tibetan Chronicles of Dunhuang] as the father of Tho-legs bTsan-po who was the first of the Six *Legs* of the Earth. No indication is given about the identity of Grang-mo gNam-gser-brtsig's father.

The sentence "when sPu-de Gung-rgyal died ..." would seem to indicate that after the death of sPu-lde Gung-rgyal, gSer-brtsig ascended the throne. Nowhere is it indicated that sPu-lde Gung-rgyal was the father of gSer-brtsig, an interesting fact, since it is impossible for King gSer-brtsig to be the son of Gri-gum bTsan-po as the *Dunhuang Chronicles* mention only Sha-kyi and Nya-kyi as his sons. As we have seen, according to the *lDe'u chos 'byung* and several other documents, the sons were three: Sha-khri, Bya-khri, and Nya-khri. Sha-khri became the king of Kong-po and initiated the royal family line known as Kong-dkar-po; Nya-khri became the king of Myang; and Bya-khri was enthroned as sPu-de Gung-rgyal; therefore none of them could have been gSer-brtsig. Also no way exists that Minister Ru-la-skyes or Ngar-las-skyes, later known as Khu-smon-gzung, could belong to the same family line. Therefore, since in the *Dunhuang Chronicles* the words "Grang-mo gNam-gser-brtsig" follow "when sPu-de Gung-rgyal died," there is a strong possibility that he was indeed the son of sPu-de Gung-rgyal.

The *lDe'u rgya bod kyi chos 'byung* affirms (Bod, 247, 5):

> Then it is said that while Ngar-las-skyes acted as overseer, Bod-'bangs Pha-dgu erected a support inside the cavity, put the corpse on it, and laid thirteen layers over it. Gri-'tsho-mi[101] and bCo-mi tried to appease [the spirit of] sDe Gri-gum bTsan-po, but did not succeed. Then the son of Pha-ba-ra,[102] Zi-rgyal rMang-po, tried and succeeded. Afterwards, they assembled at Ngar-ma-thang, circumambulating 360 times,[103] and then moved the corpse to Grang-mo Grang-chun-gi-rdza. Now [that place] is called Grang-mo'i gNam-gser-tig.

Here, even if this last expression is similar to the name Grang-mo gNam-gser-brtsig, it actually refers to the name with which the tomb of Gri-gum bTsan-po came to be known. Therefore no confusion should be made between this and the name of the king mentioned in the *Old Tibetan Chronicles of Dunhuang*.

Moreover, the *lHo brag chos 'byung* reads (Pe, Vol. I, 163, 3):

> [The body] was left [to rest] on the summit of the mountain Drang-mo Drang-chung. At that time, a golden [*gser*] drop [*thig*] fell from the sky [*gnam*] and dissolved in the corpse. [This entity] is known as gNam-lha gSer-thig. Now it is said that [this entity] resides as the deity [*lha ru bzhugs*] in that place.

It is related that when the corpse of King Gri-gum bTsan-po was placed on the summit of the mountain Drang-mo Drang-chung, a golden drop appeared from the sky and dissolved in the corpse. Because of

---

101 *gri 'tsho mi*. A Bonpo purported capable of pacifying the tormented state of the murdered king.

102 *pha ba ra'i bu*. Pha ba is a Bon gShen at the service of the father. This is the son [*bu*] of the royal Bon gShen called Pha-ba-ra.

103 *'phang skor sum brgya drug cu*. That is to say, they walked around the remains of the king for 360 times.

that happening, an entity called gNam-lha gSer-thig is said to have manifested as the grave-tending deity and is still considered to preside over that place. Even if a marked similarity exists with the name of King Grang-mo gNam-gser-brtsig, here the name refers to the deity looking after Gri-gum's grave. Therefore this name and the name of Grang-mo gNam-gser-brtsig mentioned in the *Old Tibetan Chronicles of Dunhuang* should not be confused.

Furthermore, in the *Tun hong bod kyi lo rgyus yig rnying* [Old Tibetan Chronicles of Dunhuang] (PI 553, 51) we read:

> When [Gri-gum bTsan-po] married, sPu-de Gung-rgyal [was born]. When [sPu-de Gung-rgyal] died, Grang-mo gNam-bse'-bstsig [succeeded him]. Leading the cavalry, he arrived to be the lord of the black-headed [people].

Thus, the son conceived by King Gri-gum bTsan-po and his wife was sPu-de Gung-rgyal who became the lineage holder and when he died, the royal lineage holder became King gSer-brtsig or bSe'-bstsig.

The *Byams ma* affirms (Tantra Series, TSHI, 71, 6):

> There were thirteen royal castles combined with thirteen temples at Phyi-ba sTag-rtse and other locations [*la sogs*]; the law of the ancient Bon of Existence was in place.

As we read, before the time of the Six *Legs* of the Earth, altogether thirteen temples had been erected jointly by the king and the royal Bon gShen in each royal palace or castle built for the Tibetan monarchs; a common Bon law was also codified and widespread. In this regard, a strong connection can be seen between the thirteen castles and temples and the above-mentioned Bon of Existence that spread during the time of the thirteen dynasties.

Furthermore, the *lDe'u chos 'byung chen mo* confirms that Thod-dkar was the father of bSe-rnol-nam, who was one of the so-called Eight *lDe* of the Water [Chu-la lDe-brgyad] (Bod, 104, 10):

> Of the Eight *lDe*, bSe-rnol-nam, the son of Thod-kar, was confined [*thang mtshangs su*]. Since the elder brothers of I-sho-legs and bSe-rnol-nam were also confined, the lineage of these

two is known as that of the Five Maternal Uncles and Elder Brothers [*zhang lnga gcen po*].

The meaning of this citation is as follows: since one of the elder brothers of I-sho-legs, the sixth of the Six *Legs* of the Earth, and one of the elder brothers of bSe-rnol-nam, the fourth of the Eight *lDe* of the Water, were punished and imprisoned, the descendants of these two are known as the Five Maternal Uncles and Elder Brothers. From this it can be understood that Thod-dkar, the father of bSe-rnol-nam, was a descendant of the elder brother of I-sho-legs.

About the system then in force of chastising with incarceration most of the royal heirs who were unable to safeguard the power of the royal lineage, the *lDe'u chos 'byung chen mo* affirms (Bod, 104, 13):

> At this time, if there were many [eligible] kings, the intelligent ministers would give the power to one and imprison the others.

This custom developed beginning in the Intermediate Period and was also common at later times.

The *g.Yung drung bon gyi rgyud 'bum* says (Thob, KHA, 30, 16, 1):

> Khri-thob Nam-brtsan invited many Zhang Zhung gShen-pos. Stūpas and temples were erected in the four directions. Tibet and Zhang Zhung were united as one, and since Bon was diffused and widely practiced, also the king enjoyed longevity and the subjects were happy. Then, because also the Tibetan lord practiced Bon, [his] power increased more and more, and [he] formulated the plan of conquering the borderlands[104]. The Bla-bon supported [him] from the four directions. The royal gShen Gyer-zla-med conquered evil spirits with magic, consecrated the army, and led it to 'Jang; there they battled the king of 'Jang and defeated him. This made the king rejoice. Then the Bonpos were offered insignia,[105] such as headgear with three vulture [feathers][106]

---

104 *mtha' dul bar dgongs*. This refers to seizing the opportunity to bring under submission the small princedoms that existed at the borders of the kingdom.
105 *yig rtsang*. A sign of distinction or rank.
106 *rgod gsum gyi zhwa*. A helmet decorated with the feathers of three vultures. As their plumage allow vultures to fly at high altitudes, this headdress was a

adorned with turquoise horns[107] and a cloak of white vulture [feathers][108] with the forepaws of a tiger. From that time the Bonpos began wearing feather helmets and feather cloaks.

As these excerpts explain, because the king Khri Thog-rje Thog-btsan, who belonged to the dynasty of the Five *bTsan* of the Middle, invited many Bon gShen from Zhang Zhung, the teaching of Bon flourished, and the relation between Tibet and Zhang Zhung was close.

The royal gShen Gyer-zla-med, the most powerful among the several Bonpos of the Bla [Bla'i Bon-po] who were at the king's service such as dPon-gsas lJang-tsha 'Phan-snang, lHa-bon Tha-tsha Khog-'phar, and so forth, consecrated the army of the king, led the Tibetan army to 'Jang, and defeated the king of that region.

Furthermore, in the *g.Yung drung bon gyi rgyud 'bum* (30, KA, 16, 6) we read:

> The Bon-po of Sum-pa, sPe-nag-gu, prayed to the dGra-lha, conquered the evil spirits with magic, fought in Hor, and brought that kingdom under submission.

As a token of his great prowess, he was offered the golden *gtor-ma*[109] and the turquoise offering [bowl].[110] As a sign of command, he was given the golden arrow and the turquoise spindle.[111] That is when the

---

symbol of the elevated level of awareness realized by the Bonpos. Also Guru Padmasambhava wears a headdress ornamented with vulture feathers.

107 *g.yu'i bya ru la*. A helmet decorated with turquoise horns similar to the ones worn as an insignia by the great Bon gShen and kings of ancient Zhang Zhung that had horns made of precious stones resembling those of the Great Khyung.

108 *bya rgod dkar mo'i thul pa*. A large cloak made with vulture feathers, the kind also gShen-rab Mi-bo-che wore, as described in the *Srid pa spyi mdo* (2, 2): "If [one asked] what [he would] wear on his body, [the answer would be] a vibrant [*lhams se lhams*] vulture [feather] cloak.

109 *gser gyi gsas zan*. A *gtor ma* made of gold offered to the deities of the Bon gShen; a golden *gtor ma*.

110 *g.yu'i sman bshos*. A bowl made of turquoise used to offer libations of nectar and medicine.

111 *gser mda' dang g.yu 'phang*. The image of an arrow and a spindle, or the objects themselves, called the variegated arrow [*mda' bkra*] and the variegated spindle [*'phang bkra*], were frequently used as implements in *mDos* rituals to represent male and female human beings, the arrow as a men's tool and the spindle as a women's

Bonpos started to use the arrow and spindle, precious *gtor-mas*, and bowls as supports for offerings to the deities.

The excerpt shows how a king who came after Khri Thog-rje Thog-btsan, relying on the power of Bon, led the Tibetan army to Hor, and conquered it. The same text also says (ibid., 31, KA, 16, 1):

> Another time the king of China insulted the Lord's person. The Bon-po from Zhang Zhung, Gyer-chen bTso-'phen, cast a spell on some gold, caused a [deadly] magic blast [*btso*], and punished the kingdom of China. As a token of his great prowess, the king offered him a set of turquoise stones [and] a turban of white silk. This is the reason why Bon-pos now wear a turban and gold and turquoise around the neck.

When the king of China attempted to harm the Tibetan bTsan-po, the Zhang Zhung gShen-po displayed his magic power and annihilated the Chinese assault. The same text also affirms (ibid., 31, KA, 16, 3):

> Then, leading the army to Mon, bTso-chen Thog-'bebs of Zhang Zhung hurled a magic [deadly] blast [*btso*] and conquered Mon. In recognition of his great prowess he was offered a cloak of tiger, leopard, and otter skins, and the three sweet [substances].[112] This is how the Bon-pos [began] wearing tiger skin garments on their bodies.

This makes clear that during the reign of one of the kings belonging to the lineage of the Five *bTsan* of the Middle, the Tibetan army advanced to the country of Mon and defeated that kingdom, merit of the magic power displayed by the Bon gShen of Zhang Zhung, bTso-chen Thog-'bebs.

King To-re Long-btsan had a younger brother. The *lDe'u chos 'byung chen mo* relates how the younger brother was disinherited (Bod, 105, 2):

> The younger brother of King To-to Re-long-btsan was imprisoned: he was the younger brother lTab-nag and his lineage is

---

tool. Similarly, as a sign of supreme excellence among all men and women, the Bon gShen were offered a spindle made of turquoise and an arrow made of gold.
112 *mngar gsum*. Sugar, molasses, and honey.

known as the lineage of the Five Maternal Uncles and Younger Brothers.

King Khri Thog-rje Thog-btsan had four younger brothers. The *lDe'u chos 'byung chen mo* relates how also they were disinherited (Bod, 105, 8):

> The four younger brothers of Khri Thog-rje Thog-btsan— rGung-mtha', sNubs-mtha', 'Bring-snya, and sNya-'bring—were imprisoned.

This citation reveals the names of the younger brothers and the way in which they were disinherited.
As for the identity of the great ministers of these kings, the *Yar lung jo bo'i chos 'byung* affirms (Si, 46, 12):

> During the reign of Khri-btsan-nam, gNubs-gnya' Do-re gTsug-byon and dBas-khri Zung-mong acted as ministers.

And also (ibid., 46, 15):

> During the reign of Khri-sgra sPungs-btsan, 'Gar-sgra Dzi-mun, and Thon-mi Klu-mang Dred-po acted as ministers.

These excerpts clarify that aspect.

> lHa-tho-tho Ri-snyan-btsan is a famous king in both Buddhist and Bonpo views. The *lDe'u chos 'byung chen mo* refers to him in the following manner (Bod 105, 11):
>
> The sacred *Chos* was established during the reign of lHa-tho-tho Ri-snyan-btsan. He was an emanation of the Buddha Kaśyapa ['Od-srung] and of the Bodhisattva Kṣitigarbha [Sa'i sNying-po].
>
> When he was residing at the Yum-bu Bla-sgang castle, three texts written in golden letters, the *mDo* [*sde*] *za ma tog*, the *rTen 'brel gyi phyag rgya*, and the *sPang kong phyag rgya*, and a four-storey turquoise stūpa fell from the sky in front of him. Not being able to discern [whether they pertained] to Bon or Chos and not knowing [whether they were] to be honored, feared, or regarded as powerful and dangerous, he called them the divine fruit of the secret gNyan-po [*gnyan po gsang ba'i lha 'bras*], put them in the repository of Yum-bu, and worshipped them at night with

golden and turquoise libations.¹¹³ From that moment [the king's] power increased and his life was lengthened; and it was also from that moment that the Twelve Minor Princes recognized him as the head of their combined dominions.

This event is recorded in a Bonpo source, the *Byams ma*, as follows (Tantra Series, TSHI, 71, 4):

> Words explaining the Teaching fell [from] the sky to Tho-do sNyan-shal.¹¹⁴

However, this old source does not describe what actually fell from the sky. The Buddhist version of this event and the different stories that emerge from other sources will be enlarged upon within the context of the Tibetan monarchy of the Later Period in Volume Three of this work.

Also the *g.Yung drung bon gyi rgyud 'bum* refers to the feats of lHa-tho-tho Ri-snyan-btsan (Thob, 31, KA, 16, 4):

> Thus the enemies of the Lord were defeated by Bon.
> The Twelve Princedoms were brought under control.

And also (ibid., 32, KA, 17, 4):

> At that time when the army was led to India, many small Indian kingdoms were conquered and evil spirits and demons dominated.

This excerpt regarding the feats of lHa-tho-tho Ri-snyan-btsan means that Tibet led an army to India and brought several Indian princedoms that existed at its borders under its jurisdiction.

King lHa-tho-tho-ri had a younger brother who was disinherited. In that regard, the *lDe'u chos 'byung chen mo* affirms (Bod, 106, 14):

---

113 *gser skyems dang g.yu sngon*. *gSer skyems* is a tea libation, whereas *g.yu sngon* or *g.yu skyems* is a wine libation.

114 *'chan bu gnam bab byung*. The text consulted reads *'chan bu*, although it should be *mchan bu* indicating an annotation or words which clarify the essence of a teaching.

lHa-bzangs, the younger brother of the king, was placed in confinement.

The *lDe'u chos 'byung chen mo* also says (Bod, 107, 17):

During the lifetime of sTa-gu rNyan-gzigs, the ministers of Zings-po-rje sTag-skya-bo who were Myang, dBas, gNon, and Tshe-spong-'phrin consulted each other. [They gathered an army] and overthrew the Twelve Minor Princes, bringing them under [the king's] dominion, along with [some] Zhang Zhung districts and 'A-zha localities, as well as [the area of] g.Yog [in] Dwags-po.

This means that the campaign to subject the Twelve Minor Kingdoms initiated under lHa-tho-tho-ri was concluded by those ministers who unanimously gathered troops for that purpose and also brought under control some districts of Tibet, Zhang Zhung, 'A-zha, and of the Dwags-po area.

The *lDe'u rgya bod kyi chos 'byung* affirms (Bod, 252, 4):

The son of sTag-gu gNyan-gzigs and 'Ol-god-bza' gDon-btsun-sgron was gNam-ri Srong-tsan. Due to him, six [regions of] the bordering rGya, Gru-gu, and Hor were conquered.

This quotation shows that King gNam-ri srong-btsan led the army to rGya, Gru-gu, and Hor, and that the Tibetan army defeated and subdued six regions of rGya and the lands of Gru-gu and Hor. In this respect the *rGyal rabs gsal ba'i me long* states (Pe, 61, 17):

The son of sTag-ri gNyan-gzigs was gNam-ri Srong-btsan. During his reign, Chinese medicine and astrology made their appearance [in Tibet]. rGya and Gru-gu were conquered. Salt was acquired from the north.

During the reign of this king, Chinese-style medicine and astrology were introduced from China to Tibet as an enrichment of the ancient Tibetan medicine and astrology, and rGya and Gru-gu were conquered and brought under the king's rule. It is generally maintained that Tibet conquered neighboring kingdoms only from the time of the forefather king Srong-btsan sGam-po and also that the Tibetan kings who preceded him controlled only a portion of the Tibetan territory.

However, if only for a moment we look back honestly at the creativity, determination, and heroism expressed by the forefathers of the Intermediate Period of Tibet, we would see that in modern times most of their legacy has been eclipsed, with the result that the descendants of those extraordinary forefathers perceive their own origins as dimly as wanderers in dense darkness.

 IV
The Written Language of Ancient Tibet

THE MAJORITY OF Tibetan historical documents currently available concurs that before the time of the *dharmarāja* Srong-btsan sGam-po, that is from the female Earth Ox year of the last *sMe-phreng* of the fourteenth *sMe-'khor* (Tibetan year 2486, 569 CE), until the male Iron Dog year of the first *sMe- phreng* of the fifteenth *sMe-'khor* (Tibetan year 2567, 650 CE), no tradition of a written language existed in Tibet.

These sources declare that the lores appearing before then, as well as Bonpo rituals like the *gTo*, and so on, had all been orally transmitted from generation to generation according to how they had been memorized and that a system for writing the Tibetan language was established due to the benevolence of the *dharmarāja* Srong-btsan sGam-po and of his appointed minister Thon-mi A-nu. They state that for the first time and only from then onward were all preceding history and ancient oral traditions committed to writing.

This way of seeing permeated the entire Tibetan culture of the Later Period.

1. The Initial Diffusion of the Tibetan Written Language

For illustrations of how these views have become widespread in major Tibetan religious histories, dynastic chronicles, and so on, one can refer to the *lDe'u chos 'byung chen mo* that affirms (Bod, 114, 15):

> Before then there was no written language in Tibet.

Or to the *rGyal rabs gsal ba'i me long* [Clear Mirror of Royal History] that says (Pe, 66, 10):

> Then seven sagacious ministers were dispatched to India to learn a written language, since none existed in Tibet, in order to frame a royal law [*rgyal khrims*] based upon the ten virtuous *Dharma* rules, so that the five desirable qualities [which please the five senses, such as offerings and the like] could be increased, gifts received could be reciprocated, and the Words of the *Dharma* could be expounded to subjects.

Or the *rGya bod yig tshang chen mo* that asserts (Si, 141, 2):

> One king of Tibet at the age of fourteen proclaimed, "Let the country be ruled according to the *Dharma!*" The fame [of his resolution] spread everywhere. The kings of the four directions sent [him] missives and extraordinary objects as presents. The king of Tibet sent rich gifts as acknowledgement but no missives because there was no written language. Therefore it was thought that also Tibet needed a written language.

Or the *rGyal rabs gser phreng* that states (Dha, 203, 15, 6):

> During the reign of King Srong-btsan sGam-po, emanation of sPyan-ras-gzigs, all the border kingdoms were conquered. Each monarch in turn sent gifts and letters. The deeds accomplished by this king were inconceivably successful, but no response could be made to the various letters, since no written language existed in Tibet, not even in the profound and secret objects [that appeared at the time] of the forefather Tho-tho Ri-snyan-shal [*sic*]. However, it was thought that with due modifications the written language that existed in India could serve as the Tibetan one.

To analyze the issue in an appropriate way, we must consider the following: was the tradition of a written language actually absent in Tibet prior to the *dharmarāja* Srong-btsan sGam-po or, alternatively, was a written language used to some extent? If the latter was true, was that written language called Tibetan [*bod yig*] or not? And what were the real motivations of the claim of many early historians that before the *dharmarāja* Srong-btsan sGam-po Tibet had no written language? We must carefully investigate the differences between the two affirmations, namely, that Tibet had no written language and that before Srong-btsan, the Tibetan people had no tradition of a written language, if we want to uncover their implications.

The thesis underlying this research is that it is unfounded to purport that no solid basis exists for the multifarious cultural expressions of the Tibetan people. As no survey of a castle's dimensions can be valid without examining its foundation, similarly if it is assumed that in early times Tibet had no written language and that the origin of its culture was not Tibet itself, the authentic nature, distinctive qualities, and extensive expressions of that ancient land can never be demonstrated. To comprehend and analyze in straightforward fashion the allegation that Tibet lacked a written language tradition prior to the *dharmarāja* Srong-btsan sGam-po or that the Tibetan people did not make use of a written language, we can take into account textual evidence as well as logic. Related to the first point, an important and authoritative text, the *Be ro tsa na'i rnam thar 'dra 'bag chen mo* that contains the hagiography of the Tibetan master Vairocana, affirms (Sle, JA, 489, 43, 7 / lHa, 43, 1):

> Because of the kindness of Srong-btsan sGam-po, the Indian scholar Li-byin was invited. Thon-mi Mi-chung Saṃbhoṭa transformed the written language [*yi ge bsgyur*]. Some sūtras, such as the *Tsin rda ma ni* [Skt. *Cintāmaṇi*], the *'Dus pa rin po che tog dge ba bcu'i mdo* [Sūtra of the Ten Virtues], and so on, were translated.

This excerpt is easy to understand whereas the calligraphy of the written language of the Tibetan people of ancient times made it difficult to use. Thon-mi A-nu was asked to devise a new system for the Tibetan written language, taking the Indian one as example, thus fulfilling the need of the Tibetan people for a more convenient writing style. This new system would represent at the same time a suitable tool for translating into Tibetan the Word of the Victorious One originating in India, the treatises of subsequent savants, and the numerous and extensive teachings that had appeared until then, while also facilitating discussions on the profound meanings of *dharma* terms in the Sanskrit language.

If a written language had not existed in Tibet before then, the sentence "Thon-mi Mi-chung Saṃbhoṭa transformed the written language" would be unjustified, since there would have been nothing for him to transform, just as determining the sharpness and length of the horns of rabbits and horses is impossible because their heads bear no such appendages.

An early diffusion in Tibet of Bon teachings originating from Zhang Zhung was specifically the *gSas mkhar sPyi spungs* cycle. The *rGyal rabs bon gi 'byung gnas*, relates the following from this cycle (Thob, 100, 50, 1):

> During the time of gNya'-khri bTsan-po, the teachings of the Twelve Lores [*shes pa can bcu gnyis*] [pertaining to the] Bon of the Cause [*rgyu'i bon*] spread.

And also (ibid., 100, 50, 4):

> Then the *sPyi spungs* teachings were requested from and imparted by Nam-mkha' sNang-ba mDog-can. Mu-khri bTsad-po, the son of that [king], understood the meaning of the training, accomplished the purpose of the practice, and realized the state of meditation.

As the quoted excerpt shows, from the time of gNya'-khri bTsan-po and his son, the Bon teachings of the *sPyi spungs* were diffused. In this respect, the tantra *gSas mkhar rin po che sPyi spungs gSang ba bsen thub*, root text of the *sPyi spungs* cycle, states (Thob 127, 64, 4):

> With a beautiful feather, clear letters are written in precious colors on white paper. Interrupting the silence, the letters manifest their defining characteristics. In particular, sound [arises

from] the physical body, the mind, and the deity. [Everything,] external, internal, [and] secret, is connected by the magic net [produced by the letters].

In what manner does that occur? From the innate dimension of Reality [*bon gyi dbyings nyid*], the light of unobstructed compassion spreads and interrupts the silence, emerging as magic letters. With the visualization of the forty-five deities, the forty-five defining characteristics [of the letters] are established in the physical body. In appearance, the forty-five [letters] are without substance [and represent] the Nature of the Mind. They are like the magic net of the outer, inner, and secret [dimensions].

A, Ôm, Hūm.
Pa, Pha, Ba, Ma.
Ra, La, Sha, Sa.
Ka, Kha, Ga, Nga.
Tsa, Tsha, Dza, Wa.
Ca, Cha, Ja, Nya.
Ta, Tha, Da, Na.
Zha, Za, 'A, Ya.
Ha, Ha:, Hu, He, Ho.

And also (ibid., 129, 65, 3):

The letters of the totality of existence originate from space.
The letters of the aggregates [*phung po*] originate from the Base.
The letters for communication originate from the sound [produced by] the chest, the throat, the palate, and the tongue, the teeth, the lips, and the crown of the head.
A is innate, it originates inside [the body].
Ha and 'A [originate in] the throat.
The Ma series issues from the lips.
The Ka and Ca series originate in the palate, with the distinction [that the Ka series] issues from the upper part [of the palate and the Ca series issues from] the lower part [of the palate].
The Ta and Ra series are [produced by] the play [of the] tongue.
Sha, [which is] special, [originates at the] crown of the head.
Ôm and Hūm [issue through] the head [and] nose.

Through specific ornamental and supporting elements [added] to the seed letters, distinct syllables, names, and words are produced.

As these excerpts indicate, a written language must have existed at that time; otherwise a method for pronouncing written letters would not have been created.

2. Did a Tibetan Language Exist Before the Dharmarāja Srong-bTsan?

Another evidence that a written language was used by the Tibetan people during the Intermediate Period is contained in the *Nyang gi chos 'byung* that affirms (Bod, 165, 5):

> It is also maintained that during the time of Khri-so Bud-btsan-po a Tibetan written language appeared.

Even if this king named Khri-so Bud-btsan-po is not mentioned elsewhere in the *Nyang gi chos 'byung* itself, we can confidently assume that he was a king that actually ruled in olden times because his name is reminiscent of some of the names of the Seven *Khri* of the Sky that have similar sounds and wordings, such as So-khri, Srib-khri, and so on.

Another proof of the existence of a written tradition prior to Srong-btsan is provided by a popular apotropaic ritual called *Srid pa spyi mdos*, practiced in many villages of Central Tibet and Khams.

I have obtained an original manuscript of this ritual from sDe-dge in mDo-khams, and a second one from Dol-po, Nepal. I also had access to an original albeit incomplete manuscript of the *Srid pa spyi mdos*, part of the sizeable collection of Bonpo documents that the renowned Italian scholar Giuseppe Tucci collected during his expedition to Gu-ge in Western Tibet. Thus I was able to consult three different original versions of this text. The colophon [of the sDe-dge version] of the *Srid pa spyi mdos* states (16, 2):

> It was transmitted successively [starting] from the great gShen gCe-'od.

> I, Sangs-po Khrin-khod, have put [it] in writing.
> The power [of this ritual] is revealed through the uninterrupted [lineage of the] masters of Zhang-Bod.
> This profound ritual is [hereby] completed.

As we can see, the colophon clearly mentions gShen-po gCe-'od and Ra-sangs Khri-na-khod. For what concerns the former, the *Dar rgyas gsal ba'i sgron ma* affirms (Thob, 640, 73, 6):

> The son of Ding-khri and Se-za-sman [was] So-khri bTsan-po.
> The royal gShen [was] gCo'u 'Od-dkar.

This excerpt clarifies that he was the royal gShen of So-khri bTsan-po, the fourth of the Seven *Khri* Kings of the Sky that ruled ancient Tibet. The *Gleng gzhi bstan pa'i byung khungs* says (IsMEO, 17, 7):

> His son [was] Ding-khri bTsad-po. (The mother was Sa'i Ding-ding-ma). The royal gShen [was] Co'u sMin-dkar. [The king] built the castle of Kho-ma Yang-rtse. His son [was] Mu-khri bTsan-po (the second one). (The mother was Se-za sMan-mo). The royal gShen [was] gCo'u 'Od-dkar.

Both texts agree that gCo'u 'Od-dkar was the royal gShen of the king generally known as So-khri bTsan-po who was the son of King Ding-khri bTsad-po. Furthermore, in the *sGrags pa rin chen gling grags* we read (Thob, 63, 8, 6):

> The preceptor of King Srin-btsan [was] sTag-sgra dGe-bshis. The Bonpo for the deities [was] Yi-za Khod-grags. The preceptor of rGya-wer Li-lod-btsan [was] sTong-sgra Kun-'dul. The Bonpo for the deities [was] gCo'u 'Od-dkar.

In this text gCo'u 'Od-dkar appears as the Bonpo for the deities [lHa Bon], together with the preceptor of the first king of the Five *bTsan* of the Middle, who represent the twenty-sixth Tibetan dynasty, commonly known as To-ro Lo-btsan. gCo and/or gCo'u are names generally associated with a famous ancient clan. Several gCo or gCo'u have served the Tibetan kings successively as royal gShen, preceptors, and Bonpos for the deities, for example gCo-bon, gCo'u Lan-tsha, gCo'u

Zhal-dkar, gCo'u sMin-dkar, gCo'i Bon-po Khri-phyung, gCo-stag Klu-gsas, gCo-phan-grags, and gCo-snyan-rings. Needless to say, many other clan names besides these two can be found within the ancient Tibetan population.

The version of the *Srid pa spyi mdos* found in sDe-dge in Khams contains the reading gCe-'od, while the *Dar rgyas gsal sgron*, the *Gling grags*, and the *Gleng gzhi bstan pa'i byung khungs* have a slightly different reading, gCo'u 'Od-dkar. The colophon of the version obtained in Dol-po has (16, 2), "It was successively transmitted [starting] from the great gShen gCo-'od dKar-po." Nonetheless we can understand that the text refers to gCo'u 'Od-dkar.

> About Ra-sangs Khri-na-khod, the *Gleng gzhi bstan pa'i byung khungs* says (IsMEO, 17, 7):
> The son of that (Klu-gnyan gZung-btsan) was blind. The gShen-po [magically] restored his eyesight. The first thing [that the prince] saw [*gzigs*] was a wild sheep [*gnyan*] on the facing mountain. Because of this, he was given the name sTag-gung gNyan-gzigs. The royal gShen [was] Ra-sangs Khri-na-khod.

In this textual source Ra-sangs Khri-na-khod is identified as the royal gShen of the third of the Four Bonpo Kings of Prosperity [Phun sum tshogs pa'i Bon rgyal bzhi], after the Six *bTsan* of the Middle, the Six *lDe* of the Water, the Six *Legs* of the Earth, the Two *lDings* of the Middle, and the Seven *Khri* of the Sky. Similarly, in the *Legs bshad rin po che'i mdzod* we read (Pe, 133, 7):

> The son of that (Khri-gnyan gZung-btsan) [was] 'Brang-snyan-lde'u. The royal gShen [was] Phon-po Ma-rung. The son of 'Brang-snyan-lde'u was blind. The gShen-po [magically] restored his eyesight. Because [the prince] saw a wild *snyan* on the facing mountain he was given the name sTag-gong sNyan-gzigs. The royal gShen [was] Ra-sang Khri-ne-khod. During the reign of this king, the Twelve Minor Kings [rGyal-phran bCu-gnyis] were subdued. Nevertheless, Bong-ba-rje, the ruler of lHo-brag, fought back; he captured King sTag-gong sNyan-gzigs, locked him in a dungeon, and defeated the Tibetan people.

In that time the Bonpo entrusted with the Bla rituals for the lord was Ra-sang Bon-po Khri-ne-khod. He had prodigious power and formidable capacities. He transformed himself into a vulture and arriving [in lHo-brag], made the entire retinue of Bong-rje and the prison guards drunk, severed with his wings the iron chains that were binding sTag-gong sNyan-gzigs, and rescued the prince from imprisonment. At that point, Bong-ba-rje paid [his] respects and offered [his] submission. Since gShen-po Khri-ne-khod had saved the king so skillfully, the importance of Bon in the king's eyes grew even more.

The *Dar rgyas gsal ba'i sgron ma* says (Thob, 667, 86, 3):

'Grong-snyan and 'Chin-za Klu-rgyal Ngan-na-mtsho had a blind son. Khu-bon Mang-rje Lod-po [magically] restored his eyesight, and since [the prince] saw a *snyan* on the facing mountain, he was given the name sTag-ri sNyan-gzigs. When he seized power, the Twelve Minor Kings were reduced to subjects, except for the ruler of lHo-brag, Bang-ba-rje, who fought back. Bang-ba-rje even took King sTag-gu sNyan-gzigs as captive, threw him into a dungeon, and defeated the Tibetan people. At that time the Bonpo entrusted with the Bla rituals for the lord was Khri-ne-khod, the Bon-po of Ra-sangs. Since he had enormous power, and formidable capacities, he transformed himself into a crystal vulture. When he reached [lHo-brag], he won over the external and internal retinue as well as the prison guards with his compassion, and rescued sTag-ri sNyan-gzigs from [his] imprisonment by cutting with his wings the blue iron chains that bound the prince. Bang-ba-rje declared his submission. Since the gShen-po Khri-ne-khod had so skillfully saved the king, the importance of Bon in the king's eyes grew even more.

As these two documents both reveal, Ra-sangs Khri-na-khod was the royal gShen of King sTag-ri sNyan-gzigs. The son of sTag-ri sNyan-gzigs was gNam-ri Srong-btsan and the son of gNam-ri Srong-btsan was the *dharmarāja* Srong-btsan sGam-po. Therefore, the statement that at the time of King sTag-ri sNyan-gzigs the royal gShen Ra-sangs Khri-na-khod committed the text to writing proves the existence of a written tradition prior to the *dharmarāja* Srong-btsan sGam-po.

Since the sDe-dge manuscript of the *Srid mdos* has (16, 2), "I, Sangs-po Khrin-khod, put [it] in writing," whereas the other historical texts say "Ra-sangs Khri-ne-khod," it could be wondered if the Sangs-po Khrin-khod of the sDe-dge *Srid mdos* might be different from the Ra-sangs Khri-ne-khod of the other quoted texts. Furthermore, the colophon of the *Srid pa spyi mdos* found in Dol-po, Nepal, says, "I, Ra-sang Khri-kha, put [it] in writing." However, we can be certain that Ra-sang is the same as Ra-sangs, for the following reason: generally the word *ra* of the Zhang Zhung language corresponds to the word red [*dmar po*] in Tibetan, while the Zhang Zhung term *sang* or *sangs* has many meanings in Tibetan, such as clear [*gsal ba*], pure [*dag pa*], empty [*stong pa*], noble one [*'phags pa*], and so on. In this case Ra-sang or Ra-sangs refers to the name of an ancient Zhang Zhung clan, so there can be no doubt that this word has a definite meaning.

Also the words Khrin-khod, Khri-na-khod, and Khri-ne-khod are slightly different; nonetheless, from the fourteenth sMe-'khor until now, more than 1,800 years have elapsed. During this period the manner in which words were spoken in the Zhang Zhung language became totally unfamiliar to the elderly Bonpos and Buddhists in ancient villages who were copying texts generation after generation. Therefore, it should be no surprise if at times the ancient *ne* would be stripped of its vowel *e* and become *na*, or if a mark separating syllables would find its way between *khri* and *na*. The drawbacks of those scribal errors are certainly recognizable, but at the same time the mistakes call attention to the special ancient character of those textual sources, an important aspect that also needs to be considered.

Another text similar to the *Srid pa spyi mdos* in relevance was given me by g.Yung-drung rNam-rgyal, an elderly Bonpo from Kong-po, when I traveled to Lhasa and Central Tibet in 1981 (Tibetan female Iron Bird year 3989 of the middle sMe-phreng in the twenty-second sMe-'khor). The colophon of this guide to the construction of a meditation house for the practice of Zhang Zhung Me-ri [*Zhang zhung me ri'i lcog mkhar bzhengs lugs kyi zur byang*] says (6, 2):

> I, Gu-rub gSal-'od dGa'-ba, am entrusted with the Me-ri transmission lineage.

The text does not contain even a note about the person who actually transmitted the teachings, who the text discoverer was, where it was found, and so on. Hence we can assume that this text was successively handed down by the various gShen-pos entrusted with the Zhang Zhung Me-ri cycle of whom this Gu-rub gSal-'od would have been the first representative.

Generally speaking, both Bonpos and Buddhists later developed the custom of adopting names of great sages of former times: for example the great Sa-skya teacher Mang-thos Klu-sgrub rGya-mtsho (1523-1596) chose a name emulating that of Glorious Lord Ārya Nāgārjuna [dPal-mgon 'Phags-pa Klu-sgrub]; or also, when Guru Padmasambhava arrived in Tibet, many Bonpos had the name Dran-pa Nam-mkha', inspired by the Zhang Zhung master Bla-chen Dran-pa Nam-mkha'. That notwithstanding, the surname or clan name of the person would be used to identify the individual, an impossibility if one relied solely on first names with their similarities. In this case the origin of the name Gu-rub is the name of a territory in Zhang Zhung as stated in the *rDzogs pa chen po Zhang zhung snyan rgyud kyi bon ma nub pa'i gtan tshigs* (Dhi, 266, 4, 5):

> These people of Gu-rub were given the territory of Yar-lung Sog-kha, were exempted from taxes and tributes, and were placed on the right side.

It is thus feasible that over the course of time the name of a territory could have become the identifying term for a group of people. In the *Zhang zhung snyan rgyud kyi brgyud pa'i bla ma'i rnam thar* we read (Dhi, 35, 18, 3):

> The history of dMu rGyal-ba Blo-gros has five aspects, first of all, attainment of the pure human body and the story of [his] father and mother. The father was a pauper named Gu-ru bTsu-gu [who belonged to the] Gu-rub race.

The clarity of the quotation should leave no doubt that Gu-rub gSal-'od dGa'-ba of our excerpt had a connection with the race thus named. This gShen-po is one of the teachers whose biographies appear both in the *Zhang zhung me ri* and in the *Zhang zhung snyan rgyud*. The *Zhang zhung me ri'i bla ma brgyud pa'i bstod phyag chen mo* affirms (Thob, 105, 2, 5):

> I pay homage to Gu-rub gSal-dga', the U-rgyan teacher who maintains the conduct of the single taste.

The *Zhang zhung snyan rgyud kyi brgyud pa'i bla ma'i rnam thar* contains some slight information about the transmission lineage of the gShen-pos of that time (Dhi, 25, 13, 5):

> (Ra-sangs 'Phen-rgyal) transmitted [it] to Gu-rib gSas-dga'. That teacher kept the conduct of the single taste. Gu-rib gSas-dga' transmitted [it] to Zla-ba rGyal-mtshan. That teacher abided in the nature of Reality.

And also (ibid., 26, 13, 1):

> The ultimate of all doctrines rested with sNang-bzher Lod-po.

As indicated by the excerpts, Gu-rib gSas-dga' or Gu-rub gSal-dga' was the teacher of Tshe-spungs Zla-ba rGyal-mtshan. Tshe-spungs Zla-ba rGyal-mtshan was the teacher of Gyer-spungs sNang-bzher Lod-po. Gyer-spungs sNang-bzher Lod-po was invited to Tibet from Zhang Zhung by the *dharmarāja* Srong-btsan sGam-po. This shows that the text composed by Gu-rub gSal-dga' was written before Srong-btsan sGam-po. I do not think that the Gu-rib gSas-dga' mentioned in the *Zhang zhung snyan rgyud kyi brgyud pa'i bla ma'i rnam thar* is someone different from Gu-rub gSal-dga'. The evidence for this is found in the *Zhang zhung me ri'i bla ma brgyud pa'i bstod phyag chen mo*, which specifies the succession of teachers and also the Gu-rub family name (Thob, 105, 2, 4):

> I pay homage to the Four teachers of U-rgyan!
> I pay homage to Don-kun Grub-pa [who holds] the definitive view.
> I pay homage to Ra-sangs 'Phen-rgyal [who mastered] the practice of meditation.
> I pay homage to Gu-rub gSal-dga' [who maintains] the conduct of the single taste.
> I pay homage to Zla-ba rGyal-mtshan [who has realized] the full dimension of the Fruit.

The *Dar rgyas gsal sgron* says (Thob, 642, 74, 6):

> Moreover, the Teacher Padma said, "When the Indian *Dharma* teachings were translated into Tibetan, [it was found that] it was not practicable [to adapt] the Indian written language [and] transform [it] into Tibetan. The thirty [letters] *Ka, Kha* [and so on,] became [instead] the model for [the new] Tibetan [written language]. The names of the deities were drawn from the sounds of the elements, [and] the secret formulas were not translated, but left in the Indian original."

The *Legs bshad rin po che'i mdzod* contains a similar passage (Pe, 180, 18). Although the source of the passage is unknown, if it did not exist somewhere, its incorporation in this text could not have happened. Hence, the fact that such a passage exists where Slob-dpon Padma is cited as saying, "The thirty [letters] *Ka, Kha*, [and so on,] became [instead] the model for [the new] Tibetan [written language]" clarifies the principle on which the new written language was created, that is, modeling itself on the ancient Tibetan language which was based on the thirty-letter alphabet. If this previous ancient language based on the thirty-letter alphabet had not existed in Tibet, it could not have been the template for a new Tibetan written language and Slob-dpon Padma would not have said what he did.

On the basis of this logic, we can deduce the following three facts, namely: one, that the Tibetan people made use of a written language during the Intermediate Period; two, that the origins of the Tibetan culture are indigenous; and three, that the country of Tibet and the Tibetan people are endowed with a history similar in its antiquity to that of India or China. These conclusions represent the viewpoint of a research that is scholarly, rational, and exhaustive.

Another valid argument for the existence of a written language in Tibet prior to the *dharmarāja* Srong-btsan sGam-po and for the early use of a written language by the Tibetan people can be derived by way of knowledge. In this respect the *rGyal rabs gsal ba'i me long* affirms (Pe, 57, 11):

> At the time of the king and minister (sPu-de Gung-rgyal and Ru-la-skyes) the Everlasting Bon made its appearance. The

Teacher called gShen-rab Mi-bo-che was born in 'Ol-mo'i Lung-rings [of] sTag-gzig. All the Bon-po teachings from the country of Zhang Zhung [such as] the Eight Great Spheres [*Khams chen po brgyad*] and so on were translated, diffused, and expanded. [The teachings of] Bon were divided into nine kinds: [of these nine kinds,] four [were incorporated in] the [so-called] Bon of the Cause [*rgyu'i bon*] [and] five [were incorporated in] the [so-called] Bon of the Fruit [*'bras bu'i bon*]. The Five Bon of the Fruit included the Unsurpassable, Everlasting Vehicle. It is maintained that [these Five Bon] allow the attainment of superior rebirths [as] gods [and] humans. The Four Bon of the Cause are: [the Vehicle of] the gShen of Appearance [which makes use of a] woolen turban; [the Vehicle of] the gShen of Magic [which makes use of] colored wools; [the Vehicle of] the gShen of Divination [which makes use of a system and cords called] *Ju thig*; and [the Vehicle of] the gShen of Funerary Rituals [which makes use of] ritual weapons.[115]

This last passage needs to be carefully examined. sPu-de Gung-rgyal belongs to the first Tibetan dynasty of the Seven *Khri* of the Sky and is also the last of the Two *lDeng* of the Middle who were Gri-gum bTsan-po and sPu-de Gung-rgyal himself. From the statement in this text that "[a]ll the Bon-po teachings from the country of Zhang Zhung, [such as] the Eight Great Spheres and so on were translated," one grasps that a written language existed in Tibet at that time.

The so-called Eight Great Spheres [*Khams chen brgyad*] represent a large corpus of Bon literature and are distinguished as the Sphere of Existence (*srid pa'i khams*), the Sphere of Continuity (*rgyun gyi khams*), the Sphere of Appearance (*snang ba'i khams*), the Sphere of Emptiness (*stong pa'i khams*), the Sphere of Clarity (*gsal ba'i khams*), the Sphere of Awareness (*rig pa'i khams*), the Sphere of the Everlasting (*g.yung drung gi*

---

115 [In the *Drung, Deu and Bön* the translator Adriano Clemente states (p. 239, n. 53): "It seems the expressions used to denote the attributes of the different types of gShen refer to characteristic ritual objects, but it is not easy precisely to identify the meaning of 'woolen turban' (*bal thod*—maybe a type of ritual headgear) or of 'colored wool' (*bal tshon*—used in various *glud*, *mdos*, etc., rites to construct *nam mkha'*, *rgyang bu*, and so on). *Ju thig* is the name of a kind of divination carried out using knotted cords and is also the name for the cords themselves. For the 'ritual weapons' (*mtshon cha*) used in the *'dur* rites see Chapter VII, iv [p. 93]."]

khams), and the Sphere of Equanimity (*mnyam nyid kyi khams*). Within the nine categories into which the Bonpo teachings are divided, the Five Bon of the Fruit consist of the Bon of Virtuous Devotees, the Bon of Ascetics, the Bon of the White A, the Bon of the Primordial gShen, and the Unsurpassable, Supreme Bon. The Eight Great Spheres together with the nine kinds of Bon of the Cause and Bon of the Fruit represent a vast and extremely articulate series of Bon teachings. The affirmation by some that even a short ritual in these series, such as those presented in the ancient narrations, could be retained through memory is groundless.

As I have expounded and clarified in the section referring to the origins of the ancient culture of Zhang Zhung in the Early Period [Volume One] and as illustrated by the teachings of the gShen of Prediction, the various series on divination, astrological predictions, medical science, and rituals for the ransom of life are numerous and diverse. I have also shown by citing both Bonpo and Buddhist historical documents how the different Bon teachings arose due to the widespread diffusion throughout Tibet of the Twelve Lores at the time of the Tibetan king gNya'-khri bTsan-po. Even if only those traditions, which certainly are not the only ones, were under consideration, it can also be logically inferred that many other documents related to those traditions must have existed.

If people like ourselves with our present-day understanding and skill in the Tibetan language can remember with difficulty just a few details regarding, for example, the Tibetan kings that appeared before Srong-btsan sGam-po or the types of knots utilized in the *Ju thig* divination system together with the different responses related to those knots, or about medicine, astrology, and so on, let alone the totality of all these, how can one possibly affirm that the people of those ancient times were able to commit the totality to memory? No historical records testify to such a power of retention among the early Tibetans, nor would it be easy to find a cause for such a capacity to have developed. If an underdeveloped people settled in the dark country of Tibet, unable even to read or write, had not only committed to memory the history of thirty-four dynasties and the details of the extensive and diversified

Bonpo culture, but also preserved this knowledge from generation to generation and amplified it for the sake of posterity, it would have been a task of enormous magnitude, not an insignificant one. Even for us in the present time with all our capacities, such an accomplishment would be unheard-of and impossible. In the *rGyal rabs gsal ba'i me long* we read (Pe, 64, 22):

> The Prince studied the five sciences, artistry, astrology, and crafts for a long time and became skilled and learned [in them]. The ministers said, "This Lord of ours has many qualifications and profound compassion". For this reason they called him Srong-btsan sGam-po.[116] When he reached the age of thirteen, after [his] father had died, [the king] moved to the capital.

This excerpt reveals that the *Dharmarāja* learned the five sciences prior to his arrival in the capital. The five sciences mentioned in the text consist of five major and five minor ones: the five major sciences are craftsmanship, medicine, poetry, logic, and philosophy; the five minor ones are rhetoric, ornate language, rhyming, drama, and planetary astrology. If there had been no codified language in Tibet before then, it would have been impossible for the prince to have become learned in any of the fundamental sciences, no matter which of the five major or five minor ones, just as it would be totally impossible to measure the horns on the head of a hare or a horse.
The *Deb ther dmar po* affirms (Pe, 35, 5):

> In the female Fire Ox year, King Srong-btsan sGam-po came into this world with immutable love. When he was thirteen, [his] father died, and he took power.

This excerpt clarifies the time when he moved to the capital. We also read (ibid., 35, 18):

> After the Indian teacher Ku-sa-ra and the Brahmin Sham-ka-ra, the teacher Shi-la Manju from Nepal, the teachers Ta-nu-ta and Gha-nu-ta from Kha-che, and the Indian scholars Li-byin and Ha-shang Ma-ha De-ba had been invited, the translator

---

116 [*sgam po* means profound.]

Thon-mi Saṃ-bho-ṭa together with his assistants Dharma Ko-sha and lHa-lung rDo-rje-dpal translated and systematized the teachings. Thon-mi created a Tibetan written language, taking as a model the Indian one.

Reading this passage, we discover that Indian scholars had been invited to Tibet before Thon-mi created the Tibetan written language; that the three above-mentioned translators not only translated, but also systematized the Indian *Dharma* teachings; and that only afterwards Thon-mi created a new Tibetan written language. How would it have been possible to translate and systematize those teachings if no written language had existed before then? The reason why Thon-mi set out to create a new Tibetan written language can be inferred through this passage. If those scholars had to translate and systematize the Indian teachings in the earlier Tibetan mode, rendering the meaning clearly or seamlessly into Tibetan from the Indian language would not have been possible. Given the nature of the old Tibetan, it would have been laborious as well to systematize its orthography, spelling, connecting particles, and so on.

The interpretation of this passage as meaning that Thon-mi first created a new Tibetan written language and then translated the Indian teachings together with the Indian *paṇḍitas* is highly unlikely. Why? Because it would be tantamount to implying that an author of great scholarly renown such as mKhas-dbang Tshal-pa Kun-dga' rDo-rje, also known as Si-tu dGe-ba'i Blo-gros (1309-1364), who composed many historical works such as those contained in the *Deb ther dmar po*, considered an essential account among the Tibetan dynastic histories of later times, confused the order of the words, an unreasonable claim on anyone's part.

The *rGyal rabs gsal ba'i me long* states (Pe, 86 22):

mGar[117] said: "Let us now decide carefully!" This Lord of ours is sixteen years old. Since none other is fit [to rule, he should]

---

117 [That is, Minister mGar-blon sTong-btsan Yul-srung (d. 667) who was instrumental in arranging the marriage alliances for Srong-btsan sGam-po and in deciding other major administrative, legal, and military matters for the rising Tibetan empire.]

take power. In Nepal there is a beautiful maiden [who is] the daughter of the Lord of Nepal. Similarly in China, the king has a beautiful daughter. Let us invite them both here to be queen consorts." Everybody agreed and said yes.

This passage reveals that Srong-btsan sGam-po was sixteen when he married his Nepalese spouse. Furthermore, the same text states (ibid., 87, 6):

> The king presented five strings of gold and said, "Let this gift confirm the request." Then he offered a headdress made of lapis lazuli inlaid with rubies and said, "Give this precious object to the princess." The king issued three different commands to [his] subjects. He also said, " Without failure offer each of these three [presents]." As [he] commanded, three caskets [*sgrom bu*] were [thus] sent.

This second passage clarifies, instead, how Srong-btsan sGam-po sent communications and three small coffers to the king of Nepal. *sGrom* indicates a box or chest made of gold, silver, or precious stones or wood, paper, and so forth, and corresponds currently to *sgam*. *Bu* means small, hence *sgrom bu* [small box] has the same significance as *sgam chung*. Nevertheless this type of object is not identifiable necessarily with the well-known egg-shaped treasure chests [*gter gyi sgrom bu*] of present times. Furthermore, the same text affirms (ibid., 88, 11):

> At that [point the minister] mGar [took] the first of the three small boxes and offered [it] to the king. When [the king] opened it and looked [inside, he saw that] it contained Nepali words written in gold on indigo paper.

The text says that the writing was in the Nepali language in order not to contradict the statement about the absence of a written language prior to Srong-btsan. Maybe that happened through magic or miraculous influence, but obviously the story has no connection with real history and was fabricated merely to prevent inconsistency. If Tibet did not have a written language of its own, the king himself would not know it; hence, he would also not know how to send missives to the kings of Nepal and China written in Nepali and Chinese. Royal dynasties determined by magic or miracles should be attributed to nondualistic causes and talking about dualistic dynasties according to an ordinary historical viewpoint would be pointless. Historical facts should always be judged on a realistic basis. The *rGya bod yig tshang chen mo* says (Si, 141, 2):

> One king of Tibet at the age of fourteen proclaimed: "Let the country be ruled according to the *Dharma!*" The fame [of his resolution] spread everywhere. The kings of the four directions sent [him] missives and extraordinary objects as presents. The king of Tibet sent rich gifts as acknowledgement but no missives because there was no written language. Therefore it was thought that also Tibet needed a written language. The son of Thon-mi A-nu-ra called Sam-bho-ra Mi-chung was intelligent. He was given [a quantity of] gold and sent to India to study the *Dharma* and to learn the Indian language.

Let us examine these quotations: Srong-btsan sGam-po was thirteen years old when he started to rule, but it was not until he was fourteen years old that the idea of a need for a written language in Tibet was envisaged. This new idea arose following circumstances related to the arrival of missives from foreign rulers, and it was not until then that Thon-mi A-nu was sent to India. Thon-mi A-nu could well have had a variety of admirable qualities such as a good disposition, great knowledge, intelligence, and so on. In practice however, he was sent to India, a huge, distant, and alien country, although he had no cultural background, having been born in Tibet, an obscure borderland and [according to this account] lacking a written language. In those times there were no good roads, let alone airplanes, trains, cars, or bicycles, as at present. Narrations of voyages to India undertaken by great translators, such as Vairocana and others, relate this obstacle.

Thus, firstly, how long would it have taken to go to India from Tibet? Then, a Tibetan person with no cultural background arriving in India would initially have had to study the local idioms in order to communicate minimally with the Indians. How long would that have taken? And how much time would he have needed, once arrived, to become proficient in the written language, meet with the *paṇḍitas*, and having met them, to study the Sanskrit language and the texts of Buddhist philosophy? Obviously all that could not have been accomplished immediately. Then how long would it have taken Thon-mi A-nu, once having become learned in Sanskrit and Buddhist philosophy, to return to Central Tibet? When he reached Central Tibet, how much time would the creation of a new written language and the composition of the grammatical texts known as the *Eight Vyākaraṇa* require? How long would the translation of several texts, such as the *'Dus pa rin po che'i tog*, and so forth, from Sanskrit into Tibetan have taken, in order to present, as it is claimed, a new written language to the king? If we consider all this from the viewpoint of feasibility, we can be absolutely sure of the impossibility of realizing this plethora of activity in the short period of time that extends from when Srong-btsan sGam-po was fourteen until he reached the age of sixteen.

If the information and textual evidence cited has eliminated doubts that a tradition of written language existed in Tibet before the *dharmarāja* Srong-btsan sGam-po, we have still to examine carefully how the written language was traditionally used in those times and whether that written language was called Tibetan [*bod yig*] or not. Original Bonpo historical texts are the source for this information. As a matter of fact, the *Dar rgyas gsal ba'i sgron ma* affirms (Thob, 642, 74, I):

> The old writing was changed into *smar sgrag*. That was divided into large *smar* [*smar chen*] and small *smar* [*smar chung*]. sMar chen became *dbu can* or elegant writing; *smar chung* became the regular [printed] script ['*bru ma*]. The various letters were created from the latter.

A detailed explanation of old Zhang Zhung writing and the so-called *smar sgrag* is found in Volume One, where I discuss the origins of the written language of ancient Zhang Zhung during the Early Period. The forms of writing used by the ancient Tibetan people prior to the Tibetan *dharmarāja* Srong-btsan sGam-po were none other than *smar chen* and *smar chung*.

When I was thirteen years old, an old lama called Dhi-bzod who was a famous Tibetan calligrapher from rMug-sangs in mDo-khams sDe-dge arrived at the temple Ku-se gSer-ljongs, and resided there for several days. At that time, I was studying at the school of that temple, and so I repeatedly asked him to correct my calligraphy of the printed cursive Tibetan script.

Finally one day he spoke to me in a happy way and said, "Your calligraphy is proficient and you are very talented. I can teach you an old form of calligraphy that I know, called *lha babs yi ge* [the language descended from the gods], if you wish to study it." I asked him to please teach it to me and with great kindness he spent a whole day teaching me the complete form of this so-called language descended from the gods. I applied myself to it for many days, because I liked it so much. I remember clearly that as an exercise I wrote the first three chapters of the *bsTan bcos legs bshad rin gter* by Sa-skya Paṇḍita Kun-dga' rGyal-mtshan (1181-1251) in this calligraphic style.

About two years later, I went to sGa-skye rGu-mdo to meet my parents. At that time in a place not very far from the town of sKye-rgu-mdo lived a doctor of Tibetan medicine in his fifties called Lama Tshe-rgyal who had visited many places, such as India among others and who was a famous expert in Tibetan medicine, astrology, and all the sciences. One day we went to meet Lama Tshe-rgyal. In his bedroom in a fine large bookcase I saw four verses elegantly written in the style of the language descended from the gods. I looked closely at those four verses, and slowly read them aloud. The verses were a stanza [number 129] from the eighth chapter on meditative absorption of the *Bodhicaryāvatāra* by the noble Śāntideva (mTsho 84, 6), "All happiness in the world arises from desiring happiness for others. All suffering in the world arises from desiring happiness for oneself."

Image of the Four Verses Written in Lha Babs Yi Ge by Chögyal Namkhai Norbu

Tibetan transliteration of the Verses

'Jig rten bDe ba Ji sNyed pa
De Kun gZhan bDe 'Dod las Byung
'Jig rten sDug bsngal Ji sNyed pa
Du Kun Rang bDe 'Dod las Byung

Lama Tshe-rgyal, surprised and amazed, asked me, "How did you learn to read this writing?" After I told him in detail, he was overjoyed and said, "What a good omen! This is an extremely important form of old Tibetan writing. Few people are now able to read and write it. Do not forget it! It will be useful to you one day." Apart from my former teacher bZod-pa-lags and Lama Tshe-rgyal, I have indeed met no other person who knows this form of writing, although some Tibetans must exist who do so.

In the language of Zhang Zhung, *smar* means auspicious or good. In fact, a sense of the divine [*lha*] or evil [*'dre*] is attached to the concepts of auspicious and inauspicious, or good and bad. Related to this, the *sGra 'grel* addresses the way in which the first human generations were released from the cosmic eggs (Dhi, 52, 11):

> From the essence of the five elements, [space,] air, fire, water, [and] earth, two eggs, one of light and one of darkness, appeared. From the pure essence [of] the five primary causes, because of the invocation made by the deity, g.Yag-ma-grus came into being [from] the egg of light with four sides and eight corners. From the turbid essence, because of the invocation made by Med-'bum Nag-po, Glad-shad Nyal-ba came into being [from] the egg of darkness with three corners.

This is how the original distinction between good and evil took place. Furthermore, in the *Phung po gzan skyur gyi rnam bshad gcod kyi don gsal byed pa*, the text containing the teachings on *gCod* by Ma-gcig Lab-sgron (1031-1129), we read (bKra, 91, 3):

> A conventional definition of divine [*lha*] and evil [*'dre*] commonly acknowledged by all people is this: divine is any good and lovely form related to worldly sense objects that inspires trust and joy; while evil is whatever causes harm to life by the display of hideous forms that produce fear. Moreover, whatever brings about benefit is called divine and whatever does harm is called evil.

The excerpt clarifies that these words are used on the basis of a powerful notion born simultaneously in the mind stream of all human beings whereby anything called divine [*lha*] is good and anything called evil [*'dre*] is bad. It is certain that the meaning of what is called *smar* in the Zhang Zhung language and what is called *lha* in Tibetan is the same. The special written language that is related to those two words is clearly defined as the *smar* language [*smar gyi yi ge*] or the language descended from the gods [*lha babs kyi yi ge*]. This form of writing is the written language that was used by the Tibetan people prior to the advent of the Tibetan king Srong-btsan sGam-po.

Reproduced below is a copy I made of the alphabet of the language descended from the gods, trying to avoid mistakes and imperfections. I invite those who are knowledgeable about the written form of the divine language and, whose eyes open in understanding, are able to clarify and reveal its source in all its purity to do so without hesitation and to indicate errors in the manner of writing or in any other way.

The Language Descended from the Gods

[sMar] / [Tibetan] — (script comparison table)

A critical comparison of the Tibetan cursive script with the divine language script, could lead, it can be argued, to the conclusion that the Tibetan cursive script derives from the divine language script. Even if the former may have been slightly changed and become more flowing during the course of time, in its entirety the later script still retains the original way of writing. The way of joining the subscribed letters to the vowels, the way of writing the superscribed letters *ra* and *sa* before the radical that is typical of the cursive script such as in *rtsa* and *stsa*, or *spa* and *spya*, the custom of not writing the upper part of the letters, and so on, represent a not insignificant evidence of the great similarity of these two scripts.

An extremely important factor that needs to be considered is that writing in *dbu can* proceeds from left to right, while writing in *dbu med* moves from right to left. This is true not only in the consideration of these two ways of writing; in reality the basic principle in the two modes is reflected in the ancient custom of arranging seats in rows, according to the importance of the guests, starting either from the right or from the left, and also in the way of venerating or paying respect to the supports of Body, Speech, and Mind, whereby one circumambulates either toward the right or the left. Therefore the basic difference between the *dbu can* and the *dbu med* scripts, as well as the changes that occurred over time, can also be inferred from that fact.

Even if many scholars say that the *dbu can* script written quickly becomes *dbu med*, that is not actually the case: no matter how fast *dbu can* is written, the basic way of starting in *dbu med* is different. That *dbu-can* script cannot be transformed into *dbu med* can be observed if we compare it with, for example, the calligraphic style called *lho yig* or *rgyugs yig*, which is still used in Bhutan and which is produced by rapidly writing in *dbu can*. There is no way that Tibetans can create the *dbu med* script by quickly writing in *dbu can*, nor that *dbu med* can be created just from the *rgyugs yig* script, or when the Bhutanese quickly write in *dbu can*, because the *dbu can* script derives from the Gupta model, an Indian calligraphic style, while the *dbu med* script derives from *smar*. We do not need any additional reasons beyond our common sense to be certain of that.

When I was thirteen years old, I went to visit several times a lama more than eighty years old called mDzad-rtag sPrul-sku who lived in a hermitage not far from Ku-se gSer-ljongs temple in sDe-dge. I remember that he had in his bedroom numerous old handwritten books in *po ti* form with singed traces visible on the edges of many of them. When I asked him what those old books were, he replied, "These books are the inner support of mDzad-rtag temple." When I asked the location of mDzad-rtag dGon-pa, he explained in great detail that a temple had once stood among the many ruins of mDzad-rtag on land descending from the river basin, about ten kilometers from present day gSer district; that he was the main incarnation of that temple; and that when he was young, mDzad-rtag dGon-pa was destroyed by fire but since no permission for rebuilding it was granted, he and the temple monks moved to gSer-ljongs dGon-pa and settled there. I opened some of those *po ti* texts to see what they were about: the majority of them were part of the *rNying ma rgyud 'bum* collection, although also quite a few texts of the 'Brug-pa bKa'-brgyud school were present. All were written with tall consonants and small vowels and attached letters. When I asked the lama why the writing style was different from that of other texts, he said, "This is called *smar* or *smar tshugs*." These occurrences appear to illustrate that not only the divine language, but also those types of writing known in ancient times as *smar* or *smar tshugs* were not called Tibetan [*bod yig*]. In this respect the *lHo brag chos 'byung* says (Pe, Vol. One, 178, 8):

> Do not depend on the written language of another place. The written language of Tibet proper is what is necessary.

Even if the *smar* script was used by the ancient Tibetan people, that language was one of the languages of Zhang Zhung and it was not recognized as the written language of Tibet proper. That produced the desire to create a new written language for Tibet and to discard that of Zhang Zhung. This is the meaning expressed by this quotation. Since a number of similar ways of saying this appeared in other Tibetan historical texts, how the distinct definitions of *smar* and Tibetan [*bod yig*] came about can also be understood.

Although it is certain that a written language was used in Tibet before the *dharmarāja* Srong-btsan sGam-po and that the majority of Tibetan history scholars have that understanding, the main reason for their distortion of Tibetan history is because the Tibetans held for some time such a vehement faith in and pure desire for the sacred teachings coming from India that they attributed to India also the origins of the entire Tibetan culture without exploring the cultural and historical origins of ancient Zhang Zhung. Even if the Tibetan Bonpos were the people who cared most about the continuity of the large and small aspects of the culture originating from Zhang Zhung, from the moment the sacred *Dharma* spread in Tibet, the authentic teachings of Bon weakened ever more like a lamp that flickers as it runs out of oil.

Thus, with the pretense of extolling the praises of the sacred *Dharma*, a negative attitude vilifying Bon and the Bonpos became diffused among the majority of Tibetans. As this insulting bias came to be held by most Tibetans, Bon and Bonpos became regarded as entities to be avoided or as sullied and unacceptable, and because of that also the Bonpos of later times were dominated by this perspective. Influenced by a variety of *Dharma* attitudes, just as the Buddhists attributed the origins of their teachings [*chos*] to the great country of India, so the Bonpos recognized in sTag-gzig the country of origin of Bon. Similarly, as in Buddhist fashion, Bon adopted the Three Baskets [*sde snod gsum*],[118] the higher and lower tantric series of the Secret Formulas, and so on. Whatever *Dharma* tendency spread and developed, the Bonpos felt impelled to develop and spread that tendency as well.

Consequently the sad condition arose whereby the unique and valuable nature of authentic Bon was eclipsed. More than one thousand years have passed in such circumstances and it is evident that today historical criterions have been lost and that it is extremely difficult to pursue the historical origins of authentic Tibetan culture. Because this is the case, if someone should say, "There was no tradition of a written language in Tibet prior to Srong-btsan. Through the grace of the kind king and of his minister a written language system appeared in Tibet and the lamp of *Dharma* could shine in that obscure country," no Tibetan would contest that. On the other hand, someone who declared that a written system existed in Tibet before Srong-btsan sGam-po and also that history revolved around the multifarious aspects of the Bon culture would be

---

118 [Sūtra, Vinaya, and Abhidharma.]

doubted and the reliability of such a statement questioned. Some scholars have even mocked proponents of such ideas, calling them deceitful.

However, one should not be at all amazed or even surprised by this reaction. Why? More than one thousand years have passed since the historians who deeply revered the *Dharma* distorted history, influencing many Buddhist and non-Buddhist scholars. Proving the existence of this influence, in the past many Buddhist and non-Buddhist scholars continued to write their books according to those views. Since the majority of historians who previously appeared in Tibet all became great *Dharma* teachers, it could be said that due to this particular circumstance an account of the true history of Tibet could have little hope of emerging, since the history recounted was mostly of how the sacred *Dharma* developed and spread in Tibet. Nonetheless, the real necessity of clearly drawing forth the cultural history of ancient Tibet and its authentic origins is a matter of great importance, not only for us present day Tibetans who need to recognize the extremely valuable aspects of the ancient Tibetan culture and the relevant cultural history, but also because expanding the opportunities for study by interested intellectuals everywhere would be of great significance.

There is a notable difference in saying that Tibet did not have a written language and in saying that before the *dharmarāja* Srong-btsan sGam-po Tibetans did not use a written language. It does not follow that Tibetans did not use a written language, because before then Tibet did not have a written language of its own. It would be as unreasonable to say that because we do not have textbooks by Mr. Tashi in our school, we do not have textbooks by anyone else either.

Furthermore, some histories say that Buddhism was introduced in Tibet at the time of lHa-tho-tho-ri when the texts of the *mDo sde za ma tog*, and so on, fell onto the roof of the royal palace and that since Tibet did not have a written language at that time, the king did not know how to read. Statements of that order are used as the justification for the claim of the absence of a written language in Tibet before the *dharmarāja* Srong-btsan sGam-po. In the *sNgon byung gi gtam me tog phreng ba* of Ne'u Paṇḍita [Nel-pa Paṇḍita Grags-pa sMon-lam Blo-gros, thirteenth century] we read (Dha, 13, 7, 4):

> We cite in detail the history of the introduction of the sacred *Dharma* at the time of lHa-tho-tho Ri-snyan-btsan, [recounting that] when that holy being took power, Li-the-se and the Lotsāba of Tho-gar, Blo-sems-mtsho, invited the Indian paṇḍita Legs-byin. He arrived with the intention to teach the *Dharma* to the king, but it was impossible [for the latter] to learn, since in Tibet no written language existed. Thus, having marked them with a special seal, [the Indian *paṇḍita*] presented the king with the *Za ma tog bkod pa*, the *sNying po yi ge drug ma* (this was called the yellow scroll), [and] one text written in gold (*Lan tsha* letters).

The *rGyal rabs gser phreng* says (Dha, 204, 15, 1):

> Since also the *mChod gnas gnyan po gsang ba* [cycle] of the forefather Tho-tho Ri-snyan-shal was in the Indian language, it was necessary to translate it, so as to have it in the Tibetan language.

The text, as can be clearly read, states that the books of the *gNyan po gsang ba* [Powerful Secret] were in the Indian language. If the king did not know how to read the Indian language, what assures one that he did not know *smar*, the written language used by the people of ancient Tibet? If Tibetan scholars in the majority are not familiar with English, who can say that they also do not know Tibetan? Most Tibetan histories such as the *Deb ther dmar po*, and so on, refer to Thon-mi A-nu only as the creator of a new Tibetan written language and do not say that no written language existed in Tibet before him.

However, due to the manifestation of concrete circumstances, many possible misrepresentations were advanced by those who did not accept an historical perspective and who contributed their prestige to embellish tales about the generations of *dharmarājas* that came before them, such as Tibet lacking a written language before the *dharmarāja* Srong-btsan sGam-po or that Tibet had been an obscure country populated with Tibetans for the most part wild savages living like apes. In reality those misrepresentations are as erroneous as saying that a good donkey is the offspring of a mule, or that a good *mdzo*[119] is a stud generated by a bull.

---

119 [A *mdzo* is a female hybrid of a yak and a cow.]

V

The Civilization of Ancient Tibet

THE CULTURAL EXPRESSIONS that became diffused in Tibet during the Intermediate Period can certainly be said to have arisen chiefly from the different aspects of Bon originating in the country of Zhang Zhung. However, numerous other such expressions based upon long-term experiences accumulated by human groups in various areas of Tibet and that descended from the four, six, or seven original clans,[120] the number depending upon opinion, are also a reality.

1. The Twelve Lores of Bon

The presence of these cultural expressions can be noted in total clarity in historical documents. For example the *Byams ma* affirms (rGyud, TSHI, 70, 4):

> In the country of Tibet the Bonpos sGom-lha-bo lHa-sras, lDong-lha-bon, and others who were the Bonpos of the Twelve Lores examined the marks [of gNya'-khri bTsan-po], purified [him] with lustral water, and crowned [him] as king. During his time, the so-called Twelve Lores of the Bon of the Cause flourished.
>
> They were:

---

120 [See Volume One, p. 64 et seq.]

the Bon[po] of the Deities, the Lore of Protection [*mGon shes lha bon*];

the Bon[po] of the Positive Force, the Lore of Prosperity [*g.Yang shes phywa bon*];

[the Bonpo of] Ransom Rituals, the Lore of Demons [*'Dre shes glu gtong*];

the gShen of Existence, the Lore of Funerary Rituals [*'Dur shes srid gshen*];

[the Bonpo of] Exorcisms, the Lore of Purification [*gTsang shes sel 'debs*];

[the Bonpo of] the Lore that Releases from Curses [*sGrol shes lda byad*];

[the Bonpo of] Therapeutic Methods, the Lore of Healing [*Phan shes sman dpyad*];

[the Bonpo of] Astrology, the Lore that Controls the Order [of Existence, *sKos shes rtsis mkhan*];

[the Bonpo of] *gTo* Rituals, the Lore of Proclamation [of the Origin, *sMra shes gto rgu*];

[the Bonpo of] Deer Rituals, the Lore of Soaring [*lDing shes sha ba*];

[the Bonpo of] *Cu tig* [sic], the Lore of Divination [*'Phur shes cu tig*];

the Bon[po] of Magic Power, the Lore of Ritual Destruction [*'Gro shes 'phrul bon*].[121]

As is evident from this excerpt, at that time twelve great Bon/gShen who were expert in twelve distinct specific Bonpo teachings developed and spread the knowledge of the so-called Twelve Portals of Bon [*bon sgo bcu gnyis*] in Tibet. It is possible that three Lores of the Bon teachings among the Twelve—namely, the Lore of Protection, the Lore of Purification, and the Lore of Demons—derive from teachings that gShen-rab Mi-bo-che imparted to the Bonpos of Tibet when he went there during the Early Period or that they developed as modifications

---

121 [For the order of the Twelve Lores established by the Author after collating the various texts he had examined and their relevant analysis see *Drung, Deu and Bön. Narrations, Symbolic languages and the Bön tradition in ancient Tibet*, translated from Tibetan into Italian, edited and annotated by Adriano Clemente, translated from Italian into English by Andrew Lukianowicz, Library of Tibetan Works and Archives, Dharamsala, 1995, pp. 49-50.]

of previously existent Bonpo teachings. In this respect the *gZer mig* states (Thob, KHA, 662, 51, 5):

> To the Bonpos of Tibet, gShen-rab taught two methods, [one] for worshipping deities and [one] for banishing demons. As symbolic substitutes [*yas rtags*], [he] instructed them [in the use of] ritual libation and smoke purification by burning branches[122] and aromatic shrubs.

The text refers to two Bonpo practices of deity worship such as the gTod-lha[123] and the gNyan that remove hindrances and punishments, the consequence of offensive human behavior, and to practices such as the 'Dre gdon[124] that cause harmful demons to go away after they are rewarded with suitable offerings.

Although those whom the text calls the Bonpos of Tibet [*bod kyi bon po*]—an expression that implies both the teachings of Bon and its officiants—had previously developed a way of praying to the deities and ridding themselves of demons, their methods involved sacrifices of the life, the flesh and blood of sentient beings such as goats, birds, and so on. That a Bon teaching method for praying to deities and expelling demons already existed and that gShen-rab Mi-bo-che brought changes to an old custom is demonstrated by the phrase contained in the *gZer mig*, namely, "As symbolic substitutes [*yas rtags*], [he] instructed them [in the use of] ritual libations and smoke purification by burning branches and aromatic shrubs."

Evidence for the ancient Bonpo custom of performing blood sacrifices is found in the *Srid pa spyi mdos* that reads (8, 1):

> What has gShen-rab done about the sanguinary immolations [*dmar thabs*] of the bDud-bon? [He] has subjugated [the bDud]

---

122 *zhug shang*. Sometimes also written *zhugs shing* [literally, firewood], I think it most probably refers to wooden branches and stems burned in the flames.
123 [In the *Drung, Deu and Bön* the translator Adriano Clemente specifies (op cit, n. 16, p. 253): "The *gTod* are fierce beings that dominate rocks and mountains; their worship in Bon [...] is generally associated with that of the *Sa bdag* (Lords of the Earth), the *gNyan* (Lords of Intermediate Space between earth and sky, symbolized by trees), and the Klu (Lords of Water and the Underworld)."]
124 [Spirits that disturb energy. See *Drung*, op cit, p. 68.]

> Khyab-pa [and satisfied him] with the offering of sacrificial cakes [*gtor ma*] made of white grain.

And also (ibid., 10, 1):

> What is it that pleases the Lord of the bTsan? As food, he devours flesh; as beverage, he craves blood; life [and] breath is what he takes away. [His] associates are the bGegs, [his] companions the gNyan. [His] protégés are the bTsan-bon; those [he] torments, the petitioners [*gsas*]. gShen-rab, with [his] great power, hurled the *dzwo dmar* above him. [He] entrusted the gShen with the rope of life [*srog thag*]. Symbolic substitutes were created for [supporting] the pledge. [125]

This gives an idea of how blood offerings were performed and the reason why gShen-rab taught the use of substitutes.

The Bon of the Positive Force, the Lore of Prosperity [*g.Yang shes phywa bon*] refers to what the Bonpo tradition generally calls *phywa gshen pa* [the Way of the gShen of the Positive Force], which includes medical treatment and astrology. Here the name *g.Yang shes phywa bon* [Bonpo of the Positive Force, the Lore of Prosperity] specifically refers to those Bon and gShen expert in understanding the functioning of the constructive forces or powers related to the five elemental spheres of the world and of beings. These individuals had the capacity to create happiness through meritorious accumulations and to discern and summon positive agents from among the good and bad ones in the world, fostering long life, augmenting virtues, increasing fortune, prosperity, and so on.

As to the gShen of Existence, the Lore of Funerary Rituals [*'Dur shes srid gshen*], the Tantra *gSang ba bsen thub* affirms (284, 142, 4):

> Those who lack the ability of an excellent gShen hope to be led to a place of salvation in the afterlife, [but] the confusion that guides them like a fool leading [another] fool by the hand, causes them to fall into the abyss [of transmigration]. Due to the power of karma which is the base of transmigration, the body and the mind separate [so that] the soul, the function

---

125 [See Volume One, chapter II, p. 89, for another version of this passage.]

of the mind, and the mind [*bla yid sems gsum*]¹²⁶ wander in the intermediate state [*bar do*].

Those whose three potentialities are perfected within their bodies tame [demons and spirits of the intermediate state] as when a savage is reduced to submission. Similarly, the individuals who possess intuitive wisdom [*shes rab*] reunite the soul, the function of the mind, and the mind in the Sphere [*thig le*] [of their consciousness] and are liberated without obstructions in the Expanse of Space [*mkha' klong dbyings*].

As explained above, Bonpos or gShen-pos belonging to this Lore can be any individual able to summon the soul of a living human being that is wandering or has been stolen by other entities or anyone capable of re-unifying the scattered soul, function of the mind, and mind of a deceased one, establishing them in a happy dimension. In particular, these Bonpos or gShen-pos are noted as priests familiar with rituals performed specifically for those murdered, suffering because the Shi-gshed spirits [torturers of the dead] have deprived them of their soul [*bla*]. These spirits, disguised as the deceased person from whom they have stolen the soul, lure the living left behind, so that, using deception, they can disturb or harm them. Bonpos or gShen-pos of this type of Lore are able to conquer these spirits with rituals; by reuniting the soul, the function of the mind, and the mind of the deceased, they create happiness for the living and the dead.

The real meaning of the Lore that Releases from Curses [*sGrol shes lda byad*] is based on the reading *'grol shes gtad byad* that refers to the type of Bonpo capable of releasing [*'grol shes*] someone afflicted by a curse [*byad*] or an incantation [*gtad*]. The term *gtad* [literally, handed over] involves powerful beings with a physical form such as humans as well as nonhuman beings without a physical form, such as the spirits of the Eight Classes and the gTod, that due to dissonant circumstances are able to place [*gtad*] a single individual, a household, a group of people, or an entire area in the control of the intensely wrathful Klu and Sa-bdag. As material support for this incantation, objects [*gtad rdzas*] are hidden in powerful places identified as the abodes of the

---

126 [For an explanation of these three, see *Drung*, op cit, p. 254, note 2.]

Sa-bdag or in springs inhabited by the Klu. These locations are then known as having been put under a *gtad* [*gtad 'og tu bcug*]. As long as the objects of the incantation remain underground, the individual, household, and so forth, that are the victims of the incantation experience constant impediments, illness, deaths, and all sorts of misfortunes. To release the victims from the incantation, it is necessary either to remove its material support or to perform a specific ritual called *gTad rul* to neutralize its effects.

In the other case, *byad kha* refers to offenses caused the spirits of the gTod class by someone. Here the gTod, who perceive the offender as an enemy or culprit, send maledictions, so that the person is constantly assailed by unexpected impediments.

The teachings of Therapeutic Methods, the Lore of Healing [*Phan shes sman dpyad*] are related to the medical texts that gShen-rab Mi-bo-che taught to his sons—dPyad-bu Khri-shes, gTo-'bum, and so on—and to the Eight Great Ascetics[127] during the Early Period. These were the Four Medical Treatises titled *rTsa ba thugs 'bum mkha' sngon, sMan 'bum dkar po, dPyad 'bum khra bo,* and *Nad 'bum nag po*, subsequently discovered by Bu-mtsho Srid-pa'i rGyal-po (eleventh century). These four texts and the root text plus commentary in seven chapters taught by dPyad-bu Khri-shes, titled *sMan mdo rtsa 'grel le'u bdun pa*, were found at bSam-yas by the Three A-tsa-ra [Skt. Ācārya, A-tsa-ra Mi-gsum, tenth century], together with other texts written in Tibetan. Translated from the Zhang Zhung language into Tibetan by *lotsābas* of the Intermediate Period, they thus became diffused in Tibet. There is no indication in the texts about the identity of the translators, but in the *Legs bshad rin po che'i mdzod* we read (Pe, 198, 1):

---

127 *Drang srong chen po brgyad.* The *Thugs 'bum mkha' sngon* (mDo, 5,1) specifies that these were: "lHa'i Drang-srong mNgon-par Shes-pa [the Divine Clairvoyant]; bDen-par sMra-ba [the Truthful Speaker]; Rig-par sMra-ba [the Intelligent Speaker]; Nges-par sMra-ba [the One Who Spoke with Certainty]; Yid-las sPrul-pa [Emanated from Consciousness]; Yid-las 'Byung-ba [Arisen from Consciousness]; Yid-las sKyes-pa [Born from Consciousness]; and Yid-las Grub-pa [Accomplished from Consciousness]."

> The scholar from sTag-gzig, dMu-tsa Dra-he-pa, was an expert in each of the five sciences.

And also (ibid., 198, 3):

> The scholar from Phrom, gSer-thog lCe-'byams, was an expert in the healing arts.

Among the Eight Great Lotsābas there was also a Sha-ri dBu-chen of Tibet. Thus it is more than likely that they were the translators.

As an example of a cycle dealing with healing methods, the *lDe'u rgya bod kyi chos 'byung* reads (Bod, 251, 17):

> The moment the doctor from 'A-zha opened the eyes of Prince dMus-long at Phying-nga sTag-rtse, [the prince] saw [*gzigs*] a wild goat [*gnyan*][128] on the roof of the castle; for that reason he was called sTag-gu gNyan-gzigs. During his time, all [the lords] that were not yet gathered under the dominion of the king [such as] the Lords of 'A-zha and Zings-po-rje, and so on, were subjugated.

As the excerpt reveals, we can know with certainty that a doctor from 'A-zha existed and that the country of 'A-zha fell under the political influence of Tibet.

Concerning Astrology, the Lore that Controls the Order [of Existence, *sKos shes rtsis mkhan*], the *dPyad gsum dag rtsis* says (Thob, 25, 13, 1):

> The cycle of astrological sciences [*gtsug lag rtsis*].[129] The infinite astrological series [*Grangs med sa bon gser thub*] were entrusted to 'Od-srung. In rTag-gzigs [Zhang Zhung Phug-pa, and in] Sham-bha-la, gDung-sob Chen-po systematized the commentaries and [their various] sections; in particular, he put together the essence [of the texts] and sealed [them]. In addition, the Six Supreme Scholar-Translators [*Lo tsa mkhas pa'i rgyan drug*] and others [transmitted] those good sayings to the fortunate and meritorious ones of Sham-bha-la where they flourished. The Six Great Translators [contributed to their] diffusion and dis-

---

128 [*gnyan*. The name can also refer to a type of wild goat called an argali.]
129 [*gtsug lag*. For an explanation of the term related to Tibetan astrology see *Drung*, op cit, pp. 158-160.]

semination by translating [them in the languages of] rTag-gzigs, Zhang Zhung, O-rgyan, India, China, Phrom, Ge-sar, Bru-sha, Kashmir [Kha-che], Tibet, and Li [Khotan].

This shows that the astrological texts taught by gShen-rab Mi-bo-che during the Early Period were translated during the Intermediate Period by the Six Great Lotsābas in various languages including Tibetan and that they were diffused in Tibet at that time. Furthermore, in the *rGyal rabs gsal ba'i me long* we read (Pe, 58, 2):

> With [his] tools and weapons, the Dur gShen removes obstacles for the living, builds tombs for the dead, and conquers the demons [that haunt] the little ones [Sri]. By observing the celestial bodies, he subdues the spirits ['Dre] of the earth.

This demonstrates the development of the astrological science.

Concerning *gTo* Rituals, the Lore of Proclamation [of the Origin, *sMra shes gto rgu*], the *smra* in this sentence in its real sense means *smrang*, that is, proclamation. *sMrang* is any declared truth that can transform negative forces[130] into positive ones.[131] Beneficial rites or diagnostic cures [*gto dpyad*] are performed depending on the primary causes and secondary circumstances. The rituals determine the type of relation that exists between an individual's performance and the influence of concrete factors or forces controlled by the gTod. The Bonpos or gShen-pos expert in proclaiming [those truths] and in applying the necessary methods or the numerous types of beneficial rituals are known as *sMrang shes gto rgu*.

The Deer [rituals], the Lore of Soaring [*lDing shes shwa ba*]: it is possible that this Lore derives from the famous tradition known in ancient times as bTsan Bon. Using deer antlers or a deer head as a supporting element for the image of a king is a custom shared by both Bonpos and Buddhists. Among the protectors [*srung ma*], a deer-headed one is known as Gri-btsan; and during the sacred temple dances, a

---

130 *ngam*. In the ancient Bonpo tradition the term indicated the negative side and unfavorable circumstances; its meaning is similar to darkness [*mun pa*].

131 *ye*. In the ancient Bonpo tradition the term indicated all positive, virtuous aspects; its meaning is similar to light [*snang ba*].

specific one called the deer dance [*shwa 'cham*] is performed with a deer mask. Apart from those instances, the fundamental connection of this tradition with Bon is confirmed by the existence, still today, of *mDos* rituals such as that of the Deer with Branched Antlers [*shwa ba rus rgyas kyi mdos*]. The relevant text describes the way in which the main ritual object, the figure of a deer, must be prepared (*Shwa ba rus rgyas kyi mdos chog*, I, 2):

> Mold a pleasing form of a deer about the size of a three-year-old ram in yellow clay mixed with a powder of precious substances and color it in the following way: the front half of the right flank, white; the back half, red; the front half of the left flank, blue; the back half, yellow; the tail, black; the back, white; the belly, yellow. For the right antler, use the wood of the male tree;[132] for the left one, that of the female tree.[133] [To the two horns] attach the feathers of various birds of prey, tied together with a black thread.[134]

As a sign of the successful accomplishment of the ritual, the deer image would move and rise above the surface of the *mDos*. The term *lDing shes shwa ba* may have been created to designate a type of gShen who was expert in such rituals.

Ju thig, the Lore of Divination [*'Phur shes Ju thig*][135] is one of the four types of divination in the Phywa gShen pa tradition. This tradition includes the Divination of the Manifestation of Primordial Existence [*Ye srid 'phrul gyi ju thig*]; the Clairvoyance of the sGra-bla of Primordial Knowledge [*Ye mkhyen sgra bla'i mngon shes*]; the Aspiration Dream of the Primordial Lord [*Ye rje smon lam*]; and the Oracles of the Deities of Primordial Power [*Ye dbang lha yi bka' babs*]. The *Ju thig* was first expounded by gShen-rab Mi-bo-che for the benefit of gShen Legs-rgyal Thang-po and others; during the Intermediate Period, it was diffused in Tibet through

---

132   *pho shing*. Birch.
133   *mo shing*. Alpine willow.
134   *skud pa nag po'i rgyud kha*. Many objects are used for *mDos* rituals: branches of various trees, thread crosses, *rgyang bu* [for a description, see Volume One, p. 104], arrows, and spindles to which five-colored wool threads are tied. In this case, only black woolen thread is used.
135   [See Volume One, pp. 189-191, and *Drung*, op cit, pp. 188-198.]

several texts such as the *Ju thig srid pa'i rgyud 'bum*, the *dPyad don sgyu ma gser 'bum*, and so on. Here *'phur shes* refers to the six cords used as tools for the *Ju thig* divination, five shorter [*thig gu lnga*] and one longer [*mo rta*]. The diviner ties the cords and then lets them fall [*'phur*]. Diverse types of knot combinations appear in this way according to which the hidden positive or negative aspects of a given situation can be distinguished.

The *sNang gsal sgron me* says (sDe dge, 229, 5):

> Examined in detail, the main knots [*bla mdud*] known at present are 600. [The text] explains [that the existing combinations are] 10,000 *sangs*, 100,000 *phrag*, and so on. In practice, [the knots that occur most frequently can be] subsumed into 360 with 10,000 possible combinations [*brgyag*] of which 720 are considered primary.

Furthermore, *'Gro shes 'phrul bon* corresponds to the Bon of Magic Power, the Lore of Ritual Destruction [*sgrol shes 'phrul bon*]. The most important aspect of this series of Bon teachings is found in the *Dzwo*, *This*, and *dBal* destructive actions that are related to the *gSas mkhar spyi spungs* cycle. This Lore refers to the Bonpos who possess powerful magic and who know how to destroy [*sgrol shes*] enemies of the teachings or of sentient beings, as well as particular foes of the doctrine who cannot be tamed through peaceful actions and thus require the display of wrathful force that among the gShen-pos is exemplified by the destructive actions of the *Dzwo*, *This*, and *dBal* rituals.[136]

2. The Three Cardinal Aspects of the Culture of the Intermediate Period

Thus the teachings expounded through the Twelve Lores became a foundation for the culture of the Intermediate Period. Looking closely, we can see that this culture was entirely based upon three cardinal aspects: the art of divination, therapeutic methods for the well-being of the living, and funerary practices for the peace of the deceased.

---

136 [See *Drung*, op cit, pp. 199-219.]

Firstly, without the support of divination, neither how to obtain happiness and fortune for the living nor how to get rid of unlucky and adverse circumstances that may arise could be known. Likewise, since it would be difficult to decide how to behave in order to ensure a peaceful existence for the soul [*bla*] of the deceased and which ceremonies would be propitious to sustain a harmonious rapport between the living and the dead or which funerary rituals would be needed for the spirits of the latter and for the spirits who tormented both the living and the deceased, several different divination systems were developed that included astrology [*rtsis*], *Ju thig*, and the *pra mo* methods, as well as the interpretation of dreams.

Through a detailed analysis, we can see that the ancient Bon tradition was extremely knowledgeable about and attentive to a series of methods that could:

- determine the relation between an individual and material forces or between the concrete forces of the environment and the classes of nonhuman beings able to control those forces [*gTod*];
- indicate how to obtain help to benefit an individual's potential through the power arising from white *ye* energies or show how to transform harmful circumstances arising through black *ngam* energies that could affect the strength of an individual;
- aid in assessing the relation between an individual and positive and negative energies altogether;
- make it possible to transform the power of an individual or his or her inherent positive and negative strengths by virtue of those positive and negative forces themselves;
- adequately transform the power of the positive [*ye*] and negative [*ngam*] aspects inherent in the dimension of an individual.

This is why different types of healing methods for the welfare of the living and of funerary practices for the peace of the soul of the dead were developed.

Within the healing arts for the welfare of the living, we find invocations to the gTod, to the protective forces of the primordial sGra-bla, and so on,[137] meant to develop the fortune and charisma of the individual; rituals for summoning long life, glory, good fortune, and prosperity[138] meant to restore and enhance weakened positive energies; codified beneficial ceremonies [*gto, mdos*] to prevent the presence of or banish demons and evil spirits ['Dre-srin] by binding them to an oath; and medicine which would allow people to live happily by removing damage caused the three doors[139] by illness.

Concerning funerary practices for the peace of the deceased, the *Legs bshad rin po che'i mdzod* tells us that (Pe, 196, 4):

> After the funerary ceremony for the murdered king [*rgyal gyi gri 'dur*] was performed at Kong-po Bri-sna, the world of the living was happy. sPu-lde seized the throne. The putting to rest of the deceased was easy: Gri-rum obtained salvation. Even now a teaching exists called "The Three Hundred Sixty Assistant Intermediaries of the Funerary Ceremony for the Slain of King Gri-rum" [*rgyal gri rum gyi gri 'dur yog bar pa sum brgya drug bcu*].

The history of the Profound Inner Topics [*nang don rig pa*] and the way in which the topics became diffused in the Tibetan country during the Intermediate Period is directly related to the appearance of Bla-chen-po Dran-pa Nam-mkha', sNya-chen Li-shu sTag-ring, and other great Bon gShen-pos. In this respect, the Chronological Table entitled *bsTan rtsis mgo mtshar nor bu'i phreng ba* of the great Abbot of sMan-ri Monastery Nyi-ma bsTan-'dzin (1836-1875), compiled in the male Water Tiger year of the first *sMe phreng* of the twenty-second *sMe 'khor* (Tibetan year 3819,[140] 1902 CE). It was published by his successor, the sMan-ri Abbot bsTan-'dzin rNam-dag (born 1926) in the female Iron Ox year (Tibetan year 3878 [second *sMe phreng* of the twenty-second *sMe 'khor*],[141] 1961 CE) says (Thob, 28, 6):

---

137 [See *Drung*, op cit, pp. 60-62, and n. 65, p. 247]
138 [See *Drung*, op cit, p. 63 et seq.]
139 [Body, speech, and mind.]
140 [Indicated by the Author as 22/1.]
141 [Indicated by the Author as 22/2.]

> In the Wood Mouse year, the Lord of Phya [Phya-rje] himself, Yab-lha bDal-drug, together with the royal gShen mTshe-mi [and] bCo'u, descended from the heavens in order to establish pure virtue [in] the common, untamed Tibetan subjects and [also] to assign a name to gNya'-khri bTsan-po. ([Tibetan year] 3097).

As explained here, the first Tibetan king 'O-lde sPu-rgyal ascended the royal throne of Tibet in the male Wood Mouse year (Tibetan year 781, [second *sMe phreng* of the fifth *sMe 'khor*] 5/2). We also read (ibid., 28, 19):

> In the Fire Horse year, on the tenth day of the Horse Month, the Bla-chen, embodiment of all the Victorious Ones [and] protector of the five hundred [teachings], was born. ([Tibetan year] 2875).

As it is written, Bla-chen Dran-pa Nam-mkha' of Zhang Zhung was born in the male Fire Horse year (Tibetan year 1003, [second *sMe phreng* of the sixth *sMe 'khor*] 6/2). And also (ibid., 29, 12):

> In the Earth Monkey [year] the Lord sNya-chen Li-shu requested the 1100 teachings of Bon; and from rTag-gzigs [in] Zhang Zhung Phug-pa he magically alighted in Tibet. ([Tibetan year] 2513).

This quotation clarifies how sNya-chen Li-shu sTag-ring arrived in Tibet in the male Earth Monkey year (Tibetan year 1365, [second *sMe phreng* of the eighth *sMe 'khor*] 8/2) and together with the other quotes cited above permit us to understand the time frame.

A cosmological treatise that explains the condition of Existence, the *Srid pa'i mdzod phug* is an important text belonging to the Profound Inner Topics [*nang don rig pa*] series that was diffused in the Zhang/Bod region during the Intermediate Period. The text was first transmitted by gShen-rab Mi-bo-che to the gShen Tshangs-pa gTsug-phud-can and to others who had requested it. This transmission took place in the country of 'Ol-mo Lung-ring in a location situated to the southeast of Mount Kailash called 'Od-kyi lHa-ri sPo-mthon on the mountain known in the Zhang Zhung language as Shim-phod Ngad-ldan and in Tibetan as sPos-ri Ngad-ldan [Fragrant Incense Mountain].

Successively the text was transmitted by the gShen Tshangs-pa gTsug-phud to sPang-la Nam-gshen. The latter transmitted it to rGyal-gshen Mi-lus bSam-legs, A-nu Phrag-thag of Zhang Zhung, Sad-ne Ga'u of Zhang Zhung, Mu-khri bTsad-po, the Bonpo of Mon Ha-ra Ci-par, sTag-wer Li-wer, the Bonpo of China [rGya-bon] Zing-pa mThu-chen, sPe-bon Thog-rtse, sPe-bon Thog-'phrul, and Thi-mar Thad-ge. They transmitted it to the Eight Great Translators [Lo-tsā-ba Chen-po brGyad] who were sTong-rgyung mThu-chen of Zhang-zhung, Sha-ri dBu-chen of Tibet, Ne-rgyung [lCe-tsha] mKhar-bu of Me-nyag, lDe Gyim-tsha rMa-chung, Za-rang Me-'bar of sTag-gzigs, lHa-bdag sNgags-dro of India, Ngam-pa lCe-ring of Ge-sar, and Mu-spungs gSal-tang of Sum-pa.

As the colophon of the text and the history of the commentary clarify, Zhang Zhung sTong-rgyung mThu-chen and Bod Sha-ri dBu-chen completed the text, combining the sections containing both Zhang Zhung and Tibetan words, at gTsang-bye-ma situated in the border area between Zhang Zhung and Tibet on the heights of the Eighty-two Everlasting Springs. Although many commentaries to this text exist, the most noteworthy is certainly the one compiled by Bla-chen-po Dran-pa Nam-mkha' entitled *sGra 'grel 'phrul gyi lde mig*.

The *Legs bshad rin po che'i mdzod* affirms (Pe, 197, 23):

> As for the so-called Six Great Ornaments of the World [*'dzam bu gling gi rgyan chen po drug*], the *Byams ma* says:
> The sage of sTag-gzig, dMu-tsa Dra-he-pe, was expert in the five sciences. The sage of India, lHa-bdag sNgags-dro, was expert in the Profound Inner Topics [*nang rig pa*]. The sage of China, Legs-tang rMang-po, was expert in the Outer Topics [*phyi rig pa*].[142] The sage of Phrom, gSer-thog lCe-'byams, was expert in the healing arts. The sage of Zhang Zhung, Tso-min Gyer-rgyung, was expert in philology. The sages from Me-nyag and Tibet, Nam-ra [and] Co-sku, were experts in cosmology.
> There was not one field of knowledge that they did not understand or fully master; they knew how to translate the 360

---

142 [Doctrines in the Sūtras that gShen-rab Mi-bo-che taught to Kong-tse 'Phrul-rgyal. See Volume One, passim.]

idioms, and they were all endowed with magic feet [*rdzu 'phrul gyi zhabs dang ldan pa*]. Whether all six of them went to Tibet is not clear, although many [other] sages came into contact with them.

This excerpt tells us that at that time in the Zhang/Bod region masters and translators were present who were expert in various aspects of knowledge. Since that was true, it is clear that their expertise and the relevant cultural aspects were also flourishing in Tibet.

Most historical documents such as religious and dynastic sources relate that before the advent of the *dharmarāja* Srong-btsan sGam-po, the succession of Tibetan kings held power during the Intermediate Period with the support of *sGrung* [narrations], *lDe'u* [symbolic language], and *Bon*. Different statements acknowledge this fact. For example, the *rGyal po bka'i thang yig* says (Pe, 115, 6):

> The divine religious system of the *sGrung* and *lDe'u* appeared during the life of the ruler gNya'-khri bTsan-po.

In this case, *sGrung* and *lDe'u* are considered the religious system of the gods [*lha'i chos lugs*].

The *rGyal rabs gsal ba'i me long* says (Pe, 58, 4):

> Political affairs [were] implemented [through the] *sGrung*; the *lDe'u* were changed.

In this case, the *sGrung* appear to be the major safeguard for the maintenance of power.

The *lHo brag chos 'byung* affirms (Pe, Vol. One, 166, 9):

> Before this, for twenty-seven dynasties political affairs were protected by the *sGrung*, *lDe'u*, and *Bon*.

The above examples present ways of describing the protective role of the *sGrung*, *lDe'u*, and *Bon*.

Let us examine how the first element of this triad, the *sGrung*, was customarily identified. The *lHo brag chos 'byung* contains some indicative examples of *sGrung* (Pe, Vol. One, 164, 21):

sGrung were diffused to herald the Sūtra series. The tale of the [living] Corpse that [could] turn into gold, that of the Ma-sangs, that of the Sparrow,[143] and so on, were imparted and listened to.

Several other narrations exist, but the three examples mentioned here were considered a type of narration useful for opening the mind of the subjects and were classified as one category of *sGrung*; these, however, are just claims, since how could the ancient kings of Tibet have ruled [simply] by telling the tales of the Corpse that turns into gold, of the Ma-sangs, of the Sparrow, and so on, to ministers and subjects? Actually, all narrations that came from antiquity can be called *sGrung*. The numerous narratives in the Bonpo tradition about the lHa, Klu, gNyan, and Ma-sangs state that these beings originate from the primordial cosmic egg and control the force and power of the three worlds—namely, the sky, the earth and underworld, and the atmosphere—and that from them all human beings, and especially the progeny of Zhang/Bod, gradually came into existence: these narratives can aptly be defined *sGrung*. The tales about the Ma-sangs do not fall outside this category, as it is appropriate to identify as *sGrung* all the numerous histories of kings, ministers, and subjects of worldly descent that are related to them.

Concerning the so-called *lDe'u* the *lHo brag chos 'byung* affirms (Pe, Vol. One, 164, 23):

> lDe'u were used to introduce the Abhidharma series. It is said that the funerary mounds of Lhasa had inscriptions in the style of *lde'u, sgrung,* [and] *bon*, consisting of queries such as, "What [has a] big gullet [and] notch[-like] wrinkles," to indicate a set of scales, and "What is it [that] has a head that grows and increases," to indicate a *por mgo*,[144] and so on.

Analyzing those queries, we can see that they resemble the riddles that today are commonly identified as *khegs*. This viewpoint was formulated not only by the great scholar dPa'-bo gTsug-lag Phreng-ba (1504-

---

143 [That is, the narration of the Old Speckled Sparrow [*mchil rgan rgya bo'i sgrung*]. For these three tales see *Drung*, op cit, pp. 12-14, 14-16, and 16-19.]
144 [*por mgo (por*, head), *spo mgo* or *spo tho* refers to mounds of earth covered with grass. For these two riddles see *Drung*, op cit, n. 2, p. 231.]

1566) [who authored the *lHo brag chos 'byung*], but was also shared by the majority of the scholars of ancient history.

Since these types of riddles are considered effective in developing the level of skill of one's imagination, they represent the category known as *lde'u*. In this excerpt the great scholar dPa'-bo gTsug-lag, who also had this view, utilized easy to understand examples. However, although a case could be made for identifying the *lde'u* with the *khegs* of the present time, they do not have the same significance. Even though the two examples of easily understood riddles used by that renowned scholar dPa'-bo gTsug-lag were drawn from the language of Central Tibet of his time, more than five hundred years have elapsed since then and consequently also the structure of the language has undergone transformations; hence, those examples have now become difficult to interpret. For example the first one, "What [has a] big gullet [and] notch[-like] wrinkles," to indicate a set of scales, if expressed in other words becomes cryptic words to indicate a set of scales: "It has a big gullet and the rungs of [a] ladder. What is it?" The second, "What is it [that] has a head that grows and increases," to indicate a *por mgo*, becomes cryptic words to indicate a *spo tho* or *spo mgo* found above the ground: "It has a head, gradually grows, and becomes fatter. What is it?" It is evident that it is a matter of two different sentences combined, consisting of a question and an answer.

In some documents of later times the word *khegs* begins to be written *khed* which was simply a way of putting in writing the sound of the word on the basis of its pronunciation; actually the use of the word as *khegs* is well attested to in earlier documents; therefore, depending on the pronunciation is not necessary. As seeing smoke on a mountain top is an indirect indication of the presence of fire or seeing a seagull overhead is an indication of a nearby body of water, any illustrative sentence that has a hidden way of communicating the meaning of what is to be identified can be called a *khegs*. For example, "What is that small coral purse filled with gold coins?" is a question based on its visual presentation the answer to which is a chili pepper, the meaning of the object to be identified. This kind of sentence is called *khegs*.

The word lDe or lDe'u is an archaic term commonly used in Zhang Zhung and Tibet since ancient times. The correct meaning of this term, taking into consideration modern language usage, would be identical with the term *rig pa* [knowledge or intelligence], as it is referred to in the *Legs bshad rin po che'i gter*, "Study is a must even if one is to die on the morrow."[145] A particular reason for this affirmation is the inscription carved on the eastern side of the stele erected in the year 823 CE facing the main temple of Lhasa, which reads (line 5):

> The miraculous divine king, 'O-lde sPu-rgyal,

which is the name of the first king of Tibet. Similarly, the *Tun hong bod kyi lo rgyus yig rnying* [Old Tibetan Chronicles of Dunhuang] say (PT 1286, 44):

> lDe Nyag-khri bTsan-po.

And also (PT 1286, 53):

> [...] lDe-phru-bo gNam-gzhung-bstsan.
> The son of gNam-gzhung-bstsan [was] lDe-gol.
> The son of lDe-gol [was] gNam-lde rNol-nam.
> The son of gNam-lde rNol-nam [was] bSe'-rnol-po.
> The son of bSe-rnol-po [was] lDe rGyal-po.

And also (PT, 1286, 58):

> The son of Khri-snya Zung-bstsan and 'Bro'-za Dung-pyang-bzher [was] 'Bro-mnyen lDe-ru.

And also (PT 1286, 51):

> The son of Slon-btsan Rlung-nam and Tshes-pong-za 'Bring-ma-thog [was] Srong-lde-bstsan.

And also (PT 1286, 65):

---

145 *rig pa nang par 'chi yang bslab*. This passage is clarified in the *mkhas pa* section of the first chapter of the *Legs bshad rin po che'i gter*, Bod ljongs mi dmangs dpe skrun khang, 1982 (2, 18).

The son that 'Dus-srong Mang-po-rje had from his first wife, mChims-za bTsan-ma-thog, [was] Khri-lde gTsug-bstan.

The son that Khri-lde gTsug-bstan had from his fourth wife, sNa-nam-za' Mang-mo-rje, [was] Khri-srong lDe-bstsan.

As the excerpts indicate, the word *lDe* appears repeatedly in the names of Tibet's ancient kings. Examining it, we can conclude with certainty that it has a vast and deep meaning. Also ordinary Tibetan people customarily gave names with good and auspicious meanings to their boys and girls; this is a habit that has continued uninterrupted since ancient times. Accordingly, it is to be expected that each Tibetan king necessarily had a name that was extensive and profound in significance.

lDe'u, as for example in the case of *mi'u* that indicates a small man and *rte'u* that indicates a small horse, does not have any other meaning than that of small or low.

It is also possible that the terms *lde* and *lde'u* may be related to the word *lde'u mig*, which in the common Tibetan language indicates the key that opens the door of a house, and so forth. The word *sgo* [door] refers not only to the door of a house, but is also found in references to the three doors of body, speech and mind, although to open those doors, what other than pure knowledge can do that? The authentic meaning of *lde* and *lde'u*, its ordinary definition in ancient times, is that of a total state of vast and profound cognitive knowledge that opens the door of the mind. Furthermore, that term also indicates the understanding of a range of deeply significant symbolisms. An example is found in the *rDzogs pa chen po zhang zhung snyan rgyud kyi bon ma nub pa'i gtan tshig*, where we read (Dhi, 262, 2, 2,):

> sGron-legs-ma said: "The king of Zhang Zhung has an army that covers the earth. The king of Tibet has an army that could barely [cover] the center [of the back] of a mottled cow.[146] Therefore, [you] can not defeat [him] openly. But if [you wish to] defeat him by cunning and wickedness, next month[147] the king of Zhang Zhung [will leave] Zhang Zhung [and go] to

---

146 *ba bre mo'i gzhung*. Commonly the mingled black and white hair of horses, yaks, and so on, is called *gro bo*; this expression has the same meaning.

147 *zla ba phyi ta*. The expression means next month.

Glang-gi Gyim-shod [in] Sum-pa together with his entourage[148] to join an assembly. There, lie in ambush and kill him! I will tell you what to do." She spoke those words since she had no children and [thus] no interest to further.[149] It was decided that [she would] leave a sign of the exact date at the cairn [la-btsas][150] at the summit of the pass.

When the time came, the king arrived [at the place] together with his ministers and several thousand soldiers. He was the first to arrive at the cairn, accompanied by [the minister] sNang-nam Legs grub. When he looked, he saw a pan brimming with water, inside of which were three [objects]: a small piece of gold, a conch shell fragment, and a poisoned arrowhead. The King of Tibet said, "The pan full of water means that [the King of Zhang Zhung] will arrive on full moon of the next month. The small piece of gold and the conch shell fragment mean that we have to keep the soldiers in readiness for the ambush at the Gold and Conch Caves of Dwang-ra.[151] The poisoned arrowhead means that we should waylay [the King] and kill [him]." After he said [that], they prepared themselves.

The kind of knowledge demonstrated by the king of Tibet who interpreted the meaning of the objects clearly, as well as the intelligence demonstrated by sGron-lebs-ma in the choice of those objects as symbolic signs for transmitting secret information is called lde'u. lDe or lde'u similar to this one, the knowledge of which represented a necessary condition for ruling, was not the only variety used. The use of many other methods belonging to the lde or lde'u should be acknowledged,

---

148 *sku rkyen dang chas*. This has the same meaning as the modern expression "*sku bcar dang bcas*."
149 *bu med kyi blo*. Ordinarily this phrase could be interpreted as "a woman's way of thinking" [*bud med kyi bsam blo*], but if we examine the words that follow, "*ltos pa ci yang ma 'dod*," the meaning becomes "since she had no sons from the king, she had no hope of political power."
150 [A structure situated on a mountain pass composed of a mound of rocks into which are inserted long spears with prayer flags representing a support for the cult of mountain and local deities. Although the annual renewal of spears and prayer flags is a male prerogative, the event involves the entire village as well as local religious figures.]
151 [Situated on the northwestern side of Tibet.]

such as symbolic knowledge[152] needed to introduce secret and profound principal points, as well as the science of clairvoyance [*lde'u 'phrul mo'i rig pa*] that could distinguish without error the positive or negative aspects hidden in a given situation.

The third term *bon* can be identified with the different kinds of Bon that were diffused in Tibet since very early times: that is, with all the teachings of the Everlasting Bon [*g.yung drung bon*] expounded by gShen-rab Mi-bo-che when he went to Central Tibet from Zhang Zhung more than 3,900 years ago, which are known as the Four Doors of the Bon of the Deities [*lha bon sgo bzhi*]; and, in particular, with the Bonpo methods of the Twelve Lores that developed beginning in the era of the primeval Tibetan king, 'O-lde sPu-rgyal.

Some scholars of later times expressed views such as those contained in the *Deb ther dmar po* (Pe, 35, 3): "His son was gNam-ri Srong-btsan. During his time, medicine and astrology came from China" or in the *Ne'u sngon gtam* (Dha, 5, 3, 5), "During the time of gNam-ri Srong-btsan [and his consort] (Tshes-spong-gza' 'Bri-ma Tho-ga) astrology came from China," the claim being that before that time Tibet had no medical and astrological culture, an extremely narrow way of seeing. It is evident that the real purpose of those words was to laud an extraordinary astrological system that had come from China, the diffusion of which occurred at that time in Tibet.

The *rGyal rabs gsal ba'i me long* affirms (Pe, 58, 11):

> Furthermore, the essence of burned wood [is] charcoal. The essence of liquefied leather is glue. Stones containing iron, copper, and silver were found and by fusing them with charcoal, the production of iron, copper, and silver was assured. Holes were made in wood, and thus plows and wooden yokes were crafted. The yokes were hung around the necks [of animals], and furrows were plowed. When irrigation water was brought, seeds were sown. Before then, fields were not farmed.

Discussion of the use and knowledge of iron, copper, and silver, implies that the skill of forging precious materials by reducing them with

---

152 [*brda thabs kyi rig pa*. See the examples in *Drung*, op cit, pp. 30-34.]

charcoal had already developed. Surely that was the case because it is stated that 3,800 years ago the king of Zhang Zhung, Khri-wer gSergyi Bya-ru-can, who was a contemporary of gShen-rab Mi-bo-che, as well as King sTag-rna gZi-brjid, Holder of the Iron Horned Crown [Zom-shang lCags-kyi Bya-ru-can] and King Nye-lo Wer-ya, Holder of the Meteorite Lightning Horned Crown [gNam-lcags dBal-gyi Bya-ru-can],[153] had gold or iron helmets. Also, the ancient Bonpo cycle of the *Zhang zhung Me ri* mentions a vessel needed for boiling water called a *dbal zangs* [blazing copper], which was made, in fact, of copper.

The *rGyal rabs gser phreng* relates in general terms how government was managed at the time of 'O-lde sPu-rgyal (Dha, 200, 13, 2):

> It is narrated that the Lord was given the name gNya'-khri bTsad-po and that [he] ruled the area of Yar-lung Swo-ka. He resided at the castle of Phyi-dbang sTag-rtse. Power and law were the royal ornaments. His rule accorded with the religion and the kingdom was peaceful and happy. The four royal gShen[-pos][154] protected him. The forty-four lDong chiefs conquered foreign enemies with their military units.[155] The forty-four lDong units

---

153   [See Volume One, pp. 128-129.]
154   *sku srung sde bzhi*. The *Nyang gi chos 'byung* says (Bod, 160, 4), "The officiants [*rim gro ba*, persons who perform rituals to eliminate obstacles] of the king: the royal protectors Bon-po Co-na, gShen-gyi Phyag-gar-tsha, 'Tshe-mi, [and] gShen-bu rGyal-tsha." These are probably the four Bon-gShen who enthroned Lord gNya'-khri bTsan-po as king of Tibet.
155   *rgod ldong sde mi bzhi bcu rtsa bzhi*. The *lD'eu rgya bod kyi chos 'byung* says (Bod, 273, 3), "In those areas [there were] the so-called forty military units [of] one thousand [soldiers each]." The lHo brag chos 'byung says (Pe, Volume One, 185, 5), "They were divided into sixty-one military units [of] one thousand [soldiers each]." Also (ibid., 187, 9), "The great [A-]mdo area of mDo-khams [had] eight military units [of] one thousand [soldiers each]," and so on. As at the time of the *dharmarāja* Srong-btsan sGam-po when the army was divided into many units of one thousand men each, it would seem that also during the reign of Nyag-khri bTsan-po there were military units of one thousand soldiers each that together with their chiefs formed forty-four distinct units, and also that these units were subduing foreign enemies. However, the *lDe'u rgya bod kyi chos 'byung* says (Bod, 275, 11), "It is said that those who always conquered enemies were the lDong [and] the sTong, [while] the rMu and Se were unable [to do so] for generations." Ex-

settled disputes [among] the internal tribes.¹⁵⁶ At the four borders the boundaries of the land were established.¹⁵⁷

The eight garrisons [*khrom-kha*]¹⁵⁸ kept enemies distant from the borderlands. The twenty-two treasuries [of the twenty-two] fortresses¹⁵⁹ distributed resources. Precious stones from the twelve market places were offered. Courage was rewarded whereas cowardice was castigated.¹⁶⁰ By punishing mistakes, the source of deceit was annihilated. The five types of wisdom and bravery¹⁶¹ were recompensed with gold, turquoise, and emblems

---

amining this citation, we can understand that those military heroes were mostly from the A-spo-ldong and the sTong clans.

156   *g.yur ldong sde bzhi bcu rtsa bzhi*. This indicates that the military units of one thousand soldiers each were equally divided among the internal tribes, and that together with their chiefs, they formed forty-four divisions. The use of the term *lDong* indicates that the majority of the soldiers and chiefs belonged to the A-spo-ldong lineage.

157   *so kha bzhi*. The *lDe'u chos 'byung chen mo* affirms (Bod, 111, 16), "Therefore, Tibet had eight borders [*so kha*] [distinguished] by [the following] areas [*rong kha*]: the border between China and Tibet was defined by the area of the rGod-snyan valley; the border between Zhang Zhung and Tibet was defined by the Zhang-po brGya-bcu area; the border between Tibet and Bon was established when the iron peg was planted; the border between sTag-gzigs and Tibet was defined by the Shab-shang brGya-bcu area; the border between Hor and Tibet was defined by the Zangs-thang Sha'i-gling area; the border between Khrom and Tibet was defined by the rGya-shar area; and the border between 'Jang [present day Lijiang, in Yunnan Province, China] and Tibet was defined by the Ra-ga area. In this way, the eight borders marked the [extent of] Tibetan territory." Just as Tibet had eight borders at the time of the *dharmarāja* Srong-btsan, we can understand that four great borders existed at the time of Nyag-khri bTsan-po.

158   *khrom kha brgyad*. According to the *lDe'u rgya bod kyi chos 'byung* (Bod, 264, 1), these were: "In Upper Tibet [sTod], the three big garrisons of Dru-zha, Dru-gu, and Bal-po; in Lower Tibet [sMad], the three garrisons of Gar-log, Rong-rong, and lDan-ma; in Central Tibet [dBus], the two garrisons of lDong [and] sTong."

159   *rong dor khab so nyi shu rtsa gnyis*. This means that twenty-two fortresses or lookout posts were to be found in the center of localities situated in strategic places and in the border areas.

160   *legs nyes kyi bya dgas*. Good people received rewards and bad ones, punishments.

161   *mdzangs sna lnga*. The *lDe'u chos 'byung chen mo* says (Bod, 114, 4), "Emblems of rank [were bestowed] for wisdom and bravery." The *lDe'u rgya bod kyi chos 'byung* says (Bod, 276, 4), "If the wise and brave are not gratified with emblems of rank, the interest in pursuing these two virtues will diminish." The concept expressed here

of rank. The five types of heroism[162] were acknowledged with lion, leopard, and tiger ornaments. The five types of speed[163] were practiced in horse riding, and [people] took delight in horse racing. The law of the Lord shone like the sun on snow. As a challenge the palace of 'Om-bu Bla-sgang was erected. Robbers were ousted and falsehood discarded; selling and profit were monitored. Since the whole kingdom was at peace and all the vassals were happy, good aspects such as these flourished, and [living] in the motherland was agreeable.

Since the *rGyal rabs gser phreng* was written by Kaḥ-thog Rig-'dzin Tshe-dbang Nor-bu (1698-1755), it is not an old text, although the author certainly collected the material in this excerpt from several old sources. This can be observed in the rhythm of the words and because some points are difficult to interpret in the places where the way the syllables are written is not in harmony with the meaning of the sentences.

Thus, the sentences of the above-cited excerpt, "*sKu* **bsrungs** *sde bzhi'i sku bsrungs / rgod ldong sde mi bzhi bcu rtsa* **bzhi'i** *phyi'i dgra* **'dul** */* **g.yur** *ldong sde bzhi bcu rtsa* **bzhi'i** *ni nang gi* **tsha** *kha snyoms / so kha* **bzhir** *ni so* **'dzugs**" should be interpreted as "*sKu* **srung** *sde* **bzhis** *sku bsrungs / rgod ldong sde mi bzhi bcu rtsa* **bzhis** *phyi'i dgra* **btul** */* **g.yul** *ldong sde bzhi bcu rtsa* **bzhis** *ni nang gi* **tsho** *kha snyoms / so kha* **bzhi ru** *ni so* **btsugs**."

The same applies to, "*Legs nyes kyi bya* **dar dpa' 'dzangs** *kyi shan 'byed / nongs kyi* **chad pas** *ngan g.yo'i khungs* **snubs** */* **'dzangs** *sna* **lngas** *gser g.yu dang yig tshang gis* **stod** */ dpa' sna* **lngas** *seng ge dang gung stag gis brgyan / mgyogs sna* **lngas phyibs** *mdzas nas rgyugs su spro*" which have to be read as, "*Legs nyes kyi bya* **dgar** *dpa'* **mdzangs** *kyi shan 'byed / nongs kyi* **chad par** *ngan g.yo'i khungs*

---

is similar to the one found in "The Eight Wise and Brave Tibetans" who obtained no rewards, a story set in the time of Dharmarāja Srong-btsan.

162   *dpa' sna lnga*. The *lDe'u rgya bod kyi chos 'byung* (Bod, 269, 3) affirms that, "The five types of heroism are: the virtue of the hero is to suppress enemies; the virtue of the wise and brave [is] to position themselves in the forefront of the government; the virtue of the orator [is] to successfully present reasoning; the virtue of the fierce is great courage; the virtue of the accumulator [of riches] is risking generosity."

163   *mgyogs sna lnga*. As in the case of the heroes that obtained recognition, this means that five kinds of rewards existed for skills shown in speed or running during horse racing.

bsnubs / mdzangs sna lngar gser g.yu dang yig tshang gis bstod / dpa' sna lngar seng ge dang gung stag gis brgyan / mgyogs sna lngar chibs mdzad nas rgyugs su spro." The *gSer phreng* also says (Dha, 202, 14, 4):

> The son of Tho-tho Re-long-btsan [and] sMan-tsha Glu-rgyal [was] Khri-btsan. During this time, self-defense [*bsrung*] and rights [*ldem*] spread.

bSrung and *ldem* mean that legalities were established at that time in order to discourage negative actions such as killing, stealing, or the robbing of other people's property, and to sanction the right of ownership of fields, of individual household possessions, and so forth. We also read (ibid., 203, 15, 2):

> At the time of Khri-snyan bZung-btsan, animal husbandry and the plowing of fields existed; dams were built on the lakes in order to collect water for irrigation; and by damming the streams at night, the water [accumulated] would be drawn [for irrigation] during the day. The son of Khri-snyan bZung-btsan was 'Brang-snyan lDe-ru. The son of 'Brang-snyan lDe-ru [was] sTag-ri sNyan-gzigs. During the time of this king, hybrids of yaks and cattle [*mdzo*], and [hybrids of horses and donkeys] mules [*dre'u*] were created, the value of the cattle was fixed, mountain herbs were woven into wreaths, and so on.

Statements such as these are followed by others declaring that all the above-mentioned forms of civilization and the relevant activities started from nothing at that time. What certainty can there be in making such an affirmation? The same observation that dPal Sa-skya Paṇḍita Kun-dga' rGyal-mtshan [1182-1251] made to his teacher and paternal uncle, dPal Sa-skya-pa Grags-pa rGyal-mtshan [1146-1216] could be made here: when the latter addressed words of praise to him, he responded, "The object of praise can also be the locus of criticism." As scriptures and reasoning convince us, various forms of the Zhang Zhung civilization had permeated the whole of Tibet for more than 3,800 years.

3. Royal Castles of Ancient Tibet

The level of civilization reached by the Tibetan people during the Intermediate Period became of great significance, as demonstrated by the palaces and castles gradually erected by the Tibetan kings, and also by the temples built jointly by the kings and their royal gShen-pos. A list of the temples built jointly by the latter, the names of the temples constructed individually, and so on, can be found in Chapter Two of this volume, where the origin of the Bonpo lineages of ancient Tibet is discussed.

Concerning the name of the castle erected by the first Tibetan king 'O-lde sPu-rgyal/gNya'-khri bTsan-po, the *lDe'u rgya bod kyi chos 'byung* says (Bod, 237, 21):

> Then, after [he] erected the castle [of] Yun-bu Bla-sgang, [he] conquered the king of Sum-pa-shang, prodigious feats.

The excerpt clarifies the way in which Nyag-khri bTsan-po not only erected the castle of Yum-bu Bla-sgang, but also powerfully subdued Sum-pa. The *Yar lung jo bo'i chos 'byung* says (Si, 40, 2):

> As a challenging enterprise, the castle [of] Yum-bu Bla-sgang was erected during the time of this king.

The *rGyal rabs gsal ba'i me long* says (Pe, 55, 11):

> That was the first king of Tibet. He erected the palace [of] 'Um-bu Glang-mkhar.

The *lHo brag chos 'byung* says (Pe, Vol. One, 160, 1):

> He became known by the name gNya'-khri bTsan-po. [He] created the first castle [of] Yum-bu Bla-sgang.

The *Deb ther dpyid kyi rgyal mo'i glu dbyangs* says (Pe, 12, 17):

> This Lord erected the palace [of] Yum-bu Bla-sgang.

As we can see, even if the ways of writing the name of the castle built by gNya'-khri bTsan-po differ—Yun-bu Bla-sgang, Yum-bu Bla-sgang, and 'Um-bu Glang-mkhar—the majority of Tibetan religious and dynastic histories agree on the fact that he built it.

In the *Srid pa rgyud kyi kha byang* we also read (Thob, 78, 40, 4):

> The Lord went to Yar-lung Sog-ka, and resided happily at the castle [of] Phyi-ba sTag-rtse.

The excerpt states that the first Tibetan king resided at the castle called Phyi-ba sTag-rtse, meaning that a castle called Phyi-ba sTag-rtse existed prior to the construction of the Yum-bu Bla-sgang palace. Most probably this was a castle built by the Bonpos of the Lores, such as the great gShen-pos sNang-ba'i mDog-can, Byams-ma lTar-na, sGom-lha-bo lHa-sras, and so on. It is also possible that it was a place of residence, such as that described in the *bKa'chems ka khol ma*, making it compatible with the ancient customs of Tibetan nomads (Kan, 84, 8):

> The Lord gNya'-khri bTsan-po arrived at [the location] situated in bTsan-thang sGo-bzhi [of] the Yar-lung [valley], and raised a palace. The palace was not built with earth and stones. [He] pitched a tent made with the skins of [herbivorous] wildlife, animals [such as] deer and yaks[164] and of carnivorous animals [like] tigers [and] leopards.

Most religious and dynastic histories use clear terminology when they talk about erecting a castle or palace, for example, *pho brang* or *sku mkhar brtsigs*, which is to be understood as a palace built with stones and earth. On the contrary, the original terminology to describe the building of a palace made of various kinds of skin and leather is unknown, demonstrated by the fact that the text just quoted indicates "raised a palace" [*pho brang btab*], and not "constructed a palace" [*pho brang brtsigs*].

In any case, the name of the place called Phyi-ba sTag-rtse or Phying-ba sTag-rtse and that of the castle called mKhar [castle] Phyi-ba sTag-rtse or mKhar Phying-ba sTag-rtse cannot be considered to be the same. Similarly, the name of the castle called Pho-brang [palace] Yum-bu Bla-sgang and the name that simply refers to the place called

---

164 ['*brong*: Bos grunniens, Linnaeus 1766.]

Yum-bu Bla-sgang are mutually exclusive, demonstrated by what the *lDe'u chos 'byung chen mo* says (Bod, 102, 4):

> Then [he] went to Yum-bu Bla-sgang. From the beginning, this construction was much higher [than others], [and to demonstrate its greater importance, its] administrators [were] lHo and sNyag. Then [he] traveled to Phying-ba sTag-rtse, and pitched a tent [made with] nine layers of white silk.

The *rGyal rabs 'phrul gyi lde mig* says (Dhi, 7, 12, 4):

> At that point Lord gNya'-khri bTSan-po himself arrived at Yar-lung Sog-kha. The palace 'Um-bu Glang-mkhar was erected. That was the first palace of Tibet.

If we compare the excerpts, the basic difference of the constructions becomes visible.

The Yum-bu Bla-sgang palace

Concerning the construction of castles, palaces, and other buildings carried out by the royal generations of the Intermediate Period that gradually succeeded King 'O-lde sPu-rgyal/gNya'-khri bTsan-po, the *Yar lung jo bo'i chos 'byung* says (Si, 45, 5):

> During the time of the son sPu-lde Gung-rgyal, the royal castle of 'Ching-nga rTag-rtse was erected.

The name of the castle 'Ching-nga rTag-rtse mentioned here is written in different ways in other documents: Phyi-ba sTag-rtse, Phying-ba sTag-rtse, or 'Ching-ba sTag-rtse, and it should be understood that these names refer all to the same castle. This is demonstrated by the *lHo brag chos 'byung*, which says (Pe, Vol. One, 163, 17):

> The royal castle 'Ching-ba sTag-rtse was erected. The construction of the Sham-po-mkhar was leveled, and then became the foundation [for the new castle]

and by the *Deb ther dpyid kyi rgyal mo'i glu dbyangs*, which affirms (Pe, 13, 16):

> During the time of the son (sPu-de Gung-rgyal) the royal castle Phying-ba sTag-rtse was erected.

The *lHo brag chos 'byung* says that the construction of Sham-po-mkhar was leveled and then became the foundation of the Phying-ba sTag-rtse castle that was built by King sPu-de Gung-rgyal. This occurred because Tri-rgyal Lo-ngam, having killed his father, King Gri-gum bTsan-po, seized power for twelve full years and Sham-po-mkhar was his palace. This can be understood by the following quotation taken from the *Yar lung chos 'byung* (Si, 44, 9):

> Then Ru-la-skyes surreptitiously introduced himself into a vulture's nest situated on the mountain where the castle Nyang-ro Sham-po stood, and imitating a vulture, flung himself onto the roof of the castle, and from there descended inside. He killed Lo-ngam's male retinue by crushing their chests with a pan and suffocated his female retinue with a copper vessel. He [also] killed all the young by hurling them against the rocks. The construction of the Sham-po-mkhar was leveled and became the foundation of the royal castle 'Ching-nga sTag-rtse.

Some historical sources, such as the *bKa' chems ka khol ma*, claim that the royal castle Phying-ba sTag-rtse was built during the time of the Six Legs kings (Kan, 89, 5):

> During the time (of the Six *Legs*), the royal castle Phying-ba sTag-rtse and the so-called Six Tops [rTse-drug][165] were erected.

Furthermore, the *rGyal rabs gser phreng* says (Dha, 202, 14, 1):

> His son [was] I-sho-legs. This king erected the palace Phyi-dbang sTag-rtse. That was the first royal palace to be built.

According to this source, I-sho-legs not only erected the palace Phyi-dbang sTag-rtse or Phying-ba sTag-rtse, but that it was also the first royal palace or castle to be built.

The *rGyal rabs gser phreng* discusses the deeds of gNya'-khri bTsan-po, saying (Dha, 200, 13, 2):

> [He] was named Lord gNya'-khri bTsad-po; [he] seized the area of Yar-lung Swo-ka. He resided at the castle Phyi-dbang sTag-rtse.

This means that at that time a castle called Phyi-dbang sTag-rtse existed. The text also affirms (ibid., 200, 13, 6):

> As [one of his] accomplishments, [he] erected the palace 'Om-bu Bla-sgang.

Declaring that the construction of ancient palaces started at that time and that the palace or castle built at the time of the Six *Legs* was the first one could appear as a contradiction if it is not clarified that the *gSer phreng* must really intend that I-sho-legs expanded the previously existing castle Phyi-dbang sTag-rtse by enlarging the building with new sections. For this reason the author uses the name Phyi-dbang sTag-rtse. Since the expansion of the palace is the first to be mentioned in the dynastic histories of the so-called Six *Legs* of the Earth [Sa-la Legs-drug], it is said that, "It was the first palace or castle to be built." Otherwise, there would be no way to understand the seemingly contradictory words of the great scholar who authored the text.[166]

The names of the Six Mountain-Peak Royal Castles [sKu-mkhar rTse-drug] erected during the time of the Six *Legs* and the names of

---

165 [See explanation below.]
166 [Kaḥ-thog Rig-'dzin Tshe-dbang Nor-bu (1710-1755).]

the kings who built them are found in the *lDe'u rgya bod kyi chos 'byung* (Bod, 248, 12):

> Owing to the kindness of the Six *Legs*, six castles [*phying*[167] *sa rtse drug*] were built: Phying-sa sTag-rtse; g.Yu-rtse (by The-sho); dBu-rtse (by Gur-bu); Khri-rtsig; 'Bum-stug (by 'Bro-bzhi); mThong-rtse (by I-sho).

The opinion presented in the text was that the first of the Six *Legs* was Sho-leg; therefore, he was the one who built Phying-sa sTag-rtse/Phying-ba sTag-rtse. We can also infer from the in-text notes that the fifth one, The-sho-legs, built the g.Yu-rtse castle; the third one, Gur-bu, or Gor-bu-legs, built the dBu-rtse castle; the fourth one, 'Bro-bzhi-legs, built the 'Bum-stug castle; and the sixth one, I-sho-legs, built the mThong-rtse castle. The text does not mention the castle built by the second king, De-sho-legs, but we can deduce that it was the Khri-rtsig castle because it appears in the list of the six castles and also because the *lHo brag chos 'byung* says the following about the six castles erected by the Six *Legs* (Pe, Vol. One, 165, 12):

> During the time of these Six [kings], six castles [*'ching ba*[168] *rtse drug*] were erected. These were: sTag-rtse, rGod-rtse, Yang-rtse, Khri-rtse, rTse-mo Khyung-rgyal, [and] Khri-brtsigs 'Bum-gdugs.

As the meaning infers, what is here called sTag-rtse corresponds to the Phying-sa sTag-rtse of the *lDe'u rgya bod kyi chos 'byung*; Yang-rtse corresponds to g.Yu-rtse; rGod-rtse to dBu-rtse; Khri-rtse to Khri-rtsig; Khri-brtsigs 'Bum-gdugs to 'Bum-stug; and rTse-mo Khyung-rgyal to mThong-rtse.

---

167 [Literally, felt.]
168 [Literally, ropes.]

VI

Kings, gShen-pos, and Bonpos of Zhang Zhung

An understanding of the roles of kings, gShen-pos, and Bonpos of Zhang Zhung during the Intermediate Period must necessarily be based on the history that begins with the dominion of King sTag-rna gZi-brjid Khri-ldem lCags-kyi Bya-ru-can [Holder of the Iron Horned Crown], the last of the famous Eighteen Bya-ru-can kings of Zhang Zhung.

1. KING STAG-RNA GZI-BRJID

The *Gangs ti se'i dkar chag tshangs dbyangs yid 'phrog* says (IsMEO, 24, 3):

> The sage [*drang srong*] Ye-shes rGyal-ba explained the teaching on Emptiness to the community of sixty thousand Bodhisattvas [*g.yung drung sems dpa'*] [and] Arhats [*dgra bcom*] next to the great Ghandha stūpa of the city of sTag-rna-gling, [situated] at the foothill of [the mountain] sPo-ri Ngad-ldan in Zhang Zhung. At that time, the ruling monarch was King sTag-rna gZi-brjid Khri-ldem lCags-kyi Bya-ru-can [who resided] in the fortified castle sTag-rna-dbal in the center of the city of sTag-gling on the foothill of sPos[-ri] Ngad-ldan [in] the Zhang Zhung Tsi-na region.

> Accordingly, the disciple of Ye-shes rGyal-ba, the sage called dBal-gyi dBang-phyug, spread the Vinaya teachings widely in the country of Tibet.

The excerpt clarifies how the sage dBal-gyi dBang-phyug spread the Vinaya teachings in Tibet in the second half of King sTag-rna gZi-brjid's life. This occurred when the Seven *Khri* of the Sky [gNam-gyi Khri-bdun] were ruling Tibet. In this respect, the *rTsa rgyud nyi sgron* says (Thob, 301, 149, 1):

> They were called the Seven *Khri* of the Sky. Each king had a Bon/gShen that acted as his royal protector. For this reason, the might of the Bon/gShen was great. At that time, the four [Bon/gShen] Ga-chu, Ya-gong, Phams-shi, [and] lDe-btsun built four large monastic complexes in four important locations [with] deity temples, protector chapels, and stūpas.

This shows that Ga-chu, Ya-gong, Pham-shi, and lDe-btsun were four key figures of the Vinaya teaching in the Bon tradition, a fact confirmed by the *Dar rgyas gsal sgron gyi lo rgyus kun gsal*, which says (Si, 159, 6):

> As for the Vinaya: the gShen-po of Zhang-zhung, gTsug-phud Tshul-khrims, had four disciples. These were Ga-chu gTsug-phud rGyal-mtshan, sPa-gong Ye-shes rGyal-mtshan, Pham-shi dPal-gyi dBang-phyug, [and] lDe-btsun Rab-gsal.

King sTag-rna gZi-brjid was the surrogate father of the great Bon/gShen Li-shu sTag-ring. The *Gangs ti se'i dkar chag tshangs dbyangs yid 'phrog* describes the way in which the king of Zhang Zhung Tsi-na, Khri-ldem lCags-kyi Bya-ru-can, made him his surrogate son (IsMEO, 26, 3):

> In Zhang Zhung Tsi-na on the foothill of sPos-ri Ngad-ldan in the center of the city of sTag-rna-gling in the fortified castle called sTag-rna-dbal, King sTag-rna gZi-brjid, the emanation of the great deity Yongs-su dGa'[-ba] [Complete Joy], and [his] consort called Khyung-lcem g.Yung-drung dGe-ldan-ma were living amidst retinues and riches, but did not have a son. Once, when the royal couple and the ministers had gone to the Brag[-dmar] Rin-chen sPungs-pa forest, [situated] on the southern side of Lake Mu-le-khyud, to collect flowers to offer to the

Enlightened Ones, the father picked a blue lotus with eight-petals and discovered a splendid, real baby girl inside. Amazed, he offered her to the mother. This auspicious child was given the name 'Chi-med sPrul-pa Bon-mo sTag-za Li-wer. Furthermore, because a priestess [*bon mo*] had performed a ritual on the most sacred mountain, the girl was transformed into a boy who became known as sNya-chen Li-shu sTag-ring.

Nevertheless, sTag-rna gZi-brjid rGyal-po Khri-ldem lCags-kyi Bya-ru-can is not the actual personal name of a king, but rather an important title referring to the king who was the lord of the sTag-rna-dbal fortified castle. For this reason, the *Tshangs dbyangs yid 'phrog* (IsMEO, 23, 2) in discussing a king of Zhang Zhung sTag-rna who was the main patron of the sage called rDzu-'phrul Ye-shes, the fourth lineage-holder before Sage Ye-shes rGyal-ba, says:

> The sage called rDzu-'phrul Ye-shes expounded the teaching to a community of several thousand Arhats and Bodhisattvas [who were gathered at] La-mor rDo-yi Khang-bu'i-gling, [situated] on the eastern side of Zhang Zhung sPos[-ri] Ngad-ldan. At that time, the king was sTag-rna gZi-brjid rGyal-po Khri-ldem lCags-kyi Bya-ru-can, [who resided] in the fortified castle called sTag-rna-dbal, [located] in the center of the city of sTag-rna-gling, on the foothill of sPos-ri Ngad-ldan in the area of Zhang Zhung Tsi-ṇa.

The year in which sNya-chen Li-shu sTag-ring was born was two hundred years after the birth date of gShen-rab Mi-bo-che and corresponds to the female Water Sheep year (200 BCE) of the first *sMe-phreng* of the second *sMe-'khor*. This dating has already been discussed in relation to the Bon lineages of the Early Period.[169]

Concerning the succession in the lineage of the king called sTag-rna gZi-brjid rGyal-po gZha'-tshon 'Od-kyi Bya-ru-can [Holder of the Rainbow Light Horned Crown] who was the patron of Sage Ye-shes rGyal-ba and resided in the sTa-rna-dbal fortified castle of Zhang Zhung Tsi-ṇa, the various sources that I have consulted have not contained information about the history of each dynastic lineage. However,

---

169 [See Volume One, p. 124.]

the *Bon gyi bstan 'byung nyung bsdus* presents a partial sequence (Thob, 624, 36, 3):

> Last [came] Khri-ldem lCags-kyi Bya-ru-can and Mu-wer sTag-sna rGyal-po (the latter at the time of the Tibetan king gNya'-khri). Then [came] Mu-wer Khri-'od-gsal, (the *Ge-khod* says so); Mu-khung gNam-rje; Mu-wer Seng-ge-'gram; [and] Mu-la Khyung-gi rGyal-po (*Me-ri*, *Ge-khod*, and so on, say so). Another lineage [presents] Mu-wer bTsad-po Lig-mi-skya, Mu-la Gung-sang-rje, gShen rGyung-yar Mu-khod, and so on, [as] kings of Central Zhang Zhung [Zhang Zhung dBus] while still another indicates that many [other] minor kings appeared, [such as] La-dwags rGyal-po, Shang-pa'i rGyal-po, Se-reb rGyal-po, and so on.

2. Mu-wer bTsad-po

Concerning the ruler Mu-wer bTsad-po, the *rTsa rgyud nyid sgron* says (Thob, 302, 149, 1):

> Of the four appointed kings, the king of the Bon/gShen was Mu-wer bTsad-po Li-mi-rgya. At that time, the five gShen-pos of Tibet met six great scholars trained in the wisdom lineage [initiated] by Mu-cho, five of whom were Zhang Zhung sTong-rgyung mThu-chen, Se Sha-ri dBu-chen, lDe Gyim-tsha rMa-chung, Me-nyag lCe-kha [*sic*] mKhar-bu, [and] Sum-pa Mu-spungs gSal-tang. [They also] requested oral and secret transmissions from all the Siddhas [of] important sacred places. Interpreters clarified uncertainties about the teachings. [Texts containing] external, internal, and secret instructions of scriptural, tantric, [and] quintessential nature, [such as] the Tripiṭaka, subjugating mantras, teachings of the secret formulas [related to] the tutelary deities, [and those on] the Nature of the Mind [*sems don*] were loaded on buffaloes, wild asses,[170] camels, and elephants, [and] arrived in Tibet after crossing ravines, rivers, [and] mountains passes. First Zhang Zhung [sTong-rgyung

---

170 *ku hrang*. This is written here in the Zhang Zhung language, the Tibetan equivalent of which is *sha rkyang*, the Tibetan wild ass [Equus hemionus, Onager].

mThu-chen translated from his language; then the scholars] Se [Sha-ri dBu-chen], lDe [Gyim-tsha rMa-chung], Me-nyag [lCe-kha mKhar-bu], [and] Sum-pa [Mu-spungs gSal-tang] translated the Bon language in the languages of their own places.

The excerpt clarifies how at the time of Mu-wer bTsad-po Li-mi-rgya there were six great scholars such as sTong-rgyung mThu-chen, and so on, from whom the five gShen-pos of Tibet requested cycles of Bon teachings, many of which were brought into Tibet loaded on buffaloes, wild asses, camels, and elephants; and how Zhang Zhung sTong-rgyung mThu-chen first translated from the language of Zhang Zhung in another one, and on that basis, Se Sha-ri dBu-chen, lDe Gyim-tsha rMa-chung, Me-nyag lCe-kha mKhar-bu, and Sum-pa Mu-spungs gSal-tang translated the teachings into their own languages. The text also says (ibid., 302, 149, 5):

At that time in Khyung-lung mNgul-mkhar of Zhang Zhung, Dran-pa Nam-mkha' was born.

As the excerpt states, at the time of Mu-wer bTsad-po Li-mi-rgya the great teacher [*bla chen po*] Dran-pa Nam-mkha' was born. These examples show that at the time of those great Bonpos and gShen-pos the kingdom of Zhang Zhung was under the dominion of Mu-wer bTsad-po.

3. The Bon gShen-po Dran-pa Nam-mkha'

Some scholars who have researched Tibetan history claim that the Bla-chen-po Dran-pa Nam-mkha' cited above is the same individual as the eighth century CE figure. About this, the *Tshangs dbyangs yid 'phrog* says (IsMEO, 34, 7):

The great teacher Dran-pa of Zhang Zhung, and the infant [khye'u] Dran-pa of Tibet do have the same name, but stating that they are the same [person] is possibly an error.

Furthermore, when Guru Rinpoche Padmasambhava went to Tibet, there was a Bon gShen-po called Dran-pa Nam-mkha' who later became one of his twenty-five disciples, and who could be confused with the great teacher Dran-pa Nam-mkha' of Zhang Zhung except for the fact that the latter could not have lived in the eighth century. He cannot be the disciple of Guru Padmasambhava, the Dran-pa Nam-mkha' alive during the time of the *dharmarāja* Khri-srong lDe'u-btsan (Tibetan years 2659-2714 or 742-797 CE), as the Dran-pa Nam-mkha' of Zhang Zhung authored the famous Bon text called *sGra'grel* at an earlier time. Therefore, it is not possible to confuse him even chronologically with the Dran-pa Nam-mkha' of Tibet. The certainty that it is the Bla-chen Dran-pa Nam-mkha' of Zhang Zhung is found in the history of the texts of the *gSas-mkhar spyi-spungs* cycle that all contain numerous teachings of his. An idea about the way in which the great teacher Dran-pa Nam-mkha' was born is related in the *sGra 'grel*, which says (Dhi, 3, 2):

> The father was rGyung-yar Mu-khod; the mother was Phya-btsun Gung-ma. They did not have children. Having arrived in the presence of the eight great translators and teachers, the couple [*stangs dbyal*] offered loads of the six grains [*'bras drug*][171] and of the three white and sweet substances[172] to an elephant with a gold ring in its nose. The father said: "We [as a] couple are not destitute [in terms of] food and riches. However, we do not have an heir.[173] If this is because it would not be beneficial in this life and the next one, so be it. If, on the contrary, it would be beneficial in this life and the next, we look forward to receiving your advice." Thus they made their request.

And also (ibid., 4, 11):

> Then the mother generated a son marked with superior signs. Since the father and the mother gave him names according to [their interpretations of] the [song of the] cuckoo,[174] he was

---

171 [*'bras drug*: barley, rice, wheat, beans, buckwheat, and millet.]
172 [*dkar gsum mngar gsum*: milk, butter, and curd; sugar, honey, and molasses.]
173 *chu srid 'dzin pa'i dmar dod med. Chu srid* corresponds to *chus srid* [administrative unit or political district] in current language; *dmar dod* may indicate a [patrilineal] descent line belonging to a certain lineage.
174 *bya khu byug gis mtshan khong nas btags.* The meaning of this expression is clarified in the *sGra 'grel* (Dhi, 4, 3): "Once, in the ninth month, a cuckoo, king of birds, alighted inside the She-le fortified castle. The cuckoo emitted three sounds that were interpreted in three different ways. With the first sound, the father

also called Khye'u-skye-ba Dran-pa'i Nam-mkha' and rGyung-yar Bla-chen Khod-spungs.

An excerpt that is even clearer and more articulate than the last two is found in the *Tshangs dbyangs yid 'phrog*, where we read (IsMEO, 24, 6):

> In the big city of rGyal-ba mNyes-pa [situated at] Khyung-lung dNgul-mkhar in the country of Zhang Zhung, the emanation of Tshad-med 'Od-ldan, rGyung-yar Mu-khod rGyal-po gZha'-tshon 'Od-kyi Bya-ru-can [Holder of the Rainbow Light Horned Crown] and the emanation of Zangs-za Ring-btsun, Phya-btsun Gung-ma, had perfect riches and dominions, but they did not have a son.

And also (ibid., 25, 3):

> The year after that, the mother gave birth. When the child was three months old, he [already] remembered [his] five hundred [past] lives that had been devoted exclusively to the benefit of sentient beings. He was also called Dran-pa Nam-mkha', Mind Emanation of 'Chi-med ['*chi med thugs sprul*].[175]

These excerpts show that the great master Dran-pa Nam-mkha' was born as the son of a king of Zhang Zhung and also that he was the descendant of rGyung-yar Mu-khod rGyal-po gZha'-tshon 'Od-kyi Bya-ru-can, the last of the eighteen secular kings of Zhang Zhung to hold the powerful *Bya-ru* title. With respect to the specific name of the great master Dran-pa Nam-mkha', that is, rGyung-yar Bla-chen

---

heard that 'the clear light of the sun and the moon would shine together,' while the mother understood that 'a lamp that would dispel darkness would appear.' With the middle sound, the father heard that 'the axle [*srog shing*] of Everlasting Bon would be established,' while the mother heard that 'the big hammer that would defeat perverse views had come.' With the last sound the father heard that 'the recollection [*dran pa*] of before and after was in the sky [*nam mkha'*]', while the mother heard 'it is rGyung-yar Bla-chen Khod-spungs.'"
175 ['Chi-med gTsug-phud is sometimes considered an earlier divine incarnation of gShen-rab Mi-bo-che. Zangs-za Ring-btsun is the mother of 'Chi-med gTsug-phud.]

Khod-spungs, the excerpts also show that this name is based upon [his father's name], which was rGyung-yar.

When the great master Dran-pa Nam-mkha' was born and Zhang Zhung was under the rule of King rGyung-yar Mu-khod, eight great scholars were extremely famous in the Zhang Zhung kingdom. After King rGyung-yar Mu-khod and his consort met with those great scholars and requested a method for having a son, the royal couple was blessed with the extraordinary birth of Bla-chen-po Dran-pa Nam-mkha'. General information about those scholars is found in the *sGra 'grel* (Dhi, 2, 15):

> Formerly, [near] the forest of A-pa-ra trees [situated in] the I-sho Da-na region of Zhang Zhung, in the center of the city of rGyal-ba-mnyes, also called mKhar Khyung-lung dNgul-ma-mā as well as 'Om-po sGo-bzhi, eight great scholars who became translators and masters [and who were the disciples of] the great scholar Da-mi Thad-ge and of others like him, resided in the pavilion [called] Radiating Light of the Lotus Flower. These were: Zhang Zhung sTong-rgyung mThu-chen; Bod Sha-ri dBu-can; lDe Gyim-tsha rMa-chung; Me-nyag Ne-rgyung 'Phar-bu; sTag-gzigs Za-rang Me-'bar; Sum-pa Kha-yam rLung-lce; Ge-sar Ngam-pa lCe-ring; and sTangs-chen dMu-tsa Gyer-med. Moreover, [also] rKyel-thur, Khye-nan Yo-phya, and many others resided [there].

Needless to say, during the Intermediate Period the above-mentioned Bon scholars or gShen-pos were renowned.

A reason for concluding that the time in which Bla-chen-po Dran-pa Nam-mkha' appeared corresponds to the first part of the Intermediate Period is provided in the commentary to the *gSang ba bsen thub*, the *Rin po che yid bzhin rnam par bkod pa'i rgyan*, which states (Thob, 50, 25, 1):

> (gShen-po Mi-lus bSam-legs) transmitted [the teaching] to Nam-mkha' sNang-ba'i mDog-can. Nam-mkha' sNang-ba'i mDog-can transmitted [it] to King Mu-khri bTsan-po. At that point the king who was strongly attached [to those teachings] completed blocked the transmission by keeping [them] secret and since that damaged the lineage, the virtues, power, and splen-

dor of the king declined by one-third. Then Mon-bon Ha-ra Ci-par magically received it from the Four sMan-mo.[176] Mon-bon Ha-ra Ci-par transmitted it to Bon-mo sTag-za Rlung-rgyal. Bon-mo sTag-za Rlung-rgyal transmitted it to Zhang Zhung A-nu Phrag-thag. Zhang Zhung A-nu Phrag-thag transmitted it to Zhang Zhung Sad-ne Ga'u. Zhang Zhung Sad-ne Ga'u transmitted it to the master Da-mi Thad-ke. Da-mi Thad-ke transmitted it to rGya-bon Zings-pa mThu-chen. rGya-bon Zings-pa mThu-chen transmitted it to Shad-ra-khug. Shad-ra-khug transmitted it to dPe-thog-rtse. dPe-thog-rtse transmitted it to dPe-thog-'phrul. dPe-thog-'phrul transmitted it to Zhang Zhung sTong-rgyung mThu-chen. Zhang Zhung sTong-rgyung mThu-chen transmitted it to three persons: Se Sha-ri dBu-can, lDe Gyim-tsha rMa-chung, and Mi-nyag lCe-tsha mKhar-bu. They transmitted it to sTangs dMu-tsha Gyer-med and to Bla-chen Dran-pa Nam-mkha'.

This shows the succession in the lineage of the *sPyi spung* teachings.

We have seen how King rGyung-yar Mu-khod and his consort met the great scholar Tha-mi Thad-ge [sic] and the others, and so it would seem that prior to Bla-chen-po's birth, they existed at the same time. However, even if the famous scholar Tha-mi Thad-ke [sic] and the others lived before that event, perhaps their disciples mentioned their names due to their widespread fame. On the other hand, in the Bon tradition proper, all those great Siddhas were wisdom-holders who could exercise power over life, and therefore, there would be no contradiction in thinking that their life span extended over several hundred years.

In any case, it is certain that Bla-chen-po Dran-pa Nam-mkha' appeared in the era corresponding to the reign of the eighth Tibetan king Gri-gum bTsan-po. Concerning this, the commentary of the *gSang ba bsen thub*, the *Rin po che yid bzhin rnam par bkod pa'i rgyan* says (Thob, 59, 30, 3):

Then the king [Gri-gum bTsan-po] summoned the gShen-pos; the paternal royal protectors [sku gshen] were spared and [were

---

176 [*sman mo*. A class of female beings similar to the Klu, also inhabitants of the countryside.]

allowed] to recite [liturgies], wear their headdresses, and so forth, as before. [He asked] lHa-bon sGo-bzhi, Gyim-bu Lan-tsha, and Ge-khod This-'phen to remain as his royal protectors. [He] asked the remaining ones to go [into exile] beyond the borders of the four divisions [of Central] Tibet. At that point the great minister Ra-sang Khod-ram said: "Oh Lord, King, bTsan-po! Attributing to others the responsibility for one's evil deeds causes a fall into the three lower realms of existence. Practicing virtues causes ascent to the fortunate higher spheres. The unsurpassable view is true realization. If the ministers are garrulous, the king's mind will be burdened. If the king is hostile, political power will be seized by the masses. Therefore, I request the Lord bTsan-po not to give that order!"

[But] the king did not accept [his counsel]. At that time the gShen-pos conferred, and on that occasion rGyung-yar Bla-chen Khod-spungs said: "Oh all you gShen-pos! A king's words are spoken only once. Falsities are said over and over. [This situation is like trying to] beat a hornless yak by weeping! Let us all go into exile, and let Gyim-bu Lan-tsha and the others remain!" That was his advice.

As we can see, when King Gri-gum bTsan-po suppressed Bon, Bla-chen-po Dran-pa Nam-mkha', also known as rGyung-yar Bla-chen Khod-spungs, resided in Tibet. This fact is well-attested to in Bonpo historical sources.

4. The King of Zhang Zhung Lig-mi-rkya lDe-bu

in the *Tun hong bod kyi lo rgyus yig rnying* [Old Tibetan Chronicles of Dunhuang] we read (PI, 571, 398):

During the time of this king,[177] in Zhang Zhung, [there was] lDe-bu [who] was outstanding among [his] relatives [and also] the best in combat. So that dominion could be had over the Zhang Zhung realm, the noble lady Sad-mar-kar was sent [in marriage] to Lig-myi-rhyal [*sic*].

---

177 [King Srong-btsan sGam-po.]

When the *dharmarāja* Srong-btsan sGam-po, who initiates the Later Period, was still young, the most important among his relatives, but also the one who became the worst of his adversaries, was the Zhang Zhung King Lig-myi-rhyal "lDe-bu". Because of that fact, Sad-mar-kar, the elder sister of King Srong-btsan sGam-po, was sent in marriage to the king of Zhang Zhung. We can also understand from the excerpt that the name of the king at that time was Lig-myi-rhyal lDe-bu. Lig-myi-rhyal was an epithet commonly attributed to the kings of that period: the Zhang Zhung word *lig* means *srid pa* [existence]; *myi* or *mi* means *drang po* [righteous] or *mdzangs pa* [brave]; and *rhya* or *rkya* means lord. Combined, the words result in the title Srid-pa'i Drang-rje [Righteous Lord of Existence].

This king belongs to the royal lineage of the Khyung-lung king known as rGyung-yar Mu-khod rGyal-po gZha'-tshon 'Od-kyi Bya-ru-can [the Holder of the Rainbow Light Horned Crown]. That is certain because Bla-chen-po Dran-pa Nam-mkha' and the Eight Great Scholars were active during the middle part of the Intermediate Period. Furthermore, the fact that this Lig-myi-rhya lDe-bu was a king of Zhang Zhung Khyung-lung is also reported in the *Tun hong bod kyi lo rgyus yig rnying* [Old Tibetan Chronicles of Dunhuang], where we read (Pl 571, 401):[178]

> Lig myi rhya'i so nam dang bu srid zung shig ches / spug gyim brtsan rmang cung bka' stsal te / mkhar khyung lung du mchis na / btsan mo myi bzhugs te / chab nya la rol zhing / mtsho ma pang du gshegs nas / rmang cung ma pang du mchis te / btsan mo zha sngar phyag bgyis //

The King requested sPug Gyim-brtsan rMang-chung to deliver the following command to his sister, "Take care of Lig-mi-rkya's lineage and of the prosperity of the household!" When rMang-chung arrived at the Khyung-lung castle, the queen was not present. rMang-chung was told that the queen had left for Lake Ma-pham [Manasarovar] in order to perform the ritual

---

178 [This and the following two excerpts are first given as they appear in the *Chronicles* and are then paraphrased by the Author in order to facilitate understanding, given the difficulty the Tibetan language of those sources presents, even for Tibetans. To avoid redundancy, I have opted to translate his interpretation directly, reproducing the original passages in transliteration.]

ablutions of the full moon. Thus he went there, and requested an audience with her.

The *Tun hong bod kyi lo rgyus yig rnying* [Old Tibetan Chronicles of Dunhuang] also report the way in which the Tibetan king killed Lig-mi-rkya lDe-bu, the last king of the Zhang Zhung dynasty (PI, 571, 399):

> *sNga na shud ke za stsal thing shags mchis ste / btsan mo dang ni myi brnal bar / lig myi rhya'i shud ke za stsal ting shags gnang ste / btsan mo yang lig myi rhya'i so nam dang bu srid myi mdzad cing log shig na bzhugs par / 'dir dral gyi snyan du gda' ste / btsan mo de ltar log pa bgyis na / chab srid kyi dkrugs ma 'gyur bas de lte bu ma bgyid par / lig myi rhya'i so nam dang bu srid zung shig ches / spug gyim brtsan rmang cung bka' bstsal //*

Before King Lig-mi-rkya of Zhang Zhung took Sad-mar-kar as his wife, the king already had a prior queen called Shud-ke-bza's Tsal-thing-shags. The two wives did not have a harmonious relation, and since King Lig-mi-rkya gave more importance to Shud-ke-bza', Sad-mar-kar refused to contribute to the development of Lig-myi-rkya's lineage or to the prosperity of the household, and kept to herself. When her brother, the king of Tibet Srong-btsan sGam-po, was informed of the situation, he feared that the disaccord between Sad-mar-kar and Lig-myi-rkya could become an obstacle to the political relations between the two countries. Since that was unacceptable, in order to persuade her of the necessity of her contribution to the development of Lig-myi-rkya's lineage and to the prosperity of the household, he dispatched rMang-chung to Zhang-zhung Khyung-lung dNgul-mkhar to deliver his command.

This passage reveals how the basic causes of the conflict came about, showing that at that time the *dharmarāja* Srong-btsan sGam-po did not want circumstances to occur that would hinder the political relations between Zhang Zhung and Tibet. Nevertheless, Queen Sad-mar-kar sent this reply to her brother. The event is related in the *Tun hong bod kyi lo rgyus yig rnying* [Old Tibetan Chronicles of Dunhuang] (PI, 573, 427):

> *Gyim brtsan rmang cung slar / btsan po spyan sngar mchis nas / btsan mos bka' lan yi ger gsol pa ni chang ma mchis / mgur blangs pa'i tshig ni 'di zhes mchi / phyag rgyas btab ste skur ba 'di lags shes gsol pa las / zhu*

phyag rgya phye ste / gzigs na / g.yu rnying bzang po sum cu tsam zhig byung ste / btsan po dgongs dgongs nas / yu bus lig myi rhya la rgol phod na ni g.yu thogs shig / rgol ma phod na ni bud med dang mtshungs zhu gyon chig zer ba lta zhes bka' stsal nas / rje blon blong blong de / lig myi rhya'i srid brlag go //

    Gyim-brtsan rMang-chung returned to the presence of King Srong-btsan sGam-po and said, "Queen Sad-mar-kar did not send a written reply. She sang a song, and these are the words." Repeating the words, he then said, "Also, the Queen sent something sealed. Here it is," and handed a sealed envelope to the king. The king opened the sealed envelope and looking, he saw it contained thirty pieces of old turquoise of excellent quality. The king thought intently about what meaning that could have. In the end, he concluded what its symbolic meaning was, and said: "What she means is this: "If you are capable of confronting Lig-mi-rkya, then wear these good turquoises as an emblem signifying bravery and heroism. If you are not capable of confronting Lig-mi-rkya, then wear them on your head, since you would be just like us women!" The Lord and the minister, their hearts full of apprehension, decided that Lig-mi-rkya's sovereignty had to be destroyed.

This communicates how the overthrowing of King Lig-mi-rkya of Zhang Zhung was decided, albeit with great distress, on the basis of the special appeal by Queen Sad-mar-kar, although that was not the fundamental cause. This matter is clarified in Volume Three that is concerned with the history of the Later Period and to which the reader is referred.

    Apart from saying that the decision of the Tibetan lord and ministers to terminate Lig-mi-rkya's rule was made with great anguish, none of the Tibetan dynastic and religious histories, including the *Old Tibetan Chronicles of Dunhuang*, specify how this overthrow took place. The only exception is the slight information found in the history of the Zhang Zhung Aural Transmission of the Great Perfection teachings. The *rDzogs pa chen po zhang zhung snyan rgyud kyi bon ma nub pa'i gtan tshigs* says (Dhi, 260, I, 2):

In Zhang Zhung around that time there was Siddha Tso-men Gyer-chen, [while] in Tibet [there were] sBa Ji-phrom dKar-po, sTong-rgyung mThu-chen, the Four Scholars, [and] Bla-chen Dran-pa Nam-mkha', who was in the last years of his life. The Four Emanations were: Zhang Zhung bKra-shis rGyal-mtshan; Gu-rub sTag-wer Shig-slags; Ma-hor sTags-gzigs; and Tshe-spungs Zla-ba rGyal-mtshan.

When Gyer-spungs Chen-po sNang-bzher Slod-po was the powerful and arrogant holder of the ordinary and superior instructions left by Ta-pi Hri-tsa, the Everlasting Bon declined due to the overwhelming dominion of events. The kings of that time were the king of Zhang Zhung, Lig-mi-rgya; the king of Mon, Pa-na Ra-ling; [and] the king of Tibet, Khri-srong lDe-btsan.

Before that time, when each [of these] kings was born, there were only three ministers [in Tibet]: one for external affairs, one for internal matters, and one chancellor. During the reign of Khri-srong lDe-btsan, there were ten ministers for external affairs, ten ministers for internal matters, and ten chancellors, thirty in all. Then the power of the king was great: he conquered the king of sTag-gzigs-nor who promised to build long wooden bridges to span the great rivers which interrupted the bordering trade routes and to protect them. At the time the king of Zhang Zhung was Lig-mi-rgya, Zhang Zhung had an army of 990,000 soldiers and its dominion extended to Sum-pa, where a small regiment was kept. Tibet had only 42,000 soldiers, and another small regiment, forty-three [regiments] altogether. Obviously, the king of Zhang Zhung could not be defeated by the king of Tibet; the king of Tibet reflected upon the matter, and decided to overthrow him with surreptitious means.

At that time, the king of Zhang Zhung had three consorts; the youngest of them called Gu-rub-za sNang-sgron Legs-mo was eighteen years old. A chancellor of the Tibetan king called sNang-nam Legs-grub who was a persuasive speaker with a cruel mind and a wicked disposition [met with] sNang-sgron Legs-ma, offering her as a present the horn of a wild yak heaped with gold dust that he had brought [with him] and said: "sNang-sgron Legs-ma, someone like you deserves better than being the minor consort of the king of Zhang Zhung! Also the king of

Tibet cannot tolerate [this state of affairs]. Is there a way to put an end to this? If there is, the king of Tibet will make you his primary consort and will grant you two-thirds of his realm."

sGron-legs-ma said: "The king of Zhang Zhung has an army that could cover the earth. The king of Tibet has an army that could barely cover the midsection of a heifer['s back] and cannot defeat [him] in open [warfare]. However, if he wants to vanquish him using craft and deceit, then next month, the king of Zhang Zhung will travel from Zhang Zhung to Sum-pa Glang-gi Gyim-shod together with his attendants in order to take part in an assembly. You can lie in ambush there and kill him! I will be [your] secret informer." She spoke those words since she had no children and [thus] no interest to defend.

It was decided that [she would] leave a sign indicating the exact date on the face of the cairn. When the time came, the Tibetan king arrived [at the place], together with his minister and several thousand soldiers. He was the first to reach the cairn, together with sNang-nam Legs grub. When he looked, he saw a pan brimming with water inside of which were three [objects]: a small piece of gold, a conch shell fragment, and a poisoned arrowhead. The king of Tibet said: "The pan full of water means that [the king of Zhang Zhung] will arrive on full moon of the next month. The small piece of gold and the conch shell fragment mean that the soldiers have to be kept in readiness, lying in ambush, at the Golden and Conch Shell Caves of Dwang-ra. The poisoned arrowhead means that we should wish him ill, lie in ambush, and kill [him]." Thus they waited. When the two kings met, the Tibetan soldiers killed the king of Zhang Zhung.

This excerpt describes a crucial event of great import in the concluding history of the Intermediate Period, and it is necessary to examine it carefully.

First of all, the reason why the text contains a passage saying, "During the reign of Khri-srong lDe-btsan ..." and describes some of the history occurring at the time of King Khri-srong lDe'u-btsan owes to the fact that all Bonpos are familiar with an axiom that states the *dharmarāja* Khri-srong lDe-btsan destroyed Bon. It seems obvious that the facts recounted have been confused with what happened before, namely, the decision to terminate the political rule of King Lig-mi-rkya of Zhang Zhung Khyung-lung, at the time of Srong-btsan sGam-po.

It is certain that when this historical source says:

> Before that time, when each [of these] kings was born, there were only three ministers: one for external affairs, one for internal matters, and one chancellor. During the reign of Khri-srong lDe-btsan, there were ten ministers for external affairs, ten ministers for internal matters, and ten chancellors, thirty in all. At that time, the power of the king was great [...],

it does so in reference to the situation during Srong-btsan sGam-po's time, because the *rGyal rabs gsal ba'i me long* affirms (Pe, 73, 23):

> There were six severe ministers for external affairs, six kind ministers for internal matters, and four wise chancellors,

and provides the names of each of the ministers. That notwithstanding, the textual source in question claims that before Khri-srong lDe-btsan only three ministers existed: one for internal matters, one for external affairs, and one chancellor. Besides, the text says: "Around that time, in Zhang Zhung there was Siddha Tso-men Gyer-chen, [while] in Tibet [there were] sBa Ji-phrom dKar-po, sTong-rgyung mThu-chen, the Four Scholars, [and] Bla-chen Dran-pa Nam-mkha', who was in the last years of his life." All those Bonpos and gShen-pos were definitely predecessors of Srong-btsan sGam-po who lived at the end of the Intermediate Period. Therefore, how could they be associated with Khri-srong lDe'u-btsan's time?

The *gYung drung bon gyi bstan 'byung nyung bsdus* says (Thob, 625, 37, 3):

> In the end, at the time of the Tibetan kings Srong-btsan and Khri-srong, the Zhang Zhung king of Khyung-lung, Lig-mi-skya, and the king of Dang-ra, Lig-mi-rgyal, were killed by the Tibetan lords, and consequently, most of the eastern territory of central Zhang Zhung was incorporated in Tibet.

The text thus differentiates between a king of Khyung-lung and a king of Dang-ra on one hand and between the reign of Srong-btsan and that of Khri-srong on the other. It is also possible that at the time of Khri-srong, a king ruling over part of Zhang Zhung killed the king of Dang-ra, situated on the eastern side of Central Zhang Zhung, thus bringing the area under his control. However, the Zhang Zhung king Lig-mi-rkya connected with the history of the Zhang Zhung Aural Transmission was the king of Khyung-lung, and the mandator of his destruction was Srong-btsan sGam-po. The evidence for this is provided by the *Old Tibetan Chronicles of Dunhuang*.

Moreover, given that the text also mentions the Golden Cave and the Conch Shell Cave of Dwang-ra, it is difficult to believe that a king was there. If the king of Dwang-ra was himself residing in that place, the text would not have said: "When the time came, the Tibetan king arrived [at the place] together with his minister and several thousand soldiers," because to hide such a military force in the two caves would have been impossible. Obviously that manner of speaking meant that the king of Khyung-lung would reach Sum-pa by gradually traveling eastward from the center of Zhang Zhung through the Dwang-ra region and that the Tibetan army was instructed to ambush and kill him in the Golden and Conch Shell Caves area which was situated near the Dwang-ra route.

Thus the dissolution of the political power of the kings that held such authoritative titles as the Zhang Zhung King of Existence or the Lord of Existence came about at the time of the Khyung-lung king called Lig-mi-rkya lDe-bu, representing the conclusion of the history of the Intermediate Period.

The ruins of the castle of Lig-mi-rkya, the Khyung-lung king, the last of the Zhang Zhung monarchs, are still visible today on the mountainside of Khyung-lung dNgul-mkhar. The main reason the castle is called dNgul-mkhar [Silver Palace] is because its white radiance stands at the center of a variegated panorama of land and boulders where the upper heights of the rocky mountains are tinted with rainbow-like nuances of blue, yellow, and red.

The basis for the term Khyung-lung dNgul-mkhar [Khyung Village Silver Palace] attributed to the royal fortress is due to the seemingly carved surface of the mountain and to the doors of the internal assembly hall that appear on the outside. Looking from a distance, one sees that the small doors of the assembly hall are located about halfway up the mountain. All around, many rooms are carved in the rock with inner and outer rooms rising one above the other, some of which have further chambers on the left and on the right.

In light of the nomadic lifestyle of ancient Zhang Zhung and Tibet, the existing ruins of Khyung-lung dNgul-mkhar lead to the assumption that the Zhang Zhung kings of those times resided for the greater part of spring, summer, and autumn in black yak-hair tents. They did not settle in one place, but would pitch camp in prime locations in Inner, Outer, and Central Zhang Zhung [Zhang Zhung sGo Phug Bar gsum], staying there as long as they deemed fit, taking care of local issues, and implementing crucial government activities. In winter and during part of autumn and spring, they would customarily live in various big and small caves that came to be known as the Khyung-lung Palace. The word cave [*phug pa*] may suggest a limited space, but in that area most of those ancient caves were large and even if at present many have crumbled, their roofs are still clearly visible.

Khyung-lung dNgul-mkhar was not the capital or settlement only of the last Zhang Zhung dynasty: during the Early Period, three of the eighteen Bya-ru-can kings, namely Rin-chen 'Od-kyi Bya-ru-can, king of Slas-kra Gu-ge, as well as rGyung-yar Mu-khod rGyal-po gZha'-tshon 'Od-kyi Bya-ru-can, and the king of Kyi-le Gu-ge, Un-chen Dung-gi Bya-ru-can, also resided in the area of Khyung-lung rGyal-ba-mnyes. Furthermore, since it was also the chosen seat of many *siddhas* and scholars, such as the great masters Dran-pa Nam-mkha', sNang-ba'i mDog-can, and so on, it became a special place for the gShen-pos of Bon after the end of the last Zhang Zhung dynasty.

During the Later Period, not only Bonpos, but also Buddhists arrived at Kyung-lung dNgul-mkhar and took charge of it. The Buddhists covered the surface of the caves and the internal walls with designs. Ruins of a temple built over the vestiges of the main part of the ancient Silver Castle are still clearly visible. The numerous traces of Tibetan language inside the various caves suggest that the place became a Buddhist site approximately during the time of lHa-bla-ma Ye-shes-'od (947-1024) and Lo-chen Rin-chen bZang-po (958-1055), confirmed by diverse textual fragments pertaining to the three Lower classes of Tantras found there. Because of the presence of several Sa-skya and bKa'-brgyud textual fragments, it appears that also Sa-skya-pas and bKa'-brgyud-pas gradually appropriated the place, as the Ri-bo dGa'-ldan-pas did, in later times. Before the Cultural Revolution a small dGe-lugs-pa monastery existed in Khyung-lung. Today, adjacent to this not easily accessible place, the major renovation undertaken by the local village and neighboring district can be seen.

During the last summer month of 1988 (Tibetan year 3905, male Earth Dragon year of the last *sMe-phreng* of the twenty-second *sMe-'khor*), I and a group of eight western students of mine interested in Tibetan culture went to see the vestiges of Khyung-lung dNgul-mkhar, the residence of the last king of Zhang Zhung and seat of Bla-chen-po Dran-pa Nam-mkha'. We remained for a few days, visiting with care more than a hundred caves of very early times, observing the traces of the royal residences built inside them during the various eras, and enjoying the marvels of the neighboring mountains and rivers, stūpas, and natural hot springs. Of the numerous pictures taken at that time, here is one of them.

View of cave dwellings

The cave shown here is of major importance among the hundreds present. Every room in the cave is internally connected above and below. On the upper level [see photograph below] the ruins of a temple or a palace are still clearly visible.

Chögyal Namkhai Norbu, at lower right, exploring the Silver Palace

This structure, a temple or castle, was most probably built at the time of Bla-chen Dran-pa Nam-mkha'. That afterward it became an important location for Buddhists is demonstrated by the drawings still on its walls.

Apart from this important location of Khyun-lung dNgul-mkhar, many famous pilgrimage sites connected with ancient history existed in various districts of Inner, Outer, and Central Zhang Zhung where during the Early Period and especially during the Intermediate Period many Bonpo scholars and realized beings resided and whose activities greatly contributed to the diffusion of the teachings. In this respect, the *Tshangs dbyangs yid 'phrog* relates (IsMEO, 26, 1):

At Khyung-lung dNgul-mkhar rGyal-ba-mnyes, there was Bla-chen-po Dran-pa Nam-mkha'.
At Zhang Zhung Byi-ra gTsug-ldan, there was Tshe-dbang Nam-mkha' sGron-gsal.
At dBal-gyi Brag-phug Rong-chen, there was g.Yung-drung dPa'-bo mThong-grol.
At Zhang Zhung sPos-ri Ngad-ldan, there was Slob-dpon Tha-mi Thad-ke.
On the shore of Lake Mu-le-khyud, there was Bon-mo sTag-wer Li-wer.
In the Crystal Cave of Mount Ti-se, there was Zhang Zhung A-nu Phrag-thag.
In the Secret Magic Cave of Mount Ti-se, there was Bla-ma Tshe-dbang Rig-'dzin.
In the Secret Cave of dBal-'bar Me-ri, there was Bla-chen-po Dran-pa Nam-mkha'.
At Dug-mtsho Mu-le'i Do-gling, there was Zhang Zhung This-dmar sPungs-rgyung.
In the Cave of the Elephant that Hides Itself on the Ground, there was Zhang Zhung Glang-chen Mu-wer.
At gSang-brag Brag-dmar Yang-rDzong, there was Zhang Zhung Tso-min Gyer-rgyung.
At rTag-tu Ngu-ba'i rTsi-chog, there was Gyer-chen Mar-me sGron-gsal.
At Brag-dmar Rin-chen sPungs-pa, there was Zhang Zhung sPungs-rgyung mThu-chen.
In the Cave Yongs-'dus dBang, there was Zhang Zhung Mi-bon Mu-phya.
At Zhang Zhung Shod-kyi Dum-tshal, there was Dzo-dmar Me-yi Bon-po.
At Zhang Zhung Khyung-lung dNgul-mkhar, there was Gar-ma Me-slag-can.
At Zhang Zhung Khyung-chen sPungs-ri, there was Zhang Zhung Khyung-yer dKar-po, and so on.

This shows that at that time famous masters of Bon, such as:
- the Lineage of the Thirteen [gDung-rgyud bCu-gsum], which included the renowned Nam-mkha'i sNang-ba'i mDog-can;

- the Four Scholars [mKhas-pa Mi-bzhi], which included sTong-rgyung mThu-chen;
- the Nine Translators and Paṇḍitas [Lo-paṇ mKhas-dgu], which included dMu-tsa Dra-he;
- the Nine gShen of the Blessed Lineage [Byin-rlabs rGyud-pa'i gShen-dgu], which included Bya-ru dBal-slag;
- the Nine Powerful Ones [mThu-chen Mi-dgu], which included Mi-bon Mu-phya;
- the Nine Miraculous Ones [rDzu-'phrul Mi-dgu], which included Li-shu sTag-ring; and
- the Nine Charismatic Bonpos [Zil-gnon Bon-dgu], which included rNal-'byor gTsang-gshen,

blessed all those places and greatly contributed to the diffusion of Bon teachings.

During the reign of sPu-lde Gung-rgyal, some particularly learned Tibetan Bonpos were sent to Zhang Zhung in search of Bon teachings. For this reason, it is said that the Bon gShen-pos of Zhang Zhung spread the teachings. The way in which this happened is recorded in the *rTsa-rgyud Nyi-sgron* (Thob, 304, 150, 6):

> At the time (of sPu-de Gung-rgyal), Bon spread. The twenty-seven Scholars of Zhang Zhung [Zhang Zhung mKhas-pa Nyi-shu rTsa-bdun] possessed the teachings. Sūtras and scriptures, temples, sanctuaries, and stūpas became widespread in the land of Zhang Zhung; they did not flourish in the rTsang [sic] [and] dBus [areas] of [Central] Tibet.

The *g.Yung drung bon gyi rgyud 'bum* gives an idea of whom the famous Bon gShen-pos in Zhang Zhung were at that time and how the teachings of Bon developed (Thob, KA, 60, 7, 6):

> At that time, all the Bon-gShen were invited to a conference. In order to [foster] the spreading of the doctrine, the guardians of hidden treasures [*gter bdag*], the gods, and the spirits allowed some treasures to be revealed, but not many.
>
> The gShen-pos entrusted to look for the teachings of the Everlasting Bon were laden with gold dust, pieces of silver, and

natural turquoise[179] and were dispatched to various places where different languages were spoken.

The Bonpos of Me-nyag, dPal-legs rGyal-mtshan and mTsho-mi Rings-skyol-po, went to the country of Zhang Zhung. Once they arrived, they sought out with and offered gold lamps[180] to the teacher Ma-rgyud rGyal-mtshan who knew all the treasures of Bon without exception, especially the five *'Bum* series [*'Bum sde lnga*][181] and the Twelve Categories of the teachings [*Bon sgo bcu gnyis*][182] and [to] the teacher called lHa-khyung who was an expert in the Bon of the Nine Vehicles,[183] could recite by heart the Twelve Detailed *'Bum* series,[184] and was also highly proficient in the practice of profound secret formulas. They spoke these words [...].

And also (ibid., 62, 8, 3):

---

179   *g.yu sbram po*. A natural turquoise not crafted by artisans.
180   *rin po che'i zhugs thogs*. *Zhugs* means fire or the flame of a fire; *thogs* means to carry in the hands; hence, the meaning is "a lamp made of precious gold."
181   *'bum sde lnga*. The *sKal bzang mgrin rgyan* lists them as follows (Bod, 146, 20): "*Khams brgyad gtan phabs stong phrag brgya pa'i 'bum; rGyas pa bye ma nyi khri chu rgyun 'bum; De bzhin byams ma 'bum lnga khams 'bum; dGe rgyas tshogs 'bum rnam dag 'dul ba'i 'bum; and g.Yung drung lam 'bum ye shes bkod pa'i 'bum.*"
182   *bon sgo bcu gnyis*. These seem to correspond to the "Twelve Categories of Excellent Speech" [*gsung rab yan lag bcu gnyis*] of the Buddhist tradition, which are: 1. the Sets of Discourses [*mdo'i sde*]; 2. the Proclamations with Songs [*dbyangs kyis bsnyad pa'i sde*]; 3. the Prophetic Teachings [*lung du bstan pa'i sde*]; 4. the Poetic Pronouncements [*tshigs su bcad pa'i sde*]; 5. the Special Aphorisms [*ched du brjod pa'i sde*]; 6. the Introductory Teachings [*gleng gzhi'i sde*]; 7. the Narratives [*rtogs pa brjod pa'i sde*]; 8. the Parables [*de lta bu byung ba'i sde*]; 9. the Narratives of Former Births [*skye pa'i rabs kyi sde*]; 10. the Extensive Sayings [*shin tu rgyas pa'i sde*]; 11. Marvels [*rmad du byung ba'i sde*]; and 12. Established Doctrines [*gtan la phab pa'i sde*] referring to the historical Buddha.
183   *theg pa rim pa dgu'i bon*. These are: 1. the Vehicle of the gShen of Prediction [*phywa gshen theg pa*]; 2. the Vehicle of the gShen of Appearance [*snang gshen theg pa*]; 3. the Vehicle of the gShen of Magic [*'phrul gshen theg pa*]; 4. the Vehicle of the gShen of Existence [*srid gshen theg pa*]; 5. the Vehicle of Virtuous Devotees [*dge bsnyen theg pa*]; 6. the Vehicle of Ascetics [*drang srong theg pa*]; 7. the Vehicle of the White A [*a dkar theg pa*]; 8. the Vehicle of the Primordial gShen [*ye gshen theg pa*]; and 9. the Unsurpassable Supreme Vehicle [*yang rtse bla med theg pa*].
184   *'phra ba'i 'bum bcu gnyis*. Teachings of the *Prajñāpāramitā* type.

> As requested they presented themselves to Lord sPu-rgyal and his subjects, whereupon they said, "We have received the teachings." [In this way,] since the Five *'Bum* Series, the Twelve Categories, the numerous Treasure Series teachings [*mDzod sde*], the Twelve Detailed [*'Bum* series], and the diverse tenets of the [Nine] Vehicles spread greatly in Tibet, the teaching flourished even more.

The *rTsa rgyud nyi sgron* relates how gShen-pos were sent to Zhang Zhung during the reign of King gNam-ri Srong-btsan in order to gather Bon teachings (Thob, 305, 151, 1):

> The reign of the divine son gNam-ri Srong-btsan was an auspicious one, since the Divine Son [lHa-sras] restored Bon to its former grandeur. Also, four outstanding Tibetan Bonpos—Khyung-po sTag-sgra Dung-gtsug, sNyan [*sic*] Li-shu sTag-ring, sPe-bon Shod-bkram, and gCo-bon Khri-gtsug Khyung-drag—were given yak horns filled with gold dust and were sent to the country of Zhang Zhung in search of Bon teachings. Those four gShen-pos met with the Four Scholars of Zhang Zhung.

This excerpt clarifies that four famous scholars lived in Zhang Zhung at the time of gNam-ri Srong-btsan. As we shall see in Volume Three, two of the four Tibetan Bonpos mentioned in the excerpt, namely, Khyung-po sTag-sgra Dung-gtsug and sNyan Li-shu sTag-ring, are reckoned among the illustrious figures of the Bon gShen-pos of the Later Period.

Bibliography

"bKa' chems ka khol ma"
   (*gter-ma*)
   Discoverer: Jo-bo rJe A-ti-sha (982-1054)
   Publishing house: Kan su'u mi rigs dpe skrun khang, Lanzhou
   Publishing date: 1989

"Gangs ti se'i dkar chag tshangs dbyangs yid 'phrog"
   '*Dzam gling gangs ti se'i dkar chag tshangs dbyangs yid 'phrog dgos 'dod ces bya ba*
   Author: bsTan-'dzin Rin-chen rGyal-mtshan bDe-chen sNying-po (born 1801)
   Owner: Is.IAO (Istituto Italiano per l'Africa e l'Oriente), Rome, Italy
   Type: *dbu med* manuscript

"Gab pa srog 'dzin sngags kyi don"
   gSas mkhar rin po che thig le dbyings chen g.yung drung yongs rdzogs dpal gsang ba 'dus pa don gyi rgyud las g.yung drung gab pa srog 'dzin sngags kyi don zhes bya ba (Tantra Series, vol. TA)

---

185 This bibliography, arranged in Tibetan alphabetical order, lists the three different genre of texts quoted in the present work, first with the abridged title when that has been used and then with the full title. Whenever possible or applicable, oral transmission texts [*bka' ma*], and treatises [*bstan bcos*] carry the name of the author and his dates, and/or the date of compilation; aural transmission texts [*snyan rgyud*], and texts originating from pure vision [*dag snang*] carry the name of the compiler; *gter-ma* texts carry the name and dates of the original author, of the discoverer(s) [*gter ston*], and/or of the discovery. These are followed by the name of the owner, publisher, or editor(s) or that of the review (in case of articles); the name of the place of publication or the name and place of the publishing house; the year of publication; and indications about the type of publication (manuscript, manuscript in *dbu med*, reproduction of manuscript, or xylographic edition). The same structure is followed in all three volumes of *The Light of Kailash*.

(*gter-ma*)
  Discoverer: bDe-chen Gling-pa (born 1833)
  Publishing house: Si khron zhing chen mi rigs zhib 'jug su'o Bod kyi rig gnas zhib 'jug khang, Chengdu
  Type: Reproduction of *dbu med* manuscript

"*Grags rgyal bod kyi rgyal rabs*"
  Bod kyi rgyal rabs
  in: *Sa skya'i bka' 'bum*, vol. TA
  Author: Grags-pa rGyal-mtshan (1146-1216)
  Publishing house: sDe dge lhun grub steng
  Type: Manuscript, xylographic edition

"*Gling grags*"
  sGrags pa rin chen gling grags"
  in: *Sources for a History of Bon*
  Author: Dran-pa Nam-mkha' (*sMe* 1003)
  Publisher: bsTan-'dzin rNam-dag (born 1926)
  Publication place: Tibetan Bonpo Monastic Center, Dolanji, HP, India
  Publishing date: 1972

"*Gleng gzhi bstan pa'i byung khungs*"
  Author: Khyung-po Blo-gros rGyal-mtshan (fourteenth century)
  Owner: Is.IAO (Istituto Italiano per l'Africa e l'Oriente), Rome, Italy
  Type: *dbu med* manuscript

"*rGya bod yig tshang chen mo*"
  rGya bod kyi yig tshang mkhas pa dga' byed chen mo 'dzam gling gsal ba'i me long
  Author: sTag-tshang rDzong-pa dPal-'byor bZang-po
  Compilation date: 1434
  Publishing house: Si khron mi rigs dpe skrun khang, Chengdu
  Publishing date: 1985

"*rGya'i thang yig rnying ma*"
  rGya'i yig tshang nang gsal ba'i bod kyi rgyal rabs gsal ba'i me long
  Translator and editor: sTag-lha Phun-tshogs bKra-shis
  Publication place: Dharamsala, HP, India
  Publishing date: 1973

"*rGya'i thang yig rnying ma*"
  Thang yig gsar rnying las byung ba'i bod chen po'i srid lugs dang 'brel ba'i deb ther g.yu 'brug bzhad sgra
  Translators and Editors: Don-grub-rgyal (1953-1985), and Khrin-chin-dbyin
             (Chén Jiànjiàn)
  Publishing house: mTsho sngon mi rigs dpe skrun khang, Xining
  Publishing date: 1983

"*rGyal po bka'i thang yig*"
  in: *bKa' thang sde lnga*
  (*gter-ma*)

Discoverer: Orgyan Gling-pa (born 1323)
Publishing house: Mi rigs dpe skrun khang, Beijing
Publishing date: 1986

"rGyal rabs 'phrul gyi lde mig"
rGyal rabs 'phrul gyi lde mig, or Deb ther dmar po'i deb gsar ma
Author: Paṇ-chen bSod-nams Grags-pa (1478-1554)
Publishing house: International Academy of Indian Culture, New Delhi
Publishing date: 1968

"rGyal rabs bon gyi 'byung gnas"
in: *Three Sources for A history of Bon*
Author: Khyung-po Blo-gros rGyal-mtshan (fourteenth century)
Publisher: mKhas-grub rGya-mtsho
Publication place: New Thobgyal, Tibetan Bonpo Monastic Centre, Dolanji, HP, India
Publishing date: 1974

"rGyal rabs gsal ba'i me long"
Author: bSod-nams rGyal-mtshan (1312-1375)
Publishing house: Mi rigs dpe skrun khang, Beijing
Publishing date: 1981

"rGyal rabs gser gyi phreng ba"
in: *Rare Historical Texts from the Library of Burmiok Athing*
Author: Kaḥ-thog Rig-'dzin Tshe-dbang Nor-bu (1710-1755)
Publishing house: Library of Tibetan Works and Archives, Dharamsala, HP, India
Publishing date: 1985
Type: *dbu med* manuscript

"rGyal gshen ya ngal gyi gdung rabs"
rGyal gshen ya ngal gyi gdung rabs un chen tshangs pa'i sgra dbyangs
Author: Yang-sgom Mi-'gyur rGyal-mtshan (seventeenth century)
Publishing house: New Thobgyal
Publishing date: 1978
Type: *dbu med* manuscript

"sGra 'grel"
bDen pa bon gyi mdzod sgo sgra 'grel 'phrul gyi lde mig ces bya ba
(*gter-ma*)
Author: Dran-pa Nam-mkha' (*sMe* 1003)
Discoverer: Gyer-mi Nyi-'od (1108-)
Publisher: bsTan-'dzin rNam-dag (born 1926)
Publication place: Delhi
Publishing date: 1966

"sGrags pa rin chen gling grags"
See Gling grags

"sGrung lde'u bon gsum gyi gtam e ma ho:"
  Drung, Deu and Bön, Narrations, symbolic languages and the Bön tradition in ancient Tibet
  Author: Nam-mkha'i Nor-bu (born 1938)
  Publishing house: Library of Tibetan Works and Archives, Dharamsala, HP, India
  Publishing date: 1989 (English edition, 1995)

"sNgon gyi gtam me tog phreng ba"
  in: *Rare Historical Texts from the Library of Burmiok Athing*
  Author: Ne'u Paṇḍi-ta sMon-lam Blo-gros (thirteenth century)
  Publishing house: Library of Tibetan Works and Archives, Dharamsala, HP, India
  Publishing date: 1985
  Type: *dbu med* manuscript

"rJe btsun thams cad mkhyen pa be ro tsa na'i rnam thar 'dra 'bag chen mo"
  Author: Unknown
  Publishing house: Lhasa Zhol
  Type: Xylographic edition

"Nyang gi chos 'byung"
  Chos 'byung me tog snying po
  Author: Nyang-ral Nyi-ma 'Od-zer (1124-1192)
  Publishing house: Bod ljongs mi dmangs dpe skrun khang, Lhasa
  Publishing date: 1988

"Nyer mkho bum bzang"
  gTsug lag rtsis rigs tshang ma'i lag len 'khrul med mun sel nyi ma nyer mkho'i 'dod pa 'jo ba'i bum bzang zhes bya ba
  Author: dBon-rgan Karma Nges-legs
  Compilation date: 1732
  Publishing house: sDe-dge dPal-spungs
  Type: Xylographic edition

"Tun hong bod kyi lo rgyus yig rnying"
  in: Spanien, Ariane, and Imaeda, Yoshiro (eds.), *Choix de documents tibétains conservés à la Bibliothèque nationale*, vol. II
  Publishing house: Bibliothèque Nationale, Paris
  Publishing date: 1979

"bsTan rtsis ngo mtshar nor bu'i phreng ba"
  in *bKa' 'gyur brten 'gyur gyi sde tshan sgrigs tshul bstan pa'i me ro spar ba'i rtung g.yab bon gyi pad mo rgyas pa'i nyi 'od*
  Author: Nyi-ma bsTan-'dzin dBang-gi rGyal-po (1813-1875)
  Publishing house: New Thobgyal
  Publishing date: 1965 (Śatapiṭaka Series, vol. 37, Part II, 31 pages).

"Thang yig gsar rnying las byung ba'i bod chen po' srid lugs"
  See *rGya'i thang yig rnying ma*

"Dar rgyas gsal sgron" <*Dar rgyas gsal ba'i sgron ma*>
bsTan pa'i rnam bshad dar rgyas gsal ba'i sgron ma zhes bya ba
in: *Sources for a History of Bon*
Author: sPa-ston bsTan-rgyal bZang-po
Compilation date: 1345
Publishing house: New Thobgyal, Tibetan Bonpo Monastic Centre, Dolanji, HP, India
Publishing date: 1972

"Dar rgyas gsal sgron gyi lo rgyus kun gsal"
Author: sPa-ston bsTan-rgyal bZang-po
Compilation date: 1324
Publishing house: Si khron zhing chen mi rigs zhib 'jug su'o Bod kyi rig gnas zhib 'jug khang, Chengdu
Type: Reproduction of *dbu med* manuscript

"Deb ther dkar po"
Bod chen po'i srid lugs dang 'brel ba'i rgyal rabs deb ther dkar po zhes bya ba
Author: dGe-'dun Chos-'phel (1905-1951)
Publishing house: Si khron mi rigs dpe skrun khang, Chengdu
Publishing date: 1988

"Deb ther sngon po"
Author: 'Gos-lo gZhon-nu-dpal (1392-1481)
Publishing house: Si khron mi rigs dpe skrun khang, Chengdu
Publishing date: 1984

"Deb ther dpyid kyi rgyal mo'i glu dbyangs"
Gangs can yul gyi sa la spyod pa'i mtho ris kyi rgyal blon gtso bor brjod pa'i deb ther rdzogs ldan gzhon nu'i dga' ston dpyid kyi rgyal mo'i glu dbyangs zhes bya ba
Author: Ngag-dbang Blo-bzang rGya-mtsho (1617-1682)
Publishing house: Mi rigs dpe skrun khang, Beijing
Publishing date: 1980

"Deb ther dmar po"
Deb ther dmar po rnams kyi dang po hu lan deb ther
Author: Tshal-pa Kun-dga' rDo-rje (1309-1364)
Publishing house: Mi rigs dpe skrun khang, Beijing
Publishing date: 1981

"Dri med gzi brjid"
'Dus pa rin po che'i rgyud dri ma med pa gzi brjid rab tu 'bar ba'i mdo (Dol-po Tshal-mkha' Ms., Aural Transmission)
Compiler: Blo-ldan sNying-po (born 1360)
Publisher: bSod-nams rGyal-mtshan, New Thobgyal
Publishing date: 1978
Type: *dbu med* manuscript

"mDo gzer mig"
    (*gter-ma*)
    Discoverer: Drang-rje bTsun-pa gSer-mig (eleventh century)
    Publishing house: Krung go'i bod kyi shes rig dpe skrun khang, Beijing
    Publishing date: 1991

"'Dul ba gling grags"
    (*gter-ma*)
    in: *Sources for a History of Bon*
    Publishing house: New Thobgyal, Tibetan Bonpo Monastic Centre, Dolanji, HP, India
    Publishing date: 1972

"lDe'u rgya bod kyi chos 'byung"
    mKhas pa lde'us mdzad pa'i rgya bod kyi chos 'byung rgyas pa
    Author: mKhas-pa lDe'u Jo-sras (twelfth century)
    Publishing house: Bod ljongs mi dmangs dpe skrun khang, Lhasa
    Publishing date: 1987

"lDe'u chos 'byung chen mo"
    Chos 'byung chen mo bstan pa'i rgyal mtshan
    Author: lDe'u Jo-sras (twelfth century)
    Publishing house: Bod ljongs mi dmangs dpe skrun khang, Lhasa
    Publishing date: 1987

"Ne'u sngon gyi gtam"
    See *sNgon gyi gtam me tog phreng ba*

"sNang gsal sgron me"
    Srid pa 'phrul gyi ju thig gi dpyad don snang gsal sgron me
    Author: Mi-pham 'Jam-dbyangs rNam-rgyal (1846-1912)
    Edition: sDe dge lhun grub steng
    Publication place: Gangtok
    Publishing date: 1974

"dPyad gsum dag rtsis"
    dPyad gsum dag rtsis bskal srid dus kyi 'khor lo las Zhag gsum rtsis gzhung nam mkha'i gter mdzod ces bya ba
    Author: 'Jigs-med Nam-mkha'i rDo-rje (1897-1956)
    Publishing house: New Thobgyal
    Publishing date: 1972

"sPyod 'jug"
    Byang chub sems dpa'i spyod pa la 'jug pa
    Author: Zhi-ba-lha (Śāntideva, eighth century)
    Publishing house: mTsho sngon mi rigs dpe skrun khang, Xining
    Publishing dates: 1989; 1990

"Phung po gzan skyur gyi rnam bshad gcod kyi don gsal byed
    Publishing house: Tashi Jong, Palampur, HP, India

"*Be ro ca na'i rnam thar 'dra 'bag chen mo*"
    in: *Be ro'i rgyud 'bum*, vol. JA
    Publisher: bKra-shis sGang-pa
    Publication place: Leh, Ladak
    Publishing date: 1971

"*Baiḍūrya dkar po*"
    Phug lugs rtsis kyi legs bshad mkha pa'i mgul rgyan baiḍūrya dkar po'i do shal dpyod ldan snying nor zhes bya ba
    Author: sDe-srid Sangs-rgyas rGya-mtsho (1653-1705)
    Publishing house: sDe-dge lhun grub steng
    Type: Xylographic edition

"*Baiḍūrya dkar po*"
    Author: sDe-srid Sangs-rgyas rGya-mtsho (1653-1705)
    Publishing house: Lhasa Zhol
    Type: Xylographic edition

"*Bod kyi rgyal rabs*"
    See *Grags rgyal bod kyi rgyal rabs*

"*Bod kyi rdo ring gi yi ge dang dril bu'i kha byang*" (吐蕃金石录 Tǔ fān jīn shí lù)
    Editor: dBang-rgyal (王尧 Wáng yáo)
    Publishing house: Wénwù chūbǎnshè (文物出版社), Beijing
    Publishing date: 1982

"*Bod kyi gna' rabs yig cha gces bsdus*"
    Editors: bSod-nams-skyid and dBang-rgyal
    Publishing house: Mi rigs dpe skrun khang, Beijing
    Publishing date: 1983

"*Bod gna' rabs kyi rig gnas dang chos lugs mi rigs bcas kyi 'byung khungs skor gleng ba*" (article)
    in: *Bod ljongs zhib jug*, vol. 2, Lhasa, 1984
    Author: Dung-dkar Blo-bzang Phrin-las (1927-1997)

"*Bon gyi bstan 'byung nyung bsdus*"
    g.Yung drung bon gyi bstan pa'i byung khungs nyung bsdus
    in: *Three Sources for a History of Bon*
    Author: bsTan-'dzin rNam-dag (born 1926)
    Publisher: mKhas-grub rGya-mtsho
    Publication place: Tibetan Bonpo Monastic Centre, Dolanji, HP, India
    Publishing date: 1974

"*Byang gi 'byung khungs la dpyad pa'i thog ma'i bsam tshul*" (article)
    in: *Bod ljongs zhib jug*, vol. 2, Lhasa, 1986
    Author: rDo-rje-mkhar

"Byams ma"
    Byams ma skyon gyi 'jigs skyobs (Sūtra Series, vol. TSHI)
    (*gter-ma*)
    Discoverer: Khro-tshang 'Brug-lha (956-1077)
    Publishing house: Si khron zhing chen mi rigs zhib 'jug su'o Bod kyi rig gnas zhib 'jug khang, Chengdu
    Type: Reproduction of *dbu med* manuscript

"Blon po bka'i thang yig"
    in: *bKa' thang sde lnga*
    (*gter-ma*)
    Discoverer: Orgyan Gling-pa (born 1323)
    Publishing house: Mi rigs dpe skrun khang, Beijing
    Publishing date: 1986

"Mi nyag gi skor rags tsam gleng ba" (article)
    in: *Bod ljongs zhib jug*, vol. 3, Lhasa, 1986
    Author: Reb-gong rDo-rje-mkhar

"Me ri'i lcog mkhar bzhengs lugs kyi zur byang"
    Author: Gu-rub gSal-'od-dga' (seventh century)
    Owner: Kong-bon g.Yung-drung rNam-rgyal
    Type: Xerox copy of *dbu med* manuscript, preserved at the Shang Shung Institute, Arcidosso (GR), Italy

"rTsa rgyud chen po gsang ba bsen thub kyi 'grel pa rin po che yid bzhin rnam par bkod pa'i rgyan"
    Author: 'A-zha Blo-gros rGyal-mtshan (1198-1263)
    Publisher: bKra-shis rDo-rje
    Publication place: New Thobgyal, Tibetan Bonpo Monastic Centre, Dolanji, HP, India
    Publishing date: 1985

"rTsa rgyud nyi sgron"
    Srid pa las kyi gting zlog gi rtsa rgyud kun gsal nyi zer sgron ma
    (*gter-ma*)
    Discoverer: Bra-bo sGom-nyag (pre. 1310)
    Publisher: g.Yung-drung rGyal-mtshan
    Publication place: New Thobgyal
    Type: *bdu med* manuscript

"rTsa rgyud nyi sgron" (Tantra Series, vol. TSA)
    (*gter-ma*)
    Discoverer: Bra-bo sGom-nyag (pre. 1310)
    Publishing house: Si khron zhing chen mi rigs zhib 'jug su'o Bod kyi rig gnas zhib 'jug khang, Chengdu
    Type: Reproduction of *dbu med* manuscript

"Tshangs dbyangs yid 'phrog"
    See *Gangs ti se'i dkar chag tshangs dbyangs yid 'phrog*

"*rDzogs pa chen po zhang zhung snyan rgyud kyi bon ma nub pa'i gtan tshigs*"
    Zhang Zhung Aural Transmission Cycle
    in: *History and Doctrines of Bonpo Niṣpanna Yoga*
    Author: Gyer-spungs sNang-bzher Lod-po (seventh century)
    Publishing house: International Academy of Indian Culture, New Delhi
    Publishing date: 1968

"*Zhang zhung snyan rgyud kyi brgyud pa'i bla ma'i rnam thar*"
    Author: sPa-btsun bsTan-rgyal Seng-ge dPal-bzang (fifteenth century?)
    Publishing house: International Academy of Indian Culture, New Delhi
    Publishing date: 1968

"*Zhang zhung me ri'i lcog mkhar bzhengs lugs kyi zur byang*"
    See *Me ri'i lcog mkhar bzhengs lugs kyi zur byang*

"*Zhang zhung me ri'i bla ma brgyud pa'i bstod phyag chen mo*"
    Zhang Zhung Aural Transmission Cycle
    Authors: 'Gro-mgon Klu-brag-pa, and Khyung-sgom dPal-'byor lHun-grub (thirteenth century)
    Publishing house: International Academy of Indian Culture, New Delhi
    Publishing date: 1968

"*gZer mig*"
    'Dus pa rin po che'i rgyud gzer mig
    (*gter-ma*)
    Discoverer: Drang-rje bTsun-pa gSer-mig (eleventh century)
    Publishing house: New Thobgyal
    Type: *bdu med* manuscript

"*Ya ngal gdung rabs*"
    See *rGyal gshen ya ngal gyi gdung rabs un chen tshangs pa'i sgra dbyangs*

"*Yar lung jo bo'i chos 'byung*"
    Author: Shākya Rin-chen-sde (fourteenth century)
    Publishing house: Si khron mi rigs dpe skrun khang, Chengdu
    Publishing date: 1988

"*Yum bu bla sgang gi dkar chag 'bring po*" (article)
    in: *Bod ljongs zhib jug*, vol. 4, Lhasa, 1984
    Author: lCang-glang-pa Rol-pa'i rDo-rje

"*g.Yung drung bon gyi rgyud 'bum*"
    See *Grags pa rin chen gling grags* in *Sources for a History of Bon*
    Publishing house: New Thobgyal, Tibetan Bonpo Monastic Centre, Dolanji, HP, India
    Publishing date: 1972

"*g.Yung drung bon gyi bstan 'byung nyung bsdus*"
    See *Bon gyi bstan 'byung nyung bsdus*

"Rus mdzod pad dkar skyed tshal"
    Editor: 'Bru bKra-shis rGya-mtsho
    Origin: rNga khog (Amdo rNga ba)
    Type: *dbu chen* text

"Rlangs kyi po ti bse ru"
    Author: Rlangs Byang-chub 'Dre-bkol (968-1076)
    Publishing house: Bod ljongs mi dmangs dpe skrun khang, Lhasa
    Publishing date: 1986

"Rlung rta'i gsol kha"
    Rlung rta'i gsol kha dge legs kun stsol zhes bya ba
    Author: Mi-pham 'Jam-dbyangs rNam-rgyal (1846-1912)
    Publishing house: sDe dge lhun grub steng
    Type: Xylographic edition

"Legs bshad rin gter"
    Legs par bshad pa rin po che'i gter zhes bya ba'i bstan chos
    Author: Sa-skya Paṇḍi-ta Kun-dga' rGyal-mtshan (1182-1251)
    Publishing house: Bod ljongs mi dmangs dpe skrun khang, Lhasa
    Publishing date: 1982

"Legs bshad rin po che'i mdzod"
    Legs bshad rin po che'i gter mdzod dpyod ldan dga' ba'i char zhes bya ba
    Author: Shar-rdza bKra-shis rGyal-mtshan (1859-1933?)
    Publishing house: Mi rigs dpe skrun khang, Beijing
    Publishing date: 1985

"Sha ba ru rgyas kyi mdos chog"
    Owner: dPon-slob bsTan-'dzin rNam-dag (private copy)
    Type: *dbu med* manuscript

"bShad mdzod chen mo"
    bShad mdzod yid bzhin nor bu
    Author: Don-dam sMra-ba'i Seng-ge (fifteenth century)
    Publisher: Kun-bzang sTobs-rgyal
    Publlication place: Thimphu, Bhutan
    Publishing date: 1976

"Srid pa spyi mdos"
    Author: Ra-sangs Khri-ne-khod
    Owner(s): Nam-mkha'i Nor-bu, and IsIAO, Rome, Italy

"Srid pa rgyud kyi kha byang"
    (*gter-ma*)
    Discoverer: Khod-po Blo-gros Thogs-med (fourteenth century)
    Publisher: bsTan-'dzin rNam-dag
    Publication place: New Thobgyal, Tibetan Bonpo Monastic Centre, Dolanji, HP, India
    Publishing date: 1976

Index of Tibetan and Zhang Zhung Names and Terms

KA
Kaḥ-thog Rig-'dzin Tshe-dbang Nor-bu 226, 232, 261
Ka-ra bDun-tshe 80
Kar-ma Yo-lde 49
Ku-sa-ra 188
Ku-se gSer-ljongs 193, 199
ku hrang 238
Kun-'dus Rigs-pa 81
Kun-bzang 47, 48
Kong 25, 44, 45, 56, 57, 65, 66, 109, 122, 128, 159, 163, 182, 214, 216, 266
Kong-dkar-po 163
Kong-rje 45
Kong-po 25, 56, 66
Kong-po De-mo 122
Kong-po Bon-ri 56
Kong-po Bri-sna 214
Kong-bza' Khri-lcam 45
Kong-yul Bre-sna 57
Kyi-le Gu-ge 252
Klu 34, 43, 112, 157, 161, 205, 207, 218, 243
Klu-lcam Mi-mo 68
Klu-gnyan Gung-btsan 85

Klu-gnyan gZung-btsan 68, 85, 152, 180
Klu-thang Mer-mo 125, 143
Klu-mo sByang-pa 92
Klu-sman Mer-mo 125, 140
Klu-srin Bye-ma Lag-ring 162
Klung-shod Thong-dmar 57
Klo 56
dKa'-thub-can 46
dKar-dun-rtse 83, 86
dKar-nam rGyal-ba 89, 100
dkar gsum mngar gsum 240
dkyil rgyud klung thang 38
dkrigs 36
bKa'-brgyud 253
bka' nyan bshad kyi bstan pa 57
rke'i mjing pa 121
rKong 61, 159, 160
rKong-dkar-po 159
rKong[-po] 124
rKyel-thur 242
sKar-ma Yol-lde 89, 100
sKar-zla-gdong 46
sKu-mkhar rTse-drug 232
sku gshen 68, 97
sKu-gshen gCo Gyim-bu Phyag-dkar 71

sKu-gshen gCo'u sMin-dkar 72
sKu-gshen gCo'u Zhal-dkar 74
sku srung 68, 97
sku srung gi bon po 50
sku srung sde bzhi 224
sku srung gshen po 51
sku lha 90
skud pa nag po'i rgyud kha 211
sKos 88
skos shes rtsis mkhan 52
sKyi-shod Lung-nag 57
sKyid-grong 38
sKye-rgu-mdo 193
bskal pa 88
bskal pa bas bskal 88

KHA
Kha-che 160, 188, 210
kha che'i chos 43
Kha-dang sKyol-med 89
Kha-ba Glang-ri 56
Kha-yug 56, 57
Kha-yug Khyung-lung dNgul-mkhar 56
Kha-rag gSang-phug 57
Kha-rub 37, 38
khad kyis 93
Khab-rmu-bza' mThing-khug-sman 114
Khams 24, 56, 64, 178, 180
Khams chen brgyad 186
Khams chen po brgyad 66, 67, 186
Khu 49, 159
Khu-bon Mang-rje Lod-po 126, 181
Khu-mang bZher-gnyan 78, 79
Khu-smon-gzung 162, 164
Khu'i Bon-po Mang-sgra Legs-pa 85
Khu'i Bon-po Mang-rje Lod-po 85
Khu'i Bon-po Mang-rje lHa-'od 85
khegs 218, 219
khed 219
Kho-ma Ne-chung 71
Kho-ma 'Bro-rje 88, 100
Kho-ma Yang-rtse 68, 72, 76, 179

Kho-ma Ru-ring 74
Khong-ma Ne-chung 60, 71
Khong-ma Yang-rTse 60
Khong-ma Ru-rings 74
Khom-yang-rtse 76
Khyab-pa 205
Khyim-bu Gor-gor 93
Khyung 16, 22, 52, 167
Khyung-lcem g.Yung-drung dGe-ldan-ma 236
Khyung-po sTag-sgra Dung-gtsug 258
Khyung-po sTag-sgra Dun-tsug 75
Khyung-lung 55, 245, 250, 251, 252, 253
Khyung-lung rGyal-ba-mnyes 252
Khyung-lung dNgul-mkhar 55, 56, 59, 241, 246, 251, 252, 253, 255
Khyung-lung dNgul-mkhar rGyal-ba-mnyes 255
Khye-nan Yo-phya 242
Khye'u 239
Khye'u-skye-ba Dran-pa'i Nam-mkha' 241
khra bsang 19
khrag khrig 36
khri 120, 121, 122, 124, 127, 128, 132, 155, 156, 178, 179, 180, 182, 186, 182, 236
Khri Ka-g.yu-btsan 83, 148
Khri-skor 67, 75
Khri-skor lDem-nyag 75
Khri-gar-gyi bDun-tshigs 90
Khri-rga sTag-gzigs 89, 103
Khri-rgyal-po 103
khri rgyal po bdun 94
Khri-rgyal-ba 94, 103, 104, 105, 106
Khri sGra-sgrungs-btsan 83
Khri-sgra dPung-btsan 148
Khri-sgra dPungs-btsan 128
Khri-sgra sPung-bstan 129, 148
Khri-sgra sPungs-btsan 148, 149, 169
Khri-rje 120
Khri-rje Yag-pa 113

INDEX OF TIBETAN AND ZHANG ZHUNG NAMES AND TERMS 273

Khri-gnyan Zung-btsan 151, 157
Khri-gnyan gZung-btsan 68, 85, 126, 151, 152, 180
Khri-gnyan gZungs-btsan 128, 149, 152
Khri-gnya' gZung-btsan 85
Khri-snya Zung-bstsan 129, 130, 151, 220
Khri sNya-zungs bTsan-po 85
Khri-snyan Zung-btsan 126
Khri-snyan bZung-btsan 152, 227
Khri-brten 120
Khri-thog rJe-btsan 128, 149
Khri Thog-rje Thog-btsan 86, 149, 150, 151, 167, 168, 169
Khri-thog-bstsan 129, 149
Khri Thob-rje Thog-btsan 86, 149, 150, 151, 167, 168, 169
Khri-thob rJe-btsan 128, 149, 151
Khri-thob Nam-brtsan 166
Khri-lde lCags-kyi Bya-ru-can 120
Khri-lde gTsug-bstsan 221
Khri-lde Yag-pa 61
Khri-lde Yags-pa 113, 124
Khri-lde Srong-btsan 116
Khri-ldem lCags-kyi Bya-ru-can 236, 238
Khri-nam-btsan 128, 147
Khri-ne-khod 181, 182
Khri-pan bTsan-po 73, 136
Khri-spe bTsan-po 129, 135
Khri-ba gNyis-gzig 94, 103
Khri-bar-gyi bDun-tshigs 90, 103, 121
Khri-bar-la bDun-tshigs 50
Khri-ma 60, 120
Khri-ma sTong-cho 60
Khri-sman rJe-ma 125, 145
Khri-btsan 83, 120, 129, 133, 148, 149, 169, 227
Khri-btsan-nam 83, 129, 148, 149, 169
Khri-bstsan-nam 148
Khri-btsan-po 'Od-ldan 120
Khri-btsun 65, 120, 137, 147

Khri-rtsig 77, 233
Khri-brtsigs 'Bum-gdugs 233
Khri-rtse 233
Khri-rtse dGu-rtsegs 75
Khri-wer 120
Khri-wer gSer-gyi Bya-ru-can 120, 224
Khri-'od-gsas 120
Khri-shel dKar-po 89
Khri-shor rGyal-mo 23, 24
Khri-sad 'Bar-ba 98, 103, 104, 106, 121
Khri-so Bud-btsan-po 178
Khri-srong 250, 251
Khri-srong lDe-btsan 248, 249, 250
Khri-srong lDe'u-btsan 120, 240, 249, 250
Khri-srong-btsan 117
Khri'i-bdun-tshigs 108
Khri'u-ra-tsa 120
Krig 29
Khrin 88
khrus gsol 47
Khro-ma Ye-sangs 60
Khrom 225
khrom-kha 225
khrom khrom bsang 19
mkhan po 63
mkhan bu 63
mkha' klong dbyings 207
mkha'-'gro 63
mKhar Khyung-lung dNgul-ma-mā 242
mKhar-chen Brag-dkar 57
mKhas-pa lDe'u 49, 264
mkhas pa mi bzhi 59
mKhas-dbang Tshal-pa Kun-dga' rDo-rje 189

GA
Ga-chu 63, 236
Ga-chu gTsug-phud rGyal-mtshan 236
Gangs-gnyan sTag-sgo 64
ga'u 63
Gar-ma Me-slag-can 255

Gu-ge 56, 178
Gu-ru bTsu-gu 183
Gu-rub 183, 184
Gu-rub-za sNang-sgron Legs-mo 248
Gu-rub gSal-dga' 184
Gu-rub gSal-'od dGa'-ba 182, 183
Gu-rum-legs 120, 128
Gu-rum Legs-rgyal 68, 77, 141
Gung-then-rje 93, 101
Gung-gzigs 92
Gu-rib gSas-dga' 184
Guru Rinpoche Padmasambhava 239
Gu-rub sTag-wer Shig-slags 248
Gu-rub gSal-dga' 184
Gu-rub gSal-'od 182, 183, 266
Gu-rub gSal-'od dGa'-ba 182, 183
Gu-rum Legs-rgyal 68, 77, 141, 274
Gur-bu 233
Gur-sman 125, 126, 140, 149, 150
Ge-khod This-'phen 63
Ge-god 114
Ge-mun bTsan-po 74
Ge-sar 20, 58, 210, 216
Ge-sar Kong-po 44
Ge-sar Ngam-pa lCe-ring 242
Go-ru-legs 77, 140, 141
Go-ru-legs bTsan-po 129, 140
Go-ru Legs-rgyal 77, 140
Gong-bu-me 57
Gor-bu-legs 77, 140, 233
Gyang-thog Thog-yangs 92
Gyim-bu Lan-tsha 63, 244
Gyim-brtsan rMang-cung 274
Gyim-brtsan rMang-chung 247
Gyim-shod Shel-brag 56
gyer 42
Gyer-chen Mar-me sGron-gsal 255
Gyer-chen bTso-'phen 168
Gyer-spungs Chen-po sNang-bzher Slod-po 248
Gyer-spungs sNang-bzher Lod-po 184, 267
gyer ba 42

Gyer-zla-med 166, 167
grags pa bon lugs 96
Grang-mo Grang-chun-gi-rdza 164
Grang-mo gNam-gser-bstsig 129, 131
Grang-mo gNam-bse'-bstsig 165
Grang-mo'i gNam-gser-tig 164
Gram-pa-kha'u 58
Gram-pa-tshal 60
gri 113, 124
Gri-gum 62, 65, 67, 124, 127, 128, 165
Gri-gum bTsad-po 112
Gri-gum bTsan-po 27, 61, 62, 64, 65, 74, 113, 117, 136, 137, 155, 158, 159, 160, 161, 163, 164, 165, 186, 231, 243, 244
Gri-btsan 210
Gri-'tsho-mi 164
Gri-rum bTsan-po 61, 74, 113, 124, 136, 137, 161
Gru-gu 25, 171
Gru-zha gNam-sras 62
Gro-za sKyid-rgyal 92
Glang-gi Gyim-shod 222
Glang-chen-'dul 46
Glad-shad Nyal-ba 195
glud 45
dGu-ra dGu-khyud 72
dgung 96
dGe-sho-legs 78, 141
dGe-lugs-pa 253
dgra bcom 235
dgra sri 162
dGra-lha 167
bGegs 206
mGar 189, 190
mGar-blon sTong-btsan Yul-srung 189
mgul lha mched gsum 89, 101
mgon shes lha bon 45, 52, 53, 54
mgyogs sna lnga 226
'Gar 49
'Gar-sgra Dzi-mun 169
'Gu-ru-legs 77, 125, 141

'gog pa 64
'Gos 49
'Gos-lo[-tsa-wa] gZhon-nu-dpal 36
'Gru 21
'gro shes glud gtong 53, 54
'gro shes glud bon 45
'gro shes 'phrul bon 45
'Grong-snyan 126, 181
'Grong-snyan lDe-ru 85, 126
'grol shes gtad byad 207
'grol shes 'phrul bon 53
rGa 21, 22, 35
rGa Yig-tshang-can 21
rGung-then-che 89, 101
rGung-mtha 169'
rGo 17, 18, 35
rGod-snyan 225
rGod-rtse 233
rGya 171
rGya-rje Drang-dkar 31
rGya-bon Zings-pa mThu-chen 243
rGya-'brong-nam 275
rGya-wer Li-lod-btsan 82, 179
rGya-rong 31
rGya-la 'Brong-nam 89, 102
rGya-shar 225
rGya-shod sTag-la-tshal 30
rgyang bu 186, 211
rgyal khrims 174
rgyal gyi gri 'dur 214
rgyal gri rum gyi gri 'dur yog bar pa sum brgya drug bcu 214
rGyal-bco Ye-shes 64
rgyal chen mi bzhi 21
rGyal To-ro Lo-btsan 82, 126
rGyal To-re Longs-brtsan 129
rGyal sTo-re Lo-btsan 82
rGyal Thod-re Long-btsan 82, 147
rGyal-drang 23, 31
rGyal-lde bTsun-rab-gsal 64
rGyal-po sPrin-btsan 82, 147
rGyal-po Srin-btsan 82
rGyal-phran bCu-gnyis 180

rGyal-ba-mnyes 242, 252, 255
rGyal-ba mNyes-pa 241
rGyal Zan-nam Zin-lde 78
rGyal-zi Nam-'dzin 78, 142
rGyal-btsan 82, 147
rgyal rabs sil ma bdun 128
rGyal-rong 23, 31, 33
rGyal-gshen Mi-lus bSam-legs 216
rGyal-sa rGya-mkhar Ba-chod 57
rGyal Sa-nam Zin-te 78
rGyal-srid bTsad-po 81, 145
rGyal-srin-btsan 129, 147
rgyas pa 'bum lnga 157
rgyu'i bon 51, 176, 186
rgyugs yig 198
rGyung-yar 242
rGyung-yar Mu-khod 240, 242, 243
rGyung-yar Mu-khod rGyal-po gZha'-tshon 'Od-kyi Bya-ru-can 242, 245, 252
rGyung-yar Bla-chen Khod-spungs 241, 244
rgyun gyi khams 186
sGa 18, 19, 21, 22, 23, 30, 32, 35
sGa-skye rGu-mdo 193
sGa-khog 23
sGa-mo 19
sgam 190
sgam chung 190
sGam lHa-sras 47
sGo 30
sgo 221
sgong 55
sGom-lha-bo lHa-sras 203, 229
sGor-mo 38
sgra 41
sGra-bla 211, 214
sGrang-za lHa-rgyan 61, 113, 124
sgrub pa po 59
sGrung 53, 95, 217, 218, 262
sGron-legs-ma 221, 249
sgrom 190
sgrom bu 190

sgrol shes gtad byad 53
sgrol shes lta bon 54
sgrol shes lda byad 53, 54, 204, 207
sgrol shes 'phrul bon 212
sgrol shes lha byad 54
brGya-ltangs bDud-'dul 63
brgyag 212

NGA
Nga-la g.Ya'-ma-gong 92
ngag 41
ngan 'tshang 211
Ngan-lam-ral 57
ngam 210, 213
Ngam-pa lCe-ring 216, 242
Ngam-'brang lCang-brang 90, 91
ngar pa 65
Ngar-ma-thang 164
Ngar-las-skyes 162, 164
dNgul-zla-sgang 56
mnga' sde 17
mNga'-ris 56
mngon pa sde bzhi 157
rngan 111
rngan nam mtshang 111, 114

CA
Ci-hri 28
Co 51, 60
Co-sku 216
Co-na Phyag-gar-tsha 70
Co-bu 'Tshams-dkar 61
Co-bu Zhal-dkar 61
Co-bu 'Od-dkar 60
Co-bu Shel-dkar 60
Co-bon gSang-skyes 86
Cog-la-bon 53
Co'u Phyag-dkar 70
Co'u sMin-dkar 60, 72, 179
Co'u-tshe-dkar 276
gCe-'od 178, 179, 180
gCo Gyim-bu Lan-tsha 63
gCo-snyan-rings 180

gCo-stag Klu-gsas 108
gCo bDud-kyi mDud-bkrol 76
gCo-ldan mTshe-'gron 70
gCo-phan-grags 180
gCo-phyag-dkar 72, 78
gCo-bu 50
gCo-bon 179
gCo-bon Khri-gtsug Khyung-drag 258
gCo-bon dGu-brgyud 74
gCo-bon gNyan-dkar Legs-pa 75
gCo-bon g.Yang-skyes 86
gCo-smin-dkar 72
gCo-tshem-dkar 74
gCo-zhal-dkar 73
gCo-'od dKar-po 65, 180
gCo-shang-dkar 73
gCo-gshen Phyag-dkar 50
gCod 36, 195
gCo'i Bon-po Khri-phyung Grags-pa 84
gCo'u gNyan-bzher 75
gCo'u gNya'-bzhed 67, 75
gCo'u Phyag-dkar 70, 71
gCo'u sMin-dkar 72, 180
gCo'u Zhal-dkar 74, 124 179
gCo'u 'Od-dkar 72, 123, 179, 180
gCo'u g.Yang-skyes 68, 86
gCo'u Lan-tsha 71, 179
gCo'u Shang-dkar 73
bCo Gyim-bu Lan-tsha 61
bCo-na Mi-chen 61, 73
bCo-bu Phyag-dkar 60
bCo-mi 164
bCo-btsun 64
bCo Ye-shes 63, 64
bCo'u 215
bCo'u sMin-dkar 72, 123
bCo'u Lan-tsha 71, 123
lCe-tsha mKhar-bu 27, 59

CHA
chang 24, 25, 29, 92
Chab-mdo 37
Chab-mdo Kha-rub 39

INDEX OF TIBETAN AND ZHANG ZHUNG NAMES AND TERMS 277

Char-then-che 89, 101
Char-then-rje 93, 101
Chu-sgro rDo-ring 57
Chu-lcam rGyal-mo 97
Chu-la lDe-brgyad 126, 165
chung bsang 19
chud po 43
chun po 43
Che-dgu 96
Che-chid Mang-sung 28
che gnyan che 21
Chē-hpho-kri-'phan 28
chos 169, 200
mChims 49
mChims-za Klu-rgyal Ngan-mo-mtsho 130, 151
mChims-za bTsan-ma-thog 221
mChed bzhi 93
mChog-dkon rGyal-mo-khang 57
mchod rten 63
mChod gnas gnyan po gsang ba 202
'chi med thugs sprul 241
'Chi-med sPrul-pa Bon-mo sTag-za Li-wer 237
'Chi-med gTsug-phud 241
'Ching-nga rTag-rtse 230, 231
'Ching-ba sTag-rtse 231
'Chin-za Klu-rgyal Ngan-na-mtsho 126, 181

JA
Ju-tig 58
Ju-thig 66
'Jag-ma Glu-len 57
'Jang 28, 29
'Jang-gi-bu Ru-la-skyes 65
'Jad-kyi sKyang-khor 57
'Jug-ma'i-rtse 60
rJe-btsan 86, 128, 149, 150
rJe-rigs bTsun-po 120

NYA
Nya-khyi 159

Nya-khri 66, 103, 109, 118, 122, 123, 124, 128, 159, 160, 162, 163
Nya-khri bTsan-po 103, 109, 122, 123
Nya-ro Zla-ba'i-tshal 61
Nyag-khri 118, 122
Nyag-khri bTsan-po 122, 129, 133, 220, 224, 225, 228
Nyag-nyi rGyab-dmar 92, 107
Nyag-ri 118, 121, 122
Nyag-ri brTsan-po 122
Nyang 124
Nyang-chu 39, 65
Nyang-chu sKya-mo 65
Nyang-stod sTag-tshal 57
Nyang-po 65, 66, 128, 160
Nyang-phu She-nag 57
Nyang-ro sTag-tshal 113
Nyang-ro Sham-po 113, 231
Nyan-kong 56
Nyi-khri 39
Nyi-ma bsTan-'dzin 214
Nying-khri 37, 38
Nye-lo Wer-ya 224
gNyags 52
gNyan 69, 180, 209
gNyan-chen Thang-lha 57, 112
gnyan pa 52
gNyan-po 88, 169
gNyan po gsang ba 202
gNyan-po-lha 88
gNyan-mang-mo 125, 143
gNyan-btsun Mang-mo-rje 126, 147
gNya'-khri 46, 60, 90, 111, 118, 119, 121, 124, 127, 238
gNya'-khri Gar-gyi bDun-tshigs 90
gNya' Khri-po 90
gNya'-khri bTsad-po 47, 70, 98, 118, 133, 134, 224, 232
gNya'-khri bTsan-po 10, 32, 45, 46, 47, 49, 50, 51, 52, 54, 60, 69, 70, 78, 90, 91, 92, 94, 96, 98, 103, 104, 105 106, 107, 108, 109, 110, 114, 115, 116, 118, 119, 123, 127, 132,

133, 134, 176, 187, 203, 215, 217, 224, 228, 229, 230, 232
gNya'-nang 37, 38, 39
gnya' ba 90
gnya' ba nas byon pa'i lha 90
gNye-yul Bum-nag 30
gNyer 88
mnyam nyid kyi khams 187
sNya-khri 118, 121
sNya-khri bTsan-po 121
sNya-chen Li-shu 215
sNya-chen Li-shu sTag-ring 214, 215, 237
sNya-'bring 169
sNya-gzi bTsad-po 84, 153
sNyag 230
sNyags 94
snyan 69, 180, 181
sNyan Li-shu sTag-ring 258
sNying po yi ge drug ma 202

TA
Ta-nu-ta 188
Ta-pi Hri-tsa 248
Ta-zig 58, 59
Ta-zig-rong 56
Ti-tse 56
Ti-se 7, 64
Ting-khri bTsad-po 59, 134
To-to Re-long-btsan 168
To-re Long-btsan 147, 148, 168
To-ro Lo-btsan 82, 126, 147, 148, 179,
Tri-rgyal Lo-ngam 127, 132, 137, 160, 161
Tri-rgyal Lo-ngam rTa-rdzi 124, 127, 161
gtad 207, 208
gtad rdzas 207
gtad 'og tu bcug 208
gTad rul 208
gtam [ma] 36
gtan tshigs 50, 183, 247, 267

gter gyi sgrom bu 190
gter bdag 256
gto 45, 157, 173, 204, 210, 214
gto thabs g.yen sel 58
gto dpyad 210
gTo-'bum 208
gTod 205, 207, 208, 210, 213
gTod-lha 205
gtor-ma 167
rTa-nag rKyang-bu 57
rTa-phu Gron-lhas 57
rTag-tu Ngu-ba'i rTsi-chog 255
rTag-gzigs 58, 59, 209, 210, 215
rte'u 221
lTab-nag 168
lTing-rgyu dKar-po 89, 100
ltems 49
lto shes rtsis mkhan 54
sTag-gu gNyan-gzigs 157
sTag-gung gNyan-gzigs 84, 180
sTag-gong sNyan-gzigs 69, 84, 153, 180, 181
sTag-gling 235
sTag-rna-dbal 235, 236, 237
sTa-gu rNyan-gzigs 171
sTag-gu Nyan-gzigs 157
sTag-sgra dGe-bshis 179
sTag-cha ['Al-'ol] 97
sTag-cha Yal-yol 89, 102
sTag-rna gZi-brjid 224, 235, 236
sTag-rna gZi-brjid Khri-ldem lCags-kyi Bya-ru-can 235
sTag-rna gZi-brjid rGyal-po Khri-ldem lCags-kyi Bya-ru-can 237
sTag-rna gZi-brjid rGyal-po gZha'-tshon 'Od-kyi Bya-ru-can 237
sTag-bu sNya-gzigs 130
sTag-rtse 230, 233
sTag-wer Li-wer 216
sTag-gzig 20, 54, 59, 96, 186, 200, 209, 216
sTag-gzig 'Ol-mo Lung-rings 67
sTag-gzig 'Ol-mo'i Lung-rings 66, 67

INDEX OF TIBETAN AND ZHANG ZHUNG NAMES AND TERMS 279

sTag-gzigs 216
sTag-gzigs-nor 248
sTag-gzigs Za-rang Me-'bar 242
sTag-ri 126
sTag-ri gNyan-gzigs 84, 128, 151, 153, 154, 171
sTag-ri sNyan-gzigs 126, 153, 154, 181, 227
sTag-la Me-'bar 113
sTangs-chen dMu-tsa Gyer-med 242
stangs dbyal 240
sTangs dMu-tsha Gyer-med 243
sTong 18, 20, 22, 23, 30, 32, 35
sTong-rgyung mThu-chen 55, 59, 216, 238, 239, 242, 243, 248, 250, 256
sTong-sgra Kun-'dul 179
stong pa'i khams 186
sTong-bzangs lHa-phug 84
sTong-ri sTong-btsan
sTong-re Shib-shang 75
sTod 18, 52, 57, 225
sTod-ral-lung 57
sTobs-ra Shib-shang 68, 75
bsTan-'dzin rNam-dag 214, 260, 261, 265, 268

THA

Tha-chung rTser-rtser 89, 100
Tha-nga lHa-mo 90, 103
Tha-mi Thad-ke 243
Tha-mi Thad-ge 243
Tha-tshan Hi-sang-skyes 99
Thag-ring rTse-dgu La-dgu 91
Thang-thang 90, 121
Thang-nag Bon-po 61
Than-tsho Zo-'brang 89, 94, 103
Thi-mar Thad-ge 216
Thi-sho-legs 76, 120, 128, 140, 141
Thi-sho Legs-rgyal 68, 76, 140, 141
Thi-sho-legs bTsan-po 129
thig gu lnga 212
thig le 207
This 212

Thu-bhod 28
Thu-hpha 28
Thu'u-hu-li'i-lo'o-ku 27, 29
Thu'u-hpha-li-lo'u-ku'u 28
Thu'u-hphā 28
Thu'-hphan 28
thugs dam 64
The-brang 88, 104, 106, 111, 112
the brang skyas 'debs 104
The-brang Ma-nya U-be-ra 106
The-brang Mang-snya U-be-ra 105
The-rang Mang-snya dBu-wer 113
The-sho 233
The-sho-legs 76, 125, 140, 141, 142, 233
The-hrig 28
theg pa rim pa dgu'i bon 257
Then dgu 93, 99
The'u-brang 87, 103, 105, 108, 112, 118
The'u-brang sPun-dgu 103
The'u-brang Mang-snya U-be-ra 108, 109
The'u-rang 96, 99, 103, 104, 105, 111, 112, 113, 114
The'u-rang sPun-dgu 103
The'u-rang Ma-snya U-wer 113, 124
ther 'bum 36
Tho-gar 202
Tho-tho gNyan-btsan 128, 149
Tho-tho Re-long-btsan 149, 227
Tho-tho Ri-gnyan-btsan 86, 150
Tho-tho Ri-snyan-shal 86, 174, 202
Tho-tho Ri'i-snyan-btsan 86, 149
Tho-tho-hu 38
Tho-do sNyan-shal 157, 170
Tho-lde Lo-rog bTsad-po 82, 147
Tho-ri Lung-btsan 68
Tho-re Long-btsan 148
Tho-la Da-ma Ga-'go 64
Tho-leg bTsan-po 82, 147
Thog lcags 34
Thod-kar 165

Thon-mi 189
Thon-mi Klu-mang Dred-po 169
Thon-mi Mi-chung Saṃbhoṭa 175, 176
Thon-mi Saṃ-bho-ṭa 188
Thon-mi A-nu 173, 175, 191, 191, 202
mtha' bzhi'i rgyal po bzhi 96
mThu-chen Mi-dgu 256
mThong-rtse 78, 233
'Then dgu 93, 99

DA
Da-mi Thad-ke 243
Da-mi Thad-ge 242
Dag-khri 61
Dag-khri bTsan-po 60
Dag-pa Mi-chen 73, 124
Dag-gtsang Ya-ngal 51
Dags-khri bTsan-po 73
Dang-ra 250, 251
Dang-ra g.Yu-bun 57
dam tshig 48
Dar-rgyal Srin-btsan 82, 147
Dar-khri bTsad-po 59, 73
Dar-khri bTsan-po 73, 120, 135, 136
Dar-za Zhang-zhung-ma 123, 134, 135
Dar-ha-to 75
Dar-ha-ni 79
ding 92, 120
Ding-khri 60, 123, 124, 179
Ding-khri bTsad-po 72, 134, 135, 179
Ding-khri bTsan-po 60, 72, 120, 123, 127, 129, 133, 134, 135
Ding-ri 37, 38, 39
Dug-mtsho Mu-le'i Do-gling 255
dung phyur 37
Dung-'phar-po 'Phar-chung 90, 91
Dur gShen 210
dur gshen mtshon cha can 66
De-khri bTsan-po 129, 135
De-mo 109
De-sho-legs 76, 120, 125, 140, 233

De-sho Legs-rgyal 68, 76, 140
Dog-lha Bon-po 47
Dogs-mo Dog-mo Dog-nyen 92
Don-rtogs rGyal-po 78, 79, 125
Don-kun Grub-pa 184
Dom-sgro Nag-mo sMyug-ma Bu-'khur 57
Dol-po 178, 180, 182
Dwags 124, 160
Dwags-kyi lHa-mo dKar-mo 124
Dwags-khri 124
Dwags-khri bTsan-po 73, 124, 135, 136
Dwags-po 25, 171
Dwags-yul Shing-nag 92
Dwags-yen-mkhar 92
Dwang-ra 222, 249, 251
Drag-pa 124, 160
Drang-mo drang-chung 164
drang srong 235
Drang srong chen po brgyad 208
Dran-pa 239
Dran-pa Nam-mkha' 10, 75, 183, 239, 240, 241, 242, 252, 260, 261
Dri-gum bTsad-po 74, 137
Dri-gum bTsan-po 129, 136
Dri-dmu Tri-btsan 103
Dri-rum bTsan-po 74
Drung-gi mTshal-phug 57
dre'u 227
Dre-nga Bram-sna 92
Dre-rmu Dre-btsan 103, 104, 121
gdags 94
gDags-khri bTsan-po 73, 127, 135, 136
gDung-rgyud bCu-gsum 255
gDung-sob Chen-po 209
gDong 19, 21, 30, 32, 35
gDong-lha-mo 19
gDon 112
bDud 205
bDud-'dul dGra-'joms 63
bDud-bon 205

bDun-tshig 94, 98
mDa'-then-rje 93, 101
mDo-khams 23, 178, 224
mdo khams sgang drug 56
mDo sde za ma tog 201
mdo-smad 64
mdos 67, 167, 186, 211, 214
'Da'-le 124
'Dam g.Yung-drung Khri-'dus 63
'Dam-shod sNar-mo 57
'Dar-khri bTsan-po 59, 73
'du gnas 54
'Du-phrod 86
'dur 186
'dur shes srid gshen 45, 52
'Dul ba 58, 157
'Dus-srong 117
'Dus-srong Mang-po-rje 221
'don pa 42,
'dom 44
'Dru 18, 21
'Dre 44, 52, 111, 112, 195
'dre bkar ba 45
'dre the'u rang 112
'Dre gdon 205
'Dre rMu-khri bTsan-mo 94, 10, 104
'dre shes glud gtong 53
Dre-srin 214
rDo rJe 115
rdo ring 115
lding shes sha ba 210, 211
lDing shes shwa ba 52
lDe 120, 126, 132, 155, 156, 158, 165, 166, 180, 220, 221, 222
lDe-gol 129, 145, 220
lDe Gyim-tsha rMa-chung 59, 216, 238, 242, 243
lDe rGyal-po 81, 220
lDe Nyag-khri bTsan-po 122, 129, 133, 220
lDe Nyag-ri bTsad-po 9, 103, 121
lDe gNya'-khri bTsan-po 49, 70, 133
lDe Nam-'phrul gZhung-btsan 79

lDe gNol-nam 80
lDe-rnol-po 81, 125, 146
lDe sNol-nam 79
lDe sPrul-gnam gZhung-bTsan 143
lDe-phru-bo gNam-gzhung-bstan 129, 220
lDe 'Phrul-po gNam-gzhung-btsan 129, 220
lDe-'Phrul Bon-rgyal 79, 144
lDe-bu 244
lDe-btsun 63, 236
lDe-btsun Rab-gsal 236
lDe 'O-rnal bTsad-po 143
lDe 'Od-rnol-nam 80
lDe-ru gNam-gzhung-btsan 128, 143
lDe So-pha-nam 80, 146
lDe Srid-btsan 82
lDe Srin-btsan 82
lDe gSer-gnon-rgyal 80
lDe-khri bTsad-po 73, 135
lDe-glang Ru-kar 50
lDe-rnol rNol-nam 79
lDe-nam 'Phrul-zhung[sic]-btsan 79
lDe gNol-po 81
lDe rNol-po 125, 146
lDe-bo gNam-gzhungs bTsad-po 79
lde-btsun 63, 236
lDe 'Od-nam bTsad-po 80, 145
lDe gSer-nam rGyal-po 81, 146
lDe'u 67, 70-86, 95, 130, 133-136, 138-149, 151, 153, 217, 218-222
lDe'u rGyal-po 81
lDe'u Nam-'od 80
lDe'u sNol-po 81
lDe'u sPrin-btsan 82
lde'u 'phrul mo'i rig pa 223
lDe'u-'Phrul gzhung-btsan 79, 144
lde'u mig 221
lDe'u-rje mChed-bdun 97, 121
ldem 227
lDong 17, 18, 20-27, 30, 32, 33, 35, 224, 225

lDong Che-gnyan-can 21
lDong-byang 25, 26
lDong-lha-bon 203
sde 169
sDe 19, 22, 30, 155
sDe Gri-gum bTsan-po 164
sDe-dge 23, 178, 180, 182, 193, 199, 262, 265
sde snod 58, 59
sDe-snod-sbas 128, 143
sDe-snod-ya 128, 145
sde snod gsum 200
brda rnying 42
brda thabs kyi rig pa 223

NA
Nag-chu 38
Nag-shod gZi-'phrang 30
Nags-ma Bya-tshang-can 92
nang don rig pa 214, 215
Nang-lha Gul-rgyal 89, 101
Nan-le 27, 29
Nan-leng 28
nam mkha' 186
Nam-mkha' sNang-ba mDog-can 51, 55, 176
Nam-mkha' sNang-ba'i mDog-can 242
Nam-mkha'i mDog-can 46-48
Nam-mkha'i sNang-ba'i mDog-can 46, 119, 255
Nam-ra 216
Ne-rgyung [lCe-tsha] mKhar-bu 216
Nel-pa Paṇḍita Grags-pa sMon-lam Blo-gros 201
Ne'u Paṇḍita 201
gNam-khri gZhung-btsan 79
gNam Khri-srong lDe-brtsan 127
gNam-gyi Khri-bdun 120, 236
gNam-gyi Ru-gdab 57
gNam-lcags dBal-gyi Bya-ru-can 224
gNam-then-che 89, 101
gNam-then Chen-po 93, 101
gNam-then-rje 93

gNam-lde rNol-nam 129, 145, 220
gNam-spu'o gZhung-btsan-lde 79
gNam-mu-yug 123
gNam-sman Phyug-mo 60
gNam-mtsho Do-ring 57
gNam-mtsho Phyug-mo 57
gNam-gzhung-brtsan 129
gNam-gzhung-bstan 220
gNam-ra sTong-btsan 84, 154
gNam-ri Gong-btsan 157
gNam-ri Srong-btsan 25, 69, 84, 126, 128, 132, 153, 154, 171, 181, 223, 258
gnam rim pa bcu gsum 88
gNam-ru Gong-btsan 84
gNam-la Khri-bdun 127
gNam-la Rong-rong 89, 102
gnam sa ga'u kha sbyor 88
gNam-lha gSer-thig 164, 165
gNas-'jog 46
gnas pa'i bskal pa 36
gNubs-gnya' Do-re gTsug-byon 169
gNon 171
gNo'-za Mang-mo-rje Ji-dgos 129
rNal-'byor gTsang-gshen 256
sNa-nam 49
sNa-nam-za' Mang-mo-rje 221
sNa-lag-can 46
sNang-sgron Legs-ma 248
sNang-ldan 157
sNang-nam Legs grub 222, 249
snang ba 210
sNang-ba mDog-can 51, 55, 60, 176
snang ba'i khams 186
sNang-ba'i mDog-can 46, 51, 119, 229, 242, 252, 255
sNang-bzher Lod-po 184, 267
snang gshen bal thod can 66
snal ma 92
sNubs 52
sNubs-mtha' 169
sNo-za Ma-so-rje 126

PA
Pa-na Ra-ling 248
Pu-rgyal 115
po ti 199
por mgo 218
Pra 58
dPa-yi-tshan 17
dPa' 21, 35
dpa' sna lnga 226
dPa'-bo gTsug-lag Phreng-ba 219, 269
dpa' mtshan rnam brgyad 96
dPa'-yi-tshan 22, 35
dPal-mgon 'Phags-pa Klu-sgrub 183
dPal-legs rGyal-mtshan 257
dPal Sa-skya-pa Grags-pa rGyal-mtshan 227
dPal Sa-skya Paṇḍita Kun-dga' rGyal-mtshan 227
dPe-thog-'phrul 243
dPe-thog-rtse 243
dpon gsas 60
dPon-gsas Khu-lung Gru-'dzin 76
dPon-gsas Gu-rum Tsan-de Mi-ser 77
dPon-gsas Gyim-thang rMa'o 78
dPon-gsas Gru-bon Kha-'bar 71
dPon-gsas lJang-tsha 'Phan-snang 86, 167
dPon-gsas sTag-sgra dGe-bshes 82
dPon-gsas sTong-sgra Kun-'dul 82
dPon-gsas Drag-po Kun-'dul 79
dPon-gsas Mun-sangs 75
dPon-gsas 'Ol-bon sPyan-gcig 72
dPon-gsas Li-bon sPungs-rgyud 74
dPon-gsas Sum-la Mu-phya 79
dPyad-bu Khri-shes 208
sPa-gong Ye-shes rGyal-mtshan 236
sPa-ston bsTan-rgyal bZang-po 131
sPa-tshab sGong-phug 61
sPang-ba Nam-gshen 216
sPu 67, 103, 105, 109, 110, 115, 124
sPu-rgya lDe-gung-rgyal 75
sPu-rgyal 32, 56, 115-117, 258
sPu-rgyal sTag-bu'i-snyan 117

sPu-rje Gung-rgyal 75
sPu-de Gang-rgyal 66, 138
sPu-de Gung-rgyal 118, 128, 129, 131, 137, 138, 155, 163-165, 185, 186, 231, 256
sPu-lde 61, 68, 124, 125, 160, 214
sPu-lde Gung-rgyal 66, 67, 75, 125, 137, 138, 161, 163, 230, 256
sPu-lde Gong-rgyal 75
sPu-lde'u Gong-rgyal 67, 75, 138
sPu-bo 104, 105, 107, 160, 162
sPu-yul 105
sPu-rong 56
sPu-hreng 38
sPu'i Mi-mo-btsan 105
sPu'i Mi-mo Mo-btsun 104
sPug Gyim-brtsan rMang-cung 245, 246
sPug Gyim-brtsan rMang-chung 245
sPur-rgyal 28, 29
sPur-rgyal-bod 117
sPe-nag-gu 167
sPe-bon Thog-'phrul 216
sPe-bon Thog-rtse 216
sPe-bon Shod-bkram 258
sPo 106
spo mgo 218, 219
spo tho 218, 219
sPo-bo 65, 66, 106, 117, 128
sPo'i Mi-mo Bya-btsun 106
sPo-de Gung-rgyal 117
sPo-bo Brag-thog 117
sPos-chu-ldong 35
sPos-ri Ngad-ldan 57, 215, 236, 237, 255
sPyang-khrig Ye-shes 19
spyan gyi sgros ma 88
spyan gyi gzigs stang 88
sPyan-ras-gzigs 174
sPyi-khri bTsan-po 127, 136
sPrin-rgyal-btsan 128, 146
sPrin-then-che 89, 101
sPrin-then-rje 93, 101

PHA
pha rgyud 59
Pha-dams-pa Sangs-rgyas 36
Pha-ba 113
Pha-ba mTshe-gco 51, 70
Pha-ba 'Tshe-gco 74, 113
Pha-ba-ra 164
Pha-'brum 114
phan shes sman 54
phan shes sman dpyad 52
Pham-shi dPal-gyi dBang-phyug 236
Phams-shi 236
Phu-mo Dre-rmu Dre-btsan-mo 90, 121
Phug 22
Phug-pa 59
phug pa 252
phung po 177
Phun-sum-tshogs-pa'i Bon-rgyal-bzhi 156
Pho-brang 229
Pho-'brang 114
pho shing 211
phon gyi yul 43
Phon-po Ma-rgyung 68
Phon-po Ma-rung 180
Phya-rje 215
Phya-rje Yab-bla bDal-drug 97, 121
Phya-bon-sngags 98
Phya-bon Thang-yag 51, 70
Phya-bon De-skyong 98
Phya-btsun Gung-ma 240, 241
Phya Yab-bla bDal-drug 99
Phyi-ba sTag-rtse 51, 165, 229, 231
Phyi-dbang sTag-rtse 224, 232
phyi rig pa 216
Phyi-lha Thog-dkar 89, 101
Phying-nga sTag-rtse 209
Phying-ba sTag-rtse 94, 229, 230, 231-233
Phying-yul Dar-thang 65
Phying-sa sTag-rtse 65, 233

Phywa 58, 88, 93, 114
Phywa-bon The-lag 50
Phywa-za Ye-thang-ma 89
Phywa Yab-bla bDag-drug 109
Phywa Yab-bla bDal-drug 98
Phywa-rje Yab-bla brDal-drug 114
Phywa Ye-mkhyen Chen-po 88
phywa gshen ju thig can 66
phywa gshen pa 206
Phywa-lha Bram-chen 89, 93, 102
phrag 212
Phrug-shor-ba rKya-bdun 44
Phrom 141, 209, 210, 216
'Phags[pa] sKyes-po 46
'phags pa'i dge 'dun 64
'Phan-myi 28, 29
'Pham-shi 63
'Phar-po Zo-brang 93
'phur shes 212
'phur shes cu tig 53, 204
'phur shes ju thig 53, 54, 211
'Phen-yul Brag-dkar 57
'Phyongs-rgyas 116
'phra ba'i 'bum bcu gnyis 257
'phrul gshen bal tshon can 66

BA
Ba-glang-gnas 46
Ba-rabs 97
Bang-ba-rje 181
ban bon 107
Bam-brag brTsegs-pa 57
bar 22, 37, 66, 88, 136-137, 147-149, 158, 166, 207, 214, 246, 252
bar gyi bskal pa 88
Bar-gyi bDun-tshigs 90
Bar-gyi lDeng-gnyis 125
Bar-gyi bTsan-lnga 126
bar do 207
Bar-lha 'Od-'bar 89, 101
Bal-then-rje 93, 102
bal thod 66, 186
Bal-po 20, 225

INDEX OF TIBETAN AND ZHANG ZHUNG NAMES AND TERMS   285

bal tshon 66, 186
bu gcig khos srel 98
bu de kun las rgyal 66
Bu-'bor-sgang 56
Bu-mtsho Srid-pa'i rGyal-po 208
Bu-ram Shing-pa 46
Bum-thang sMad-mtsho 68, 138
Bum-thang sMan-mtsho 125, 137
Bong-rje 181
Bong-ba-rje 180-181
bod kyi bon po 205
Bod Khams 91
Bod-khams Gling-dgu 43
Bod-'bangs Pha-dgu 164
bod yig 117, 130, 156, 174-175, 191-192, 199
bod lwa 24
Bod Sha-ri dBu-chen 216
Bon 6-10, 19, 33, 40-48, 50-67, 69-86, 92, 96, 107, 112-113, 119-120, 123, 130, 133-134, 136-142, 144-147, 149-154, 156-157, 159, 161, 164-170, 176-177, 179-181, 183, 185-187, 199-200, 203-206, 209-215, 217-218, 221, 223, 225, 236-244, 247-250, 252, 255-258
bon chen 59
bon chos 66-67
Bon-kyi-rong 38
bon gyi dbyings nyid 177
bon sgo bcu gnyis 204, 257
bon pa 42
Bon-po 7, 47, 61, 70, 80-82, 84-86, 98, 126, 167-168, 180-181, 186, 224, 255
Bon-mo sTag-wer Li-wer 55, 255
Bon-mo sTag-za Rlung-rgyal 243
Bon-mo Mang-rgyud 85
Bon-mong Mang-rung 85
Bon-ri 56, 61
Bon-ri-dgon 61
Bya-khri 66, 117, 128, 159-160, 162-163

Bya-mo-btsun 105
Bya-ru 241, 256
Bya-ru-can 120, 223-224, 235-238, 241, 245, 252
Bya-ru dBal-slag 256
byang 24-26, 29, 35, 37, 48, 51, 54, 57, 96, 100, 116, 121, 130, 155, 182, 229
Byang-khri bTsad-po 73, 135
Byang-khri bTsan-po 61
Byang-pa 25
byad 49, 52-54, 204, 207-208
byad kha 208
Byams-ma lTar-na 229
Byi-ba sTag-rtse 51
Bying-nga sTag-rtse 66
Byin-rlabs rGyud-pa'i gShen-dgu 256
Bye-ma g.Yung-drung-tshal 126
Bra-la sGo-drug 92
Brag-gi dBrag-mar-po 92
Brag-dmar Ri-'dus 58
Brag[-dmar] Rin-chen sPungs-pa 236, 255
Bru-sha 210
Brud-kyi mKhar-gdong 57
bla 30, 32, 41, 59, 96, 105-106, 167, 181, 183-184, 207, 212-213, 239, 257
Bla-chen Dran-pa Nam-mkha' 183, 215, 240, 243, 248, 250, 254
Bla-chen-po 214, 216, 239, 242-245, 253, 255
Bla-chen-po Dran-pa Nam-mkha' 214, 216, 239, 242-245, 253, 255
bla mdud 212
Bla-bon 166
Bla-'brum Gyang-mdo 92
bla ma che drug gi bon 59
Bla-ma Dangs-ma 'Bring-bcu 92
Bla-ma Tshe-dbang Rig-'dzin 255
bla yid sems gsum 207
bla'i sku 94
Bla'i Bon-po 167

Blo-ngan Bya-mgo 62
Blo-sems-mtsho 201
blon chen 61
blo'u rin chen mched bdun 90
dBa' 117
dBal 17-18, 21, 35, 55, 88, 124, 157, 212, 224
dBal-gyi Brag-phug dGu-rong 56
dBal-gyi Brag-phug Rong-chen 255
dBal-gyi dBang-phyug 236
dBal-'bar Me-ri 255
dBal-za Khri-btsun 67, 136
dbal zangs 224
dBal-yi-tshan 22
dBas 171
dBas-khri Zung-mong 169
dBu-khyud 60
dbu can 192, 197-198
dBu-rtse 77, 233
dBus 44, 57, 92, 225, 238, 256
dBus-gtsang 23, 25, 56
dByal-cha Ma-ting 89, 102
dByings-kyi sKyol-med 89, 100
dBra 18, 21, 35
'Bi-sho 'Ching-rgyal 78, 142
'Bum-khri Dar-ba 82
'Bum-stug 77, 233
'Bum sde lnga 257
'Bum gser thang sha ba can 95
'byung rtsi 30
'Brang-rje-legs 77, 141
'Brang-rje Legs-rgyal — 'Brong-rje Legs-rgyal 77, 141
'Brang-snyan-lde'u 68, 180
'Brang-snyan lDe-ru 152, 227
'Brang-zhi Legs-rgyal 68, 77, 141
'Brang-bzhi-legs —'Brong-bzhi-legs 77, 128, 140, 141
'bras drug 240
'bras bu'i bon 46, 51, 186
'Bri 32, 35
'Bri chu 38
'Bri-bon Shod-tri 86

'Bring-snya 169
'Bru 17-19, 21-22, 30, 32, 35, 111, 192
'Bru Byas-pa-can 21
'bru ma 192
'Bru-mo 19
'Brug 44
'Brug-pa bKa'-brgyud 199
'Bro 49
'Bro-mnyen lDe-ru 130, 151, 220
'Bro-snyan lDe-ru 85
'Bro-bzhi 233
'Bro-bzhi-legs 77, 233
'Bro'-za Dung-pyang-bzher 130, 151, 220
'brong 65, 229
'Brong-gnyan lDe-ru 85, 128, 151-152, 157
'Brong-gnyan lDem-ru
'Brong-gnyen lDem-ru 85, 151
'Brong-gnyan-lde'u 85
'Brong-zhi-legs bTsan-po 129, 141
'Brong-bzhi-legs 77, 128, 140-141
'Brong-bzher-legs 77, 125, 141
'Brong-za Dar-ma g.Yang-bzher 126, 151
sBa 49, 248, 250
sBa Ji-phrom dKar-po 248, 250
sBo 52
sBra 17-19, 21-22, 30-32, 35
sBra Ming-rna-can 21
sBra-mo 19
sBrang-bza' lHa-rgyan 113

MA
ma rgyud 59, 198
Ma-rgyud rGyal-mtshan 257
Ma-gcig Lab-sgron 195
Ma-snya U-be-ra 104-105
Ma-tro Sa-rab 57
Ma-dros mTsho-shod 57
Ma-pang 245
Ma-pham 245

Ma-mo 92
Ma-mo Dro-zhal sKyid-lding 92
Ma-sangs 104, 112, 160, 217-218
Ma-hor sTags-gzigs 248
Mang-mkhar lCags-'phrang 57
Mang-mkhar Bon-phug 58
Mang-snya Mu-wer 113
Mang-snya U-be-ra 105, 107-110
Mang-thos Klu-sgrub rGya-mtsho 183
Mang-yul Gung-thang 58
Mang-sung 28
Mi-nyag 20, 22-24, 26-27, 30-33, 243
Mi-nyag lCe-tsha mKhar-bu 243
Mi-bon Mu-phya 255-256
Mi-mo-chung 68, 76
Mi-yul sKyin-thang 92
Mi-yul Gyi-'thing 92
mi la chad rnam gnyis 95
Mi-la Ras-pa 36
mi gsang snar mo 92
mi'u 18, 33, 221
mi'u gdung drug 18, 33
mi'u rigs drug 18
mi'u rigs bzhi 18
Mu-khung gNam-rje 238
Mu-khri 46, 54-55, 58-60, 71-72, 120, 123, 127, 129, 133-134, 176, 179, 215, 242
Mu-khri bTsad-po 54-55, 58, 133, 176, 215
Mu-khri bTsan-po 46, 54-55, 60, 71, 120, 123, 127, 129, 133-134, 179, 242
Mu-cho 97, 238
Mu-cho lDem-drug 97
mu stegs lugs 107
Mu-spungs gSal-tang 216, 238-239
Mu-tsa Dra-he 59
Mu-wer Khri-'od-gsal 238
Mu-wer sTag-sna rGyal-po 238
Mu-wer bTsad-po 6, 238-239
Mu-wer bTsad-po Li-mi-rgya 238-239
Mu-wer bTsad-po Lig-mi-skya 238

Mu-wer Seng-ge-'gram 238
Mu-zi gSal-bzang 64
Mu-ya 90
Mu-la Kha-'bras 73
Mu-la Khyung-gi rGyal-po 238
Mu-la Gung-sang-rje 238
Mu-le-khyud 56, 236, 255
Mu-le Grum-shing 93
Mug-khri bTsan-po 71, 133
mun pa 210
Me-nyag 59, 216, 238-239, 242, 257
Me-nyag lCe-kha mKhar-bu 239
Me-nyag lCe-tsha mKhar-bu 216
Me-nyag Ne-rgyung 'Phar-bu 242
Me-tog 39
Me-tog-rdzong 37
Me-dur 114
med 88, 120, 158, 197-198, 209, 222, 240, 247, 257
Med-'bum Nag-po 195
Mer-khri bTsan-po 127, 135-136
Mes-rnam-la Kar-gsum 89, 100
mo 6, 18-19, 49, 60, 87, 92, 96, 99-100, 105-107, 110, 117, 130, 155-156, 159-161, 165-166, 168-171, 174-175, 184, 191, 211-213, 225, 230, 237, 243, 245-246
mo rta 212
Mo-btsun Gung-rgyal 103
mo shing 211
Mong-then-che 89, 102
Mong-then-rje 93, 102
Mon 56, 168, 215, 248
Mon-bon Ha-ra Ci-par 243
Mon-rdzu Nag-po 19
Myang 117, 159, 163, 171
Myang-po 25
Myang-ro sTag-tshal 113
Myes gNam-lha dKar-gsum 97, 100
dMag-mi Ma-sangs 160
dmangs 22, 220
dMa'-she-le 57
dmar mchod 25

dmar thabs 205
dmar po 130, 155, 182, 188-189, 202, 223
dMu 21, 35, 60, 88, 90-91, 98-99, 121, 183
dMu rGyal-ba Blo-gros 183
dMu-lcam Khab-'bring-ma 98
dMu-lcam mChong-ron-ma 98
dMu-lcam Dra-ma-na 68
dMu-lcam rMang-legs 125, 142
dMu-lcam La-na 125, 139
dMu-rje Thum-thum rNal-mad 97
dmu thag 60
dMu-bon-thugs 97
dMu-bon The-yan 50
dMu-tsa Dra-he-pa 209
dMu-tsa Dra-he-pe 216
dMu-btsan 83, 149
dMu-btsun rGyal-mo 97
dMu-tsha-dga' 35
dMu-tsha-rga 21, 35
dMu-za gNyi-mthing-ma 98, 103-104, 121
dMu-za Dung-lcam Ral-mo-che 97, 102
dMu-yi Bon-po Gong-chung 98
dMus-long 209
rMa-ge-god 114
rMa-rgyal sPom-ra 56, 112
rMa-chu 27-29
rMa-chen sPom-ra 28-29
rMa-bon 53
rMa-tshes 114
rMang-cung 245-246
rMang-chung 245-247
rMu 18, 20-23, 35, 49-50, 90-91, 94, 224
rmu skas 50
rMu-rgyal-tsha 50
rMu-rje bTsan-po 90
rmu 'brang zangs yag 91
rMu-'bring Zang-yag 50
rMu-btsun 50, 89, 102, 121

rMu-btsun Gri-sman 89, 102, 121
rMu-yul 121
rMug-sangs 192
rMu'i Bon-po sKye-ngo-mtshar 86
rMur-dgu-khyung 72
sman dpyad 52-54, 58, 204, 208
sman dpyad 'bum bzhi 58
sMan-bu-mo 68, 141
sMan-mo 179, 243
sMan-btsun Lung-gong 126, 146
sMan-tsha Glu-rgyal 227
sMan-za Klu-stengs 126, 148
sMan-ri 214
smar 192, 195, 197-199, 202
sMar-khams-sgang 56
smar gyi yi ge 195
smar sgrag 192
smar chung 192
smar chen 192
smar tshugs 199
sMug-po-gdong 18
sMe-'khor 29, 173, 182, 237, 253
sMe-phreng 29, 173, 182, 237, 253
sMon-gzung 162
sMra shes gto 53-54, 204, 210
sMra shes gto rku 53
sMra shes gto dgu 54
sMra shes gto rgu 204, 210
smrang 45, 210
smrang shes gto dgu 45
sMri-ti Chu-nag 30

TSA
(Tsan)-dang sGo-bzhi 93
Tsi-ṇa 235-237
Tso-min Gyer-rgyung 216, 255
Tso-men Gyer-chen 248, 250
gTsang 52-54, 91-92, 204
gTsang-po 159
gTsang-gyi Bye-phug 57
gTsang-chung 56
gTsang-bye-ma 216
gTsang shes sel 'debs 52-54, 204

gTsug-lcam Ngang-ma 120
gTsug-phud Tshul-khrims 236
gtsug lag 58, 95, 157, 209
gTsug lag dbal 157
gtsug lag rtsis 209
gTso'u-phyag-mkhar 50
bTsad-po Tho-yag 76, 140
bTsad-po 'Brong-'dzin-yag 77, 141
bTsad-po A'i-sho-yag 75, 140
bTsad-po 'O-ru-yag 76
bTsan 43, 52, 86, 88, 126-128, 132, 146-150, 155-158, 167-168, 179-180, 206, 210, 245-247
bTsan-thang Gong-ma 118
bTsan-thang sGo-bzhi 109, 229
btsan pa 52
bTsan-po 6, 10, 27-29, 32, 45-47, 49-52, 54-55, 60-62, 64, 69-74, 78, 85, 90-92, 94, 96, 98, 103-110, 113-124, 127, 129, 131-137, 139-142, 155, 158-165, 168, 176, 179, 186-187, 203, 215, 217, 220, 224-225, 228-232, 242-244
bTsan-bon 206
bTsan Bon 210
bTsan-mo Gur-sman 125, 140
bTsan-gzher Me-lha 62
btsun pa 52
bTsun-mo Gur-sman 68
btso 168
bTso-chen Thog-'bebs 168
rTsang-thud-gsum 93
rTsibs-kyi lHa-skar-ma Yol-lde 49
rtsis 52-54, 204, 209, 213-214
rTse-drug 232
rTse-mo Khyung-rgyal 233

TSHA
Tsha-ba-sgang 56
tsha zhing 22
Tshangs-pa gTsug-phud 216
Tshangs-pa gTsug-phud-can 215
Tshangs-lha 114

Tshad-med 'Od-ldan 241
tshan khrus 118
Tshigs-la bTsan-lnga 128
Tshe 51, 60
Tshe-rgyal [Bla-ma] 193-194
Tshe-spungs Zla-ba rGyal-mtshan 184, 248
Tshe-spong-'phrin 171
Tshe-dbang Nam-mkha' sGron-gsal 255
Tshe-dbang Rig-'dzin 255
Tshe-mi Kun-snang 75
Tshe-mi g.Yung-drung 61
Tshe-za Khyad-khyud 89, 102
Tshe'i rGyal-po 75, 125
Tshes-pong-za 'Bring-ma-thog 153, 220
Tshes-spong-gza' 'Bri-ma Tho-ga 223
mtshang 111, 114
mtshan nyid 157
mtshan nyid sde lnga 157
mTshams 88
mTshe-bon 'Dul-srong 86
mTshe-bon 'Phrul-gsas 82
mTshe-bon Ba-nam 79
mTshe-bon Bya-slag-can 83
mTshe-bon 'Ug-ru 79
mTshe-bon Yag-rgyal 80
mTshe-bon g.Yag-zhu 83
mTshe-bon gSas-chen 81
mTshe-mi 50, 68, 70, 73, 86, 125, 214
mTshe-mi-rgyal 70
mTshe-mi 'Du-'phro 68, 86
mTshe-mi dMu-rgyal 70
mTshe-mi gShen 50
mTshe-gshen lDe-grags 86
mTshes-pa gNam-'dul 68, 77
mTsho-rNgas Dril-chung 57
mTsho-gnyis 38
mTsho-mgron 118
mTsho-dang-sko 92
mTsho-bon dGu-brgyud 68, 82-83, 86
mTshe-bon 'Od-dkar 78

mTshe-mi Zung-sman 73
mTsho-mi Zung-smon 73, 123
mTsho-mi Rings-skyol-po 257
mTsho-sman 'Brang-ma 68, 140-141
mtshon cha 66, 186
mTshon-sman Khri-dkar 125
mTshon-sman 'Brong-mo 125, 141
'Tsham-za 97, 102
'Tshe-'gron 119
'Tshe-gco 74, 113, 124
'Tshe-mi 50, 70, 79-81, 224
'Tshe-mi-rgyal 50, 78
'Tshe-mi Bon-po 'Du-'phrod 80-81
'Tshe-mi dMu-rgyal 70
'Tshe-mi gShen-bu rGyal-tsha 70
'Tshe-mis 'Tshe-btsugs 91
'Tsho-bon dGu-rgyud 82
'Tshos-pa rNam-'dul 77

DZA
Dzo-dmar Me-yi Bon-po 255
dzwa dbal 55
Dzwo 206, 212
dzwo dmar 206
mdzangs sna lnga 225
mDzad-rtag 198
mDzad-rtag dGon-pa 198
mDzad-rtag sPrul-sku 198
mdzo 202, 227
mdzod 6, 19, 21, 32, 35, 42, 44-45, 53-54, 58, 62, 67, 69, 96, 106-108, 110, 118, 131, 156-157, 180, 185, 208, 214-216, 258
mDzod sde 258
'dzam bu gling gi rgyan chen po drug 216
'Dzi-bon Kha-tor 78
'Dzi-bon Khod-ge 76
'Dzing 57
'Dzin-bon Khog-der 68, 76
rDzu-'phrul Mi-dgu 256
rDzu-'phrul Ye-shes 237
rDzogs-pa Chen-po 47

ZHA
zhang lnga gcen po 166
zhang po 90
Zhang-po brGya-bcu 225
Zhang-Bod 179
Zhang Zhung 6, 7, 9, 10, 12, 17, 18, 22, 23, 25-27, 30-33, 42, 50, 53-56, 58, 59, 61, 62, 66-68, 72, 74, 75, 77-83, 85, 86, 90, 99, 112, 114, 119-122, 125, 126, 159, 163, 166-168, 171, 176, 182-184, 186, 187, 192, 195, 199, 203, 208-210, 215, 216, 219, 221-225, 227, 235-258
Zhang Zhung Kun-rigs rGyal-po 72
Zhang Zhung bKra-shis rGyal-mtshan 248
Zhang Zhung Khyung-chen sPungs-ri 255
Zhang Zhung Khyung-yer dKar-po 255
Zhang Zhung Khyung-lung 245, 250, 255
Zhang Zhung Khyung-lung dNgul-mkhar 255
Zhang Zhung Khri-lde 77
Zhang Zhung mKhas-pa Nyi-shu 75, 256
Zhang Zhung mKhas-pa Nyi-shu rTsa-bdun 256
Zhang Zhung Glang-chen Mu-wer 255
Zhang Zhung sGo Phug Bar gsum 252
Zhang Zhung sGo-mo 56
Zhang Zhung Nga-sa Ha-ti 81
Zhang Zhung Ta-ra La-ha-te 82
Zhang Zhung sTag-rna 237
Zhang Zhung sTong-rgyung mThu-chen 55, 216, 238, 239, 242, 243
Zhang Zhung This-dmar sPungs-rgyung 255
Zhang Zhung Da-ra Ma-ha-ti 81
Zhang-zhung Dar-ma Ha-ti 125
Zhang Zhung Don-rtogs rGyal-po 79, 125

INDEX OF TIBETAN AND ZHANG ZHUNG NAMES AND TERMS 291

Zhang Zhung sPungs-rgyung mThu-chen 255
Zhang Zhung sPos[-ri] Ngad-ldan 237, 255
Zhang Zhung Phug-pa 59, 209, 215
Zhang Zhung Bon 53, 120
Zhang Zhung Bon-po Mi-tshe Lang-rung 85
Zhang Zhung Byi-ra gTsug-ldan 255
Zhang Zhung dBus 238
Zhang Zhung Mi-bon Mu-phya 255
Zhang Zhung Mu-la Ma-ho 82
Zhang Zhung Mu-la Ha-rgyal 83, 86
Zhang Zhung Tsi-ṇa 235-237
Zhang Zhung Tso-min Gyer-rgyung 255
Zhang Zhung Tsha 85
Zhang Zhung Tsha-la-rgyung 68, 85
Zhang Zhung Tsha-la-rung 85
Zhang Zhung Tshe'i-rgyal-po 75, 125
Zhang Zhung mTshe-mi Kun-snang 125
Zhang Zhung 'Tshe-mi Kun-snang 79
Zhang Zhung g.Yung-drung rGyal-po 78
Zhang Zhung Shod-kyi Dum-tshal 255
Zhang Zhung Sad-ne Ga'u 243
Zhang Zhung lHa-'od 74
Zhang Zhung A-nu Phrag-thag 243, 255
Zhang Zhung A-la Dan-ci 80, 125
Zhang Zhung A-so gTsug-phud 80,
Zhang Zhung A-so gtsug-phud 125
zhang gsum blon bzhi 49
Zhal-dkar 61, 74, 124, 180
zhal ngo 160
Zhing-rgo 35
Zhing-bo-rgo 35
Zhing-bo lHa-rigs-rgo 21
zhug shang 205
zhugs shing 205
bzhed rnam lnga 95

ZA
Za-nam-zin 78
Za-nam Zin-lde 78, 125, 142, 143
Za-nam-legs 128
Za ma tog bkod pa 201
za ma phud 89
Za-rang Me-'bar 216, 242
Za-lha dBang-phyug 69, 84
Zang-zang lHa-brag 57
Zangs-thang Sha'i-gling 225
Zangs-za Ring-btsun 241
zangs yag 91
zar 96
Zi-rgyal rMang-po 164
Zing-pa mThu-chen [rGya-bon] 216
Zing-po-rje 117
Zings-po-rje 171, 209
Zings-po-rje sTag-skya-bo 171
Zin-nam Zin-lde 78, 143
Zil-then-che 89, 101
Zil-gnon Bon-dgu 256
Zo-bo Khyung-lag 73
Zo-bo dBu-dgu 60
Zom-shang lCags-kyi Bya-ru-can 223
Zo'u-khyung-lag 73
Zwa-gnam Zin-te 129, 143
Zla 17, 18, 35, 123, 221
Zla-ba rGyal-mtshan 184, 248
Zla-yi-tshan 17, 22, 35
gZi 7, 8, 34, 120
gZer-thung rMa-rgyal sPom-ra 56
bZod-pa-lags 194
bzla ba 42

'A
'A-zha 22, 23, 25, 30, 32, 33, 171, 209
'U-de Gung-rgyal 75, 161, 162
'Um-bu Glang-mkhar 228-230
'O 88, 114
'O-de Gung-rgyal 89, 102
'O-de sPu-rgyal 115, 118
'O-lde sPu-rgyal 109, 115, 116, 118, 215, 220, 223, 224, 228, 230

'O-za Ti-mo-mtsho 125
'O-yug Nag-thang 57
'Od-kyi lHa-ri sPo-mthon 215
'Od-de Gung-rgyal 93, 102
'Od-srung 169, 209
'Om-rgod Za-stong bTsun-'gro-skar 126
'Om-po sGo-bzhi 242
'Om-bu Bla-sgang 226, 232
'Or-bon 'Phan-grag 84
'Ol-kha Shug-gcig 57
'Ol-god Za-stong Tsun'bro-ga 130
'Ol-god-bza' gDon-btsun-sgron 171
'Ol-mo Lung-ring 215
'Ol-mo'i Lung-rings 66, 67, 186

YA
Ya-gong 63, 236
Ya-gyal 37
Ya-ngal 51, 60, 61
Ya-ngal gSas-skyabs 61
ya bzhi zung brgyad 55
Yag-drug bTsan-po 78
yang dag pa'i sems bon 52
Yang-rtse 60, 68, 72, 76, 179, 233
Yangs-pa 108
Yab sTag-cha 'Al-'ol 97
Yab sTag-cha Yal-yol 89, 102
Yab-bla bDal-drug 50, 97-99, 102, 121
Yab-bla brDal-drug 114, 121
yab 'bangs 53
Yab-lha bDag-drug 108
Yab-lha bDal-drug 98, 214
Yab-lha brDa'-drug 93, 94, 102
Yab-lha brDal-drug 89, 90, 102
Yar-lha Sham-po 56, 65, 118
Yar-khyim Sog-ka 93
yar g.yen gnyan po bcu gsum 88
Yar-lung 50, 51, 56, 57, 93, 108, 109, 118, 183, 224, 229, 230, 232
Yar-lung Swo-ka 224, 232
Yar-lung Sog-ka 50, 51, 57, 93, 108, 229

Yar-lung Sog-kha 51, 183, 230
Yar-lungs 60, 66
yas rtags 205
yi dam bka' chen brgyad 55
Yi-za Khod-grags 82, 179
yig tshang drug 96
yig tshang sde dgu 96
yugs phud pa 45
Yun-bu Bla-sgang 228
Yum-bu Bla-sgang 6, 93, 94, 169, 228-230
ye 100, 120, 210, 211, 213, 257
Ye-khri bTsad-po 59
Ye-khri bTsan-po 120, 136
Ye-mkhyen sGra-bla 157
Ye mkhyen sgra bla'i mngon shes 211
Ye-rje sMan-bla 157
Ye-rje sMon-pa 98
Ye rje smon lam 211
Ye-byed Gung-rgyal 61
Ye-dbang-sa 157
Ye-dbal mThu-stobs 157
Ye dbang lha yi bka' babs 211
Ye-smon Nag-mo 19
Ye-shes Khri-po 73, 135
Ye-shes rGyal-ba 235-237
Ye-gshen bDud-'dul 68, 76, 77
Ye-sang dKar-po 19
Ye srid 'phrul gyi ju thig 211
Yer-pa-brag 61
Yo-phyal 114
Yogs 88, 89
Yongs-'dus dBang 255
Yongs-su dGa'[-ba] 236
yod 88
Yod-kyi lHa-mo Gang-grag 97, 100
Yol-zhabs lDing-po-che 30
g.Yag-ma-grus 195
g.Yang shes phya 'dod 54
g.Yang shes phya bon 52, 53
g.Yang shes phywa bon 54, 204, 206
g.Ya'-li 38
g.Ya'-lung Gang-bar 57

g.Ya'-le-gong 105, 106
g.yas ru 57
g.yu sbram po 257
g.Yu-rtse 76, 233
g.Yu-yul Drang-pa 91
g.Yu-yul Bar-do 91
g.Yu-yul g.Yam-khang 91
g.Yu-ri Phyug-mo 89, 100
g.Yung-drung Khri-brtsegs 61, 63
g.yung drung gi khams 186
g.Yung-drung rGyal-po 73, 78
g.Yung-drung rNam-rgyal 182
g.Yung-drung dPa'-bo mThong-grol 255
g.Yung-drung Bon 45
g.Yung-drung Ya-rab rGyal-mo 97, 101
g.Yung-drung Rol-pa 64
g.Yung-drung Sems-dpa' 158
g.Yung drung sems dpa' spros med pa 158
g.Yung-drung lHa-rtse 60, 70, 73
g.Yog 171
g.yon ru 57

RA
Ra-ga 225
Ra-sa Thang-bdun 58
Ra-sang 69, 84, 120, 179-182, 184, 244
Ra-sang Khod-ram 244
Ra-sang Khri-ne-khod 84, 180
Ra-sang Bon-po Khri-ne-khod 181
Ra-sangs Khri-na-khod 84, 120, 179-181
Ra-sangs Khri-ne-khod 69, 84, 182
Ra-sangs Khre-ne-khred 84
Ra-sangs 'Phen-rgyal 184
Rag-za g.Yung-drung Rol-po 64
Rang-ldan 157
rab bkram 36
Rab-sgang 56
Ri-thog 56, 128, 129, 149, 150, 153
Ri-bo dGa'-ldan-pa 253

Ri-rab Lhun-po 108
Ri-gsum 'Dus-pa 56
rig pa 120, 186, 214-216, 220, 223
rig pa'i khams 186
rigs ngan pa 22
rig 'dzin 55
rigs bzang po 21
Rin-chen Zur-mang 68, 77
Rin-chen Zur-mangs 77
Rin-chen 'Od-kyi Bya-ru-can 252
Ru-than 28
Ru-thog 38
Ru-dam Zil-khrom 56
ru tshod sngar ran 92
ru mtshon rnga ring 92
Ru-yang Za-steng rGyal-nam-mtsho 126, 149
Ru-yong Za-stong rGyal-mtsho-ma 129, 149
Ru-la-skyes 65, 66, 162-164, 185, 231
Ru-lag 57
ru'i sbal bdar 50
rum 113, 120, 124, 214
rus chen bzhi 18
Re-rkyang Sha-'thab 57
rong kha 225
rong dor khab so nyi shu rtsa gnyis 225
Rong-pa 38
Rong-rong rTsol-po 89, 94, 103, 114
rlung 41

LA
La-stod 57
La-do 91
La-dwags 238
La-dwags rGyal-po 238
La-mor rDo-yi Khang-bu'i-gling 237
la-btsas 222
La-li-gu 50
Lan tsha 201
Li 20, 210
Li-ngam 160
Li-the-se 201

Li-byin 175, 188
Li-yul 20
Li-yul-sgang 57
Li-yul-ba 20
Li-lo'u-ku'u 28
Li-shu sTag-ring 76, 214, 215, 236, 237, 256, 258
Li-sho-legs 128, 140
Lig-mi-rkya 6, 244, 246, 247, 250, 251
Lig-mi-rkya lDe-bu 6, 244, 246, 251
Lig-mi-skya 238, 250
Lig-mi-rgya 248
Lig-mi-rgyal 250
Lig-myi-rhya 245
Lig-myi-rhya lDe-bu 245
Lig-myi-rhyal 244, 245
Lig-myi-rhyal lDe-bu 245
Lin-sung 28
Lug-rar 38
le le bsang 19
Le'u-rje mChed-bdun 98
Legs-rgyal Thang-po 211
Legs-tang rMang-po 216
Legs-drug 120, 125, 127, 232
Legs-pa'i Hor-drug 88, 100
Legs-byin 201
lo skor gcig 161
Lo-ngam 64, 65, 113, 124, 127, 132, 137, 158-162, 231
Lo-ngam rTa-rdzi 113, 124, 127, 158, 159, 161
Lo-ngam Byi-khrom 159
Lo-chen Rin-chen bZang-po 253
Lo-paṇ mKhas-dgu 256
Lo-ban-shel 64
Lotsāba 201
Lo tsa mkhas pa'i rgyan drug 209
Lo-tsā-ba Chen-po brGyad 216
Long-ngam 65, 66, 162

SHA
sha rkyang 238
Sha-khyi 159
Sha-khri 66, 128, 159, 160, 162, 163
Sha-ri dBu-chen 209, 216, 238, 239
Shang-pa'i rGyal-po 238
Shangs-kyi Zhing-tshal 57
Shad-ra-khug 243
Shan-sbi'i 27, 29
Shan-rtswa 38
Shan-tsha 39
Shab-shang brGya-bcu 225
Sham-ka-ra 188
Sham-po-mkhar 231
Sham-bha-la 209
Shar-la 'Bring-lung 92
Shi-la Manju 188
Shing-rje 122
Shing-mu Le-grum-shing 92
Shim-phod Ngad-ldan 215
Shugs-mgon-mo 19
Shud-ke-bza' sTsal-thing-shags 246
Shun-gyi Brag-dmar 57
She-le 240
shes pa can bcu gnyis 45, 176
shes rab 207
Shes-rab lDems-pa 84
Sho-tse dMar-yag 85
Sho-legs 75, 78, 125, 129, 139, 140, 142
Sho-legs bTsan-po 129, 140
shwa 'cham 210
shwa ba rus rgyas kyi mdos 211
gShen 6, 11, 44-48, 50-55, 57, 60-62, 66-86, 97, 99, 112-113, 118-121, 123-124, 127, 157, 159, 164-168, 178-181, 186, 187, 204, 206, 210, 211, 214, 215, 224, 236, 238, 243, 256, 257
gShen rGyung-yar Mu-khod 238
gShen Ya-ngal 61
gShen-po 68, 71, 168, 179-181, 183, 236, 239, 242
gShen-po Mi-lus bSam-legs 242
gShen-po Tshe-rgyal 71
gShen-rab 43-46, 66-67, 120, 167,

186, 204-206, 208, 210, 211, 215,
216, 223, 224, 237, 241
gShen-rab Mi-bo-che 43, 45-46, 120,
167, 186, 204, 205, 208, 210, 211,
215, 216, 223, 224, 237, 241

SA
Sa-skya 183, 193, 227, 253
Sa-skya Paṇḍita Kun-dga' rGyal-mtshan 227
Sa-khyon brGya-po Gang-byu 56
Sa-ding-ding 129, 133, 134
Sa-bdag 207, 208
Sa-sman Ting-ting-ma 123
Sa-sman Bu-mo 125, 141
Sa-btsun sNyan-rje 125, 146
sa rim pa bcu gsum 88
Sa-la Legs-drug 125, 127, 232
Sa-le lJon-phyug 68, 75
Sa-le lJon-byug 75
Sa-le Bang-bang 68, 76
Sa-le Byed-tshang 61
Sa-le Bye'u-tshang 74
Sa-lha Bon-po 70
sangs 48, 84, 182, 212
Sangs Khre-ne-khod 84
Sangs-po Khrin-khod 179, 182
Sangs-po 'Bum-khri 17, 33, 34, 97-100, 157
Sad-ne Ga'u 215, 243
Sad-mar-kar 244-247
Sa'i sNying-po 169
Sa'i Ding-ding-ma 179
Sam-gha 32
Si-tu dGe-ba'i Blo-gros 189
Si-le Bang-ba 77
Sum-pa 20, 22, 23, 25, 30, 32, 57, 59,
167, 216, 221, 228, 238, 239, 242,
248, 249, 251
Sum-pa Kha-yam rLung-lce 242
Sum-pa Glang-gi Gyim-shod 57, 59, 249
Sum-pa Mu-spungs gSal-tang 238, 239

Sum-pa-shang 93, 228
Sum-bha 30, 32
Se 8, 18, 20, 21, 23, 30, 35, 52, 59, 80,
145, 167, 224, 238, 239, 243
Se-snan Phyug-mo 61
Se sNol-lde 80
Se sNol-po-lde 80, 145
Se-snol gNam-lde 79, 125, 144
Se-bon 53
Se-za-sman 123, 134, 135, 179
Se-za sMan-mo 179
Se-reb rGyal-po 238
Se Sha-ri dBu-chen 238, 239
Se Sha-ri U-chen 59
Seng 18, 22, 23, 33, 120, 226, 227
Seng-khri bTsad-po 59
Seng-ge-'gram 46, 238
Seng-ge-sgra 46
Seng-ge'i sPa-gro sTag-tshang 57
sems don 238
Sems tsam pa 157
gsal ba'i khams 186
gsas 46, 47, 54-56, 58, 60, 63, 67, 167,
176, 206, 212
gser skyems dang g.yu sngon 170
gSer-brtsig 163, 165
gSer-bstsig 129, 131
bSe-rnol-nam 146, 165-166
bSe-rnol-po 146, 220
bSe'-rnol-po 129, 146, 220
so kha bzhi 225-226
So-khri 59, 60, 72, 123, 127, 129,
134, 135, 178-179
So-khri bTsad-po 59, 72, 134
So-khri bTsan-po 60, 72, 123, 127,
129, 134-135, 179
So-ste 128, 146
So-tham-tham 129, 133-135
Sog-yul 23
Sor-rno-nam 128, 145
Sos 29
Sri 162, 210
Srid 6, 11, 17, 34, 42, 45, 52-54, 69-

86, 88-89, 96, 100-104, 121, 130, 133-135, 137-143, 145-148, 150, 151, 153, 155, 157, 167, 178, 180, 182, 186, 204-206, 211, 215, 229, 240, 245-247, 257
Srid-lcam Le-dur 97, 100
Srid-rje 'Brang-dkar 97, 100
Srid-pa 34, 51, 88, 97, 98
Srid-pa Phywa'i rGyal-po 88
Srid-pa Sangs-po 34, 97, 98
Srid-pa Sangs-po 'Bum-khri 34, 97
srid pa'i khams 186
Srid-pa'i Drang-rje 245
Srid-pa'i lHa-dgu 64
srid pa'i lha rabs mched bzhi 89, 102
Srid-za lHa-mo-thang 97, 100
Srin-po 44
Srin-btsan 82, 147, 179
Srib-kyi lHa-dkar Mang-po-sde 49
Srib-khri 74, 137, 178
Sribs-kyi lHa-mo dKar-mo 124, 135
Sribs-khri bTsan-po 72, 74, 124, 134, 136-137
srung ma 210
srog thag 206
srog shing 241
Srong-lde-bstsan 220
Srong-btsan 6, 25-27, 43, 49, 69-70, 84, 95, 96, 116, 123, 126, 128, 132, 153-154, 171-175, 178, 181, 184, 185, 187-192, 195, 199-202, 217, 223-225, 245-247, 250, 251, 258
Srong-btsan sGam-po 6, 26, 27, 49, 69, 70, 95, 123, 172-175, 181, 184, 185, 187-192, 195, 199-202, 217, 224, 245-247, 250, 251
Slas-kra Gu-ge 252
Slon-btsan Rlung-nam 130, 153, 220
Slob-dpon Tha-mi Thad-ke 255
Slob-dpon Padma 185
gsang gros rnam gsum 95
gSang-brag Brag-dmar Yang-rDzong 255

gsas khang 67
gSas mkhar 46, 47, 54-56, 58, 60, 63, 176, 212
gSum-ka 159
gSer 95, 131, 134-141, 143-146, 148, 149, 151, 152, 154, 156, 164, 167, 170, 174, 198, 201, 209, 211, 224, 226-227, 232
gSer-ljongs dGon-pa 198
gSer-thog lCe-'byams 209, 216
bSam-yas 57, 208
bSam-yas Khri-thang 57
bSe 6, 18, 21-23, 35, 129, 146
bSe-khyung-sbra 21, 23
bSe-lde gNol-nam 79
bSe-lde gNol-po 80
bSe-bon-la gNam-rings 79
bSe'-bstsig 165
bsrung 227

HA
Ha-ra Ci-par 215, 243
Ha-shang Ma-ha De-ba 188
Has-po Khri-Thang 57
Hig-we 28
Hu-hu-zhi-li 38
Hun-nyi 27
Hor 20, 167, 168, 171, 225
Hrin-ros 28, 29
Hre-kri-hru'e 27

LHA
lHa-khyung 257
lHa-khri Shel-dkar 89
lHa-ga-ya 90
lha gos bsil le ma 92
lha rgod lcam 62
lHa-lcam 124, 137, 160
lHa-tho-tho-ri 170, 171, 201
lHa-tho-tho Ri-snyan-btsan 156, 169, 170, 201
lHa-tho-tho Ri-snyan-shal 68, 86, 150
lHa-tho-do sNya-brtsan 129

INDEX OF TIBETAN AND ZHANG ZHUNG NAMES AND TERMS   297

lHa-tho-do sNya-bstsan 129, 149
lHa-bdag sNgags-dro 216
lha babs kyi yi ge 195
Lha Babs Yi Ge 6, 193, 194
lHa-bu mGo-dkar 163
lHa-bu rGyung-then 97
lHa-bu Chags-then 97
lHa-bu Drum-then 97
lHa-bu mDa'-then 97
lHa-bu gNam-then 97
lHa-bu sPrin-then 97
lHa-bu Bal-then 97
lHa-bu Mang-then 97
lHa-bu gTsug-then 97
lHa-bo lHa-sras 53
lHa-bon 68, 75-79, 82, 86, 167, 244
lha bon sgo bzhi 62, 223
lHa-bon sGo-bzhi 244
lHa-bon gCo-snyan-rings 77
lHa-bon gCo-stag Klu-gsas 75
lHa-bon gCo'u 'Od-dkar 82
lHa-bon Ches-pa gnam-'dul 79
lHa-bon sTong-dra Zhing-sha 78
lHa-bon Tha-tsha Khog-'phar 86, 167
lHa-bon bTso-nyag gZher-thod-dkar 76
lHa-bon bTso-mo Gung-rgyal 75
lHa-bon Yi-za Khod-grags 82
lHa-bon Ye-gshen bDud-'dul 68, 76
lHa-bon gShen-thang Mi-chung 79
lHa-bon Seg-gshen bDud-'dul 76
lHa-bla-ma Ye-shes-'od 253
lHa-mo Gos-dkar-ma 97
lHa-mo dPal-bskyed-ma 97
lHa-mo Phya-g.yang bDag-mo 97
lHa-mo rTsad-dkar bDag-mo 97
lHa-mo Tshe-'dzin-ma 97
lHa-mo Zhim-dgu'i Dag-mo 97
lHa-mo gSal-skyed-ma 97
lHa-sman dKar-mo 60
lHa-rtse 56, 60, 70, 73
lHa-bzangs 171
Lha-'od-grags 92

lHa-rab gNyan-rum 121
lha rabs mched bdun 94, 103
lha rabs mched bzhi 89, 93, 100, 102
lHa-rabs gNyan-rum-rje 97, 100
Lha-ri Gyang-to 108
Lha-ri Gyang-tho 50, 55, 56, 107-109
lHa-ri Gyang-mtho 60
Lha-ri Gyang-do 91, 108, 109
Lha-ri Rol-po 109, 118
lHa-rigs-rgo 21, 32
lHa Rong-rong rTsol-po 94, 103
lHa-lung sTag-pa 92
lHa-lung rDo-rje-dpal 189
lHa-sa Yer-pa 57
lHa-sras 47, 53, 203, 229, 258
lha gsang gar bu 92
lha gsol ba 45
lha'i chos lugs 217
lHun-grub dByings-kyi gSas-khang 78, 126
lHun-grub dByings-kyi lHa-khang 126
lHe-glang Ru-kar 90
lHe-rje Gung-rtsan 90, 103
lHe-rje Thog-rtsan 90, 103
lHe-rje Zin-gdags 90, 103
lHe-rje Yang-btsan 94, 103
lHe'u-rje Gung-btsan 94, 103
lHe'u-rje Zin-btsan 94, 103
lHo 6, 18, 24, 25, 30, 35, 52, 94-96, 130, 133, 135-142, 144-147, 149-150, 152, 154, 156, 164, 198, 199, 217, 218, 224, 228, 230, 231, 233
lHo-pa 25
lHo-brag 18, 161, 180, 181
lHo-rdza-sgang 56
lho yig 198

A
A-lcags-'bru 35
A-thang-'bru 21, 32, 35
A-nu Phrag-thag 215, 243, 255
A-pa-ra 242
A-spo-ldong 18, 21-23, 35, 224, 225

A-mye rMa-chen 28
A-tsa-ra Mi-gsum 208
A-la Dun-tsug 76
A-la Dun-tshe 76
A-sho-legs 75, 120, 125, 139, 142
A-sho Legs-rgyal 68, 139
A-sho Legs-rgyal bDud-'dul 75
A-so gTsug-spud 77
An-zhi 28
I-sho Da-na 242
I-sho-leg 129
I-sho-legs 75, 78, 120, 128, 129, 139-143, 165, 166, 232, 233
I-sho Legs-rgyal 68, 78, 142, 143
I-sho-legs bTsan-po 129, 142
U-rgyan 184
U-pe-ra 103, 105
U-be-ra 104-110
Un-chen Dung-gi Bya-ru-can 252
O-rgyan 210

GHA
Gha-nu-ta 188
Dha 27, 174, 201, 223, 224, 227, 232
Dharma Ko-sha 189
Dhi-bzod 192
Dhe-ba Za-rong Me-'bar 55

BHA
Bha'i Bon-po Shog-'brag 82

Index of Tibetan Textual Sources

bKa' chems ka khol ma 155, 160, 231
bKa' chems bka' khol ma 109, 130
bKa' thang 115, 127, 130, 133-137, 139-143, 145-149, 151, 153
bKa' thang sde lnga 115, 127, 130
bKa' la nyan pa'i chad mdo 44
sKal bzang mgrin rgyan 157, 158, 257
Gangs ti se'i dkar chag tshangs dbyangs yid 'phrog 235, 236
Gab pa srog 'dzin sngags kyi don 47
Ge khod 238
Grags rgyal bod kyi rgyal rabs 130, 155
sGrags pa rin chen gling grags 69, 179
Glang ru lung bstan gyi mdo 20
Gling grags 63, 69-86, 179-180
Gleng gzhi bstan pa'i 'byung khungs 69
rGya bod yig tshang chen mo 117, 130, 156, 174, 191
rGya'i thang yig rnying ma 27
rGyal po bka'i thang yig 43, 115, 116, 127, 155, 217
rGyal po'i bka' thems bka' bkol ma 109
rGyal po'i bka' thems shog dril ma 109
rGyal rabs 'phrul gyi lde mig 131, 156, 230
rGyal rabs bon gyi 'byung gnas 46, 130
rGyal rabs gsal ba'i me long 65, 66, 118, 130, 156, 171, 174, 185, 188, 189, 210, 217, 223, 228, 250
rGyal rabs gser gyi phreng ba 131

rGyal rabs gser phreng 156, 174, 201, 224, 226, 232
rGyal gshen ya ngal gyi gdung rabs 51, 60, 99, 121
sGra 'grel 113, 195, 216, 240, 242
sGra 'grel 'phrul gyi lde mig 216
sNgon byung gi gtam me tog phreng ba 201
Ju thig srid pa'i rgyud 'bum 211
Nyang gi chos 'byung 69, 130, 155, 160, 178, 224
Nyang gi chos 'byung me tog snying po 69
Nyer mkho bum bzang 6, 30, 35
rNying ma rgyud 'bum 198
Tun hong bod kyi lo rgyus yig rnying 108, 116, 117, 122, 128, 130, 131, 155, 158, 159, 163, 165, 220, 244-246
gTo 'bum 31
rTen 'brel gyi phyag rgya 169
bsTan bcos legs bshad rin gter 193
bsTan pa'i rnam bshad dar rgyas gsal ba'i sgron ma 123
bsTan rtsis mgo mtshar nor bu'i phreng ba 214
Thugs 'bum mkha' sngon 208
Dar rgyas 6, 53, 69-86, 98, 113, 123, 127, 130, 131, 133-137, 139-143, 145-149, 151, 153, 155, 158, 160, 161, 179-181, 185, 192, 236
Dar rgyas gsal sgron 6, 53, 69, 98, 131, 155, 158, 160, 161, 180, 185, 236

Dar rgyas gsal sgron gyi lo rgyus kun gsal 236
Dar rgyas gsal ba'i sgron ma 113, 123, 130, 179, 181, 192
Deb ther kun gsal me long 39
Deb ther dkar po 43
Deb ther sngon po 115, 130, 156
Deb ther dpyid kyi rgyal mo'i glu dbyangs 19, 131, 156, 228, 231
Deb ther dmar po 130, 155, 188, 189, 202, 223
Dri med gzi brjid 120
mDo [sde] za ma tog 169
'Dul ba rgyud drug 46, 63, 157
'Dus pa rin po che tog dge ba bcu'i mdo 175
'Dus pa rin po che'i tog 192
lDe'u rgya bod kyi chos 'byung 6, 46, 49, 69, 88, 96, 99-105, 107, 111, 114, 119, 160-162, 164, 171, 209, 224-226, 228, 233
lDe'u chos 'byung 6, 49, 50, 87, 93, 95, 96, 99-107, 130, 155, 159-161, 163, 165, 166, 168-171, 174, 225, 230
lDe'u chos 'byung chen mo 6, 49, 87, 99, 100, 105, 155, 159-161, 165, 166, 168-171, 174, 225, 230
Nad 'bum nag po 208
Ne'u sngon gtam 223
Ne'u sngon 'byung gi gtam 155
Ne'u paṇḍi ta'i sngon gyi gtam 130
rNam 'byed 'phrul gyi lde mig 127
sNang gsal sgron me 212
dPyad don sgyu ma gser 'bum 211
dPyad 'bum khra bo 208
dPyad gsum dag rtsis 209
sPang kong phyag rgya 169
sPyi spungs 46, 47, 51, 54, 55, 60, 176, 212
sPyi spungs g.yung drung thig le dbyings chen 55
Phung po gzan skyur gyi rnam bshad gcod kyi don gsal byed pa 195
Baiḍūrya dkar po 6, 22, 30, 35
Be ro tsa na'i rnam thar 'dra 'bag chen mo 175
Bod kyi deb ther dpyid kyi rgyal mo'i glud byangs 107
Bod kyi rdo ring gi yi ge dang dril bu'i kha byang 116
Bod kyi gna' rabs yig cha gces bsdus 109, 116
Bod kyi yig tshang 118
Bod ljongs zhib 'jug 37, 105
Bon gyi bstan 'byung nyung bsdus 238, 250
Bon gyi gzhung gri bshad kyi lung 161
Bon 'byung 6, 54, 69-86, 130, 133, 134, 136-142, 144-147, 149, 150, 152, 154, 156
Byams ma 6, 52-54, 58, 59, 131, 156, 165, 170, 203, 216, 257
Byams ma skyon gi 'jigs skyobs 52
Blon po bka'i thang yig 87, 96, 103, 105, 123
dBang chen 63
Ma ni bka' 'bum 109
Mi nyag gi skor rags tsam gleng ba 24
Me ri 184, 224
sMan mdo rtsa 'grel le'u bdun pa 208
sMan 'bum dkar po 208
Tsin rda ma ni 175
rTsa rgyud nyi sgron 98, 112, 236, 258
rTsa ba thugs 'bum mkha' sngon 208
Tshangs dbyangs yid 'phrog 235-237, 239, 241, 254
rDzogs pa chen po zhang zhung snyan rgyud kyi bon ma nub pa'i gtan tshig 221
Zhang zhung snyan rgyud 183, 184, 221, 247
Zhang zhung snyan rgyud kyi brgyud pa'i bla ma'i rnam thar 183, 184
Zhang zhung me ri 184, 224
Zhang zhung me ri'i lcog mkhar bzhengs lugs kyi zur byang 182
Zhang zhung me ri'i bla ma brgyud pa'i bstod phyag chen mo 184
gZer mig 88, 205
Ya ngal gdung rabs 61
Yar lung chos 'byung 231
Yar lung jo bo'i chos 'byung 130, 155, 159, 163, 169, 228, 230

Yum bu bla sgang gi dkar chag 96, 105, 106
Yum bu bla sgang gi dkar chag 'bring po 105, 106
g.Yung drung thig le dbyings chen gsas mkhar gsang ba sgo dgu 55
g.Yung drung bon gyi rgyud 'bum 50, 59, 61, 62, 113, 166, 167, 170, 256
g.Yung drung bon gyi bstan pa'i byung khungs nyung bsdus 265
g.Yung drung bon gyi bstan 'byung nyung bsdus 238, 250
Yo ga lha gyes can 93, 103, 107, 110, 114, 121
Yo ga lha gyes can gyi lo rgyus 103
Rin po che yid bzhin rnam par bkod pa'i rgyan 242, 243
Rus mdzod pad dkar skyed tshal 21, 32
Legs bshad rin po che'i gter 219-220
Legs bshad rin po che'i mdzod 44, 45, 53, 62, 67, 69, 108, 118, 131, 156, 180, 185, 208, 214, 216
Shwa ba rus rgyas kyi mdos chog 211
bShad mdzod chen mo 19, 96, 106, 107, 110
Srid rgyud 69-86, 96, 100-104, 130, 133-135, 137-143, 145-148, 150, 151, 153
Srid mdos 182
Srid pa rgyud kyi kha byang 100, 130, 155, 229
Srid pa spyi mdos 178, 180, 182, 205
Srid pa'i mdzod phug 42, 157, 215
Srid pa'i mdzod phug g.yung drung las dag rgyud 157
gSang ba bsen thub 47, 48, 176, 206, 242, 243
gSas mkhar spyi spungs 46, 54, 176, 212
gSas mkhar spyi spungs kyi bshad byang 54
gSas mkhar rin po che thig le dbyings chen g.yung drung gsang ba 56
gSas mkhar rin po che spyi spungs gsang ba bsen thub 47, 176
gSer phreng 131, 134-141, 143-146, 148, 149, 151, 152, 154, 156, 174, 201, 224, 226, 227, 232
lHa bsang rgyag brngan chen mo 18
lHo brag chos 'byung 6, 18, 30, 35, 52, 95, 96, 130, 156, 164, 199, 217, 218, 224, 228, 231, 233
lHo brag chos 'byung mkhas pa'i dga' ston 156

Index of Sanskrit Names and Terms

Acārya 208
Abhidharma 88, 157, 200, 218
Arhat 235, 237
Avalokiteśvara 109
Ārya Nāgārjuna 183
Ikṣvāku 46
Ulkāmukha 46
Karakarṇaka 46
kalpa 36, 88
Kaśyapa 169
Kṣitigarbha 169
Gupta 198
Guru Padmasambhava 167, 183, 240
Gautama 46
Gośṛṅga Vyākaraṇa sūtra 21
Goṣṭha 46
Ghandha stūpa 235
Cittamātra 157
Cintāmaṇi 175
Tripiṭaka 238
Ḍākinī 62
Dharma 58, 174, 176, 185, 189, 191, 199-201
dharmarāja 95, 96, 123, 173, 175, 181, 184, 185, 188, 192, 199, 201, 202, 217, 224, 225, 240, 245, 246, 249
Nūpura 46
Paṇḍita 193, 201, 227
Padmasambhava 19, 167, 183, 239-240
piṭaka 58-59

Prajñāpāramitā 58, 66, 67, 257
Pratyekabuddha 158
Buddha Śākyamuni 36
Bodhicaryāvatāra 6, 193
Bodhisattva 169
Madhyamaka 158
Mahāyāna 158
Yogācāra 158
Rūpati 17, 87, 110
Licchavi 108
Vasiṣṭha 46
Vinaya 46, 200, 236
Virūḍhaka 46
Vaibhāṣika 158
Vairocana 175, 191
Vaiśālī 108
Vyākaraṇa 192
Śākya 110
Śāntideva 6, 193
Śrāvaka 158
Saṃgha 64
Siddha 248, 250
Siṃhanāda 46
Siṃhahanu 46
Sūtra 21, 44, 58, 175, 200, 217
Sautrāntika 158
stūpa 58, 64, 169, 235
Hasti-niyaṃsa 46
Hīnayāna 158

Index of Chinese Names and Terms

Běi Zhōu cháo 北周朝 28
Cháng'ān 长安 27
Chángjiāng 长江 38
Dǎng Xiàng Qiāng 党项羌 18
Gānsù 甘肃 24, 25
Hàn 汉 26, 29, 38
Huáng Hé 黄河 27
Hòu Hàn Shū Xī Běi Shǐ 后汉书 西北史 38
Hòu Wèi 后魏 29
lǐ 里 27, 28
Níngxià 宁夏 26
Qiāng 羌 24, 25, 29
Qīnghǎi 青海 24, 25, 27, 38

Shǎnběi 陕北 26
Shǎnxī 陕西 26
Shén Ruì 神瑞 29
Sìchuān 四川 24, 25, 38
Súi cháo 隋朝 28
Táng 唐 27, 28
Táng cháo 唐朝 27
Xī'ān 西安 27
Xī Hàn 西汉 27
Xī Xià 西夏 26, 27
Xià 夏 26, 27
Xīnjiāng 新疆 20
Yúnnán 云南 28
Zhōngyuán Dìqū 中愿地区 38

www.ingramcontent.com/pod-product-compliance
Lightning Source LLC
Chambersburg PA
CBHW020057020526
44112CB00031B/208